THE BOOK OF HERMITS

THE BOOK OF HERMITS

A History of Hermits
from Antiquity to the Present

ROBERT RODRIGUEZ

© Robert Rodriguez, 2021

LIBRARY OF CONGRESS
CATALOGING-IN-PUBLICATION DATA

Names: Robert Rodriguez, author.
Title: The Book of hermits: the history of hermits from antiquity to the present /
Robert Rodriguez.
Includes bibliographical references and index.
Identifiers: ISBN 978-1-7368665-0-4 (paper)
Subjects: LCSH: Hermits—History. | Recluses—History | Solitude—History |
Subjects: BISAC: HISTORY / World | BIOGRAPHY & AUTOBIOGRAPHY / Historical
Classification: LCC BJ1499.S6 | DDC 204.247–dc23

Published by Hermitary Press (hermitarypress.com).
Cover design and typesetting by riverdesignbooks.com.

For Noelia, Thomas and Michael

Living in retirement beyond the World,
Silently enjoying isolation,
I pull the rope of my door tighter
And stuff my window with roots and ferns.
My spirit is tuned to the Spring-season:
At the fall of the year there is autumn in my heart.
Thus imitating cosmic changes
My cottage becomes a Universe.

— "The Valley Wind," by Lu Yün (third century, CE)

Contents

PREFACE

I started the Hermitary website twenty-some years ago because so little information about hermits was available on the web at the time. A web search would typically pull up Herman's Hermits, hermit crabs, or hermit thrush. (Actually, results have not changed much!) Something about Catholic and Orthodox hermits was always to be found, mostly hagiography, hardly challenging the definitive status of older books such as those compiled by Helen Waddell and Benedicta Ward. Not surprisingly, information relating eremitism to larger issues of solitude, psychology, society, and world culture, was quite absent on the web.

My curiosity about hermits piqued in the nineties with books such as Bill Porter's wonderful *Road to Heaven: In Search of Chinese Hermits*, and the sympathetic *Hermits: The Insights of Solitude* by Peter France. Invaluable studies on the psychology and philosophy of solitude from Anthony Storr and Philip Koch, while not directly addressing historical hermits, rounded out context. I launched Hermitary to tie together hermit and solitude threads. Many threads got tied but many did not (and have not) because of the wealth of information about historical hermits available today.

Why hermits anyway? I might find them historically intriguing, a confirmation of my personality and interests, perhaps, but not everyone will. What is persuasive about hermits is that they have grasped something important to convey to us all.

While each hermit is different, coming from different eras and mindsets, cultures and geographies, this book hopes to impress upon you the universal wisdom of the historical hermits, their discernment of life, nature, and society. In a world in crisis, among societies beset by alienation, anxiety, and insecurity, a consistent message of self-awareness, mingled with the appropriate degree of self-effacement, is the delicate and soulful fruit of the lives of the hermits, their aesthetics, and their philosophy of life.

I will contend that the hermit ethos is the grand intersection of many sages, writers, thinkers, and poets reflecting on solitude and its valuable role in the lives of all of us. That is why a significant portion of the book is given over to the creative voices in history, philosophy, and literature who were solitaries at heart but not formal hermits.

This books is a popularization—not in the sense of trying to make hermits popular, but in bridging the gap between scholarly research and what the intelligent reader really whats to know. A mix of history, biography, psychology, art, and philosophizing.

Meanwhile, the Hermitary website complements this book. The web site offers information about current hermit topics, key articles and reviews, plus galleries of hermits and eremitic themes in art, photos, film, music—among other resources and media that couldn't fit into this book. I hope you will happily avail yourself of the world of hermits.

INTRODUCTION

This book describes historical and modern hermits: hermits East and West, hermits in lore and literature, and the many motives behind their eremitism— that is, their practice of being a hermit. The motivations range from religious and spiritual to philosophical and aesthetic, from psychological disposition to a love of wilderness to the anonymity of the "hermit in the city."

What is a hermit?

Hermits have thrived in every era, geography, climate, culture, and society. Hermits have been eccentric, pious, irreverent, sociable, reclusive, and wise. Within these pages you will find like–minded souls—men and women—who reflect a profound part of each of us longing for wholeness, understanding, simplicity, and harmony. The pursuit of hermits is a search for an integral part of humanity.

Before pursuing the hermits, a few related ideas should be identified, solitude, aloneness, and loneliness, among others. We all have ideas or stereotypes of hermits. Real people often intersect with our stereotypes, but in unique ways. For example, most of the people we encounter are not hermits but some may exhibit one or several characteristics of a hermit. Similarly, many historical personalities were not, technically speaking, her- mits, but contributed to a universal understanding of solitude. Among poets, artists, and thinkers, we may call them "philosophers of solitude." They serve to contribute ideas that clarify the eremitic project, the purpose of the hermit's life and lifestyle.

We find such personalities throughout history. Think of a homeless urban man loudly proclaiming his public search for any intelligent person (Diogenes of Sinope, the Greek philosopher). Consider a public official quitting service to a corrupt government on ethical grounds to instead live in a forest or on a farm (Tao–Chien or Tu Fu, China's greatest poets). What about a worldly urbane writer longing for the solitude of a country home (Petrarch and Montaigne)? Finally, what about a woman poet living in uneventful reclusiveness in her family's large, busy house (Emily Dickin- son), or a twentieth–century woman philosopher, teacher, laborer, activist, mystic, and prolific writer (Simone Weil)?

These historical figures, thoughtful, observant, reflective, are all philosophers of solitude and help define eremitism. They do not fit the stereotype of a hermit, but calling them hermits would not be wrong. The historical hermits are often not as deep or creative, but many, surprisingly, are. Together with the perceptions of the philosophers of solitude, the lives and thoughts of the hermits will overthrow our stereotypes.

All hermits are solitaries, but not all solitaries are hermits. Hermits consciously pursue the complete benefits of solitude. As Kahlil Gibran put it, "A hermit renounces the world of fragments to enjoy the world wholly, without interruption." Hermits want, as Thoreau proposed of himself, to "live deliberately." Their solitude is not alienation from others but a pursuit of "engaged disengagement," as philosophy scholar Philip Koch puts it.

Historically, hermits are motivated by psychology, religion, spirituality, philosophy, or aesthetics. They perceive a life task, a mission, a project, a conscious purpose. Most solitaries lack this single-minded intentionality. Solitaries bridge the gulf between solitude and self, but not to the point of crafting an alternative life. Their aloneness is the result of personality and circumstance, often the product of fate. For typical solitaries, aloneness is no benefit, merely loneliness. Sometimes even the hermit is lonely, but the hermit extends such feelings beyond self to a universal poignancy.

The word "hermit" is based on the Greek word *eremos*, meaning desert or wilderness. Ancient Athenians prized citizenship and social participation, but these civic benefits could be forfeited by the formal process of ostracism, a punishment that decreed exile or banishment from the city to a perceived desert or wilderness. Athenians dreaded such a punishment. In contrast, the first hermits in the West, Christian monks of third and fourth–century Egypt, Palestine, and Syria, actively sought out desert and wilderness. They deliberately ventured from cities and monasteries on the edge of the desert to live alone in the heart of wilderness. Their motive was spiritual excellence, the pursuit and perfection of a form of life without distraction by people, comforts, and the familiar.

A few hermits lived in complete isolation from others, such as the legendary Saint Paul of Thebes, the supposed first Christian hermit of this era. Most hermits of the era followed the example of the famous Saint Anthony the Great, successor to Paul of Thebes and the first historical Christian hermit. Anthony lived alone but he recommends to aspiring hermits that they live as solitary individuals in huts proximate to one another for mutual well–being and spiritual communion.

From Anthony's example emerge the hundreds of desert hermit cells of both men and women, well–documented by testimonies of eye–witnesses including Evagrius, Rufinus, and John Cassian, and by anonymous collections of "sayings" of the Desert Fathers (*abbas*) and Mothers (*ammas*).

The desert model of eremitism spread to Europe and existed throughout the Middle Ages, especially in Greece, Russia, Italy, France, the Low Countries, and the British isles. In Italy, however, the abbot St. Benedict of Nursia (d. 547) limited the eremitic status among his monks to only the most adept, reflecting the practice of Eastern Christian monasteries on Mount Athos in Greece. Centuries later, St. Romuald (951–1027) consciously revives the desert tradition, creating the Camaldolese order, modeled on a community of individual cells.

In England, Ireland, and Scotland, hermits are celebrated for feats of survival, prayer, and solitude, popularized in the religious and literary imagination. In the later Middle Ages, anchorites emerge in Britain and in continental Europe.

Anchorites reside their entire lives in walled-off cells, called "anchorholds," usually attached to churches. Anchorites were attended by helpers. Anchorites renounce all visitors and outside comforts, leading lives of solitude and renunciation. Many anchorites, predominantly women, are known for their spiritual and mystical writings.

With the modern era of Renaissance and Reformation, eremitism throughout Europe recedes. Hermits virtually disappear in the West, though occasionally outstanding secular examples reappear both in England and later in the United States. The Romantic era rehabilitates hermits and the values of solitude through literature, philosophy, and art.

Eremitism is common in the ancient and medieval Asian world because spiritual and religious traditions encourage the eremitic state. Hinduism in India, Confucianism and Taoism in China, Buddhism in Thailand, Sri Lanka, China, Tibet, and Japan—all nourish strong eremitic traditions.

A philosophical eremitism emerges in China as "reclusion," where officials in imperial government service leave the imperial court due to its moral corruption, the officials quietly "reclusing" alone or with their families to distant villages, farms, and mountains. Reclusion becomes a solution to the moral dictum of the Confucian tradition: "When the emperor is good, serve; when the emperor is evil, recluse." China continues to be the home of the most active aspirants of eremitism in the world, with a number of genuine hermits, plus today's young urbanites heading to the mountains as weekend hermits.

With the modern era, East and West, eremitism mingles with solitude. Great modern philosophers, poets, and fiction writers have taken up the dilemma of society, alienation, and the values of hermits and solitaries. The roster of hermits, too, has, perhaps, increased.

But is there a place for hermits in today's world? Psychologists often condemn eremitism as anti–social behavior, unless, perhaps, it is practiced within a religious context. On the one hand, solitude is often thrown into the basket of philosophical individualism and egoism. On the other hand, today's popular psychology writers are distressed by the inability of moderns, especially younger people, to genuinely socialize, risking a society of atoms and automatons, all within the context of urban stress, suburban alienation, technological communications, and the breakdown of civility. To these extremes, the historical hermits have evolved careful and wise responses that we do well to take into account concerning self, others, and the environments of our daily worlds.

This book may reintroduce you to recognizable names—or introduce you to many new names, faces, and inspired writings and sayings. The ancient quests of the hermits resonate with our modern searches for meaning, understanding, and a fruitful, reflective life.

What the hermit is not

This book includes many non-hermits with important roles in the expression of solitude and self. But some exclusion of supposed hermits can be made, too, based on specific criteria. For example, a famous historical personality, the medieval priest Peter of Amiens (1050–1115), was a war leader during the First Crusade between 1095 and 1099. He is called Peter the Hermit—except that there is no evidence that he was a hermit, or used to be, or even became one. This is one instance of a hermit who was not a hermit.

A more subtle and important definition of "hermit" exists. Modern dictionaries make the words "hermit" and "recluse" mean the same, but in this book exception is made because "reclusion" has a historical definition, first, in the Eastern world (the Chinese examples mentioned) and, second, with regards to medieval women in the West, namely anchoresses, also called recluses by contemporaries. Indeed, women with eremitic aspirations have often been channeled toward reclusive lives.

By our stricter definition, too, a recluse shuns people due to psychological reasons, and lacks the sense of purpose and intent of the historical hermits. Thus, two misnamed "hermits" are examples of who are not hermits. The fearful and timid Jimmy Mason described in Raleigh Trevelyan's book *A Hermit Disclosed* (1960) was severely abused as a youth and shunned people in later life. Christopher Knight, the so–called "North Pond hermit" of Maine, described in Michael Finkel's *A Stranger in the Woods* (2017) as the "last, true hermit," hid from people precisely because he stole from them. He was a thief, not a hermit.

On the other hand, American poet Emily Dickinson has often been called a recluse because she was not strictly a hermit. Her creative drive and guarded intent as a poet and personality, as well as her occasional public mingling, grant her near status of a hermit.

A widespread phenomenon of extreme social reclusion among Japanese adolescents and young adults today is called *hikikomori*, but these disaffected youths are not, strictly speaking, hermits.

One misnomer often wrongly identified with hermits and eremitism is "hermeticism" or "hermetism," which is an esoteric tradition based on teachings of the ancient Greek–Egyptian mystic Hermes Trismegistus. Hermes was sometimes identified with the Greek god Hermes, equivalent to Roman Mercury. The twentieth–century occultist P. D. Ouspensky makes this mistake, as will be seen (section 62). Hermes Trismegistus had nothing to do with hermits.

Terms

The Greek word *eremos* (ἐρῆμος) is the root of "hermit" in English and "eremite" in Latin, Old French, and Old English; the word "eremite" (pronounced "air–eh–mite") was common in medieval Britain. As mentioned, the practice of being a hermit is called "eremitism." The adjective form "eremitic" means having to do with hermits.

At the same time, the Greek word *monos* is the root for "monk," and means "one." Originally, hermits were monks, designated as a particular type of monk not dwelling in a communal or "cenobitic" setting nor following a communal practice. But historical hermits include both solitaries and those living in small dwellings or proximate to communities.

The word "anchorite" (and the feminine "anchoress") is sometimes used synonymously with hermit. The Greek word *anachōréō* means to withdraw or retire (from the world). "Anchorite" had a specific meaning in the Western Middle Ages because such religious hermits did not leave their immediate dwelling or "anchorhold," often an enclosed room next to a church.

One last note on terminology: verbs such as hermitize, nouns like hermitry, hermitism, hermitship, or eremiteship, and adjectives such as hermitic and hermitical, may sound authentic but are all derivatives. The Oxford English Dictionary dates their usage to the seventeenth century, in some cases to the nineteenth, but their usage today is outdated, if not quaint and archaic.

Origins

The origins of eremitism may lie in deep psychology, yet eremitism can be discerned (and speculated about) in the very beginnings of human social groups. Here are some examples:

- Anthropology of paleolithic hunter–gatherer culture suggests that male hunting groups were characterized by strong social and authority bonds. As clan populations grew, exceeding the typical two dozen persons, so did competition for resources and a group power dynamic among males. Some individuals likely left the clan intentionally. Others were defeated in challenges or ostracized by the group leader. These individuals became wanderers and solitaries, at least for a time. The familiar biblical stories of Cain and Esau suggest the original group's opposition to nomadism and eremites. Good illustrations of this dynamic are found in several short stories of Hermann Hesse (see section 54).

- Medieval European ecclesiastical and civil authorities distrusted forest hermits as criminals preying on travelers. Forest–dwelling women may have been suspected of being witches. The status of hermits in Christianity varies by epoch and sect but usually looks upon hermits with suspicion. In the other scriptural religions of the West, Judaism and

Islam, only mystics defend eremitic traditions and solitary practice. The shaman tradition of East Asia offers a clear continuation of legendary solitaries gaining wisdom from their solitude. In China and Japan, this example closes the eremitic circle through the sage reflections of numerous hermit-poets.

- In his classic 1921 *Psychological Types* and related essays, psychologist Carl Jung (1875–1961) identified a psychological criteria that is useful to a consideration of hermit personalities. Jung defines attitudes of expression as extraversion and introversion, further refining expressions as functions of consciousness in thinking, feeling, sensation, and intuition, types Jung demonstrates specifically in historical expressions of philosophy and religion. Jung refines the categories of extroversion and introversion with specific historical examples that overlap the historical contexts of hermits and solitaries.

- In his book *The Hero with a Thousand Faces* (1947), mythographer Joseph Campbell (1904–1987) identifies the stages of the mythical and psychological journey to self–realization. The hero strengthens his resolve, embarks toward a remote goal, undergoes many trials and dangers, and returns with a boon for self and community. Along the way, the hero receives advice and assistance from archetypal figures, namely, wise old crones (also described by Jung) or wizened old men living alone in a forest (typical of fairy tales). Such archetypal figures are hermits, and represent a profound aspect of the subconscious. This notion of the hermit is reproduced in the modern Tarot.

- Anthropologist Ernst Becker (1924-1974), author of *The Birth and Death of Meaning* (1971), elaborates on Campbell's observations about archetypal figures in myth. In psychological development, the emergent personality, challenged by the necessity of self–development, can either resolve to pursue the hero's journey—or turn away. Becker (and Campbell) identify weakness of will at the moment of challenge as the source of infantilism, a paralysis of will that makes for anti–social neurosis, withdrawal, and isolation. But, notes Campbell, embracing the hermit option is positive, the source of artistic creativity, the elevation of the creative self transcending the temptation of fear and withdrawal.

Jung distinguished between active introversion (creativity) and passive introversion (neurosis), as did the psychoanalyst Otto Rank (1884-1939) interpreting the creative impulse in the artist.

- As originally described by the mythologist Mircea Eliade (1907–1986), the religion of shamanism in northern and eastern Asia involved solitary introspection and wandering as the shaman sought ideal conditions for developing spiritual insight. In Bill Porter's book *Road to Heaven: Encounters with Chinese Hermits* (1993), the author considers the rich tradition of shamanism in ancient China, originating in neolithic times, as a transition to eremitism. The proliferation and persistence of hermits in ancient China resists increasing bureaucratization of central authority and control of religious practice.

- The dominant Enlightenment concept of a "state of nature" was built around two sources: 1) the religious definition of original sin and loss of paradise, and 2) the parallel notion of primitive (paleolithic) society being what British philosopher Thomas Hobbes calls "nasty, brutish, and short." But in his second *Discourse*, French philosopher Jean–Jacques Rousseau (1712–1778) identifies a different state of nature, one based, rather, on free and mutual association, a state of peace and accommodation. In his later *Social Contract*, Rousseau sees modern society as a necessary renunciation of individual autonomy for a general will. In Rousseau can be found a reservoir of solitary–minded thinking pertinent to an anthropology of eremitism. Based on his personal experience, Rousseau wrote a final (and incomplete) set of short essays he titled *Reflections* [or *Reveries*] *of a Solitary Walker*.

- In modern Western European history, centralization and social alienation profoundly affect positive perceptions of solitude, especially in nineteenth– and twentieth–century philosophy, society, and literature. Sociologists like Hannah Arendt, Richard Sennett, and Robert Sayre, among others, touch upon solitude as a context of modernity. Historically, solitude was a punitive tool of authority through banishment and exile. In modern times, negative isolation and alienation continues to negatively affect society and individuals.

At the same time, solitude as positive and creative withdrawal from society has always attracted philosophers and thinkers, even if as a social and economic privilege. A chief characteristic of solitude understood thusly is its positive and voluntary nature. The historical hermits pursued solitude consciously, even as a life project, whether based on temperament, personality, psychology, aesthetics, or a spiritual ideal. For them, solitude became a life project. The solitude pursued by modern creative artists, writers, and thinkers, reveals the place of solitude in the human condition in identifying the positive psychological and social responses of solitaries to modern cultural and social breakdown.

• The psychiatrist John M. Oldham developed a profile of personality types while participating in the compilation of the third edition (1980) of the *Diagnostic and Statistical Manual of Mental Disorders* (*DSM*), published by the American Psychiatric Association. Oldham identified fourteen personality types for average people, among them "solitary," but indicates that most people include a range of characteristics across personality types. Subsequent editions of the *Manual*, *DSM-IV* (2000) and *DSM-V* (2013) elaborate spectrums of social personality disorders evidencing significant disfunction and representing mental illnesses. The *DSM* does not make broad cultural statements or use psychohistory but remains critical of solitude behaviors while refraining from causation or explication.

Such are a few of many available tools for the exploration of eremitism, and some surmises about its origins. In the following pages, we explore the historical hermits themselves.

PART I

THE WESTERN WORLD: ANTIQUITY AND MIDDLE AGES

CHAPTER 1

EREMITISM IN WESTERN ANTIQUITY

1. Diogenes of Sinope

Greek philosophy diverges between Plato (428-348 BCE) and Aristotle (384-322 BCE). This divergence, inherited by Western thought, contrasts metaphysics and abstraction (Plato) with logic and science (Aristotle). Yet both philosophers ground their thinking in authority, conformity, and an implied social order. Their ideas become fundamental to later Rome and the entire West.

In contrast to ancient Greek values promoting communal conformity and social civility, the philosopher Socrates (d. 399 BCE), who flourished in the brief era between Plato and Aristotle, is a severe social critic. He dresses shabbily, eats little, and publicly scorns the unreflective lifestyles coveted by his contemporaries. By Plato's account, Socrates is a gadfly who actively engages people. He is no solitary—the first individual, perhaps, but not the first hermit.

Inheriting and extending the style of Socrates is Antisthenes (446-366 BCE), a philosopher opposed to Plato's abstract theory of ideals. Antisthenes pursued Socrates in personal ethics and asceticism, garnering the attention of a disciple, Diogenes of Sinope (412–323 BCE). Antisthenes was nominally the founder of the school of Cynics, in part for the simplicity of his life but also because the Stoics wanted a chain of successive founders among the schools of philosophy culminating in their own.

To the staid Greek authorities, simplicity suggested scorn of established convention, hence the modern notion of "cynicism," of skeptical mockery and sardonicism. The true origins of the term is only clarified in the eccentric Greek philosopher Diogenes of Sinope (412–323 BCE).

In the biography of Diogenes written by Diogenes Laertius, we find the classical world's prototype of the urban hermit. Diogenes describes himself as "a homeless exile, to his country dead; a wanderer who begs his daily bread." Diogenes flagrantly violates social propriety by begging for food, publicly sleeping in a barrel, eating in the marketplace, performing bodily functions in public, and openly defying figures of authority and repute. Plato called him "Socrates gone mad." Diogenes was also called a dog, in Greek *kuvikoi*, from which is derived the word "cynic," the name given to the school of philosophy he helped engender: Cynicism.

In a famous anecdote about Diogenes, he is lounging on the roadside when King Alexander the Great and his retinue pass. Eager to confront Diogenes, Alexander dismounts and walks over to him. After a few coaxing words fail to get Diogenes to speak, Alexander asks him, "What do you want, Diogenes?" Diogenes replies at once, "For you to go away. You are blocking the sunlight."

Another familiar anecdote about Diogenes describes him carrying a lantern in the night streets to shine into the faces of others, claiming that he is looking for an honest or intelligent person. This anecdote is the basis of German philosopher Friedrich Nietzsche's story of the madman in the marketplace (section 52), as well as the famous image of the hermit in the Tarot deck of cards (section 62).

While Socrates and Antisthenes can be cited as predecessors of Diogenes, a remote precursor is the Greek philosopher Heraclitus. Heraclitus, who lived in the 500s BCE, is known for his philosophy of flux; his famous saying is "You cannot enter the same river twice." Heraclitus stood in sharp contrast to his contemporary, Parmenides, who maintained a philosophy of monads and absolutes anticipating Plato. Biographer Diogenes Laertius (who also described the life of Diogenes of Sinope) intensely disliked Heraclitus, portraying him as dismissive of others, garrulous, melancholic, and misanthropic, the "dark" philosopher. Eventually Heraclitus ended his days a vegetarian in self–exile on a deserted island, an example of Greek banishment to *eremos* but confounded by the voluntary character of eremitism.

2. Stoics & Epicureans

From the example of Diogenes rose a Greek school of Cynicism, fore-shadowed by the ascetic Antisthenes, student of Socrates, but furthered by Crates of Thebes (365–285 BCE). Given its foundation on one individual's personality, Cynicism was inevitably short-lived. Crates taught Zeno of Citium (fl. 300 BCE), the founder of Stoicism. Among later Roman thinkers, Seneca the Younger (4 BCE–65 CE) and Lucian (125–180) praise the ethical tenacity of Cynic thinkers, but the school waned in the rise of Stoicism.

Stoicism advocates no eccentric behavior. It maintains that virtue is suffi-cient for *eudaimonia*, or happiness and contentment of mind. This happiness is comprised of *ataraxia* ("imperturbability") and *apatheia* ("equanimity" or "freedom from passion"). These virtues promote a state of tranquility, immunity to the vicissitudes of fortune, and steadfastness before either pleasure or pain. The virtues point to the ideal state of mind of the rational individual. Roman Stoicism demonstrates the universality of its principles in its two most famous and very different advocates: the Greek Epictetus (50–135), a tutor and former slave, and Marcus Aurelius (121–180), Rome's greatest emperor.

A contemporary alternative to Stoicism is the thought of Epicurus (341–270 BCE). While embracing the basic concepts of Stoicism in terms of tranquility of mind, Epicurus expected from society and individuals no more than a minimum of virtue. He advocates *aponia* ("absence of pain") as the most logical goal or state of mind. The individual should pursue plea-sure, not as hedonism but in order to identify those activities and personal relations that particularly foster tranquility and quietude. This tenet implies withdrawal from worldly activity.

Because of its emphasis on "pleasure" versus "virtue," Epicureanism has often been distorted as egoism. Understood philosophically, Epicureanism converges with Stoicism, only differing in emphasis and personality.

Stoicism establishes the philosophical foundations of early Christianity in the realm of ethics. In its emphasis on tranquility of mind and attainment of virtue, Stoicism furthers the psychology of the individual disengaged from the world, a necessary trajectory to justify eremitism.

3. Early Judaism

Historical Judaism does not encourage or foster eremites. Social and religious activities are communal. Jewish youth were expected to marry and raise families. Tradition and Talmudic scripture and authority crafted religious expression of prayer and ritual to require group settings that could not be performed alone or in solitude.

In anthropology, strict adherence to socially–sanctioned expression is a representative remnant of historical clan and tribal societies in geographical isolation. The ethnic Hebrews of history and scripture cultivated not only a people exclusively chosen by God but an indivisible cultural identity. Folkloric clues to tribal separatism include stories like the those of Cain and Esau, failed brothers exiled into nomadism and solitude. Another clue is the set of formulaic commandments safeguarding tribal identity and tribal members, each imprecation beginning with the familiar phrase "Thou shalt not …." The object of each commandment is not universal ethics but social order within the clan or tribe.

Solitude is the privilege of prophets such as Moses and Elijah. According to the Book of Exodus, Moses "entered a cloud" for forty days, a mystical and solitary state. Elijah, or Elias, described in the Book of Kings, devotes his life to a fierce opposition to the Canaanite king Ahab, a life–long dedication on behalf of but physically separate from the Jewish community.

Two Jewish religious communities of the first century CE represent nascent cenobitic (that is, communal) monasticism: the Essenes and the Therapeutae. The Essenes were small monastic groups of men living under common rule governing prayer, ritual, meals, and daily life. The male monks emphasized asceticism, including prayer, fasting, and celibacy. The Greek–speaking Jewish philosopher Philo of Alexandria (20 BCE–50 CE) describes the Therapeutae as Egyptian monastic adherents emphasizing ascetic practices, including contemplation. The Therapeutae are distinctive for their inclusion of women, who lived in separate quarters but who participated with male adherents in a weekly communal meal.

But little else is known of these Jewish monastic movements. They appear to have been limited to one–time short–lived efforts. Did Jesus or John the Baptizer visit the Essenes? Were the Therapeutae a disguised Christian or Gnostic group? These are speculations, for nothing else is known of them, except that they were distinctly transient.

A Jewish pursuit of eremitic life and an intrinsic view of solitude as integral to religious insight first arises among Jewish mystics of the Middle Ages. These Jewish mystics will be visited in section 33.

4. Early Christianity

Inheriting the anti–eremitic tradition of Judaism, the earliest generation of Christians maintained the idea of tight–knit identity, highlighted by the communal sharing of goods, as described in the Acts of the Apostles. But Christianity had broken from the exclusivity of Judaism, universalizing its faith to include Jewish and pagan converts. Succeeding generations of Christians abandon the millennial expectation of Christ's second coming. The need to establish a firm foundation for the future arises. Household and communal ritual and prayer was eventually ceded from community to a priesthood and an ecclesiastical structure that forcefully identifies the priorities of religion as dogma and ritual.

The process of consolidating a church structure further distinguishes the historical Jesus from the ecclesiastical Jesus. Some recent scholars identify the historical Jesus as a Cynic in style, espousing poverty, simplicity, and the primacy of individual virtue, opposing the corruption of authority and wealth, and eschewing complex theology and ritual for personal behavior and discipline.

As already noted, the Greek word *eremos* means "desert." The famous temptations of Jesus at the end of his solitary period of prayer in the desert suggests that Jesus pursued a period of solitude exceptional to Judaism. John the Baptizer clearly dwells in a desert setting from whence he emerges from its obscurity to promote Jesus. "Desert" becomes synonymous with a "place of desolation." Thus the setting of the temptations of Jesus is extrapolated to all deserts, all places of desolation, full of countless demons tormenting hermits.

An enormous increase in the number of hermits in the deserts of Egypt, Palestine, and Syria marks the third century. Monasteries barely exist at this time, bypassed by hermits and the small networks of hermit communities. The growth of eremitism within such short centuries comes at a specific time within the Roman Empire, with its unrelieved persecutions of Christians. Ultimately, the Christian heroes of faith become not the perseverant and the martyrs but those who renounce an unredeemable world. This renunciation is subtle, spiritual, and a dramatic reshaping of the Christian narrative, a renunciation not only of the world but of the church in the world.

5. Paul of Thebes, the first Christian hermit

In the later fourth century, the Roman scholar Saint Jerome (347–420) was to spend five restless years as a desert solitary. For him everything goes wrong. Jerome complains that the desert heat is oppressive, his skin is dry, his thirst perpetual, his hunger unabated. He is surrounded by scorpions and haunted by dreams of Rome and dancing girls. Jerome finally quits the hermit experiment and returns to urban life, to his precious books and the company of intellectual friends, thereafter busily writing eloquent prose: from biography and invective to the influential Latin translation of the Bible from Hebrew and Greek. And he becomes a cardinal.

But Jerome's masterpiece is his short "life" or *vita* of the first Christian hermit Paul of Thebes, a hagiographical sketch of perfect eremitism. The medieval *Golden Legend* includes Paul of Thebes, but in a spiritless crib of Jerome's animated account.

Though some contemporaries called Anthony the first desert hermit, Jerome maintained otherwise. In Jerome's account, Anthony leaves Egypt for the desert, interpreting a sign of God, and searches for Paul. He finds Paul's cave. Paul welcomes the visitor, greeting Anthony's timely arrival to bury one who will soon be dust. They sit and converse. Paul asks, in a memorable passage:

> Tell me, how fares the human race?
> Do new roofs rise in ancient cities?
> Whose empire now sways the world?
> Do any yet survive, snared in the errors of demons?

As they speak, a crow flies near, depositing before them a loaf of bread. Paul explains that every day for sixty years his portion has been half a loaf, but now God had sent enough for both of them. They eat, and drink water. Paul resumes speaking of his imminent death, and a weeping Anthony begs him to stop. Paul insists, asking Anthony to return to Alexandria and bring a cloak Paul had once given to Bishop Athanasius, that it may serve as Paul's burial cloak. Anthony promises, reluctantly retracing his steps back to civilization.

Along the way, two disciples intercept Anthony and ask where he has been for so long. "I have seen Elijah, I have seen John in the desert," replies Anthony. As he feared, however, Anthony receives a vision of Paul's death, seeing the soul fly to heaven, accompanied by angels.

After reaching Egypt and retrieving the cloak, Anthony hurries again into the desert to fulfill his promise to bury Paul's body. Returning to the cave, he wraps the body in the cloak he has brought. He realizes that he has no spade. Two lions near Paul's cave are in apparent lamentation. The lions begin to paw the ground, making a hole the size of a man. Anthony deposits the body of Paul into the grave and covers it with dirt. Anthony had used Paul's cloak for burial garb, and now takes Paul's woven palm-leaf tunic with him to Egypt, the tunic which he will thereafter wear every Easter and Pentecost.

6. Anthony (the Great)

Jerome's biography of Paul of Thebes prominently features Anthony, who considers Paul the perfect hermit. Within a generation, Anthony would become the influence for hundreds of hermits populating the deserts of Egypt and adjacent regions.

As a young layman of comfortable means, Anthony had lost his parents and been swindled of inheritance by his sister's fiancé. Despairing of his future, Anthony one day hears preached the Gospel passage wherein Jesus teaches that to be perfect one must give all one's possessions to the poor and follow him. For Anthony, following Jesus does not mean entering a monastery or becoming a priest, but a more radical vision of simplicity and solitude in the desert. Few hermits lived in the desert in his day, but by the end of his life Anthony enjoyed the distinction of popularizing eremitism to an entire generation.

Anthony's repute stems from the biography written by Athanasius, bishop of Alexandria. As a writer, Athanasius lacked the empathy and rhetorical skill of Jerome, and instead populates his story with demons, temptations, and dramatic miracles. This version of Anthony would attract latter–day painters (section 41) and inspire the famous nineteenth–century French novelist Gustav Flaubert to write *The Temptation of Saint Anthony* (section 50). Athanasius was a busy apologist and heresy–fighter unfamiliar with hermit life. We learn far more about Christian desert hermits from compilers of their deeds and sayings.

7. Christian Desert Hermits

Eremitism in Christianity emerges in specific geographical locations and in specific modes of expression. Because Anthony lived and traveled in Lower Egypt, the region close to the Nile river delta and westward towards Alexandria, the first significant population of hermits emerged there in the later fourth century. In Upper Egypt, the mountainous southern regions closer to the origins of the Nile, cenobitic monasticism emerges under the tutelage of Pachomius (292–348). Unlike eremitism, monasticism organizes men as brothers or monks in a communal setting under an abbot. Monasteries often grew large and complex, requiring a consistent set of rules and practices. They become the default mode of religious organization in the Western, Orthodox, and Coptic worlds.

A third pattern between solitaries and monastics emerges around Mount Nitria and Scete, the crossroads of monks and hermits. Here *laura* or *lavra* (Greek: Λαύρα) served as individual accommodation (huts and cottages) around separate communal meals and rituals. A *skete* (Greek: σκήτη) refers to an accommodation where two or three hermits live in isolation under a single roof. Inhabitants of *laura* and *sketes* were reputedly more intellectually–minded, but their practice emphasized prayer and manual labor, not scholarship. The deserts of Nitria and Scete were soon dotted with hermitages close to or farther from one another, but hermits regularly checked on fellow hermits.

In Syria, Palestine, and Asia Minor, still more eremitic expressions emerged. Asia Minor was populated by urban and ecclesiastical centers fostering liturgically–based monasticism. Palestine's deserts evolve systems of eremites similar to the laura and sketes of Egypt. Some of the earliest hermits known by name lived in greater Syria. In Syria, as historian Peter Brown has shown, hermits lived proximate to villages and farms and come to be incorporated into the social and economic lives of poor farmers, pastoralists, and villagers. These "holy men" were esteemed for overseeing religious ceremony, encouraging mutual aid, mingling with average people and sharing their labor. Syria also hosted more eccentric hermits pursuing extremes of ascetic practice, such as living in wilderness, wearing chains, eating only foraged foods, "holy fools" judged mad by the world. A few hermits were celebrated *stylites*, or "pillar–dwellers," living atop pillars and never descending them, dependent on alms. The most famous of these is Simeon Stylites (section 9).

8. Sayings of the Christian Desert Hermits

We know a great deal about the ethos of the desert hermits from the diligently compiled collections of their deeds and sayings by their contemporaries.

An early source on the Egyptian hermits is a now lost original manuscript titled *Historia Monachorum* (or "History of the Monks of Egypt"), composed by an anonymous Jerusalem monk but attributed by some to Evagrius Pontius (349–399), a friend of contemporaries from Jerome to church historian Palladius. The work is based on personal travels in Nitria and Scete, translated into an empathetic Latin by Rufinius, who had replicated the travels himself.

Subsequent collections of sayings comprise what scholar Helen Waddell called "the kernel of the desert tradition." The *Verba Seniorum* ("Sayings of the Fathers") was translated from the Greek by Pelagius the Deacon, recording the sayings of hermits from Nitria and Scete between the mid–fourth to mid–fifth century. The fathers or *abbas* range from scholars to illiterate shepherds, from lofty Greek–speakers to speakers of classical Egyptian. Later collections include a translation by Paschasius of Dumium (sixth–century), the reflective compilations by John Cassian titled *Institutes* and *Conferences*, and works of Palladius, author of *Lausiac History,* and John Moschus, author of *Pratum Spirituale* or "Spiritual Meadow." Of these writers, Cassian will prove most influential in the West because after wide travels in hermit lands he settled in Gaul and founded two monasteries.

These collections arrange hermit sayings by topic, such as quietude, compunction, self–restraint, patience, discretion, hospitality, or contemplation, and are called systematic collections. The *Apophthegmata Patrum*, also translated as "Sayings of the Fathers," is arranged alphabetically by person, thus providing a catalog of relevant hermits as well as aphorisms, sayings, and anecdotes. The chief work lists 131 hermits by name. A third category of collections is anonymous, sayings not attributable to a specific person.

Among famous hermits are Anthony, Arsenius, Bessarion, John the Dwarf, Macarius, Moses, Pambo, and Poemen. Moses was Black, perhaps Ethiopian, often suffering the bias of his fellow hermits. A small but significant number of hermits were women, called *ammas* or desert mothers, among them Sarah, Theodora, and Syncletica. Here we shall look at a few of the hermits and record a telling anecdote or saying:

- A monk asked Anthony what he, the inquiring monk, must do. Anthony's advice: do not trust one's righteousness, do not pay attention to the past, and control the mouth and stomach. Every year, three monks visited Anthony. Two discussed their thoughts openly while the third always remained silent. One year, Anthony asked the third monk why he remained silent. It is enough to see you, replied the monk.

- In old age, Arsenius (360–449) was tall, austere, long-bearded, and self–effacing. His cell was miles away from anyone. In church he sat behind a pillar in order not to be seen or distract others. He was born in Rome and raised in privilege but had long ago fled for the Egyptian desert. Despite education he read little. Asked why he spoke with peasants, Arsenius replied that they acquire virtue by hard work, not education.

- When archbishop Theophilus came to visit Arsenius, seeking advice, Arsenius asked him if he would take the advice to heart, to which Theophilus agreed. Then do not come and see me, Arsenius told him, for I cannot refuse you or anyone else, and if you come I will have to leave this place.

- When Arsenius was close to death, his disciples confessed to him that they did not know how to bury a body. Arsenius replied that they should just put a rope around his feet and drag his body into the mountains.

- Moses had reputedly been a robber. Many monks abused him until he became a priest. Moses is famous for saying to Poemen that a monk should go to his cell and remain there, for his cell would teach him everything. One day, Moses walked to a crossroads when a party of travelers asked him directions to the cell of Moses. Why do you want to see that old fool? Moses tells them. They insist, so at last Moses points down the road. "That way," he said—pointing in the opposite direction to his cell.

- Poemen was in his cell when an acquaintance brought a learned man to see him. The learned man spoke incessantly about theology, Scripture, and heaven. Poemen remained silent. The learned man went out, complaining to Poemen's acquaintance. The acquaintance went in to Poemen, asking why he would not speak in the learned man's presence. He speaks of things of which I know little, replied Poemen. I only know the passions of the soul. The acquaintance returned to the learned man, explaining what the hermit said he knew. The meeting resumed, and the learned man was edified.

- Bessarion was in church one day when a young brother was expelled by a priest for sin. Bessarion rose to leave, announcing that he, too, is a sinner. It is said that Bessarion lived in open air, not in a cell, wandering from place to place, saying of himself that he is like a bird or animal content with every place he encounters, and just as content to move on. Always, he says, I must wander in order to finish my course.

- Amma Syncletica recommended balance: do not fast a long time only to then break the fast sumptuously; do not grieve the sins of others only to succumb to *accidie* (melancholy). Do not preach to others without practical knowledge of the desert life. Do not pursue asceticism only to ignore discipline. Do not live as a solitary in the mountains only to have a soul crowded with thoughts.

A literary trope of the era is the repentant woman, extrapolating the Gospel figure of Magdalene. The subjects of this genre of *vitae* (lives) include Pelagia, Mary (called "Peccatrix"), and Thais, the latter depicted in the anti–clerical 1890 novel *Thais* by Anatole France, complementing Flaubert's hostile depiction of St. Anthony. The lives of the repentants are composed in the context of the sayings tradition that pits the solitary monk and hermit against temptation to save the fallen woman, and therein themselves.

9. Simon Stylites: Pillar Hermit

Early Christian Syria witnessed an eccentric asceticism pursuing self–mortification: cave–dwelling, food–foraging, wearing of chains, feigning of madness ("fool for Christ"), and pillar–dwelling, practices believed to be accelerated paths to personal salvation, often with a public face. Though Palladius of Antioch, Gregory Nazianzus, and Theodoret reported seeing pillar–dwellers (*stylites*) in deserts, Simon (or Simeon) is the first confirmed pillar–dweller. Simon occupied the top of a column from the year 423 to his death in 460. Successors include Daniel, Simeon the Younger, and Alypius of Hadrianopolis.

More than a thousand years later, Simon Stylites provoked the rationalist historian Edward Gibbon (1737–1794) to articulate invective in his famous *History of the Decline and Fall of the Roman Empire*, where he writes of Simon (volume 1, chapter 37):

> In this last and lofty station, the Syrian Anachoret resisted the heat of thirty summers, and the cold of as many winters. Habit and exercise instructed him to maintain his dangerous situation without fear or giddiness, and successively to assume the different postures of devotion. He sometimes prayed in an erect attitude, with his outstretched arms in the figure of a cross; but his most familiar practice was that of bending his meagre skeleton from the forehead to the feet; and a curious spectator, after numbering twelve hundred and forty–four repetitions, at length desisted from the endless account. The progress of an ulcer in his thigh might shorten, but it could not disturb, this celestial life; and the patient Hermit expired without descending from his column. … This voluntary martyrdom must have gradually destroyed the sensibility both of the mind and body; nor can it be presumed that the fanatics who torment themselves are susceptible of any lively affection for the rest of mankind.

A century later, British poet Alfred Lord Tennyson (1809-1892) composed a long poem titled "St. Simeon Stylites," published in 1842. The poem inherits the contemporary repugnance for ancient hygiene and religious arrogance assessed of Simeon. It is neither satire nor scorn, wavering between.

> Altho' I be the basest of mankind,
> From scalp to sole one slough and crust of sin,
> Unfit for earth, unfit for heaven, scarce meet
> For troops of devils, mad with blasphemy,

I will not cease to grasp the hope I hold
Of saintdom, and to clamour, morn and sob,
Battering the gates of heaven with storms of prayer,
Have mercy, Lord, and take away my sin. ...
Patient on this tall pillar I have borne
Rain, wind, frost, heat, hail, damp, sleet, and snow;
And I had hoped that ere this period closed
Thou wouldst have caught me up into Thy rest,
Denying not these weather-beaten limbs
The meed of saints, the white robe and the palm ...

Despite his virulent anti–clericalism, the Spanish filmmaker Luis Buñuel (1900–1983) treated Simon Stylites with considerable empathy in his 1965 film *Simon of the Desert* (*Simón del Desierto*). Perhaps Buñuel is a surrogate Simon, looking down in disdain at the follies of the bourgeoisie. The pious come to Simon seeking boons but contradicting their own beliefs. A thief whose hands were cut off as punishment asks for favor and Simon restores his hands, upon which the man slaps his fidgeting child. Elders quarrel about trivia and status in front of Simon. A delegation of priests vainly quarrels among themselves about their virtues. The devil in the form of a seductive woman repeatedly tempts Simon, who resists with exasperated patience. At film's end, she transports Simon, now groomed and dapper, to a modern dance club where youths gyrate to a song called "Radioactive Flesh," the "last dance," she points out. Simon insists on returning to his pillar, but the devil demurs.

CHAPTER 2

EREMITISM IN MEDIEVAL WESTERN EUROPE

10. Eremitism Comes to the West

By the end of the seventh century, Christian hermits nearly disappeared from their traditional geographic locations. Persia expanded into part of Byzantium, then Islam overtook Egypt, Syria, Palestine, and Asia Minor up to the Black Sea. Christian eremites retreated to Ethiopia, Greece, and nascent Russia.

When knowledge of the desert hermits reaches Western Europe through John Cassian, among other sources, a rigid ecclesiastical system had already been in place for centuries. Monasticism remained elective and fluid, chiefly modeled after the Eastern experience of small communities based on contemplation and manual labor. Monasticism spread widely in Italy, Gaul, Spain, and leaped to Celtic Ireland and Anglo–Saxon Britain, the latter two lands especially favoring eremitic traditions of peregrination or wandering.

Ecclesiastical authorities had been slow to regulate monasteries, but explicit when they did. One of the prescriptions of the Council of Vannes (Gaul) in 465 maintained that monks could not inhabit solitary cells unless they were of exceptional virtue, and even so were not to leave the precincts of their abbey. The anonymous early sixth–century *Regula Magistri* ("Rule of the Master") begins a shift in monasteries from contemplation to rote prayer and ritual.

In the first chapter of his famous monastic *Rule*, Saint Benedict of Nursia (480–543) described four classes of monks. Cenobitic monks living in community are the only genuine monks. Hermits are monks experienced in spiritual practice, presumably capable of pursuing their practice without community help. But Benedict expresses a resentment toward hermits, further evoking the third and fourth categories of monks, both nefarious and proscribed: *sarabaites* and *gyrovagues*. Both types are labeled religious frauds. Sarabaites are monks living in groups of two or three, and gyrovagues are wanderers. Although Benedict's sarabaites and gyrovagues parallel Eastern skete–dwelling desert hermits, his comments suggest a deep hostility towards any form of non–cenobitic monasticism.

Allusions to wandering monks and hermits are found in John Cassian and St. Augustine, the latter calling them *circumcellions*, meaning "those who go round and round," referring specifically to Donatist heretics. Synods at Angers (453), Vannes (465), and Toledo (633) condemned *religiosi vagabondi*. The triumph of the Benedictine *Rule* in established monasteries under abbots also enforced the expectation of a monk's permanent residence in his first choice of institution.

While in part an ecclesiastical issue, landlopers or gyrovagi represent a social and economic manifestation of the chaotic conditions of the late Empire and early Middle Ages, wherein wanderers might be displaced homeless as much as tricksters and thieves. The freedom of the gyrovagi foreshadows the preaching element of later orders, which would evolve separately from monks as friars.

As the social and economic collapse spanned successive centuries, monasticism itself was impacted, retreating into a rigid mode of self–serving survival and convenience. Monasticism atrophied into multiplying rote prayer, offices, and ritual, with some scholarship for the few literate, while the eremitic balance of prayer, labor, and service diminishes. Constantly increasing their landholdings, monasteries became increasingly dependent upon benefices and the labor of lay brothers.

The *Regula solitariorum* ("Rule for Solitaries") by the Carolingian prelate Grimlaicus (issued in 900) demonstrates that while monasticism remained uncomfortable with eremites, ongoing interest in eremitism was reluctantly addressed. Grimlaicus reiterates the spirit and strictures of the *Rule* of St. Benedict, but specifically addresses cenobitic solitaries dwelling in a monastery.

Also representative of the "rule" genre are two discrete writings by

Guigo (1083–1136), the fifth prior of Chartreuse. The *Consuetudine* or "Customs" covers routines from the shaving of monks to meal schedules. Chapter 4 explicitly states that "Our chief purpose is to study the silence and solitude of the cell," and illustratively notes that the monks rarely sing (that is, chant) the Mass because of the priority of silence and solitude. *Meditations* also extols solitude. Both manuals are intended for use within Guigo's Carthusian monastery. Among the eremitic figures inspiring Guigo is St. Eucharius of Lyon (380-449), who pursued the hermit life of solitary study after the death of his wife.

11. Early Medieval Hermits of Britain

The circumscribing influence of Benedict on eremites may be reflected in the scarcity of hermits and their influence in continental Europe until the twelfth century. Yet eremites prove very successful in early medieval Britain. Perhaps the relative absence of urban and dominant ecclesiastical centers favor hermit development in this era. Or, as Thomas Merton quips in his book *Wisdom of the Desert*, the early Christian hermits prospered by not having bishops too close to or too interested in the desert.

A deep psychology of solitude dominates the early medieval Anglo–Saxon mentality, receptive to hermits and solitary places. Five Old English poems share this profound sensibility: "Wanderer," "Seafarer," "Deor," "Resignation," and "Ruin."

"Wanderer" presents the despair of a vassal whose lord and retainers were slain in an attack by marauders, with the whole town and its residents wiped out. The poet survives, but the horrors of that day haunt him. He takes up a little boat to seek out a new lord and welcoming village, but everywhere he goes he encounters the same carnage and destruction. The poet is a wanderer on the face of land and sea, suffering a grim and irreconcilable solitude.

"Seafarer" and "Resignation" present the laments of an exile not unlike the poet of "Wanderer" except that the motive of exile is penitential, not lamentational. A better description than penitential would be ascetic, for exile is pursued in these poems as an ascetic exercise, in keeping with the motive of the early medieval English hermits and wayfarers.

"Deor" lists historical and fabulous names of heroes and others whose misfortunes turned around—or did not. The poet's solace is only in the notion that everything changes. In "Ruin" an ancient ruined city is described. As in "Deor," the poet imagines what and who filled the city in its heyday and are now gone. Scholars point to the ancient Roman town of Bath as the probable site described by "Ruin," but the poet intends to identify all earthly projects as evanescent. The sentiment of all of these poems echoes the question of Paul of Thebes: "What empire holds sway these days?"

Though broadly contemporary with the famous epic poem "Beowulf," these poems share none of its violent triumphalism, the remnant of a demonstrable paganism. Instead they forecast the melancholy that situates eremites squarely within a world–weary view. Two contemporary Old Irish poems offer further confirmation: "Hermit's Song," and "Hermit and King: A Colloquy Between King Guaire of Aidne and His Brother Marban," both poems echoing the themes of the Anglo–Saxon poems.

Images of the heroic hermits Cuthbert and Guthlac emerge in biographies of the era: Bede's *Life of St. Cuthbert*, Felix's *Life of St. Guthlac*, and the anonymous *Guthlac the Hermit* (or "Guthlac A") once ascribed to Cynewulf. These works emphasize the insular conditions of Britain and Ireland that replicate the desert hermit setting of Egypt. Ancient trade routes from the Mediterranean, Spain, and Gaul brought the tradition of the desert hermits via John Cassian and others to a receptive environment, with the Celtic and Anglo–Saxon trait of wanderlust an additional influence.

Bede tells us that the seventh–century monk Cuthbert left the monastery of Lindisfarne in Northumbria for a small deserted island where he built a hut. Regular visitors seek his advice and consolation, including the king. After forty years as a hermit Cuthbert is elected bishop of Lindisfarne, and he dutifully departs his island in tears. But soon Cuthbert resigns his duties to return to the island, where he died shortly afterwards.

Guthlac of Crowland (673–714) was a cenobitic monk for two years before leaving his monastery to live as a hermit. His biographer Felix crafts Guthlac's life after that of St. Anthony, replacing the desert setting with a demon–infested boggy swamp. Eventually, Guthlac takes a ship to Crowland, imitating the peregrinations of St. Columbanus the missionary, traveling as much as Anthony in the desert. Guthlac's sister Pega (673-719) was an anchorite, with her own peregrination to Rome, where she died.

A later example of an English hermit in this model was Godric (or Goderic) of Finchale (1065–1170). Godric traveled on pilgrimage to Jerusalem twice before living most of his life as a hermit.

12. Hermit Revival in the Central Middle Ages

The decline of Benedictine monasticism, due to the rigidities already mentioned, prompted inevitable movements of reform. The eleventh–century monastic reforms are led primarily by spiritually–minded monks strongly favoring eremitism. Among reform monks on the continent of Europe are Romuald of Ravenna (951–1027), Stephen of Muret (1025–1124), Robert of Arbrissel (1045–1116), Bruno of Cologne (d. 1101), and Robert of Molesmes (1029–1111). They create alternative religious communities based on new spiritual priorities.

While retaining the culture of monasticism, the new founders sought a return to the values of poverty and asceticism, a shift from rote prayer and ritual in physically comfortable settings to contemplation and work in the "desert" and "wilderness." They did not want to be poor within a rich community but to go where poverty and simplicity exists naturally. They wanted the insecurity of the daily life of Jesus versus the comfort of dependence or charity. They wanted physical labor and to grow their food rather than employ others to serve them. Eremitic cenobites evolved from these reforms into new orders: Cistercians, Camaldolese, and the Hermits of St. Augustine.

These founders, influential eremitic figures, are:

- Robert of Arbrissel (1045–1116), Fontevrault, France
- Stephen of Muret (1045–1124), Grandmont, France
- Bruno of Cologne (1030–1101), Chartreuse, France
- Romuald of Ravenna (951–1027), Camaldolese order, Italy
- Peter Damian (1007–1072), Fonte Avellana, Italy
- Nilus of Rossano (910–1005), Grottaferrata, Italy
- Guillermo of Vercelli (1085–1142), Williamite order, Italy
- John Buoni of Cesena (1168–1224), Bonite order, Italy
- Blasius of Brittinis (12th century), Brittinian order, Italy

Additionally, central Italy in this era is dotted with hermitages concentrated in Montagna du Fiori, Ascolo, Monte Pisano, Luca, Pisa, Monteluco, and Spoleto.

The hermits of the era maintained that the divergence of spiritual values and expression between hermits and monks is caused by the monastic departure from the teachings of Jesus. The hermits do not advocate apostolic property in common but evangelical poverty. Giovanni Gualberto (985–1073) tried to reconcile eremitism and monasticism in the Vallambrosan movement—based on his monastery and its austerities—but failed because his order remained rooted in Benedictine practice. Peter Damian (1007-1072) writes to a hermit Leo explaining that the hermit turns the world inside-out, renouncing the world for the sake of the world. Peter Damian described his biographee Romuald of Ravenna (951–1027) as a gadfly to abbots, a tireless proponent of eremitism who would turn the whole world into a hermitage.

Evangelical poverty could not be reconciled within the existing monastic structure. To be free of the world and to apply oneself entirely to spiritual pursuits diverged from monastic collectivism and toward material and spiritual self–sufficiency. As William of Saint–Thierry (1080–1148) put it to fellow hermits, while others were to serve God, they were to cling to God.

In his *Thoughts*, Stephen Muret (1045–1124) writes that there is no rule but Christ. In contrast, the monasteries are notable for spacious quarters, fine meals, great expanses of land, and large flocks of sheep. Though he "founded" the monastery of Grandmont, Muret himself intended only to set up small communities of forest–dwelling hermits.

Each founder perceives the freedom of the hermit as a rejection of the safe refuge of the monk, at once a defiance of the world and its temptations while yet living in the world and interacting with those who would support the hermit's material needs.

13. Women Hermits in the Central Middle Ages

Several women hermits are mentioned in collected sayings of desert hermits; a larger number are named in the "post–desert" sixth century but without detail: Anastasia, Apollonaria, Athanasia, Euphrosyne, Hilaria, Theodora, Matrona, Eugenia, Marina, Eusebia, Hospitia, Pelagia, Marana, and Cyra. In medieval times, women hermits lived in Britain, Italy, Gaul, and Ireland. Several British women hermits of this era include Ethelthrith of Crowland (England's most popular female saint), Milburga, Frideswide, Hilda, and the aforementioned Pega.

In ancient and medieval patriarchal society, women were physically and socially vulnerable. In the desert era, women traveled little, often concealing themselves in men's garb when in public. Euphrosyna of Alexandria disguised herself as a man to enter a monastery and quietly reside there for nearly forty years! A desert ideal was expressed by St. Jerome's praise of Sophronia of Tarentum (Spain), who lived a life of solitude in a forest; later hagiography relates that upon her death, birds brought twigs, leaves, and flowers to cover her body. More realistically is the experience of Hermelindis, a sixth–century resident of Flemish Brabant who fled marriage to retain her virginity and live a life of abstinence, an example anticipating the women of the central medieval era for whom the dilemma of marriage versus eremitism and abstinence became a central issue.

Meanwhile, the familiar harlot trope of the desert era, using the term "peccatrix" or "sinner," began with elaborations on legends about Mary Magdalene, and culminated with the lives of Maria Peccatrix and Thais, their counterpart rescuers being the hermits Abraham (Maria's grandfather) and Paphnutius (who reclaims Thais). Both women were early characters in two medieval dramas by the talented German nun–playwright Hrotsvitha of Gandersheim (935–1002).

In the European Middle Ages, women were not permitted to live alone. For women with a religious or spiritual inclination, convents were the only practical option. But nuns, too, were forbidden a life of eremitism or even significant solitude in convents. Many women, like Hermelindis, became religious–oriented recluses, concealing themselves from abusive men and protecting themselves from domestic violence by dwelling in solitude outside of populated areas, like Sophronia. Early synods reiterated the prohibition of reclusion for women. The Second Lateran Council of 1139 expressly forbad reclusion to women.

The mix of religious with social and cultural thinking on the part of ecclesiastical authorities points to the specific notion of women as the traditional "weaker" sex for whom contemplation in solitude was not possible and even dangerous to their fragile minds. Women seeking to avoid arranged marriage often insisted on refuge in convent, or reclusion, and when forced into marriage insisted on "virginal" relations, as in the case of the British mystic Christina of Markyate (1096-1155), who fled her husband to live as a hermit before her marriage was annulled. Married women in distress thus depended on sympathetic clergy not frequently accessible. More examples in the thirteenth century are discussed below.

In the later twelfth century, a rise of eremitic movements sweeps Europe. Rules for women recluses, circumscribed to the status of anchorites (or "anchoresses"), were no longer in favor on the continent, though the alternative term "inclusion" was employed. A unique social form evolved among the Beguines (section 15).

In England two outstanding rules address women recluses, offering evidence of the influence of reclusion as a spiritual alternative to monastic life. While an eleventh–century guide by Goscelin of St. Bertin titled *Liber Confortatorius* ("The Book of Encouragement and Consolation") is closer to the genre or style of Augustinian consolation, two specific English manuals or guides establish the eremitic genre for women.

Aelred of Rievaux (1110–1167) wrote his *De institutione inclusarum* ("Rule for an Incluse") for his inclused sisters. A second famous work, composed in the thirteenth century, is attributed to an unnamed Augustinian monk: *Ancrene Wisse* ("Rule for Anchorites"), called by historian Wolfgang Riehle a "magnificent exemplar of early English mysticism." Both rules for female recluses are spiritual guides fostering reclusion (or inclusion) and, indirectly, nascent forms of mysticism.

Aelred's sisters lived on their own property, confining themselves to their own quarters, as opposed to the later anchoritic practice (reflected in *Ancrene Wisse*) of dwelling within a small building or room attached to a municipal church as an anchorhold. Aelred does not mention the later devotional nor communitarian emphasis on the Mass and Communion. Presumably, the sisters depended on the occasional visits of priests for counsel and sacraments. Aelred's guide specifically identifies the anchorite's firm basis in the poverty and solitude of the desert hermits, describing the anchorite's material conditions in detail and emphasizing the importance of contemplation over rote prayer.

In the twelfth century, the Alsatian abbess (and accomplished artist) Herrad of Landsberg declares (in her compendium *Hortus deticiarum* ("Garden of Delights") that women recluses are only second to hermits—that is, male hermits— and are free to pursue their religious inclinations outside of monasteries and churches. On the continent, the notion that recluses should be restricted to anchorholds attached to churches, as in England, was not universal. In Germany, the countess Jutta von Sponheim (1091-1136) became an anchorite while yet presiding over an abbey. Among the young charges in Jutta's hermitage is the child Hildegard of Bingen (1098-1179).

The saint and mystic Hildegard one day succeeds Jutta as abbess, though not as an anchorite.

Records indicate that women recluses of the era lived in cells within cemeteries, at city gates, on bridges, and even on river islands—in Paris, Bonn, Toulouse, Auvergne Gaul, and the Hungarian Danube.

Anecdotes about women solitaries in Italy are numerous. During the thirteenth century, Chelidonid lived as a solitary among rocks and caves until becoming a sponsored hermit under the monastery of Subiaco. Santa Franca of the Marches retired to a hermitage. Bona of Pisa made a pilgrimage to the Holy Land and lived briefly as a hermit. Sperandea of Umbria would live as a solitary during Lent. Margherita Colanna dwelt in a cave on the Prenestina Hill in Rome before entering a community of Poor Clares. Umiliana Cerchi aspired to live in her family's palace tower without a door or window, or to live in mountainous wilderness eating only herbs. Clare of Montefalco is one of the few recluses to live in a cenobitic community.

In fourteenth–century Italy, reclusion is maintained by specific sponsors: abbots, secular clergy, lay orders, even local civil authority. Among such recluses are Giana Braccus of Florence, who lived on a bridge at Rubaconte, and Maria Gherardhetta of Pisa, sponsored by Camaldolese. Verdiana of Castelfiorentino lived under the authority of secular clergy, as did Margaret of Cortona and Sibyllina of Pavia, a Dominican penitent.

Documentation on women hermits and recluses of the thirteenth century is chiefly found in wills and benefices lacking biographical or hagiographical detail. Documentation on central Italy especially suggests the prevalence of non–institutional recluses living in and outside of urban centers, on or under bridges, city gates, and roadsides, and in or on churches, mountains, and forests. These documents point to networks of alms or pecuniary distribution to hermits and recluses—not by indifferent bishops but chiefly by laity. The situation contrasts with that of institutionalized anchorites (especially in England), declining eremitic orders, and cenobitic hermits.

During the twelfth and thirteenth centuries, a new vocabulary emerges, reflecting the varied locations of the recluses: *portiuncula* (little place), *casula* (cottage) and *domincula* (little cabin). Even the roles of the recluses are refined in central Italy: *reclusi* becomes a generic term that includes *carcerati* (enclosed) or *incarcerati* (literally, incarcerated), *hermitae* (living outside of formal buildings), *frates et sorores* (brothers and sisters, in lay roles) and *pauperes monialis* (reclused or poor enclosed nuns). Not included as eremitic are the *bizzoca* or penitentials, specifically of third order laity.

In contrast to the old monastic orders, the emphasis of the new eremitic movements of this era is simplicity, poverty, asceticism, and solitude, values attributed to the desert hermits which also specifically nourish feminine qualities of spiritual expression.

The life paths of women recluses varied greatly from those of men. The most typical conflict arose when parents opposed their daughter's vocation and husbands opposed their new wife's insistence on chastity. For example, Jeanne–Marie de Maille (1331–1414) of the diocese of Tours, denied a vocation as a nun and obliged by her family to marry, lived in virginal marriage and became a recluse in widowhood. She then tried living in an anchorhold, quit to live in a convent, but returned to the solitude of her cell. Similarly, the aforementioned Christina of Markyate (1097-1161) insisted on a virginal marriage despite her parents and husband. When her husband at last changed his mind, she nevertheless leaves him to be enclosed as a recluse by a sympathetic hermit. Virginal marriage becomes a medieval hagiographic theme or archetype in this era, reflecting women's spiritual model of solitude as mystical marriage to the bridegroom Christ.

Other instances of women's opposition to convention confirm historical obstacles to women seeking solitude and reclusion. Rosanesa of Faenza (1226–1310) married at fifteen, lost two sons, then convinced her husband to mutually enter celibacy and monastic life. As the nun Umiltà, Rosanesa did not become a recluse but became an abbess, founder of convents, and composer of sermons. Dorothea von Montau of Marienwerder (fourteenth–century Germany) married and became a mother, but when her children reached adulthood created of her room what her biographer describes as reclusion-in-family, remaining in her house on her own property. Caesar of Heislerbach mentions a nun of Wurzburg who rejected her parents' insistence on marriage, is finally given permission to leave, and obtains the local bishop's support of her reclusion under the authority of the abbot of the Cistercian monastery at Brombach.

Eve of St. Martin (1190-1265) in Liege—to whom Goscelin addressed his *Book of Encouragement*—was prompted by pious parents to a monastic life. She lived a while in England under Goscelin's direction but returned to France seeking reclusion. Eve first found a reclusive place in St. Laurent, then St. Eutrope in Angers, and finally, with the assistance of a hermit named Herve, a cottage adjacent to his hermitage.

Yvette d'Huy (1158-1228) married, became a mother, then a widow, after which she worked in a leprosarium, finally becoming a recluse at Orval.

Filippa Mareri (1190-1236) of Italy was a recluse in her family's home, then a hermit in a solitary place, and finally entered a community of Poor Clares.

Having experienced the typical social stages of average women in the Middle Ages, the women enumerated above nevertheless achieve a level of spirituality that clerical critics could not comprehend. The women hermits inhabited a state not so much of abstinence or self–discipline but what may be called non–temptation. Anecdotes record a feminine strength not tempted by lust, gluttony, or power. But some suffer *acedia* (melancholy), doubt, and visions. Among visionaries are the recluses Herluca of Epfach and Alpais of Cudiet, who visualize the wounds of Christ, in anticipation of Francis of Assisi, though in their feminine sensibilities do not comprehend the visions in terms of suffering. Similar visions affected Yvette d'Huy and Julian of Norwich, the latter extrapolating the meaning of her visions in her famous book, *Revelations of Divine Love*. Later beguines also experience visions.

While the historical momentum of eremites in the central Middle Ages appears unstoppable, a decline of eremitism begins abruptly in the thirteenth century, due in part to the Church's intense pressure to regularize hermits and recluses into established monastic or other orders, but also due to the rise of monastic alternatives in third order and lay religious organizations. Perhaps the fatal blow to eremitism are the negative views found in authoritative figures such as Bernard of Clairvaux and Thomas Aquinas.

14. Hermit Mystics of England

Mysticism arose in fourteenth–century England based on the solitary spiritual experience fostered by eremitism. Mysticism was rooted in the practice of penitential, contemplative, and individual prayer versus the rote prayer and ritual of contemporary monasticism and the Church. Mysticism bypasses the intellectual edifice of scholastic and scriptural theology to apprehend God and the divine directly. What distinguishes men from women is the style and expression of their mysticism. While men compose crafted theological documents based on insights, women mystics write more openly of experiences, visions, and passions.

The English mystics are all hermits and anchorites. Among men are Richard Rolle (1300–1349), Walter Hilton (1340–1396), the anonymous author of *The Cloud of Unknowing* and *The Book of Privy Counseling*, and the obscure Roger Whiterig (d.1371). Women mystics include Margaret Kirby (1322–1394), Julian of Norwich (1342–1416), and Margery Kempe (1373–1438).

The earliest mystic writer in England was Richard Rolle, a layman living under various patrons, and perhaps having studied in Paris. His popular *Fire of Love* was based on his mystical experiences. His *Form of Living* is a guide for the anchoress Margaret Kirkby, herself considered a contemporary mystic. Rolle unravels a theological treatise in his subtleties and distinctions, evoking ecstatic images and anthropomorphized roles for God and soul. The state of solitude, Rolle writes, is perfect for the received revelation of the Holy Spirit. Rolle sees the hermit's love of God transcending worldly circumstances, thus avoiding the need of loving God amidst the temptations of the world.

Walter Hilton renounced a career in canon law to become a solitary layman. Like Rolle, Hilton addresses an anchoress; unlike what he calls Rolle's "enthusiasm," Hilton's *Scale of Perfection* attracted a large readership in its day because of his emphasis on practical contemplation. He contrasts contemplation with the grappling over bodily expressions of greed, lust, idleness, and the like, offering practical refuge in contemplation to overcome bodily inclinations.

Appearing in the late fourteenth century, authorship of both *The Cloud of Unknowing* and *The Book of Privy Counseling* is anonymous. Unlike the theology of Rolle and Hilton, these works are based on the earlier mystical tradition of Pseudo–Dionysius the Areopagite and Christian Neoplatonism. The mystic impulse in these works is less austere and more accessible than the author's predecessors, positive and encouraging to the reader, emphasizing the reader's spiritual resources, rooted in contemplation, against worldly temptations and a distracted mind. An example of the author's encouraging instruction:

> I bid you do of God so that you be one with Him in
> spirit, as thus, without departing and scattering, for
> He is your being and in Him you are what you are, not
> only by cause and by being but also He is in you, both
> your cause and your being.

The English mystics draw from their own pastoral and personal experiences; there is no evidence that the fourteenth–century Rhineland mystics such as Meister Eckhart, Johannes Tauler, and Henry Suso had any influence on the classic English mystics. Nor, indeed, did the Dominican mystics recommend eremitism.

Finally, among men hermits of this era is the obscure John Whiterig (d. 1371), a hermit on Farne (a small isle of Lindisfarne), and a successor to St. Cuthbert. John composed *Meditations of a Monk of Farne*, a modest work of reflections on the crucified Christ, similar to the mystical work of Julian of Norwich.

Among women mystics little is known of Margaret Kirkby except that she received the guidance of Richard Rolle as anchoress, and provided anecdotal material about Rolle for subsequent biographical projects about him. She suffered seizures earlier in her life. Though she wrote nothing, Margaret probably influenced Julian of Norwich, whom she visited.

Julian of Norwich (or Lady Juliana) was an anchorite at the Church of St. Julian in Norwich. Her own identity and whether she was a nun or layperson is unknown. She composed *Revelations of Divine Love* based on sixteen visions received during a period of illness. The theology of Lady Juliana is heavily conscious of sin but expresses optimism in the love of God. Describing herself as "a simple creature, unlettered," she recounts revelations or "showings" during which she receives three gifts: to know the Passion of Christ, to suffer illness in youth, and to receive the gift of three wounds: contrition, compassion, and "steadfast longing for God."

Margery Kempe was born and grew up in humble circumstances. She was probably illiterate, dictating the first English autobiography, known as *The Book of Margery Kempe*. She married and bore children, but early suffered visions and hallucinations. She was prone to wailing and bouts of melancholy. Restless in maturity, she once traveled with a hermit guide, of "short cheer and dismal countenance," and later to Jerusalem, Netherlands, Germany (where her son resided), and back to Canterbury. She preached publicly and insistently, arrested several times in England for public disorder.

15. Beguines and Brethren: Hermits of Continental Euope

In the early thirteenth century, women in the Low Countries embarked upon a grand experiment based on the inspiration of the desert hermits. They called themselves beguines (the meaning of the word is uncertain). Their laura and communities are called beguinages.

A century later, a parallel movement founded by Gerard Groote (1340-1384) initiated the Brethren of the Common Life, a lay movement of communities for both women and men, and the monastic-like Windesheim Congregation based on the Augustinian rule, wherein adherents were lay followers of "Devotio moderna" or "Modern Devotion."

Both movements originated in the Low Countries and spread to Germany, organizing spiritual and religious communities without formal orders, based on desert eremitism that emphasized personal spirituality and withdrawal from the world, in contrast to what was perceived as ecclesiastical and monastic wealth and power, to the neglect of souls.

Among the beguines, many women lived alone, devoting themselves to prayer and good works as lay people. Others were propertyless and poor. Women of better means owning purchased houses often shared living spaces with other spiritually–minded women, sometimes including entire urban neighborhoods.

The beguines were not nuns, took no vows, did not reside in convents, and could return to the world and marry if they chose, not renouncing their property. If a beguine was without means, she did not seek alms but supported herself by manual labor. During the time of her novitiate, a beguine lived with a "Grand Mistress" of her cloister, but otherwise no rule or order governed the beguine, bound to her companions only by common spirituality.

Beguine religious life also fostered a mysticism typifying the era. Not surprisingly, spiritual expression by lay women often challenged ecclesiastical authorities. Dutch beguine Hadewijch (1200-1248) wrote poetry and a *Book of Visions*. In Germany, Mechthild of Magdeburg (1207–1294) composed *The Flowing Light of Divinity*, a record of her visions of God. Her criticisms of ecclesiastical authorities threatened her late years. Agnes Blannbekin (1244–1315), an Austrian beguine, recorded controversial mystical visions published posthumously. The Low Country beguine Marguerite Porete (d. 1310) compiled *Mirror of Simple Souls*, describing the workings of divine love.

In Paris, she was burnt at the stake for the heresy of Free Spirit. Thereafter, a series of popes and synods suppressed the beguinages for spreading heresy, and the beguines largely scattered.

Male equivalents of beguines, called beghards, arose parallel to the women's movement. Beghards were laymen of humble means, usually weavers, dyers, and fullers living in small communities. Far less is known of the beghards, and, like the beguines, the beghards were eventually suppressed.

The Brethren paralleled monastic life as laymen copying manuscripts and assisting intellectual work, but also included men (and women) of modest means engaged in mundane work, living by and spreading the spiritual tenets of the Modern Devotion.

The codification of the ModernDevotion is exemplified by *The Imitation of Christ*, written by Thomas à Kempis (1380–1471). In succeeding years, the Brethren made hundreds of copies. The *Imitation* consists of four parts, the first two offering counsels and directives on the interior life. The link to desert spirituality is established early in chapter 20, titled "On the Love of Solitude and Silence":

> If you desire true compunction of heart, enter into your secret chamber and shut out the tumults of the world. Commune with your own heart, and in your chamber, and be still. In your cell you will find what abroad you would often lose.

> Your cell, constantly dwelt in, grows sweet; rarely occupied, it becomes loathsome. If in the beginning of your conversion you are content to remain in it, and keep to it well, it will afterwards be to you a dear friend, and a most pleasant comfort.

The significance of the Beguines and the Brethren of the Common Life lies in the medieval extension of eremitism and new permutations to the hermit life within new religious and theological expression in continental Europe.

16. Hermits in Medieval Arthurian Lore

Paralleling the historiography of saints and hermits in Britain is an imaginative legendary genre represented by the *Historia regum Britanniae* ("History of the Kings of Britain") by Geoffrey of Monmouth (d. 1155). Geoffrey's history extends Virgil's founding legend of Rome by the Trojan hero Aeneas to Roman Britain and thereafter, and is particularly noted for introducing Arthurian legends into literature: King Arthur, Gawain, Merlin, and the Round Table. However, Geoffrey's work only mentions one hermit, a bishop Dubricius who "from a pious desire of leading a hermit's life, made a voluntary resignation of his arch-episcopal dignity" (9. 15).

The Arthurian themes were quickly taken up by French poet Chrétien de Troyes (1135-1185), who created several legends: *Lancelot* ("The Knight of the Cart"), *Yvain*, or "Gawain" ("The Knight of the Lion"), and *Perceval* ("The Story of the Grail"). There are no hermits in *Lancelot*, although one character fumes: "I don't have the cowardly heart of a hermit, or do-gooder or almsgiver…." But a forest-dwelling hermit feeds the forlorn Yvain, and Perceval seeks out a "holy hermit" in his spiritual angst.

In the Perceval story of German poet Wolfram von Eschenbach (1170–1220), titled *Parzival*, the hermit Trevrizent is a major character. The knight Parzival regrets a life of violence and crime. Angry at God's punishment, he seeks redemption by finding the Grail. He is advised to seek out the hermit Trevrizent, whose holiness is described:

> Poor was his fare, and no richer it waxed as the week wore on.
> Nor wine nor bread he tasted, nor food that with blood was red.
> Fish nor flesh, but his life so holy on the herb of the ground was
> fed. And ever his thoughts, God–guided, were turning to Heaven's
> land. And by fasting the wiles of the Devil he deemed he might
> best withstand.

Trevrizent reveals to the sorrowful Parzifal the mysteries of the Grail, the Bleeding Lance, the Knives of Silver. He explains the fate of King Anfortas, of which Parzifal felt guilty. The hermit comforts him, revealing the successors to the Grail king, starting with Parzifal himself. Finally, too, the hermit reveals himself to be Parzifal's uncle. Trevrizent confesses and absolves him. They part, ending the tale.

Almost contemporary with Eschenbach is a version of Old French Arthurian legends collected in the Vulgate or Lancelot-Grail cycle, prominently featuring a hermit named Nascien. This collection, with its continental predecessors, was a chief source for the *Morte d'Arthur* by Thomas Malory (1405–1471). Malory confirms the popular image of the forest–dwelling hermit. Relating the last days of the Arthurian circle, the tale is less complex than earlier versions. A hermit does not appear until half–way through the work.

In Book 12, chapter 3, Sir Lancelot kills a boar but is himself wounded by it, reminiscent of Percival's symbolic wound. A hermit in the forest hears the commotion and comes to the knight's aid, but Lancelot refuses, even threatening him. The hermit runs off, encounters several knights in another part of the forest, bids them help, and they agree. They take Lancelot to the hermit's dwelling, where the hermit heals his wound thanks to his herbal skills. But Lancelot cannot be healed spiritually due to his consciousness of his past sins. Only the Grail can do this.

Lancelot stays overnight with the hermit, observing his kindness and wisdom, asking the hermit for advice concerning a vision or dream. The hermit reveals to him that Galahad is Lancelot's son.

In another section (16.3–6), Gawain and Hector come to a hermitage occupied by the hermit–priest Nacien, where the hermit gathers worts (that is, herbs), having "tasted none other meat of great while." The visitors confess to him, and he interprets their dreams. Sir Bors comes later for the same boon.

In 8.22, a hermit heals Lancelot of an arrow wound. Is it the same hermit in all three incidents, or is Malory deliberately not distinguishing them? The hermit is not important enough to be remembered but not obscure enough to be ignored.

In 21.6–11, Sir Bedivere comes to a chapel where a hermit prays for a dead man. The land is now a chaos of violence and recrimination. The noble goals of the Round Table are irretrievably lost. Camelot is over. Bedivere is the last surviving knight. The hermit is revealed to be the former Bishop of Canterbury. Bedivere wants to imitate the hermit's piety but realizes that the dead man is king Arthur himself, and swoons. When he awakens, he asks the hermit if he might stay to live, fasting and in prayer. From Malory:

> "For from hence will I never go," said Sir Bedivere, "by my will, but all the days of my life here to pray for my lord Arthur." "You are welcome to me," said the hermit, "for I know you better than you know what I do."... "Sir Bedivere put upon him[self] poor clothes, and served the hermit full loving in fasting and in prayers.

Lancelot happens upon the same hermitage, finding the hermit and Sir Bedivere, and insists on being shriven, renouncing all worldly ambition.

Next arrives Sir Bors, who does likewise, plus seven other knights, seeing Lancelot's example, vow to take monk's vows and never leave.

The powerful spirituality of the hermit's example engenders a virtual monastery! After six years of penitence, Lancelot takes Holy Orders from the former bishop's hands. In a vision Lancelot sees Queen Genevieve dead. He and the others journey to bring her body for entombment next to Arthur. The sight of Genevieve kindles remembrance in Lancelot against which the hermit cautions, but it is sorrow and repentance that now grieve Lancelot. In a year, Lancelot is dead, and his monk–companions wonder if his penitence sufficed. The hermit quietly reveals to them his vision (or dream) wherein he saw Lancelot escorted to heaven by angels.

17. The Hermit in Langland's *Piers Plowman*

Piers Plowman is an allegorical poem composed by William Langland (1332–1386). The poem features a journey through society by the honest and humble laborer Piers, whose candid view of the world reflects that of the fool of myth on a hero's journey. The story's device is a dream. The unnamed narrator, a modest, unpretentious observer, sets out.

> In a summer season, when soft was the sun,
> I enshrouded me well, in a shepherd's garb,
> And robed as a hermit, unholy of works,
> Went wide through the world, all wonders to hear.

No class of society is spared in Langland's critique of the immorality of pilgrims, priests, peasants, townsfolk, and lords. Was Langland a social radical? Or a satirist like Geoffrey Chaucer (1343–1400), author of *Canterbury Tales*, whose poem *House of Fame* was clearly inspired by Langland? Langland's clear moral vision puts him in the radical camp, though unnecessarily identified as a Lollard. The dream–journey of the poem is no mere metaphor but a search for truth, pursued in the real world, in later medieval society, among all kinds of people, high and low, going about their worldly affairs. On the dream–journey, the narrator encounters embodiments of virtues who assist the narrator in his journey (Patience, Conscience, Intelligence) and of vices who obstruct it (Gluttony, Crime).

Among the social classes Langland excoriates are false hermits, vagabonds. They dress "in pride of apparel" and "costliest clothing," in contrast to true hermits and anchorites "who held to their cells, not caring to roam through the country around for doles of sweet dainties, their flesh to delight." The narrator witnesses troops of false hermits "with their wenches following after" ... "These great long lubbers, who hated work, were got up in clerical garb to distinguish them from laymen, and paraded as hermits for the sake of an easy life."

In contrast is Piers, a plowman who labors in the fields of Truth. Piers witnesses the slothful, immoral, false laborers, likening them to the false hermits. The latter represent all the social classes that hypocritically profess truth. Piers is incensed at the false hermits, by extension at all hypocrisy and worldliness. He renounces the plow to trust God in prayer, penance, and simplicity. He embraces the true hermit life.

At this point the dreamer awakens. The narrator determines to find Do–well (and other personifications of virtue) to learn how to pursue his intended life of prayer and penance. He encounters Study, Theology, Scripture, and Reason, but rejects their authority, considering them corrupted by the world. Imagination corrects many of the dreamer's misconceptions about the proper role of learning and wisdom. The proper interpretation of Scripture, for example, would show that Muslims and Jews leading virtuous lives can enter heaven regardless of baptism—but not so according to the teaching of the Church. Langland inexorably moves his reader to a new concept of virtue.

The dreamer's journey continues. He roams the earth. Fortune repeatedly fails him, and Old Ages looms. The friars despise the poor and solicit the rich. The priests lay out intolerable imprecations. But Nature is benign to all. The figure Conscience comforts the dreamer. Together the two visit Learning and Patience, the latter dressed in rags and begging like a poor hermit. They enter Learning's castle, where a Doctor of the Church asserts that to do well is to follow what the clergy teach, to do better is to teach others, and to do best is to put into practice true virtue.

Langland advises not withdrawal from active life nor spiritualized poverty but an economic and social ideal based on an eremitic view not espoused by extent religious orders. The narrator comes to see that Charity is a tree in a garden planted by God, on land leased to the caretaker by Free Will, to be cared for, as will Piers Plowman. In a final chapter, Conscience makes a fateful decision, asserting that he will quit the world and the struggle to fix it, and instead emulate the search undertaken by Piers the Plowman, whose virtues alone can set the world aright.

18. The Last Hermits of Medieval Europe

Hermits in the European Middle Ages championed a theology of evangelical poverty versus ecclesiastical centralization, control, and corruption. From the point of view of ecclesiastical authorities, however, eremitic spirituality was too mystical, and, in its last centuries, too concerned with individual contemplation.

As late as the early fifteenth century, the last medieval guide for recluses, the *Speculum inclusorum* (or "Mirror for Recluses") couched its directives disparagingly. Historian E. A. Jones notes that the guide warns against conversation with visitors, idleness, and sloth. It chastises aspiring anchorites for potential bad motives: seeking reclusion for its supposed ease (versus living in the world), using reclusion as penance for past sins (versus having a spiritual positive aspiration), and for pursuing reclusion as escape from the world and its temptations.

Ultimately, hermits proved unable to resist church authority or the suppression of anchorites accused of being heretics and vagabonds. The subsequent Protestant reformers and secular authorities completed the suppression of monks, priests, and nuns in key countries.

The three hermits highlighted below are not literally the last hermits of the Middle Ages, but their stories are representative of the fate of eremites in the waning centuries of the medieval era.

1. Hermit and Pope: Pietro Murrone & Celestine V

In the late thirteenth century, Italy was a battlefield of religious controversy, political intrigue, and incessant warfare. The pro–papal Guelphs fought the imperialist Ghibellines, authoritarian Dominicans opposed Spiritual Franciscans, and rival Roman families, the Colonna and the Orsini, fought for control of the Church. In the last decades of the 1200s, France, England, Spanish Aragon, and the reigning popes fell into bitter conflict over ecclesiastical and secular prerogatives such as taxation of clergy and control of Naples and Sicily. Into this whirlwind comes Pietro di Murrone (1215–1296), a life–long hermit.

At the age of twenty–five, Benedictine monk Pietro Angelerio left his monastery for Mt. Murrone to become a hermit. After five years living in a cave he joins two companions to form a laura on Mt. Majella. News of his piety spreads. A community of fellow hermits develops. Pietro calls them "Hermits of St. Damiano" and gives them a rule. With Pietro as superior and with papal approval, the order grows and spreads over the next twenty years with thirty–six monasteries and hundreds of hermit–monks. Pietro intended to retire at sixty but returns to work helping construct a church in Aquila. With a new superior for the order, the nearly seventy–year old Pietro withdraws at last to Mt. Majella.

Amidst ongoing war and conflict, Pope Nicholas IV dies in 1292. The rival Colonna and Orsini families fight a two–year stalemate to have their preferred papal candidate elected. The ideal candidate must not represent a faction, but at the same time be malleable to the stronger family. An Orsini cardinal reports that God has told him to elevate a pious hermit to the papacy or face divine chastisement, and that the hermit is the unpretentious, retired lover of solitude Pietro Murrone. In the spring of 1294, Pietro Murrone accedes to the demand of cardinals and kings and is crowned as Pope Celestine V.

How miserable the old hermit must have been in the midst of the corruption and intrigue of Rome! For all his simplicity, Pietro clearly refused to submit to the farce, instead cranking out lofty spiritual correctives. From the start, Pietro threatened to resign. An exasperated Cardinal Caetani, the very Orsini who appointed Pietro in the first place and who continued to insist on Pietro's cooperation, accedes at last to papal resignation—in order to himself succeed Pietro as Pope Boniface VIII!

Boniface rightly fears that the secular powers competing for control of Italy will challenge the validity of Celestine's resignation. Pietro had been winding his way back to Mt. Majelli when Boniface orders his arrest and detention, to assure that all parties will accept the resignation. Pietro's friends hide him for months. They prepare his escape to Greece but the old man is caught. At first Boniface puts Pietro in the cardinal's residence, insisting on statements to mollify the secular powers that Boniface fears. Getting nowhere, Boniface imprisons Pietro in a prison cell for nine months, where the exhausted old man dies in 1296 at the age of eighty-one, though many sources believe that Pietro Murrone was murdered at Boniface's order.

2. Nicholas of Flue, Hermit of Switzerland

Nicholas of Flue (1417–1487), also called Nikolaus or Claus, is Switzerland's only canonized saint. The eremitism of Nicholas is a paradox to contemporaries, representing two psychological dimensions of his personality: eremitism and a political–mystical persona.

The late Middle Ages was a chaotic time throughout Europe, as mentioned, including Switzerland. The contest of great powers around Switzerland exacerbate its historical mix of languages and cultures, as does the traditional absence of young Swiss men perennially seeking their fortunes as mercenaries in the wars of neighboring powers. Young Claus spent his youth in such wars.

Son of well–to–do peasants, the piety of Nicholas was unexceptional and predictable. He settled into marriage with a local peasant girl. They raise ten children while he continues heeding soldierly calls when summoned, rising to the rank of captain. Nearly illiterate and without practical political experience, Nicholas is elected or appointed to his town council, then to a judgeship he holds for nine years. Among other accomplishments, Nicholaus resolves a dispute between the local parish and neighboring Engelberg monastery. Nicholas is even offered the governorship of his canton (which he declines). This staid life may have led Nicholas to deep reflection. By design, or because of a vision of God, the fifty–year old one day announces to his family his urgent desire to become a wandering hermit.

Nicholas declares his intent to travel to foreign lands, but walking to Basel, divine inspiration bids him stop and take up residence in Ranft, about an hour's walk from his home. Here he built a crude hut for his dwelling, renouncing winter clothing for a mere gown, and refusing food and drink for nearly two decades. He called himself "Brother Klaus."

When a dangerous fire in the nearby town of Sarnen miraculously extinguishes itself, the prayers of Nicholas are credited. His fame spreads. Civil authorities build a cell and chapel for him, the latter dedicated by vicar–general and bishop of Constance. After the pope grants an indulgence for pilgrimage to Nicholas's hermitage, visitors from throughout Europe stream to his quarters seeking counsel, both personal and political. The Ranft location is declared part of the Way of St. James, the route to the pilgrim shrine of Santiago de Compostela in Spain.

In 1480, Swiss delegates attending the Diet of Stans threatened one another with dissolution of the confederacy. The pastor of Stans hastened to Nicholas, begging his intervention. But Nicholas had vowed to never leave his cell. Instead he entrusts a simple statement to the pastor, urging a peaceful settlement of the issues, with a few modest propositions. The pastor hurries back to Stans. The delegates heed the advice of Nicholas, averting disastrous civil war. Though the content of the advice was never publicized, letters of thanks to Nicholas from the cities of Berne and Soleure survive.

Popularizations of the life of Nicholas of Flue conflate his influence on contemporary events with his mysticism. Throughout his hermit life, Nicholas experienced visions. A significant dream justified his eremitic life, wherein he saw a pilgrim approaching him, who is transformed into Christ but also into Wotan, berserker and wild man, like a bear. Psychologist Carl Jung interpreted this dream as Nicholas identifying himself with animal or subhuman shadow, bearlike and cold, as in his separation from family, committing a necessary "sin" that removes him from human accretions and the world.

Saint and beast are reconciled opposites. For the eremitic life means reconciling the impulses and instincts of aggression, anger, lust, and pride with the spiritual values of renunciation, disengagement, humility, and non–possession. The Christ–figure has never completely engaged the worldly, never been fully understood as anything but pain and suffering. Jung understands this representation of opposites at the heart of the psychological tension within Christianity.

Jungian psychologist Maria–Louise von Franz notes that "compared to such holy sages as Lao Tzu or Chuang Tzu, Brother Klaus as a solitary hermit is a humbler figure." The identification of eremitic solitude as a vocation not only exempts him in the eyes of his Swiss compatriots as a gifted person, but gives Brother Klaus the psychological space to grow as a hermit reconciling the opposing needs of spirituality and sociability, of mystical vision and contribution to others. His abandonment of the world is an abandonment of its false values, but not of his fellow human beings in their simple yearnings.

3. Thomas Parkinson, Thirsk Hermit

The tragic story of the Catholic hermit and anchorite Thomas Parkinson (1489–1558) is ironic in several ways, one being that the life of Parkinson was brought to prominence by John Foxe (1516–1587), the polemical English Protestant and author of *Acts and Monumentes or Book of Martyrs* chronicling those who suffered under Catholic and Anglican regimes.

Parkinson's father was bailiff of Thirsk (Yorkshire, England) and apprenticed his son to a tailor. By the age of twenty, Thomas is able to earn his own living. He marries Agnes Hollywell and two years later she gives birth to a child. However, the child is stillborn. Because the child could not be baptized and was therefore excluded from burial in the churchyard, the little body is buried in a nearby field. Apparently the burial was slipshod and weeks later a raven scratched up the soil, fed on the corpse, and flew to roost in a tree. Some townsfolk see the gruesome sight and report it to the parish priest, who informs the recently bereaved parents. Thomas and Agnes Parkinson take it as a sign from God. They vow, as Foxe put it, to "live chaste and solitary." They formally separate and each goes by individual way into religious life.

Thomas joins a Franciscan order and may have been ordained a priest. But he is far more disposed to eremitism and solitude and is eventually granted a hermit's life in a chapel on the outskirts of Thirsk. Meanwhile, Agnes had sought entrance into the order of Poor Clares. There being no convent in the district, she pursues the habit and rule on her own, eventually becoming a nun in a hospital, then an anchoress under a wealthy patron who offers room and board in exchange for her prayers.

Thomas proves such an exemplary friar and hermit that he is persuaded to take up the more rigorous life of an anchorite. The parish embraces his intention by lodging him in a new structure of the local church, supported by the entire community. Two years later, under the auspices of the Carthusian order, patronage of Queen Catherine of Aragon (wife of King Henry VIII) is secured. Thomas moves to an anchorhold in a Mount Grace priory under the administration of the archbishop of York. But though his wife Agnes died several years before Thomas's move to Mount Grace, what should have been a happy ending turns into tragedy.

Twenty years after becoming an anchorite at Mount Grace comes the dissolution of monasteries under King Henry VIII. This monastery lasts longer than most, but in 1539, several monks are granted pensions and Mount Grace is suppressed. Thomas Parkinson is given nothing, cast out to survive as he can. He keeps his Carthusian habit. He is homeless and destitute. He travels incessantly, begging, seeking fruitlessly for an anchorite patron.

His situation worsens. Thomas's reluctant attempts to become a secular clergyman prove unsuccessful. As the years pass and traditional religious life disappears in England—and with it chanceries, schools, and hospitals, let alone orders and anchorites—Thomas's plight becomes desperate.

After years of wandering and no prospect of a religious life, Thomas Parkinson finds himself in Shropshire, where in 1552 he marries a poor widow, Elizabeth Romney. He returns to tailoring. Unemployment is rampant and he has to go far to find work, spending weeks away from home to provide for his wife and her children. This isolation rekindles his desire for solitude and the anchorhold. His old vocation comes to the attention of a Lady Gifford, who arranges for Sir Thomas Fitzherbert (who had supported an anchorage now vacant) to become Thomas's new patron. Thomas Parkinson makes an arrangement with his second wife, who would become an anchoress in Worcester. Unbeknownst to him, she falls ill and does not make the journey.

Here is the final and tragic irony. With Mary Tudor ascending the English throne in 1553, a favorable climate for Catholic practice emerges, but also the revival of the canon law which forbade clergy to marry. Thomas Parkinson is brought before an ecclesiastical tribunal, where he and his wife are interrogated and Thomas's violation of canon law confirmed. At age seventy he is sentenced to imprisonment for as long as is "the bishop's pleasure." He probably died in prison. If he had survived a few years longer, to 1558 and the accession of Queen Elizabeth, Thomas Parkinson may have found himself alive but again cast out into destitution and solitude.

CHAPTER 3

EREMITISM IN MEDIEVAL EASTERN EUROPE, WEST ASIA, & ETHIOPIA

19. Orthodox Christian Hermits: Greece

The isolated hermits of early Christian Egypt formed by the desert experience differ from the socially–available hermits of Syria, as already mentioned. But the Christian experience at this time was largely expressed in the Greek and Coptic languages in Egypt, Syria, and the Levant, all within what became the Eastern Roman Empire.

The names of numerous hermits in Syria are only recalled in brief hagiographical sketches mentioning geography. In fifth–century Syria these include Akepsimas of Cyrrhus, Auxentius of Bithynia, Simeon of Emessa, Jacob of Nisibus, Palladius of Antioch, Peter of Galatia, Rubin of Kartamin, and Maron, the fifth–century founder of the Maronite order. Fewer named hermits are recorded in Greece proper in this period, exceptions including John the Silent (454–558) and David the Dendrite (tree–dweller) of Thessaloniki (sixth century).

The consolidation of major monastic foundations at Mt. Athos and Mt. Meteora in Greece established the three forms of monastic life: cenobitic, laura and skete, and eremitic. In the ninth century, Euthymios the Younger reputedly created the first skete. Basil the Confessor and Ioannis Kolovos respectively founded monasteries. An imperial decree reserved the entirety of Mt. Athos to monks, forbidding laity. Monastery foundations increased thereafter throughout the tenth century when Athanasios of Athos founded the monastery that was to remain the largest of Mt. Athos. A later emperor confirmed protection of the cenobitic and eremitic structures. By the end of the subsequent century, the twenty monasteries of Mt. Athos, with their numerous laura and hermit cells, were completed. From the spectacular cliffs of Mt. Meteora arise five monasteries for men and one for women.

The desert hermit spirituality maintained in Greece was expressed as *hesychasm*. The term *hesychastis* means "stillness," referring to contemplation and the state of mystical prayer. The person who prays is the hesychast, synonymous with hermit or solitary, or if the person is within a laura, the term hesychast is used for each resident. Initial sources of hesychasm were four outstanding personalities: Armenian–born John the Silent, or John the Hesychast (454–558), Sabbas the Sanctified (439–532), founder of monasteries in Syria, Palestine–born Cyril of Scythopolis (525–559), author of *Lives of the Monks of Palestine*, and Mark the Ascetic (fifth century), born in Athens but who spent his life as a hermit in Egypt.

With a major military victory of Persia against the Byzantine Empire in the earliest decades of the seventh century, Christian control of Syria and Palestine ended. The spiritual tradition of eremitic thought and practice in Syria ceased. The definitive presentation of hesychasm fell to Syrian–born John Climacus (or Klimakus), a seventh–century hermit living on Mount Sinai, Egypt, who spent a short time as a monk in what is today called St. Catherine's Monastery. (A predecessor who collected ascetic maxims at the same monastery was Hesychios, about whom little is known.)

John Climacus composed *The Ladder of Divine Ascent* as the epitome of desert hermit spirituality, considered a basic text of hesychasm. The image of the ladder evokes steps ascending from basic virtues to important practices towards attaining ascetic virtues such as stillness, detachment, and, finally, achieving love of God. John Climacus remains one of the few Greek sources of mystical thought well received in the West.

In 1782, two Mt. Athos monks, Nicodemus the Hagiorite and Makarios of Corinth, publish the *Philokalia*, a compilation of ancient sayings on hesychasm. The selections range from the fourth century to the compilers' eighteenth century, featuring some well–known writers (Evagrios, John Cassian) but chiefly less familiar sources from Greek tradition (Isaiah the Solitary, Thalassios the Libyan, Ilias the Presbyter). The *Philokalia* remains an important inspirational source in Orthodoxy from Greece to Russia and beyond.

20. Orthodox Christian Hermits: Russia

In 988, Prince Vladimir I officially converted Kievan Rus to Christianity, decades after Byzantine missionaries had reached Rus and Eastern Slavic lands. Literature came to Russia as biblical scripture and hagiography, the latter in the form of *paterikon* ("Lives of the Fathers") introducing saints and sages from the desert hermit traditions of Egypt, Syria, and Palestine. But ebb and flow in Russia's political fortunes—first under Tartar rule, then the fall of rival Constantinople and the Byzantine state in 1483—further exacerbated the absence of cultural and religious maturation.

Three events affected the nature of religion in Russia: 1) national consolidation around the Principate of Moscow, 2) the autonomy of the Muscovy Patriarchate from the Byzantine Patriarch of Constantinople, and 3) emergence of tsardom and the political theory of Moscow as the "third Rome," promoting consolidation of power around Church and state.

A monastic revival paralleled an art movement. Monk–painters and patrons emerge in the late fifteenth century: Stefan of Perm, Sergij of Radonez, Krill, Epifanij the Wise, and Andrej Rubljov. Church hierarchy and control discouraged hesychasm, but led by Nil Sorskij (1433–1508), an eremitic movement emerges during this period of uncertainty.

Nilus of Sora (Nil Sorskij or Sorsky) composed the *Predanie* or "Instruction," modest guidelines for monks and hermits. The rule's influence and that of Sorsky's hermitage were instrumental in a widespread eremitic movement in Russia that persisted for centuries, shaping the concept of "non–possession."

Sorsky was a well–born, educated monk who spent years in both a Russian monastery and at Mt. Athos, a careful student of desert hermit spirituality, theology, and hesychasm. Upon returning to Russia, he established a hermitage on the model of a skete, geographically remote from existing monasteries and church authorities, across the Volga River traditionally demarcating state and wilderness. Hence, the hermits were called "trans–Volga elders." This deliberate remoteness and simplicity of practice attracted others, who created nearby hermitages, all viewed by ecclesiastical authorities as a threat, for existing monasteries (as in the West) were large institutions with vast lands and working serfs, paralleling the properties of the Russian landed nobility.

A secularizing movement in Russia at the time maintained a radical theology denying trinitarianism and the efficacy of sacraments, and advocating separation of church and state. Attacking this movement was abbot Joseph of the Volokolamsk Monastery, a leading advocate of state control over the church. Joseph (1440–1515) described the secularists as "Judaizers" and heretics. At a Moscow church council in 1503, Joseph urged authorities to arrest and punish secularist adherents. While Nil Sorsky upheld orthodoxy against the sectarians, he nevertheless argued against coercion and punishment as inherently unjust, contending that Christians who advocate violence and intolerance betray their own teachings. Sorsky believed that forgiveness and example could dissuade the sectarians of their errors.

Not surprisingly, the overwhelming number of attendees at the council sided with Joseph. The heretics are arrested, imprisoned, and tortured. Late in 1504, many are burned at the stake in Moscow, and more burned at the stake in Novgorod. Nil Sorsky did not attend the Council, but a trans–Volga representative Vassian Patrikeyev and probably others did. Their dissent from Joseph set further actions into motion.

The trans–Volga elders came to be called "non–possessors" for their views on property and landholding. The hermits considered monastic property an aberration of the spiritual purposes of monasticism. Monastic wealth and landholding, with its rents, labor, peasants, and slaves, violated the monastic vows of poverty, self–sufficiency, labor, and spirituality. The life of the monk should be one of prayer, contemplation, simplicity, and detachment from worldly concerns, Sorsky maintained.

Conversely, Joseph Volokolamsk and defenders of monastic and ecclesiastical property were called "possessors." They argued that property assures the vitality and independence of the Church and its monasteries. The configuration of society and the world (and Russia) is ordained by God, they argued, and the position of the Church is part of an inviolable order. Ecclesiastical authority worked closely with the state to regulate the needs of society. Joseph Volokolamsk argued that the Church and its monasteries maintain schools, hospitals, and food dispensaries with their incomes.

At this stage in the sixteenth century, outright secularization was not an issue among the non–possessors. The tsar was not considering state confiscation of Church land or holdings. Nor were the trans–Volga elders advocating on behalf of a land–hungry petty nobility. As hermits without worldly goods, their ideas of evangelical poverty and spiritual simplicity, somewhat analogous to the Spiritual Franciscans in Europe, was perceived as a threat to the established order. Suggesting that the elders would secularize church property was Joseph's way of identifying the non–possessors as heretics.

Vasilii (Vasily or Basil) III (1479–1533) became grand prince of Muscovy in 1505 or 8. One of his earliest acts was to support Joseph Volokolamsk and the possessors. The tsar's unflagging efforts to expand and consolidate Russia enhanced the status of the church, in turn encouraging his state centralization. In 1510, the monk Philotheus of Pskov writes to Vasilii praising the tsar's power over church and state as heir of the third Rome, adding that there would be no fourth.

In turn, Vasilii's position encouraged two eloquent defenders of the non–possessors to emerge in court. The first is prince and monk Vassian (Ivan) Patrikeyev (1470–1532), mentioned above. As a young nobleman, Vassian had been accused by Ivan III of conspiracy, forced to take the tonsure at the Kirillo–Belozersky Monastery (where Nil Sorsky had been a monk). Vassian acquainted himself with the ideas of Nil Sorsky, emerging an articulate defender of the non–possessors.

The second prominent figure to support the non–possessors is Maximos the Greek (1480–1556), a Russian–born scholar familiar with Renaissance humanism in Florence and Venice, once a Dominican, and subsequently a monk resident at Mt. Athos. In 1517, he is invited by the grand prince Vasilii to come to Moscow to translate Greek liturgical books and amend Russian service books, such as the psalter. Like Vassian, Maximos supported the non–possessor views of the trans–Volga elders, and though styled as more of a scholar and intellectual than hermit–monk, he, too, adhered to hesychasm.

But in 1523, Daniel (1492–1547) is elected Metropolitan of Russia. He is a protege of Joseph Volokolamsk and had served as administrator at the Volokolamsk monastery. Daniel immediately takes steps to break up the non–possessors, convening a 1525 inquest that excommunicates Vassian and orders him confined at the Volokolamsk monastery, where he dies soon afterwards. Then Daniel attacks Maximos for heresy and treasonous relations with Turks. He has him thrown into a dungeon, where he dies shortly afterward.

The passing of Vassian and Maximos effectively ended the non–possessor movement. Many hermitages are dissolved during this period, and their monks and hermits dispersed. The hesychasm of the hermits largely devolved to the formulaic "Jesus Prayer." Church and state in subsequent years grow more autocratic and powerful. The vision of Nil Sorsky is virtually expunged.

21. Hermits in Russia: Pilgrim & Old Believer

As a Russian spiritual classic, the anonymous nineteenth–century *The Way of a Pilgrim* is an apologia for silent prayer in the Orthodox Christian tradition, namely, the "ceaseless" prayer or the so–called Jesus prayer. The tradition cites the *Philokalia* and hesychasm as its sources. But *The Way of a Pilgrim* is also a literal presentation of a mendicant hermit life. The narrator is a solitary and a wanderer calling himself a pilgrim. The wandering hermit's example is presented as the model existence for leading a spiritual life.

The pilgrim's contemplative method is silence, gentle breathing, centering of thought on the heart, and the repeating of the Jesus Prayer, the phrase "Lord Jesus Christ, have mercy on me," what religion historian Huston Smith considered a "Western mantra if I ever heard one." The pilgrim repeats the prayer six thousand times a day, and upon the advice of a *starets* he had encountered, increases to twelve thousand a few weeks later! As the *starets* had suggested, the pilgrim found the prayer at his lips and in his mind every waking hour, as spontaneous and effortless as breathing itself.

The pilgrim walks by night, spends the day under a tree in the forest reading the *Philokalia*, and begs bread and salt in the villages he encounters. Positive moments include when children bring him to their parents' house, where he spends a week in deep conversation with the adults. Among negative experiences, the pilgrim encounters a wolf, and when he speaks to a young woman reluctantly about to enter a forced marriage, the groom has him jailed. The local judge releases him the following morning, but only after having the pilgrim flogged.

The pilgrim reveals that he is an orphan who lived as a child with his grandfather until the latter's death. The hostility of his older brother drove the pilgrim away and on the road. He tells us that he has come from Siberia, is bound for Kiev, but ultimately is on his way to Jerusalem, where he hopes to die.

Agafya Lykov (b. 1946) is a contemporary Russian hermit, made famous by the 1994 book, *Lost in the Taiga: One Russian Family's Fifty–Year Struggle for Survival and Religious Freedom in the Siberian Wilderness*, by journalist Vasily Peskov. Since publication of the book Agafya continues to garner frequent Russian media coverage. Agafya's family left Russia in 1937 to preserve Old Belief, an adherence to ritual in Russian Orthodoxy dating before the seventeenth century. The Lykovs move to the isolated wintry lands of Siberia, called the *taiga*, where they were cut off from social and technological changes of the subsequent twentieth century, such as electricity and radio. Agafya is the last survivor of the family. Except for occasional visiting journalists and forestry officials, Agafya lives in solitude, growing her own food, chopping wood, and maintaining her hut. Only in recent years has she accepted medical attention and supplies.

22. Orthodox Christian Hermits: Ethiopia

Christianity reached Ethiopia in the fourth century when Frumentius of Tyre was ordained bishop. He converted the Aksumite monarch, and Christianity took root in urban and elite circles. In the fifth century, the reputed "Nine Saints" come to Ethiopia, escaping Byzantine approbation of their Monophysitism. They translate scripture and documents from Greek to native Geez, founding monasteries, and converting laity.

Monasticism shaped the tenor of religion in Ethiopia in contrast to secular clergy. Monks early adapt the desert model of the laura. Nearly all Ethiopian monasteries were located in remote geographic areas far from urban centers, often on mountainsides. Even when a monastery was large, monks lived in individual huts and came together only for religious services. Like desert hermits, they are not scholars but often labor in agriculture, joined by students and laypeople in growing food, the surplus of which is sold to support the monastery, where schoolboys live at no cost as students, novices, and helpers. Monasteries are administered not by resident abbots but by off–site clergymen, who assign spiritual directors and govern by example, assessment, and advice.

Ethiopian monks require no regimen or permission to become hermits. They might vacate their huts to more isolated quarters on mountainsides or caves, eat what is brought to them by lay people, and pass all of their time in prayer and contemplation. Their participation in the monastic community as laborers, attending services, or joining in leisured conversations, is entirely voluntary. Thus eremitism shaped Ethiopian monasticism.

As evocative as eremitic practice has been in Ethiopia, a more radical and eccentric form emerged among the *bahtawi*, popularly known as holy men. Not all were monks. They recluse to obscure dwellings in mountains, caves, and forests, living off wild food, pursuing their own mystical persuasions, and seldom attending religious services. A distinct physical feature, besides their often gaunt appearance, is their dreadlocks, a Hindu sadhu–like emblem of their eremitism.

23. Eremitism in Medieval & Later Judaism

As already mentioned, Judaism's emphasis on family and community dis-couraged eremites and practice of solitude, contemplation, and—more practically—celibacy. Allusion to the biblical Moses entering a mystical cloud or Elijah hearing the "still small voice" of God in contrast to the noisiness of the world does not constitute an alternative to the Jewish tradition of communalism.

Instead, solitude emerged as a byproduct of eccentricity, such as celibacy, wandering, or mystical and Kabbalist interests. The scriptural figures of Elijah and Elisha are cited as celibates, as are Simeon ben Azzai (second century), devoted to Torah studies, and Shem–Tov ben Joseph ibn Falaquera (Palquera, 1225–1290), a promoter of philosophy. Among wanderers are the medieval Spaniards Abraham Abulafia (1240–1291), mystical writer and teacher, and the philosophical writer Abraham Ibn Ezra (1089–1137), though their wanderings were prompted not by a search for solitude but by forced exile.

Among famous Jewish thinkers espousing solitude, at least as a regular spiritual practice, is Maimonides (1135–1204), who considered the meditative mind a prerequisite to communication with the "Divine Spirit." Among Kab-balist writers on moral practice is Elazar ben Moshe Azikri (1533–1600), who advised withdrawing regularly from the company of others to enjoy solitude as companionship with God, and Isaac Ben Solomon Luria (1534–1572), who only saw his wife and children on the Sabbath. Luria developed the notion of *tzimtzum* as mystical inclusion into the divine, and *shevirah* as the infusion of the divine into the finite and mortal.

The eighteenth century represents the fullness of Jewish mystical and contemplative thinking in the figures of Baal Shem Tov (1690–1780) and Nachman of Breslov (1772–1810), both of Ukraine. The founder of Hasi-dism, Baal Shem Tov adapted Kabbalist language to a broader Talmudic mysticism and to a non–dualism he called *devekut* or "adhesion," meaning adherence to God in all thought and act. Baal Shem Tov was by turn an herbalist, teacher, and community leader. Nachman is closely identified with the concept of *hitbodedut* (which had existed since medieval times), the practice of "self–seclusion," of direct prayer to God, alone in a meditative setting, particularly in nature.

In general, Jewish contemplatives concentrated on the mechanics of devotion and derived solitude as a practical method, but not separating themselves from the social and communitarian setting, a separation that distinguishes historical eremitism. Only with the flowering of mysticism does Judaic thought develop the potential of a personal eremitism.

24. Eremitism in Medieval and Later Islam

Like Judaism, Islam arose as the religious expression of a society emphasizing community, marriage, and child–rearing. The prophet Muhammed observed Jews, Christians, and pagans, and reflected upon their beliefs and social highlights. Among these observed social phenomena were Christian hermits, whose lives may have influenced Muhammed, though not as thoroughly as Western scholar Duncan MacDonald remarked in 1903 that "the very soul of Islam sprang from these solitary hermits."

An early component of Islam is *zuhd*, meaning "asceticism." Its practitioner is the *zahid* or ascetic. Hasan of Basra (642–728) became a leading theologian and mystic, and a strong advocate of asceticism, abstinence, and disengagement from worldly values and interests. In part, Hasan's teachings consciously opposed the materialism and wealth that the conquests of the Umayyad caliphate, from Persia to Egypt to Spain, had suddenly brought to Islam.

The mysticism of Hasan is an important early source of Sufism, an ascetic mystical movement within orthodox Sunni Islam. The concept of *tasawwuf* ("inner development") distinguishes the spiritual from the formal and exterior (such as *sharia*) in Islam. Sufism developed under many convergent thinkers, such as Persian–born Bayazid of Bastami (804–874), whose notion of "self–union" was the basis of *shukr*, or ecstatic mysticism. The Spaniard Ibn Arabi (1165–1240), author of the mystical manual *Journey to the Lord of Power*, developed the use of *dhikr*, or dwelling within God.

In Sufism, the practitioner is bidden to embrace solitude and silence, but does not ignore the precept to directly serve fellow Muslims. With time, this paradox was reconciled by Sufi community and discipleship, as when the celebrated Sufi poet Rumi (1207–1273) remonstrates his readers to move outside of the tangle of fear–thought to live in silence, that the flower grows in silence and one's tongue should be that flower, and that wandering talk closes the path to knowledge.

Ibn Tufayl (1110–1182), called Abubacer in the West, inherited Aristotelian rationalism and the philosophy of Ghazali, Farabi, his teacher Ibn Bajjah (Avempace), and the celebrated Ibn Sina or Avicenna. This school of thought criticized logic and mathematics, affirming the human soul's innate capacity to discover natural law and the most abstruse mystical doctrine. Ibn Tufayl presents this view in his tale *Hayy Ibn Yaqzan*.

The protagonist in the *Hayy Ibn Yaqzan* allegory grows to adulthood on an uninhabited island, as a wild child. By presenting this prototype human being as a solitary, a social *tabula rasa*, Ibn Tufayl can show his reader how reason guides the human intellect naturally and that learning follows the same logical path identified by the methods of the philosophers. Moreover, the solitude of the uninhabited island is a model of the natural development of the mind in the absence of the diversions and distractions of society, showing that the cultivation of self–discipline requires a state of solitude. (In the story, Ibn Tufayl's protagonist returns to the island after adulthood to resume his eremitic life.)

Ibn Tufayl reflects the direct influence not only of Arabic thinkers already cited but of the Sufi tradition. He anticipates discussions of Rousseau, Defoe, William Golding, and other Westerners speculating on social isolation and its consequences.

PART II

THE EASTERN WORLD:
ANTIQUITY TO THE PRESENT

CHAPTER 4

EREMITISM IN INDIA, TIBET, & SOUTH ASIA

25. Hermits in Hindu India

Intricacies of social structure dominate the history and religion of ancient India. The origins of Hindu culture are historically attributed to either an early second millennium BCE migration of Indo–Europeans (called "Aryans," a term meaning "nobles") into the northern Indian subcontinent—or simply to indigenous Indic peoples.

The religion of ancient India, epitomized by its chief scriptural document *Rigveda*, presents a panoply of multiple deities and their complex interrelations both as personalities and forces. Though traditionally attributed to Vyasa as founder (or scriptural compiler), no central authority governs Hinduism. Multiple religious elements merge to develop notions of God–realization, *dharma* as social and spiritual order, and sage interpreters.

The familiar caste system originates from earliest Aryan society, evolving from nomadic to settled to urban society. The caste system formally comes into existence around the third century BCE, epitomized by the *Manusmriti* or "Law of Manu." The configuration counts four castes: priests (*Brahmin*), kings, nobility, and warriors (*Kshatriya*), merchants, craft workers, and small farmers (*Vaishya*), and peasants and manual laborers (*Shudra*).

The historical Vedic idealizes the Brahmin–born youth who becomes a priest, the nobility represented by the Kshatriyas class, and the married adult householder of the Vaishya class. The adult householder's duties in every caste is to offer ritual sacrifice and to procreate. Not unlike other nomadic cultures (Hebrew, Islamic), ancient sources celebrate the social ideal (and obligation) of marriage and the raising of sons.

By the fifth century, the agrarian village is no longer the cultural core. Kings in emerging cities begin to augment their administrative territories, with the need for administrators in law and mercantile affairs. Cities increasingly centralize as urban populations grow, economic efficiencies are implemented, and migration fosters divergence of thought.

But, in fact, the original stratification may have been based on life stages, not on economic and social classes, on *asrama*, or "path," the same root word used for "ashram." Importantly, the life stages of an asrama are not prescriptive but elective paths.

Like castes the asramas also number four: student (*brahmacarya*), householder (*garhasthya*), hermit or forest dweller (*vanaprasthya*), and ascetic or renouncer (*sannyasi*). Ascetics could emerge from among Brahminic students, or from youths who could elect householder life or the celibate ascetic life. This path is fostered and encouraged by spiritualized Brahmins themselves. Householders traditionally retired from business or office when sons achieved self–sufficiency and daughters had been married. A third–stage retirement is either at home in separate quarters of the family estate or in a forest setting, often receiving necessities from a servant in the household. Ascetics renounce all relations with society and often become wanderer–mendicants.

Although hermits and ascetics existed in the Vedic era, reassertion of the asrama system explicitly promoted eremitic options. Forest hermits appear in classic literature of the new era, the fourth–century BCE *Ramayana* and the *Mahabharata*. The *Mahabharata* specifically records the story of king Muchukunda, who at Krishna's behest renounces power and his past cruelties to follow the life of an ascetic wanderer.

Written over centuries and culminating in the classical era, the treatises comprising the *Upanishads* introduce a spiritualizing anti–ritual thought, emphasizing *samsara* (suffering and rebirth), *karma* (actions as determinants of suffering and rebirth), and *moksha* (liberation as the ultimate goal). The old Vedic belief system was interpreted as an obstacle to liberation and a cause of rebirth, for ritual and sacrifice did not account for individual ethical actions, representing only "ignorance," as the *Mundaka Upanishad* (1.2.6–10) puts it. Gautama Buddha, Jain founder Mahavira, and the presentations of Rama and Krishna in the *Bhagavad Gita* reflect the shift of sentiment in the Indic nobility during this period.

The sources of this era and thereafter perceive *vedanta* ("end of the vedas") to be based upon *samnyas* or renunciation, renunciation of Brahminical ritual, sacred fire, the sacred string, the householder life, marriage, children, and property. The classic text on renunciation in Hinduism is *Vairagya Shatakam*, composed by Bhartrihari (450–510 CE). The evolution of vedanta into non–dualism and yoga maintains the primacy of the ascetic in classic Indian philosophers from Patanjali (third century) to Shankar (seventh century). The eleventh–century *Rules for Brahmanical Asceticism* by Yadava Prakasa attempt to categorize hermit practices in ritual, penance, physical appearance, and alms–begging to conform to Brahmanical control, what Indologist scholar Patrick Olivelle calls "domestication."

While the historical Hindu hermit remained obscure, hidden within forests, the ascetic *sadhu* (Sanskrit for "mendicant") represents a more eccentric form of eremitism closely associated with adherence to gurus, deities (Shiva, Vishnu), and prescribed attire summarized by Yadava: triple staff, loincloth, ochre robe, bowl, water strainer, and such. Of the estimated millions of sadhus in India today, many attend the Kumbh Mela, a colorful religious festival held near the Ganges River every twelve years.

26. Hermits in Jain India

Like Hindus, Jains evolve ascetic monks or sadhus, but unlike Hinduism, the Jain source of spiritual authority originates directly in ascetic experience versus ritual, scripture, or writing. The priest or monk system is ascribed to the ascetic example of the founder Mahavira (6th century BCE). The Jain monk is called a sadhu or sadhvi (female). The monks of Jainism are of two traditions: Shvetambara and Digambara. The two orders have minimal doctrinal differences, upholding the same vows or acts of renunciation, namely, renunciation of killing, lying, grasping or taking, of sexuality, attachment, or possession.

Shvetambara means white–clad, and refers to the color of the plain cotton garment worn by members of this order, both male and female. Digambara means sky–clad, referring to the fact that the males of this order are without clothes. (The nuns of the Digambara order are clothed like the Shvetambara).

The usual historical explanation for the chief difference between Shvetambara and Digambara is one of geography, that the ascetics of northern India could not tolerate cold or were not as isolated from other people, while those of southern India were mostly forest hermits and wanderers. The story of Alexander the Great's encounter in India with "naked philosophers" refers to either Hindus or Jains. Plutarch (46-120) calls them Gymnosophists. Arrian (86-146) records an Indian philosopher telling Alexander that he wants nothing from the king for he has all that suffices. In that passage, Arrian seems to allude to the famous response of Diogenes of Sinope to that same king.

The path of the Jain monk is a rigorous one. The great vows already enjoin non–violence or non–injury (*ahimsa*), a practice prescribed less absolutely for the householder than the monk. Among external austerities (*tapas*) the monk observes the following: fasting one or more days per week (*anasana*), eating less than what hunger demands (*avamaudarya*), reducing possessiveness (*vrttisamksepa*), renouncing non–necessities (*rasapartiyaga*), residing in isolated places (*viviktasayyasanasamlinata*), and mortifying the body (*kayaklesia*).

In the case of the Digambara, too, austerities define daily life and practice. Digambara usually live alone, typically in temples and in forests. They travel alone (unlike Shvetambara). They have no possessions except a whisk of found peacock feathers for dispersing insects and a bowl for hygiene water (washing of feet and hands only is permitted). Sometimes they may carry a parasol. Neither order can use any conveyance but must walk from place to place on foot. They must not stay anywhere more than a day except during the rainy season, and must accept whatever non–animal food offered by those whom they encounter upon entering a village. Unlike the white–clad who carry bowls for begging food, Digambara neither beg nor carry a bowl, accepting what is offered to them into open cupped hands, eating without utensils. The Digambara says nothing, but if requested may give a brief spiritual talk to the assembled. And then he moves on.

27. Buddhist Hermits of Tibet

Buddhism in Tibet is constructed as Mahayana theory and practice, the "greater vehicle" that addresses both monks and popular adherents, in contrast to the Theravada ("lesser vehicle") route that concentrates on the moral discipline and ethics of the *bikkhu*, the monk. The current anthropological interpretation contrasts the Tibetan Buddhist clerical–monastic control of political and social administration with the less engaged and less informed popular sentiment that looks primarily for spiritual favors from the monks, holding far less interest in ritual and metaphysics. In this scheme, Tibetan priests and monks function as "civilized shamans" amalgamating indigenous spirit cults of the original Bon religion with Indian Buddhism to shamanistic effect. Pursuit of enlightenment is essentially reserved to the minority clergy which produce shamanistic services for the average Tibetan.

Tibetan Buddhism incorporates Vajrayana or tantric practice, which includes extreme and eccentric austerities akin to magic. Application of tantric practice is limited, unauthorized, and often unofficial, but the tradition lingers as a contrarian path.

In Tibetan Buddhism, volitional and practical expressions of compassion, culminating in the figure of the *bodhisattva*, offer enlightenment and salvation. Buddhists in India may have scorned hermits or sitting forest meditators for abstaining from mingling with common people to preach the bodhisattva message of compassion. Tibetan Buddhism extended original Indian religious communalism, but the chief external aspects of practice within Tibetan monasteries are ritual and scholarship—paralleling medieval European monasticism.

Tibetan Buddhist monks were scholars of scripture and commentary, of which there is a massive amount: Vinaya on ethics and discipline, Sutras on meditation, Abhidharma on philosophy and Tangyur as commentary. As in Europe, eremitism exists as a practical extension of existing discipline. Tibetan hermits usually pursue solitude and meditation in caves, cottages, or a hermitage administered by the hermit's teacher or guru on behalf of a given monastery. The hermits were closely overseen by their respective monasteries, and did not function autonomously.

Perhaps the most famous figures utilizing eremitism are Milarepa (1052–1135), Shabkar (1781–1851), Patrul Rinpoche (1808–1887), and Domo Geshe Rinpoche Ngawang Kalsang (1866–1936), the latter known as Geshe Rinpoche.

Milarepa practiced black magic in youth before renouncing this path to study under the harsh discipline of the Buddhist guru Marpa, after which Milarepa utilized a cave now identified with his name and which he described as "the monastery of the uninhabited mountain." Milarepa identified with Vajrayana. He is noted for his poetry or *Songs* (dohas), compositions of instruction, reflection, and inspiration. Prominent among Milarepa's poems is his embrace of nature:

Three winters have I delighted in the deep forests;
three summers have I delighted in the snow–peaks;
three springs have I delighted in the alpine meadows;
three autumns have I sought alms of whatever sort.

(Shabkar will be considered in section 28.)

Patrul Rinpoche practiced Dzogchen, a Vajrayana or tantric practice utilizing caves as meditation sites. Geshe Rinpoche left a monastery to live in mountain solitude for twelve years. After discovery by a local herdsman he was persuaded to construct a monastery near the site of his retreat, where his disciplines recorded his visions.

Throughout history, the role of women in eremitism has always been limited, due to cultural, societal, and psychological norms, physical vulnerability in patriarchal systems, and the simple prejudice of male organizations. Thus the limited number of women hermits in Western settings, as noted in section 13, was similar in Asia. Though women disciples were associated with the historical Buddha of India, and a prominent nun Zong Chi is associated with the disciples of Bodhidharma (5th-6th century), the Indian missionary to China and founder of Chan/Zen, the exclusion of women religious in Tibetan Buddhism was conspicuous. In eighteenth–century Tibet, Orgyan Chopyi (1625–1729) is distinguished as a Tibetan Buddhist nun, whose attributed autobiography, while a work of hagiography, consciously crafts an empathetic and respectful story of a Tibetan woman, however, exceptional, presenting stolid courage and determination.

Not unlike traditional societies, Tibetan culture was based on a misogynous social structure which came to be incorporated into religious doctrine through the identification of liberation for male human beings only. This context and the sufferings Orgyan Chopyi experienced are strong themes in her autobiography, as is the bleak physical environment of her northeastern Nepal birthplace: a short growing season, arid rocky terrain, pastoralism, recurrent patterns of warfare, famine, disease (smallpox, leprosy), and enforced labor. These conditions contribute to the centrality of suffering in Buddhist themes.

The mingling of Bon and Buddhism spawned an elite culture of lamaism but also a popular one of deities, magic, and superstition. In such an atmosphere, both scholarship and eremitism are discouraged. Wealthy patrons favor monastic flatteries and attentiveness to pilgrimage over spiritual practices.

A respected lama of the era, Tenzin Repa (1646–1723), emphasized individual character and intuitive understanding. He maintained that the most important source of spiritual growth resides in the relationship of teacher and disciple, wherein the lama's word and example is scripture itself, living and authentic. These ideas strongly influenced Orgyan Chokyi, for women could not enjoy monastic privileges as men did, instead being more disposed to beneficent teachers and the solitary path.

Moreover, Tenzin Repa welcomed women to his monastery, actively teaching them meditation. His disciple Orgyan Chopki emulates her master. He becomes her lama, and texts survive of his complimenting her mild temperament, forbearance, kindness, and compassion, confirming her spiritual progress in aspiring to the status of *dakini*, or spiritualized female.

Orgyan's childhood was difficult, with a sick, resentful father and intolerant mother. She recalls this period of suffering in poetry that resents being born a woman, a "broken vessel." The female body is itself samsara, she laments. But Orgyan also experiences mystical events and writes of moments of pervasive joy. For a while she works in monastery kitchens, but finally resolves to pursue meditation on her own. About to travel on retreat, her lama Tenzin Repa assents to Orgyan accompanying him to live in solitude.

Even in solitude, Orgyan experiences melancholy. After further counsel from her lama, she invigorates her meditation and prayer, eventually able to embrace a happiness that reconciles suffering with kindness. At age fifty, Orgyan Chokyi enters a cave in solitude, and in succeeding years, does not descend from it in winter. When she visits her old master, Tenzin Repa only recommends that she work towards her next life; at a later meeting, he tells her not to practice austerities anymore. Orgyan Chokyi died in 1729.

28. Shabkar: Tibetan Buddhism's "Perfect Hermit"

Shabkar Tsogdruk Rangdrol, or Zabs–dkar Tshogs–drug–ran–grol (1781–1851), is called by his translator Matthieu Ricard the "perfect hermit." So much is he a model hermit that contemporaries considered Shabkar the reincarnation of Milarepa, ninth–century Tibetan Buddhist hermit and composer. Shabkar's songs are part of the autobiography he dictated to a disciple in 1837 at the age of fifty–six as the first part of his life.

At thirteen years of age, Shabkar's lama presented him with Milarepa as model hermit. Shabkar entered a year–long retreat, followed by several years of monastic study. Sometimes he sang the spiritual songs of Lord Kalden Gyatso expressing joy in solitude:

> If you aspire to mountain solitudes under peaks wrapped in mist, there are natural caves in steep, rocky cliffs. To stay in such places will bring immediate and ultimate joy.

At twenty, Shabkar journeyed to Mongolia to study and practice with a notable lama, who advises Shabkar to "wander from one solitary mountain retreat to another, without preference." So he becomes a hermit.

Shabkar's parting from his mother is full of sadness and tears, a characteristic of his relations with people, a humane and emotional man of sentiments not always attributed to hermits. In his writings, for example, Shabkar describes his grief in departing from disciples or at news of the death of an acquaintance. Visiting his childhood home once, his mother deceased and the house half–ruined, sadness wells up in him. Shabkar is known for congeniality and a talent for telling stories and entertaining others. This is the personality of a "perfect hermit."

When Shabkar says that from age twenty to thirty he practiced to perfect himself, and that from thirty to fifty he worked for the good of others, he refers to ten years of physical isolation and twenty years of travel and teaching. In Mongolia he had found a pleasant cave for solitude, facing south, sunny in winter, cool in summer, where Shabkar pursued the practice of prostrations, recitations, and meditation, mastering control of channels, energies and *tummo*, the self–generated heat that enables the practitioner to withstand mountain cold. One of his prayers:

> I bow down at the feet of the hermits of the past who lived in mountain retreats. Grant your blessings that I and others may remain in mountain solitudes.

Shabkar records meeting a hermit in a cave while wandering the mountains, exchanging pleasantries, and being filled with admiration. He advises that renouncing possessions, kin, and homeland, troubles will fall away of their own accord.

For Shabkar, solitude is a preparation for life–long insight and practice, built upon a guru's initial guidance—but not within a monastery nor by pursuing study or even remaining in an informal community. He identifies ten treasures or actions leading to wisdom, seven noble riches of virtues, and the four preferences for the hermit life: simple food, simple clothing, simple dwelling–place, and simple possessions. Plus the four dharmas of training in virtue, based on the same theme: not returning anger for anger, insult for insult, slander for slander, or blow for blow. With the combination of virtues and practice, the hermit could make progress. Shabkar advises ignoring externals and turning inward, staying in mountain solitude, reaping what he calls the ten benefits of living in isolated places, which he enumerates as fewer (or less) activities, noise, distractions, quarrels, harm, emotions, or discord, and more tranquility, self–control, liberation, and complete freedom.

Shabkar identifies "ascetic virtues" specifically for hermits: clothing from rubbish heaps, a limit of three robes, clothing and shoes of cloth, eating a meal in one sitting, living only on alms, not eating after midday, sleeping in a sitting posture, and living in secluded places or under trees or in the open air or in cemeteries, or wherever one happens to be. Shabkar's succinct advice: "Meditate like the rishis... Stay alone, and be diligent in your practice." And his songs extol the virtue of solitude, for example:

> In the pleasant groves of wild mountain solitudes, where wise and accomplished beings attain supreme realization, one is not distracted by worldly affairs.

Shabkar's reputation spread widely. He began wandering throughout Nepal and Tibet, counseling disciples but also peasants and villagers, pilgrims and travelers. In this period, he describes his home as no particular place, his wanderings as in no particular direction. He calls himself "Hermit Protected by the Three Jewels," and describes his body as a hut swept clean by emptiness. Death, he writes, is the tearing apart of the boundaries and the net. He relates that his travel supply of food consists of *tsampa* (barley bread), barley, flour, butter, black tea, plus edible plants and wild garlic, but never animals. Among Shabkar's stories are many displaying compassion for animals: singing to or instructing bees, ducks, and crows, rescuing insects from a pond surface, and preventing the slaughter of sheep with his teachings to herders.

Shabkar deliberately intended to leave two images of himself to posterity: teacher and hermit. As teacher he exhorted others to practice, a teaching based solidly on experience, showing that monastic learning is not only unnecessary to enlightenment but can be a hindrance because of the absence of solitude. As hermit, Shabkar was eminently practical, from mountain solitary to wandering peacemaker among feuding nomads, from inveterate meditator in solitary places to benign teacher and poet.

29. Buddhist Hermits of Sri Lanka

Buddhism in Sri Lanka arrived in the fourth century BCE after the reign of Buddhist monarch Ashoka in India. Early in this era, Sri Lanka's Great Monastery is founded, with its commitment to preserve the earliest Buddhist documents, the Tipitaka and Commentaries, utilizing the native Pali language for scholarship. Monastery sponsorship originated with the king at the time. When a rival sectarian Abhayagiri Monastery emerged, centuries of contention darkened Sri Lankan history.

Buddhaghosa (fifth century) restored the Great Monastery, Pali ascendance, and Theravada scholarship. Buddhaghosa's classic text is *Visuddhimagga*, or "The Path of Purification." The epic poem "Mahavamsa" of Mahanama (sixth century) informally confirms highlights in Buddhist Sri Lankan history. Establishment of Dimbulagala, a famous twelfth-century hermitage, confirmed the viability of forest ascetic eremitism.

Unlike Mahayana, Theravada recreates the earliest and most direct sentiment of the historical Buddha, soberly excluding myths, deities, and powers to concentrate on the ethics and discipline of the monk or *bhikku*. From earliest time, the scholar monk and forest hermit are the models of Theravada. The hermit is nominally attached to a monastery but freely relates to the community. Buddhaghosa recommends that the ascetic adhere to a teacher as long as helpful, select a meditation subject, and then go to the forest to meditate and study. Buddhaghosa lists eighteen reasons to avoid a monastery, based on its size, newness, proximity to natural resources (food, water, timber, gardens), social atmosphere, and the presence of distracting visitors. The five factors favorable to a hermit's dwelling-place are: location (not far, not close); little human contact or sound; environment (few insects, no harsh sun, heat, or wind); availability of clothing, alms food, and medicine; and, finally, access to learned elders.

The forest ascetic Pannananda (1807–1878) promoted the pre-Pali Jakata stories about the Buddha as a more literary and folkloric ascetic source.

His disciple Subodnanda developed a village asceticism based on a discipline for laity excluding scholarly or monastic models. He also introduced the notion of self–ordination when the *sanghas* in cities and towns refuse to cede their authority. From village–based asceticism in Sri Lanka came the creation of small monastic communities based on non–authoritarian decision–making and forest–dwelling. These small communities of monks (largely self–ordained) are conceived of as a primeval sangha in a style that the historical Gautama would have approved, according to its Sri Lankan champion Ratanapala Asmandale, who lived through the mid–twentieth century.

The twentieth century also brought European converts to Sri Lanka. Among British–born monks is the hermit and writer Nanavira Thera, originally Harold Musson (1920–1965), who is described in section 56.

30. Buddhist Hermits of Thailand

As in Sri Lanka, Buddhism arrived in Thailand associated with King Ashoka of India (fourth century BCE), Thailand eventually embracing Theravada directly from Sri Lanka centuries later. As in Sri Lanka, the progress of monastic Buddhism in Thailand focuses on scholarship and ritual, dominated by monarchical control and sponsorship. This relationship continues to the present. Hindu–derived folk elements of magic, amulets, astrology, and such are endemic in the Thai population, while Buddhist reform movements, including *thudong*, or forest–dwelling, remain on the cultural fringe.

The forest–dwelling ascetic movement of Thailand known as *thudong* is a nineteenth–century reform movement intrinsically related to the forest setting. Thudong is attributed to the acetic practices recommended in Buddhaghosa's *Visuddhimagga*, which presents three essential components of asceticism: virtue or discipline (*sila*), concentration or meditation (*samadhi*), and wisdom or insight (*panna*). The ultimate goal of the path is purification (*visuddhi*). Purity is the essential metaphor of practice: purity of mind, heart, and body. At the same time, the ascetic path here recommended is marked by a psychological pragmatism that emphasizes concrete results versus speculation and metaphysics.

The *Visuddhimagga* considers the optimum physical setting for the path of purification to be one of isolation, seclusion, or reclusion (*viveka*). As the *Sutta Nipiti* 1.3 states:

Unfettered, like a deer in the forest,
Which browses wherever it will,
A wise man minds his freedom;
Like the one–horned rhinoceros: wander alone!

The *Visuddhimagga* recommends *dhutangas* or ascetic practices, which become emblematic of Buddhist asceticism by the time of the influential 100 BCE *Milindapanho* or "Questions of Milinda." The dhutangas are: wearing rag robes, having only three robes, begging alms, not omitting any house while begging, being satisfied with what one receives, eating only from one's bowl, eating no second helping, only eating in the forest at the foot of a tree, living in open air or in a cemetery, and sleeping in a sitting position.

The forest monk is to employ discarded cloth to make his robes, only secondarily accepting cloth deposited at his dwelling or along his daily path. The monk does not store or cook food but daily enters the nearby village (which could be several miles distant) and begs. Begging alms entails visiting each house in succession, not going to the wealthiest house or the most generous household first but to each in order. The monk presents his bowl in silence; Sri Lankan monks held a fan to their face, like Japanese Zen monks whose large headgear effectively covered their face. Food must come from householders' excess, and not be specifically prepared for the monk's coming nor prepared for them upon being sighted. These latter prescriptions correspond to the practice of Hindu and Jain sadhus.

The daily routine of forest monks consists in setting out for alms at midmorning, and allowing time to return to their dwelling places by about midday. If the forest monks form an organized hermitage, they assemble in a separate edifice or dining hall, redistribute the food as needed, and eat from their bowl in silence, without utensils and without taking a second helping. Excess food is given away. Typical Thai fare was rice, often with a sauce of chilies, some vegetables, and occasional fruit—whatever a typical household happened to have, which was often only rice. The monks normally used a well or stream as a water source. The midday meal constituted the only meal, but an afternoon tea from gathered herbs was acceptable.

Where the ascetic monk lives reflects his practice. Developed hermitages followed a pattern like the skete of the West among desert and mountain hermits, suggestive of individual dwellings in proximity to one another characteristic of Carthusian monks. The individual hut is called a *kuti*, in Thailand made of bamboo, palm, or other already–fallen wood; in Sri Lanka, the *kuti* is often made of concrete and wood, with concrete floors. When a master and disciple dwell together it is in a single edifice. If stationary for a period of time, the hermit monk might live in a previously–occupied hut or cave. The hermit's dwelling must be in a forest with no village or other habitation visible or readily accessible.

Individual practitioners pursued more rigorous settings. In Thailand, wandering monks carried a *klot* or modest tent–like cloth and mosquito netting, which could be set up in the open air, a cave, at the foot of a tree, or in a cemetery. The wandering monk was not to complain about whatever setting he pursued, discovered, or was obliged to use. That he never lay down to sleep but only sat is a common ascetic practice throughout Buddhist tradition into later centuries. Only a monk who is sick lies down.

The forest monk's typical schedule: sleep from 10 p.m. to 2 a.m.; meditation from 2 a.m. to 6 a.m.; wash up, clean, and sweep until going out for alms, from 6 a.m. to 10 a.m.; return to eat and rest, from 10 a.m. to 2 p.m.; attend to other chores, from 2 p.m. to 6 p.m.; spend another four hours in meditation, 6 p.m. to 10 p.m.

Village monks pursued a set of chores—those who lived close to villages in open air as well as those who lived in hermitages. Chores included manual labor to assist villagers in times of need, such as well–digging, house–building, or harvesting. Village monks did not refrain from contact with people when the purpose was well–defined and a helpful means of expressing compassion and loving–kindness. The active model of eremitism is reminiscent of the ancient Syrian hermits.

Wandering elders or masters with one or two disciples or younger monks might take up a months–long regimen of travel, sometimes without a particular itinerary, following rivers, forest highlights, mountains, valleys, and the thread of isolated villages for their food. Sometimes wandering monks would pass days without food when they lost their way. Such monks could readily pursue the practices of sleeping in the open air under trees, in caves, or in cemeteries, all the while adhering to a discipline of meditating in the wilderness.

The novice monk encounters three fears, the first being encounters with wild animals, namely tigers, elephants, and snakes. Encounters summon a confidence in *metta* (loving–kindness). A second fear is of corpses and spirits. The *Visuddhimagga* teaches that corpse meditation is a way of inculcating a spirit of impermanence and a practical way of conquering sexual temptation and fear of illness and disease. This second practice enjoined spending a night in a cemetery. Cemeteries of southeast Asia were not the tombstones and spacious lawns of the Western world. Corpses were regularly brought and deposited in shrouds on the ground for makeshift cremations incomplete or left unfinished by nightfall.

The third fear is fear of bodily suffering. The widespread contraction of malaria by forest–dwellers coexisted with the unavailability of palliative drugs in isolated locales. Conquering the third fear meant overcoming the fear of solitude and of suffering or dying alone.

Historically, the forest–monks and hermits of southeast Asia adhered to the discipline of their practice without other regulation. In Thailand, the Sangha Act of 1902 is the first formal attempt by the state and ecclesiastical bureaucracy to centralize monastic practice under the power of the king. The act curtailed the autonomy of monks by controlling the power of abbots to ordain new monks or to establish hermitages. In Sri Lanka, similar legislation led to a "self–ordination" movement, though this movement was short–lived.

In 1962, a second Sangha Act in Thailand ushered in the "forest invasion" period running through the late 1980s, during which authoritarian governments centralized rural and agricultural lands and resources, and industrialization and deforestation destroyed the habitat of the forest–dwelling monks. Forest monks were labeled pro–Communist by the government, and the forests were seen as hiding places for insurgents, a view held by the Thai government throughout the Vietnam War era. The particular targets of repression were the wandering and village–laboring monks. Most hermitage monks were forcibly moved to centralized monasteries.

The thudong tradition in Thailand has largely ended, the tradition essentially passing out of existence with the destruction of its natural setting. The last major figure of the original generation of notable Thai forest monks was the celebrated Ajahn Chah (1918–1992).

CHAPTER 5

EREMITISM IN ANCIENT CHINA

31. Eremitism in Ancient China: Confucianism to Taoism

Legends about hermits already existed in earliest Chinese antiquity, the hermits extolled as archetypes.

Among the archetype hermits are Xu You (Hsü Yu, third millennium BCE), who washed out his ears at the emperor's request that the hermit succeed him, and the brothers Boyi and Shuqi (Po I and Shu Chi, second millennium BCE), who became mountain recluses starving to death rather than assenting to join their corrupt father's war against a neighboring province. The legends illustrate the high moral principles of the learned official serving the emperor, king, or provincial lord: serve when the ruler is moral, but withdraw from service when the ruler is immoral.

Paralleling the hermit legends are ancient texts advocating the wisdom of withdrawal. The thirty–third hexagram of the *I Ching* ("Book of Changes") advises retreat or strategic withdrawal, suggestive in a military context but widely applicable to the larger context of reclusion. A verse in *Shi Jing* ("The Book of Songs") notes that "When words are well-considered, respond; when words are slanderous, withdraw." Witnessing his ruined city, a figure in *Shangshu* ("The Book of Documents") expresses a desire to "withdraw to the wilds." And a court official longs to "withdraw from public life." Not unexpectedly, folklore ascribed moral wisdom to solitary professions:

woodcutter, gatekeeper, farmer, or fisherman, for example. These figures are popularly conflated with hermits into eremitic archetypes.

In ancient China, tradition maintained that the emperor or king held the throne by virtue of the gods, a "mandate of heaven," or of fate—not unlike the divine right concept of the Western world. The philosopher K'ung Fu-tzu or Confucius (551–471 BCE) proposed that the criterion for holding power should be not heredity, conquest, or circumstance, but moral disposition. Confucius identifies the ideal as the *junzi* or "gentleman," often translated as "moral hero."

The moral hero applies an ethical criteria to life and society—versus convention or expediency—based on the Way, on the nature of the universe, as the true moral compass. The Way contrasts with the world, court life, and official service. In the *Analects*, Confucius praises the gentleman who shuns the world, and describes Boyi and Shu Chi as "excellent men of old" who sought virtue and did not complain of fate. Confucius echoes the ancient dictum to a moral hero to serve when good is in ascendancy but recluse when evil prevails.

Confucius spent his life as a "traveling scholar," journeying from province to province seeking out moral rulers, instructing rulers falling short, often fleeing hostile rulers—with little success. Eager to promote worthy gentlemen, Confucius doubtless lamented, like the historian Ssu-ma Chien (Sima Qian, 145-90 BCE), that "the hermit–scholars hiding in their caves may be ever so correct in their givings and takings, and yet the names of them and their kind vanish away like smoke without receiving a word of praise." This fate, however, was not to be completely so, even in ancient China.

Later interpolations in the *Analects*, repeated by Ssu–ma Chien, show Confucius confronting hermits on three occasions. In one instance, Confucius encounters the madman Chieh Yu loudly prophesying the destruction of the emperor. Feigned madness was a frequent device for speaking truth. Chieh Yu fled when Confucius approached. In another instance, Confucius encounters two brothers, Chang Chu and Chieh Ni, cultivating a field. A disciple of Confucius alights the carriage to ask directions. The brothers tell the disciple that the world rushes on like a torrent, and that Confucius should flee the world now and stop trying to reform it. Rather than follow one who avoids certain people, why not follow one who avoids society altogether? The brothers return to their hoes, and the disciple reports back to Confucius, who mildly protests that he cannot herd with birds and beasts, living in a haphazard world and duty–bound to promote virtue.

In a third instance, the disciple of Confucius has fallen behind the entourage, and encounters an old man in a field. He asks if the man has seen his master. The old man rebukes the disciple, telling him that a master is simply one who has never worked a field and cannot distinguish one grain from another. The old man resumes hoeing, but invites the disciple to his house because the hour is late. He gives the disciple a meal and introduces his two sons. The next morning, the disciple resumes his journey and meets Confucius, relating to him what had happened. Confucius listens and nods, saying "He is a hermit." Confucius asks the disciple to return and talk further with the old man but by the time he arrives the old man is in the fields. The disciple berates the sons for not serving the state as is their duty. Then he leaves. In berating the youths, the disciple represents the Confucian paradox of service versus reclusion. The old man and his sons are not hermits proper but archetypes of "wise rustics."

Thus Ssu–ma Chien depicts Confucius reflecting on the paradox of withdrawal versus going from one province to another in futile search of a worthy lord amenable to moral teachings.

From the death of the historical Confucius in the late fifth century BCE through the chaotic and violent Warring States era to the rise of the Han dynasty in 212 BCE, the era of the "Hundred Schools" dominated ancient Chinese thought. The Confucian thinker Mencius (Mengzi, 485–393 BCE) tried to recreate the methods of Confucius, traveling widely, promoting virtue based on the goodness of human nature. But his contemporary Yang–zhu (Yangzi, 440–360 BCE) promoted a philosophy of ego, condemned by Mencius as immoral hedonism. Confucian Mo–tzu (Mozi, 470–390 BCE) proposed an egalitarian social and political order promoting reason, social benefit, economic equity, and ethics. In contrast, the Fajia or Legalist school openly advocated an authoritarian state ruled by the wealthy with a strong military oppressing the common people. The Nung–chia School of the Tillers represented a breakthrough of thought, to be succeeded by the Taoists.

In Mencius, the contemporary philosopher Hsü Hsing (Xu Xing) represents Agriculturalist or Tiller thought, arguing that the king (or emperor) should plow his own land side by side with the people instead of maintaining his own granaries and treasuries, proof that he exploits his subjects. The Tillers extrapolated this core belief from the legendary rule of Shen–nung (or Shennong), a sage who reigned in peace over an ideal empire of peasants whom he governed without issuing decrees or imposing punishments. Shen–nung worked in the fields side by side with his subjects and shunned luxuries. In contrast to Legalists he does not coerce. In contrast to Confucius he does not moralize. Shen–nung is practical, ruling according to nature, human and otherwise. The *Tao te ching* of Lao–tzu (Laozi, fifth century BCE) echoes the Tillers' ideal society, going further to note that the wise and efficacious ruler is not even seen by the people, as Hsü Hsing noted.

The Tillers version of the story of the Boyi brothers, who recluse on moral grounds, refers to Shen–nung's model of good government. Both the brothers and the Tillers protest the swearing of oaths and making of covenants. They reject ritual prayers soliciting blessings, believing that prosperity is the result of labor, not blessings. The Legalist thinker Han Fei (279–223 BCE) acknowledged that the two brothers rightly reject state plaudits in their insistence to work as laborers and farmers, but he criticizes hermits because their withdrawal from society deprives the state and army of strength.

The Taoist Zhuang-zi or Chuang–tzu (370–283 BCE) celebrates Shen–nung as the culmination of the ideal state. The Taoists strongly identify with the eremitism of the Shen–nung ideal, especially Lao–tzu's *Tao te ching*, Chuang–tzu affirming, too, the Tillers school's rejection of the moralizing of Confucius and Mo–tzu, instead basing the eremitic motive on personality and self–actualization.

At the end of the Warring States period in 221 BCE, a fuller conceptualization of a Taoist ideal state emerges in the *Huainanzi*, compiled by King or Prince Liu An (179–122 BCE) and scholars of his court in the state of Huainan, a small realm within the Han empire. The *Huainanzi* praises the skills of Shen–nung in mastering knowledge of water, soil, grains, and herbs. The head of state is identified with the sage, universalizing the values of the hermit as the basis for a harmonious society governed by a sage philosopher–king, further corresponding to Lao–tzu. The *Huainanzi* mentions several famous hermits:

> Xu You, Fang Hui, Shan Juan, and Pi Yi all attained their Way. Why was this? The rulers of the age had the mind that desires to benefit the world; thus the people could enjoy their ease.

Hermit Xu You famously washed out his ears at the suggestion of taking office. The Taoist hermit Shan Bao lived alone on a cliff for seventy years. These recluse archetypes exemplify the virtues of the sage–ruler, such as tranquility, non–action, and adherence to the Way.

32. Eremitism in Ancient China: Han Dynasty

Just as Confucius conceived of the Moral Hero, Taoist advocates of eremitism during the Warring States period cultivated counterpart archetypes.

Taoists considered the times inappropriate to Confucian moralizing. The
Moral Hero no longer flourished and must become the Hidden Dragon. But
some Confucians flouted their high principles in refusing service, calling
themselves Paragons of Extraordinary Conduct, assuming the mantle of
the Boyi brothers and Xu You. The Taoists countered by proposing simpler reclusive heroes in the Wise Rustic (gatekeeper, gardener, woodcutter,
fisherman), socially anonymous figures in solitary occupations who do not
moralize but instinctively show themselves wise and practical. In reply to the
Paragon archetype, the Taoists proposed the archetype of the Perfect Man.

The Perfect Man abides in Attentive Transcendence, indifferent to fate,
desire, or injury. The goal of the Perfect Man is intentional anonymity, a
method for achieving union with the Way or Tao. This withdrawal does
not require formal reclusion, or external sign, but is a deep identification
with the flow of the Tao. The Perfect Man becomes Mr. Inconspicuous.

Nevertheless, the recluse may dwell in wilderness, however harsh and
off–putting it may seem to others. The recluse delights in mountains, waters,
and forests. The wilderness–dweller is an idler in the world's eyes, but the
Taoists consciously proposed the archetype of Untroubled Idler as a portrait
of disengagement, equanimity, and withdrawal. Such withdrawal can be
anywhere, hence the notions of a recluse in court and a hermit in the city.
The Taoist philosophy of non–action or withdrawal from action is *wu–wei*.

But Confucianism clung to power. The first Han emperor after the end of
the Warring States period was an illiterate peasant Gaozu (d. 195 BCE), who
thought inculcation of Confucianism would restore the empire to stability,
order, and morals. Under emperor Wu Di (140–87 BCE), Confucianism
becomes state policy and practice, elevating the Confucian philosophy of
the scholar Dong Zhongshu (179–104 BCE). The reunification of the
empire, the relative peace of the Former Han, and contemporary literary
resources served to disparage eremitism.

Among mythologized hermits and other Taoists of the Han dynasty are
"eremitic advisors" such as Sir Ge, Master Wang, and Mei Fu, the alchemist
Sir Yellow Stone, philosopher Zhuang Zun (or Yan Junping, according to
his student Yang Xiong), Zhi Jun (perhaps fictional), Anqi Wangshu, com-
mentator on Lao–tzu, Li Hong, who disappeared after being summoned

to service, and Zhang Zhong Wei, living in anonymous poverty, noted for his practice of virtue.

Among other figures with a popular story of reclusion are Song Sheng–zhai, Xun Yue and his brother Xun Xiang, Zhong Fu, and Han Fu. Song Sheng-zhai refused a proffered court post and left the capital to herd sheep. In his rural setting, he learns the zither and becomes adept at calligraphy. The fame of Song Sheng-zhai's simple virtue spread and he was sought out again for appointment to the court. Sheng–zhai disappeared further into anonymity, and could not be found.

Xun Yue and his brother Xun Xiang refused an invitation to court with the excuse of illness. The latter brother was imprisoned and died, the other fled. Zhong Fu declined an appointment to office and left his home to work anonymously on a farm, quietly pursuing study and practice. Confucian Han Fu (80 BCE) disappeared shortly after receiving summons to court service.

In his *Gaoshi zhuan* ("Biographies of Lofty Men" or "Biographies of Eminent Gentlemen"), Huangfu Mi (215–282) writes as a Confucian but relishes stories about Taoist recluses. In one instance, he tells the story of Zhi Jun, who retired to the mountains. Huangfu Mi's historian friend Sima Qian criticizes Zhi Jun for wasting his talent during such a favorable era. But Zhi Jun reputedly replied that he wished no more for his remaining years than to lie on his back gazing about without care.

According to historian Sima Qian, the Four Graybeards (or Hoaryheads) were four elderly men who had withdrawn to the Chang Mountains towards the end of the Warring States era. The four elders refused the solicitations of Gaozu to return from reclusion to serve. However, the emperor's strategist Zhang Liang privately urged them to present themselves in court not on the emperor's behalf but on behalf of the Empress Lui, mother of the young heir–designate. The emperor was about to assign the son of a favorite concubine to succession against his own legitimate son. The Four Graybeards complied, appearing in court at a banquet held for the heir–designate, thus silently rebuffing the emperor and his intent. Having made their point, the four then immediately depart, never to be seen again. Gaozu renounced his scheme. Another story postulates a fifth Graybeard who had refused to return to court for any reason. Later religious Taoists apotheosize all of the Graybeards.

Another important set of recluses is the Five Scholars–at–Home, for whom public summons were issued in 159, recognizing their high virtue and anticipating their valued contribution to the emperor. But none of them responded to the summons. One of the five, Xu Zhi (d. 168) was poor and humble, a student of classics, *feng–shui*, astrology, and *I Ching*. He had never accepted office but had been praised for his virtue by officials eager to present him to his fellow villagers as a model of quiet fealty.

Zhuang Zun, already mentioned as a philosopher, typifies the "hermit of the marketplace" of Chuang–tzu's Taoism. Zhuang Zun drew a modest living in the capital as a diviner but would cease his day's work when it suited him in order to teach Taoism. His student Yang Xiong describes him as living in deep obscurity, believing that reputation would bring him harm.

Other sources echo the sentiment of Zhuang Zun. Historian Ban Gu (32–92) says of Zhuang Zun that the people of Shu loved and respected him, and in his *Chronicle of the Hoayang Region*, historian Chang Qu (291–361) describes Zhuang Zun as noble and of tranquil manner.

Fa Zhen (d. 188) was a Confucian scholar summoned to court several times, refusing office repeatedly. In Ye Fan's *Houhanshi* ("Book of the Later Han"), the historian records an anecdote wherein Fa Zhen confronts an administrator intent upon recruiting him. Fa Zhen tells the administrator that he would go further north than the northernmost mountains and further south than the southernmost mountains rather than serve the court. Fa Zhen often lamented himself unworthy to drink the water that rinsed the ears of Xu You.

Han Kang (fl. 160) similarly sought anonymity. Though of a prominent family and expected to serve, he instead went off to pick herbs in the mountains that he would then sell cheaply in the capital. One day, a little girl recognized Han Kang in the marketplace. He fled. Summons followed. Obliged to return to the capital in the company of an imperial envoy, he escaped.

Fan Ying (d. 130) was a Confucian scholar with a hundred disciples. Summoned to office at age seventy, he was obliged to offer an inaugural lecture, which was (intentionally) so mediocre that the appointment was withdrawn. The next year, however, Fan Ying was summoned again, whence he vehemently insisted to Emperor Shun that he wished to remain a recluse. Despite his protest, Fan Ying was assigned office. He then pleaded illness, and was dismissed. A reclused contemporary criticized him for neither serving nor reclusing sooner.

An illustration of Confucian eremitism at the end of the Former Han is the story of Gong Sheng, who reclused from office with the overthrow of the Han and rise of usurper Wang Mang. The high–profile reclusion was particularly irksome to Wang Mang, who interpreted it as a refusal to acknowledge his legitimacy. The emperor sent minions to badger Gong Sheng to return to service. Instead Gong Sheng quit all food and drink, and died. Already dubbed Moral Hero for his reclusion, Gong Sheng became Paragon of Extraordinary Conduct. But historian Han–shu reports that at the funeral, an old man (later known as the Old Man of Peng–cheng) publicly criticized Gong Sheng (like Fan Ying) for not having reclused long before.

Women played a role in reclusion, as in the first century CE story of Meng Guang. Her future husband Liang Hong had studied at an imperial academy but upon finishing studies departed to herd swine. When discovered to be an educated man, he fled to his hometown. He rejected marriage until he met Meng Guang, a strong, practical woman who could sew, weave, and master household tasks. On their nuptial night she adorns herself with cosmetics and silks. Liang Hong becomes aloof and silent. Meng Guang asks her husband what is wrong. He tells her that he had wanted someone to accompany him into reclusion, as they had agreed, but that now she seemed unready, adorning herself like a court lady. At once Meng Guang returned to homespun. They soon depart for the hills to pursue farming and weaving. Liang Hong later wrote poetry and Meng Guang became famous as a woman of virtue, not mere deference, inspiring a husband's reclusion.

The wife of Laolaizi, upon learning that her husband had accepted an invitation to serve the King of Chu, tells him firmly that anyone who can offer meat and wine can follow up with floggings, that anyone who can offer office can follow with the executioner's axe. She avers that she will not be the wife of one who is under the control of another. She makes ready to go. Laolaizi follows. They recluse.

Historian Huangfu Mi relates another example of a strong–minded woman's reclusion. The wife of Jieyu returned from market one day to find her husband contemplating bags of gold just delivered by an emissary of the king of Chu to entice Jieyu to accept office. His wife tells Jieyu that she had herself tilled the fields for their self–sufficiency and herself woven their clothing. Having attained a comfortable living, now is the time to recluse. Jieyu agrees. The couple leaves for the mountains, living under different names.

Reclusion continued to interest Chinese historians and biographers after the Han Dynasty, nourished by Taoist religion and wilderness eccentricity. The recluses are described as archetypal, historical, and legendary. Sun Deng (third century) was an avid student of the *I Ching* and adept player of the *qin* or zither. Shi Yuan or Shi Tan (third century) is depicted as a supernatural, a Taoist immortal. Other famous recluses include Guo Wen (d. 333), who lived in mountains with wild animals, poet Lu Chi (fifth century), apotheosized alchemist Deng Yu (d. 515), and the eccentric thaumaturge Baozhi (d. 514).

33. Eremitism in Medieval China: The Poets

The arrival of Buddhism in China at the end of the Warring States era did not affect eremitism significantly because Mahayana Buddhism's emphasis on asceticism and monasticism differed from Chinese motives for reclusion. However, with the reputed arrival of Bodhidharma (483–540) to China, Buddhism's philosophical Chan (or Zen) component—centered on individual effort in meditation versus study of sutras and commentaries—found greater compatibility with eremitism, though Chan took several centuries to spread.

The Tang Dynasty era from the seventh through tenth century represents a Golden Age of poetry in China—and the poets were often recluses and hermits. Before the Tang, however, two important hermit–poets emerged. Hsieh Ling–yün (or Xie Lingyun, 385-433) filled his work with lavish descriptions of nature in its wild mountains and rivers. But Hsieh Ling–yün was a conflicted official, outspoken in the midst of contemporary political intrigues. He was exiled during the period of his poetry, returned, and was eventually executed. Hsieh Ling-yün presents a discomforting eremitic creativity.

Tao Chien (or Tao Yuan–ming, 365–427) was a scholar–gentleman writing of his indifference to notoriety, his penchant for quiet study, his small house without dust, noise, or busyness: a torn robe, meagre meals, and the forbearance of wife and children. Having reclused from government bureaucracy, Tao Chien pursued self–sufficiency by farming, reluctantly returning to service twice due to poverty. At night the poet browses through pictures in the *Classic of Mountains and Seas*, a collection of stories about ancient Chinese kings and sages. Tao Chien's poems reflect Taoist sensibilities.

Tu Fu (or Du Fu, 712–770) is considered by many to be China's greatest poet, recognized for his lyricism, sentiment, use of precise imagery and metaphors, his treatment of self, ambition, war, culture, fate—and the dilemma of service and duty versus reclusion. Born into a comfortable family, Tu Fu professed Confucianism but failed the civil service exam to enter office, perhaps deliberately. Taking his portion of family wealth, he traveled, enjoyed aesthetic pleasures, and remained skeptical of service.

With rising violence and civil war, conscription swept the countryside. The powerful warlord An Lu–shan seized power in 755. Impoverished, with a household of ten, Tu Fu decides to serve and is appointed as a low–level functionary. Shortly afterwards, An Lu–shan is assassinated and the court, including Tu Fu, fled the capital. The rebels are defeated, but Tu Fu ends up in a distant mountain post far from family. The prospect of reclusion gives him vague hope, inspired by a visit to an old acquaintance ("hermit" or "scholar") now living in the mountains with his own family, surrounded by children, a garden, and ample food.

Tu Fu had been writing poetry all these years; in this period the poems are somber and pessimistic reflections on war and the hardships of common people. He feels old and wonders how recluses tolerate poverty. Finally, he quits office, moves his family again, then several times more in coming years. Tu Fu writes his best, most compelling poetry, consistently Confucian, regretting instability and personal hardship. Only in his last years is he reconciled to simplicity and eremitism.

Hanshan (eighth–ninth century) served as a modest official when forced to flee with his wife and son during a court purge in the An Lu–shan Rebellion (755–763). He successfully concealed his identity by calling himself Hanshan ("Cold Mountain"), living in the Tientiei Mountains, farming, and writing poetry.

Hanshan was well–versed in literature and philosophy, but a severe critic of both professed monks and scholar gentlemen. His wife and son left him due to their poverty. Sources describe Hanshan thereafter as an eccentric hermit living in a cave, writing poems on trees, rocks, and monastery walls. His poems are inspired by Taoism and Chan, heartfelt revelations of life as a wandering hermit.

Two contemporary itinerant monk–poets associated with Hanshan are Fenggan (Fengkan, or "Big Stick") and Shide (Shih-te, ShiDe, or "Pickup"). Subsequent legends provide biographical detail. The tall (hence "big stick") Fenggan lived at the outskirts of the temple where Hanshan resided, writing poetry. Fenggan discovered the orphan Shide and raised him (hence "pick–up" or "foundling"). Shide, too, became a poet. Fenggan became popular in Japan as Bukan, an imposing figure depicted accompanied by a tiger.

Li Po (or Li Bai, 701–762) fell from favor at court in youth and wandered his entire life, occasionally taking informal service in minor courts, mingling with elites as a favored poet, then capriciously disappearing. His poetry extols the classical style even while often reflecting a life of dissipation. Li Po knew Tu Fu but is distant from the latter's sense of gravitas.

Wang Wei (701–761) was a minor official. Inspired by Buddhism, he chose not to pursue worldly advancement. He built a hermitage he dubbed "Bamboo Retreat" and left office to live there the rest of his life.

The poet Wei Yingwu (737–792) remained an official all of life, but his poetry reflected, like Tu Fu, the unease of his era. Though not a recluse, he was strongly influenced by Tao Chien. Wei Yingwu represents the cultural affinity to hermits. In one poem he remembers an old friend reclused on Chuanjiao Mountain whom the poem would like to cheer, but regrets that he would not be able to find him.

Po Chu–i (or Bai Juyi, 774–846) was a government bureaucrat transferred to distant Mount Lu because of his court criticism. Enamored of wilderness, he built a small house he called "Thatched Hall" for occasional stays. Anticipating retirement and reclusion, he frequently took his wife and daughter to the house. He wrote meticulously about his beloved hut, but did not live to retire.

Chen Tuan (817–989) built a hut at the foot of the Hua–shan Mountains when he was young, then journeyed to the capital seeking to serve as an official. He was so disgusted by court life that he spent the rest of his life as a hermit, pursuing Taoist exercises, for which he was apotheosized as a Taoist immortal.

Complementing the themes of reclusion are the hermit–poets of nature composing verse of "rivers-and-mountains." The poets of the *shanshui* tradition in China were concerned not merely with literary aesthetics but what translator David Hinton considers a conscious presentation of a cosmology based on the Tao or Way of philosophical Taoism and Chan Buddhism. In this tradition, the poet is not merely an observer but integral to the transformative process. The poet presents seasonal cycles built upon a larger ontological process called *tzu–jan*, the self–generative process wherein the human being becomes an integral and conscious part of nature. This process is achieved through reclusion and eremitism, and is given expression in poetry, painting, and calligraphy.

Properly speaking, Tao Chien inaugurated the more modest "fields–and–gardens" poetic tradition, with its more circumscribed natural subjects, while Hsieh Ling–yün (385-433) inaugurated "rivers–and–mountains" poetry, actively referencing key philosophical concepts in a larger natural setting. The key concepts are three: *li* (inner pattern), *shang* (aesthetics of wholeness), and *hsin* (identity of mind and heart). For example, Hsieh Ling–Yün conceives mountain landscapes as reflecting emptiness or non–being.

Among Tang Dynasty poets in the rivers–and–mountains tradition enumerated by Hinton are Meng Haoran, Wang Wei, Li Po, Tu Fu, Wei Ying–Wu, Hanshan, Meng Chiao, Liu Tsung–Yuan, Po Chu–i, Chia Tao, and Tu Mu. Many of these poets have already been mentioned. The poets form a unique introduction to and maturation of ideas based on their experience as hermits in wilderness, building a vocabulary and set of poetic themes. Thus Meng Haoran (689–740) introduces the element of enigma into landscape poetry. Wang Wei (701–761) extends the theme into both poetry and painting, wherein enigma transitions into silence, the silence of wilderness. Consciousness of wilderness is the contrasting backdrop of Tu Fu's world–weariness. Wei Ying–Wu (737–792) embodies the reclusiveness of Wang Wei and the sensitivity of Tu Fu.

Hanshan wrote entirely within a wilderness setting. Meng Chiao (751–814), also a deliberate hermit, crafted a dark poetic sense akin to Tu Fu's introspection. The poetry of Liu Tsung–yuan (773–819) was influenced by his monastic Chan studies. Once a contemplative monk, Chia Tao (779–843) became an impoverished poet. Tu Mu (803–853) remained a career government official acquainted with both nature and Chan, both reflected in his poetry.

The rivers–and–mountains genre continued into the Song Dynasty era of the late tenth to late thirteenth centuries. Taoist poet Lu Yu (1125–1210) retired from government employment to become an impoverished recluse on a farm in his ancestral village, where he wrote poetry. The poetry of both Fan Cheng–ta (1126–1193) and his contemporary Yang Wan–li (1127–1206) express Chan Buddhism as context for enlightenment.

Perhaps the last great hermit–poet of this era is Shiwu Qinggong, or Stonehouse (1271–1352), a Chan Buddhist monk, once a meditation master and abbot. In middle age he moved to a Zhongnan Mountain hut, composing poetry that intimately details daily life in wilderness solitude. Stonehouse describes his hut in the clouds, his few belongings, his busy days growing and foraging food, chopping wood, drawing water, wearing ragged clothes, occasionally reading poems or a sutra. From his hut, Stonehouse views nature as microcosm of the world. His poems are among the more accessible and representative works of Chinese eremitism, reflecting the hermit sense of deliberately being, as he writes, "out of touch with the world's rise and fall."

The rivers–and–mountains poets represent the culmination of Chinese philosophy and aesthetics in this era, as well as iterations of eremitism.

34. Eremitism in Medieval China: The Painters

Just as nature and wilderness inspired eremitic poets in medieval China, painters also took up reclusion themes in the Song Dynasty (960-1279) and thereafter. While some poets were hermits themselves, most painters and calligraphers were Confucian scholar–literati who remained at court, admiring reclusion as amateur or "anti–professional" painters. Just as wilderness poets saw in nature reflections of their eremitism, painters might present objects in their works—from mountains and forests, birds and flowers, plum trees and fishermen–hermits —as suggestive of hermit life.

The modest reclusion process among Song painters began gradually. Painter Dong Yuan (932–962) remained at court as an official, becoming a paragon of style and brushstroke. Guo Xi (1020–1090) wrote about artistic theory and technique while painting mountain landscapes. Su Shi (1036–1101, also called Su Dongpo) was several times exiled from court for his criticisms but as often recalled. Though chiefly a calligrapher, Su Shi's few paintings reflect natural settings, among them the famous Red Cliffs. On the other hand, Ma Yuan (1160–1225) served comfortably as a court painter. Zhao Mengfu (1254–1322), renowned for his striking depictions of nature and animals, descended from elites.

The outstanding shared premise of these painters was their amateurism, deeming themselves unworthy or lacking in skill to paint formal court themes—or simply reluctant to do so. Their status concealed an admiration for wilderness settings and the superiority of reclusion.

Four outstanding hermit–painters of the Yuan Dynasty period following the Song are Huang Gongwang (1269–1354), Wu Zhen (or Wuzhen, 1280–1354), Ni Zan (1301–1374), and Wang Meng (1308–1385). The "Four Masters" combine calligraphy and painting, usually depicting stylized natural settings that reflect their iconoclastic world view as hermits. The rise of Mongol rule, the artists's clashes with authorities, and their dissenting behavior eased their decisions to recluse.

Of an elite family, Ni Zan gave up his property to live on a houseboat. Huang Gongwang was born poor, was never a scholar, and early reclused to mountain dwelling, professing Taoism. His subjects are mountains, peaks, ranges, and forests. The titles of Wu Zhen's paintings are apt: "Poetic Feeling in a Thatched Hut," "Reclusion Among Mountains and Streams," and "Manual of Ink Bamboo." Though bamboo is a natural object, bamboo became symbolic among painters: bamboo reeds are empty (like the poet's ambitions), flexible in adverse conditions, strong when tested. Titles of Wang Meng's paintings are also suggestive: "Thatched Cottage in Autumn Mountains," "Ge Zhichuan Moving to the Mountains," "Dwelling in Reclusion in the Fuchen Mountain," and "The Simple Retreat."

By the Ming era (1368–1644), the contrast between traditional "professional" styles and individual "amateur" styles with their subtle interest in eremitic themes emerged more clearly, though eremitic themes persisted. A leading professional advocate was Jai Din or Tai Chin (1388–1462), though one of his works is titled "The Hermit Xu You Resting by a Stream." Shen Zhou (1427–1509) was not an official but mingled comfortably with established painters, promoters of traditional styles and themes. Some of his suggestive eremitic titles include "Poet on a Mountain Top," "Atop a Mountain,"Chanting Poems in Leisure Among Pines," and "Peach Blossom Study" (alluding to Tao–Chien).

Tang Yin (1470-1524), a protege of Shen Zhou, was denied an official career, and became a typical "amateur," selling his wares, to the scorn of professional painters. Many of his works are based on reclusion themes, the most famous titled "Scholar–Hermits in the Autumn Mountains." Other works by Tang Yin include "Scholar Playing the Qin," "Wuyangzi in Self–cultivation," "Reclusion by the Eastern Hedge," and "Thatched Cottage in the Western Hedges."

Most painters of the Ming era were "professional" painter–officials, such as Fa Ruozhen (1613-1696), who held a succession of government posts, including in the judiciary. His landscape paintings are eccentric but their spirit unpersuasive. Similarly, Wang Hui (1632–1717), of a long line of family successors as court painters, was celebrated by the emperor; he helped solidify the triumph of tradition over innovation.

Perhaps the most significant expression of eremitism in painting during this era is in the work of Shitao (or Zhu Ruoji, 1642–1707). Of an elite family, Shitao escaped the Manchu invasion and collapse of the Ming dynasty, first concealing his real name and then traveling to remote locales, finally entering a Buddhist monastery. For forty years Shitao roamed China as a hermit, using various names. Finding no religious patron, he became a Taoist, resumed his travels, and began to paint late in life.

The outstanding characteristic of Shitao's technique was simplicity and boldness in color, brushstroke, perspective, and use of space. Fresh and attractive calligraphy accompanies his paintings. He wrote several instructive manuals of art theory.

Shitao's subjects are chiefly landscapes: mountains, rivers, and vistas, but also detailed fruit, insects, and flowers. The hermit Shitao's many eremitic allusions include his twelve–piece series inspired by the Taoist poet Tao–Chien (Tao Yuanming), titled "Poetic Feeling of Tao-Yuanming," "Hermitage at the Foot of the Mountain," "Lonely Mountain," "Conversation With the Mountain," "Hermit Lodge in the Middle of the Table," and "A Friend of Solitary Trees."

NOTE: The popular Chan/Zen Buddhist illustrations to the *Ten Bulls* or *The Oxherding Pictures* originated among twelfth–century Chinese artists. The best–known series are by artists Kuòān Shīyuān (called Kakuan in Japanese), Ching-chu (called Seikyo), and Tzu-te Hui (1090–1159, called Jitoku). In China, no particular influence of the theme of the *Ten Bulls* is identifiable, but the series enjoyed great interest in Japanese Zen circles.

CHAPTER 6

EREMITISM IN JAPAN

35. Eremitism in Shinto Japan

The physical settings of great eremitic austerities have been deserts and mountains. For Japan, like China, the setting is mountainous.

Shinto is the indigenous nature religion of ancient Japan and evolved Shugendo, an asceticism of mountains. Shugendo is derived in part from Shinto's designation of sacred places in nature, wherein mountains are dwelling–places of spiritual beings, as are rivers, springs, and forests, in the tradition of animism. Incorporating Shinto with esoteric Buddhism and philosophical Taoism, Shugendo appeared at the end of the Heian period (794–1184).

Mountain asceticism appeared very early in historical Japan, extending to a whole class of male adventurers, soldiers, penitents, and strength–builders not necessarily imbued by religion—or, rather, carving out a martial religiosity akin to eternal combat against a panoply of gods and demons.

Shugendo is dominated by the image of Enno Gyoja, a seventh–century historical figure whom legend transformed into a "founder." The name means "En the ascetic." According to legend, Enno was exiled by the gods for trespassing on a forbidden mountain in order to pursue religious practice, but every night Enno would fly back to his favorite mountain, defying exile. Enno is closely associated, like nineteenth–century artist Hokusai, with the sacred Mount Fuji, appearing as its patron in the artist's renowned "One Hundred Views of Mt. Fuji."

In Hokusai's modern but spiritualized portrait, Enno Gyoja is depicted as a powerful and self–disciplined figure, capable ascetic, neither god nor warrior but a hermit or holy man renouncing the world and pretensions to supernatural powers. The descendants of Enno Gyoja are the *yamabushi*, who pursue mental discipline and martial arts in mountainous dwellings or retreats, though not as religion or shamanism. Eremitism did not emerge from Shugendo or the yamabushi, however, who only forecast the parameters of Japanese sentiment. This would be the work of a Chinese cultural influence among poets and thinkers.

36. Eremitism in Buddhist Japan: The Poets

The eighth–century arrival of Chinese culture irrevocably transformed Japan. Confucianism and Buddhism were the first new cultural elements. The former attracted elite classes and imperial authorities establishing a Confucian political and familial order. With proliferation of Buddhist shrines, temples, and monasteries, Buddhism gradually eclipsed Shinto, which lacked priesthood, scriptures, and popular ritual. Chinese cultural influences were decisive, from language, alphabet, and vocabulary, to architecture, clothing, and household objects.

By the twelfth century, Japan's samurai military culture with its internecine warfare, plus a series of natural disasters, provoke a cultural crisis marked by widespread popular pessimism. The crisis prompts the growth of Pure Land Buddhism, oriented to other–worldly salvation, and Zen Buddhism, based on meditation, enlightenment, and self–sufficiency.

The first eremitic figures reflecting these intellectual trends in Japan are near contemporaries: Saigyō (1118-1190), the Buddhist hermit–poet, and Kamo no Chōmei (1153–1213), hermit and author of *Hojoki* ("An Account of My Hut") and compiler of *Hosshinshu*, a collection of hermit stories. The poet's influence on literary and aesthetic issues complements the chronicler's influence on religion and biography. Kamo no Chōmei is considered here first.

In the *Hojoki*, Kamo no Chōmei applies his insight to an understanding of the era in an account of his times and of his final dwelling–place. Chōmei transforms the rarified Buddhism of his day into a tragic sense of life, lyrical and reflective, representing *mappo* or the degenerate last age, and *mujo*, the sense of impermanence.

In the *Hojoki*, Kamo no Chōmei describes a succession of recent calamities: a fire consuming Kyoto, a windstorm that levels much of the city, and a famine that lingers for the next two years, devastating town and country and leaving anguished and sickly residents wandering aimlessly, corpses littering the streets. A calamitous earthquake follows. These historic events provoke Chōmei to reflect on impermanence, suffering, and reclusion. At the age of fifty, having lost his ancestral home and livelihood, Chōmei becomes a hermit–monk, renouncing the world. At age sixty, he builds a ten–foot square woodland hut, described in detail in *Hojoki*.

In *Hosshinshu*, three types of recluses are presented: 1) *hijiri*, holy men completely rejecting the world and reclusing themselves from society as hermits, itinerate holy men, or wanderers without home or possessions; 2) *tonsiesha*, those who admire the *hijiri* and even imitate their eremitism but who cannot embrace the harshness of their material life nor the absolute human separation it entails, and 3) *inja*, those who reject society and relationships to pursue aesthetic expression in reclusion.

Here are some representative *hijiri* in Chōmei's *Hosshinshu*. The virtue of self-effacement characterizes the hermit in each story:

- Gempin Sozu, an educated monk, built a thatched hut by a river, contemptuously refusing an emperor's appointment to religious office. Years later, an old disciple of Gempin, traveling to a far northern province, comes to a river crossed by a ferry. The traveler recognizes the disheveled old ferryman as Gempin. He holds back tears, revealing nothing. At the same time, Gempin has recognized the traveler. When the traveler comes to the river on his return trip, the ferryman is gone, another having replaced him. The traveler asks the residents about the previous ferryman. Yes, a monk had been here as ferryman, they tell him, not the usual low fellow who takes such work. He never accepted a fare, wanting only a little food and to purify his heart repeating the *nembutsu*. (The *nembutsu* is the prayer–recitation of Pure Land Buddhists, "Namu Amida Butsu," meaning "I take refuge in Amida Buddha"). Something must have happened one day, they tell the traveler, because the ferryman vanished and no one knows where he has gone.

- Byodo Gubu was an eminent monk of the Buddhist Tendai sect who one day experienced enlightenment. At that moment he left everything, went out dressed as he was, and walked to the river. He takes a boat to a distant province, begging his food, wandering and sleeping anywhere. A certain Acarya, administrator of the provincial governor, had once been a disciple of Byodo Gubu. Returning from travel one day and arriving at the governor's mansion, Acarya sees a beggar–monk in the courtyard being pursued and harassed by an unruly, jeering crowd. Recognizing the old emaciated monk and overcome with pity, Acarya descends to the courtyard to bring Gubu into shelter. But Gubu refuses, and leaves. Acarya orders a search for the old man but Gubu is not to be found. Years later, a dead man is found near an unfrequented mountain stream, facing west, hands clasped in prayer. Acarya goes to the site and, tearfully recognizing Gubu, performs the last rites.

- A certain man owned fifty hectares of prosperous grain fields. One day he realizes the vanity of possessions, the impermanence of hoarded goods, and of life itself. He sets out for the capital to wander and beg. His thirteen–year old daughter finds him and pleads that he return, but the man puts her off, even drawing a sword, leaving her in tears. He ascends Mt. Koya, builds a hut, and takes up religious austerities. The fame of his virtue spreads. His daughter becomes a nun. She lives at the foot of the mountain, serving her father's needs the rest of his life.

- An articulate monk made an unusual request of the master of the governor's house. He explained that a certain young lady of his acquaintance had come into a certain condition and that he needed provisions for her. The monk asks to take the things to her himself. The governor's administrator is scandalized but says nothing. He brings the provisions but puts a servant to follow the monk. The monk departs for a deep mountain valley and a thatched hut where he lays out the provisions. The servant takes note of all this. With darkness upon him the servant settles to sleep. During the night the servant is awakened by the monk's sublime recital of the Lotus Sutra, and is unable to check his tears. In the morning, the servant returns and relates the details to the astonished governor, who wonders at the monk's ruse. He sends the servant back to the monk with more provisions. The monk accepts these without reply. Some time later, wanting to confirm the monk's well–being, the governor sends his servant again. This time the hut is empty. The first set of provisions is gone but the second set lies where the servant had placed them, now scattered by birds and wild animals.

One of the more famous *hijiri* of this era was Ippen Shonin (1238–1289), proselytizer of Pure Land Buddhism noted for his itinerancy and the fervor of his teaching. He is equally notable as the object of a famous 1299 scroll by the painter Hougen Enni depicting Ippen's life in painted scenes and accompanying text. Ippen is a model *hijiri* because he rejects both the life of the householder and of the institutional monk in a temple or monastery setting. Ippen promoted solitude, itinerancy, and self–effacement.

In his thought and teaching, Ippen incorporated a complex of Buddhist and Shinto traditions that addressed the needs of his diverse audiences from poor to wealthy, humble to noble. Ippen was a mountain hermit but incorporated into the core of his spirituality pilgrimages, rituals, dream divination, temple and shrine offerings, distribution of slips of paper with holy inscriptions, and the recitation of the Buddha's name in the *nembutsu*.

The Japanese Buddhist monk–poet Saigyō (1118–1190) is a significant figure in the literary transition to a poetic style and a shift in voice and imagery from courtly drama to nature and self as subjects. Saigyō lived as a mendicant and hermit. As translator Burton Watson notes, Saigyō's poetry evokes thatched huts, mountain settings, blossoming cherries, the moon in a night sky, and the poignant evanescence of the world.

In Saigyō's *Sankashu* ("Mountain Home Collection"), the mountain home to which he refers is his own hermit hut, and, by extension, himself and the vision of life of the hermit. While he traveled extensively in mountains and by seashores, visiting temples and shrines, staying with friends and acquaintances, Saigyō's most descriptive poems reflect his observations from his mountain dwelling. He writes with strong personal sentiment attuned to a love of nature, but also with melancholic feeling, such that the poems contribute to both the sense of *sabi* (solitude) unique to Japanese aesthetics and to use of seasons as a regulating poetic image.

The Japanese Nō play evolved from a medieval form of indigenous theater called Saragaku, which combined music, dance, song, and story with interludes of comic relief. By the fourteenth century, the Nō play had become serious and stylized, reflecting Japanese aesthetic, dramatic, and folkloric religious themes with local, historical, and legendary materials. Among the themes and figures comprising Nō subjects is Saigyō himself.

Saigyō is the only poet central to a Nō play, and certainly the only hermit. Saigyō appears directly in the fourteenth and fifteenth–century plays *Euguchi*, *Saigyō–zakiura* ("Saigyō's Cherry Tree"), and *Yugyo yanagi* ("The Priest and the Willow"). The dramatic subjects of the latter two works derive from specific poems by Saigyō. He had written about a cherry tree outside his hut, and about an ancient willow whose spirit achieved enlightenment so that the tree could now die.

Yoshida Kenkō (1283–1350) represents Chōmei's *inja*, a solitary with aesthetic rather than philosophical or religious motives. Kenkō's *Tsurezuregusa* ("Essays in Idleness") is a posthumous collection of essays and aphorisms. Retiring at forty–two, he becomes a Buddhist monk residing alone the rest of his life in a temple outside the capital Kyoto. Kenkō admires resourceful forest hermits, their simplicity and sense of detachment, referring to famous Chinese hermit–poets Tao Chien and Po Chu-i (Bai Juyi) and to the Taoist classics of Lao–tzu and Chuang–tzu. Kenkō advises the misfortunate to shun worldly ties, seek seclusion, and hasten to practice the Way, ever conscious of impermanence.

Over subsequent centuries, Japanese eremitism becomes intimately tied to Zen cultural and aesthetic expression, especially in poetry, painting, and the concepts of *wabi* and *sabi*. Matsuo Bashō (1644–1694) standardized the poetic form of the *haiku*, which he presents in individual poems written in the context of several travel journals as an itinerant Buddhist monk, including *Nozarashi Kikō* ("Journals of a Weather–Beaten Skeleton"), *Oi no Kobumi* ("Notes in My Knapsack"), and *Oku no Hosomichi* ("Narrow Road to the Far North"). A representative work befitting the genre of the hermit hut is Bashō's brief narrative of his last dwelling place, *Genjuan no Fu*, translated by Burton Watson as "Record of the Hut of the Phantom," and by Donald Keene as "The Unreal Dwelling."

The last great eremitic Japanese poet and Zen monk is Ryōkan (1758–1831). The quiet, sensitive youth trained in Zen Buddhism, Ryōkan traveled for several years, studying Chinese poetry and calligraphy, and returned to the mountain outskirts of his native village to establish his hermit hut, which he calls "Gogo–an," literally "hut of half–day's rice," a statement of his intentional poverty.

Ryōkan's poetry largely revolves around daily life at his hut, four bare walls with a window, a hearth, and a few books. He evokes the seasons in detail, the deep stillness of winter, the wild colors of spring flowers, the bamboo surrounding his hut, and the thousand peaks and ten thousand mountain streams without signs of anyone. The only poet he mentions is Hanshan. Ryōkan depicts autumn reflectively: gathering firewood, listening to evening rain. He admits that winter is harsh, with the path to the village for occasional supplies impassable. In melancholy moments, he wishes for a visitor. But the sadness Ryōkan feels is for the sad people of the world, he tells us: he wishes that his priest's robe could gather all who suffer.

37. The Aesthetics of Eremitism: *wabi, sabi, aware, yugen*

Japanese aesthetics incorporates principles of Chinese Taoism and Zen Buddhism. The primordial cosmology of China centered on observed patterns of nature which present a philosophy based on a path or way (Tao) of life. The chief phenomenon to observe is the contrast of light and dark in the universe, popularized as *yang* and *yin,* the latter identified with the fecund creative source of the "ten thousand things" in the universe originating in darkness and mystery. The ancient second–century Chinese dictionary *Shuowen jeizi* (or *Shuo wen chieh tzu*) uses the term *hsuan* ("darkness") to identify this generative reservoir with the female (yin), resting in quietude, non–action, and potentiality. Lao–tzu observes that the sage holds on to "dark virtue" to safeguard self, which entails withdrawal to observe in non–action, humility, simplicity, and adherence to the mysterious. That which is nebulous, silent, and elusive permits the truths of nature to emerge, if the sage is perceptive. Lao–tzu describes presence as visible nature but absence as that which gives presence its functionality.

Zen Buddhism brought a rigorous vocabulary to Taoism, introducing Void and Emptiness, for example, and strengthening organic Taoist thought. These two philosophical systems proved compatible with the culture and psychology of the two great civilizations. The historical hallmark of a masterpiece of Chinese or Japanese art is naturalness, the uncontrived, the accidental appearance of the art piece. The highest achievement of Taoist and Zen art is produced by one who harmonizes nature with its universal accidents.

The first principle of Japanese aesthetics is *yugen,* which is in fact the translation of the Chinese "hsuan." Yugen is employed with the same meaning of darkness, emphasizing the mystery that is the ontological reality behind phenomena, their context, and their setting. An observer cannot readily package or circumscribe this aesthetic element because yugen yields its insight through conscious and pursued attentiveness and openness. Identified as one of the seven basic principles of Zen, yugen comes to mean "subtle profundity," an experience of profundity or mystery of circumstance or object that cannot be expressed in words, hence an ideal philosophical term for an aesthetic experience in art and poetry, but also an ideal aesthetic term for a philosophical experience of nature or meditation.

Elements of yugen appear early in Japanese literature. The works of Kamo no Chōmei present reflections on the hermit life, the world, and nature, all brushed with yugen, expressed as poignant melancholy. Beside using established images and themes in his poems, Saigyō's images of nature and seasons specifically build feelings of grief, melancholy, and the sensibilities of Buddhist psychology, anticipating yugen. The preeminent haiku poet Bashō would describe himself as merely plodding in Saigyō's path.

Yugen was consciously advanced by Zeami Motokiyo (1363–1443), who virtually established the Nō drama as a literary genre. For Zeami, yugen means "what lies beneath the surface," hence, the subtle and mysterious. For the drama, Zeami sought to express subtle profundity in the elements of grace and beauty, where yugen establishes a hidden beauty to the play's theme, a deepened beauty that enriches the bare plot and action of the play with powerful emotion.

The Buddhist poet–monk Shinkrei (1405–1475) grounds the phenomena of yugen in more specific metaphysical terms, writing in his *Sasamegoto* ("Whisperings") that "You find mystery and depth as well as the sad beauty of things where things are left to be said and logic is absent."

Philosophy historian T. D. Suzuki (1870–1966) originally described yugen as "intuitive prehension," eventually preferring the simpler description of "feeling." As Suzuki puts it, yugen is "the experience the human mind has when it is identified with the totality of things, or when the finite becomes conscious of the infinite residing in it." The experienced moment of such feeling engenders "the most primary feeling which lies at the basis of every form of psychic functioning we are capable of." Profound mystery is thus perceived or felt from the most profound source in the human mind, which Suzuki identifies in Zen tradition as *mushin*, "no–mind."

Yugen is perhaps perceived as a small product of enlightenment or *satori*, where a configuration of beauty, bound in its evanescence, strikes the observer and elicits feeling. Such concepts engender in Japanese artists and poets a sense of both awareness but also detachment, the latter a refraining from contriving a feeling, which aesthetically would reveal itself to be inferior art. The haiku of Bashō represents the culmination in a long historical struggle to purge poetry of contrivance and artificiality, to reach a form that would scan immediately in its simplicity and aesthetic character, directly imparting the poet's feeling and perception, capturing yugen.

British literary historian R. H. Blyth suggested that the element of mystery in yugen is originally closely synonymous with Zen master Rinzai's "profound essence," which, in turn, refers to the core of Buddhism. The transition from concept to feeling requires a literary context, where feelings can be actively demonstrated and not simply described. The first major poets after Saigyō to address yugen are Sōgi and Sosetsu, then the Ushin School of poets through the medieval era, extending the poetic genres of waka and renga. But the mature consciousness of yugen culminates in the haiku, specifically in Bashō.

Bashō argues for yugen insight in poetry not as a mere poetic element but intrinsic to the authenticity of the successful poem. This success is only achieved when the poet identifies with nature itself:

> You must leave your subjective preoccupation with yourself.
> Otherwise you impose yourself on the object and do not learn.
> Your poetry issues of its own accord when you and the object
> have become one —when you have plunged deep enough into the
> object to see something like a hidden glimmering there. However
> well phrased your poetry may be, if your feeling is not natural—if
> the object and your self are separate—then your poetry is not true
> poetry but merely your subjective counterfeit.

In this passage, Bashō makes oblique reference to yugen as the "hidden glimmering" of a natural object. At the same time he offers direct instruction (perhaps to his many disciples) concerning a prerequisite to good poetry, one that he himself ardently pursued. In his preface to *The Records of a Travel–Worn Satchel*, Bashō reiterates his advice about identification with nature, mentioning paragons of art:

> Saigyō in traditional poetry, Sōgi in linked verse, Sesshū in paint-
> ing, Rikyū in tea ceremony, and indeed all who have achieved
> real excellence in any art possess one thing in common, that is, a
> mind to obey nature, to be one with nature, throughout the four
> seasons of the year....The first lesson for the artist is to learn how
> to overcome barbarism and animality, to follow nature, to be one
> with nature.

Contemporary critics identify many technical aspects of writing successful haiku poetry, such as association, comparison, metaphor, simile, and the like. These techniques are common to most poetic forms. Similarly, elements of Japanese aesthetics, from yugen to *aware*, *wabi*, and *sabi*, are used as descriptive forms to take into account when crafting a poem, as with structural techniques. Bashō argues that neither techniques nor aesthetic elements by themselves address the authenticity of a poem, which must be derived from the identification with nature and must express a sense of the mystery of being that is inspired by deep feeling.

The second major aesthetic principle is *aware*, meaning pathos or poignancy. The phrase *mono no aware* means "the pathos of things" or "the poignancy of things" and captures the Buddhist sense of transience or impermanence, *mujō*. With *aware*, the artist or poet attempts to portray the evanescent beauty that touches the spirit and culminates in a feeling about life, nature, and the universe. *Aware* presupposes the mature culture's ability to cherish beauty and therefore to reflect the melancholy or poignancy of its passing. In his *Essays on Idleness*, the hermit–monk Kenkō reflects on how a cold pursuit of worldly goods stifles the mind's ability to appreciate the evanescence of nature and self. The philosopher and literary critic Motoori Norinaga (1730-1801) extended "mono no aware" to the unique status of a national cultural expression.

The two dominant principles of Japanese art and culture are *wabi* and *sabi*. Wabi literally means poverty, not as the absence of material possessions but as non–dependence on material circumstances. Wabi is divestment of the material, surpassing material wealth. Wabi is simplicity that has shaken off the material in order to relate directly with nature and reality. This absence of dependence also frees itself from indulgence, ornateness, and pomposity. Wabi is quiet contentment with simple things. Simple, worn, or imperfect objects reflect wabi.

Sabi is literally solitude or even loneliness. Sabi is the atmosphere of the best Tang poetry of China and haiku poetry of Japan. Where wabi is material non–dependence, sabi is non–dependence in a psychological and spiritual sense. This position rejects all contrived attachments in favor of reality and nature. Sabi embodies imbalance and asymmetry, avoids contrived order, and rejects the abstract and intellectual. Like Zen, sabi emphasizes the completeness of simple, even primitive, experiences (moon–gazing, gardening, tea ceremony) and objects (bowls, tea cups, brush–stroked calligraphy). These pursuits and objects display utter grace in execution, but also a conscious and deliberate roughness or antiquarian primitiveness bordering on imperfection and lack of polish or sophistication.

The life of the hermit came to be called *wabizumai* in Japan, essentially "the life of wabi," a life of physical solitude and simplicity. The transition from wabi to sabi was an organic one over centuries, occurring among poets, artisans—and Japan's best known poet-hermits.

38. Aesthetics of Eremitism: Japanese Painting

The theme of eremitic reclusion dominates medieval Japanese painting, poetry, and literature during the era from the twelfth to seventeenth centuries. Reclusion as a classic Confucian theme was extended to painting by presenting as subjects the scholarly–gentleman, always Chinese, always pursuing an eremitism without hardship of poverty, vicissitudes of weather, or a sense of isolation. The recluse in these paintings was shown engaging in activities reflecting higher culture, such as conversation, poetry, music, calligraphy, and the viewing of nature, not alone but in groups, with the centrally–placed hermit's hut projecting a simple refinement, what came to be called "elegant rusticity," later evolving into the tea hut.

The Chinese eremitism depicted or implied in Japanese paintings of this era deliberately intended to satisfy all Japanese elite classes: officials, military, politicians, and religious. Confucian figures are scholar–gentlemen; Taoist figures are immortalists, literati, and eccentrics. Overtly Buddhist figures are downplayed. The staid government officials reading literature or viewing the eremitism depicted in these paintings as leisure and refinement do not feel threatened. At the same time, philosophical observers and skeptics can perceive the same paintings as a tacit "aesthetics of discontent," as veiled criticism of the existing political and social order.

In literary circles, early Chinese classics were read avidly, from the *Wen Xuan* ("*Selection of Refined Literature*") collected in the fifth century to the standard poets Tao Chien, Tu Fu, and Hanshan. Compiled in the eighth century, the *Manyoshu* ("Collection of Ten Thousand Leaves") is the first major anthology of Japanese poetry. Poetry in Japan evolved quickly through the genres of Gozan (Zen), *renga* (a genre reflecting collaborative socializing parlor games of class elites), culminating in the early tenth–century anthology *Kokin Wakashū* (or *Kokinshu*) and the genre of *waka*, the dominant poetic genre of the medieval centuries.

Paintings reflect the culmination of Japanese enthusiasm for Chinese culture. A popular subject of painting was Hanshan and his circle. The Japanese artist Mokuan Reien (d. 1345), who spent the latter part of his life in China studying Zen and art, introduced the theme with his painting "The Four Sleepers." The painting depicts Hanshan, Shide, and Fenggan sleeping while sitting, plus the tiger that reputedly accompanied Fenggan everywhere. The symbolism suggests perfect contentment in Zen practice.

In other painters, Hanshan is depicted alone, as in "Portrait of Kanzan," by Kaō Ninga (fourteenth century), or with Hanshan's sidekick Shide, as in "Zen Eccentrics Hanshan and Shide," also by Kaō Ninga. Another painting is "Hanshan and Shide," by Yintuoluo (fourteenth century). Fenggan is included in a painting by Reisai (early fifteenth century) titled "Fenggan, Hanshan, and Shide." All of the portraits exaggerate the hermits in their eccentricity, reminiscent of "holy fools."

A second popular Chinese image in Japanese painting is the Four Graybeards of Mt. Shang. In China, the Graybeards represented discontent with the court, for the historical Graybeards had reclused (as the story in section 32 relates). However, "The Return to Court of the Four Graybeards of Mount Shang" of Kanō Mitsunobu (1565–1608) depicts the reverse of the original Chinese story, with the Graybeards returning in this version not as critics but to resume favor and remain at court! The revised theme conforms to official tolerance of Chinese eremitic themes that altered their original (and threatening) meaning.

"The Four Accomplishments" of Kanō Motonobu (1476– 1559) refers to the four skills of the Confucian scholar–gentleman: music (specifically the *qin* or koto), calligraphy, painting, and games of strategy (such as *go*). The work fuses Taoist and neo–Confucian virtues in aesthetic reclusion. "The Four Admirers" of Kanō Tsunenobu (1636–1713) depicts classic Chinese poets (including Tao–Chien) with flowers representing preferred seasons.

On the same screen as the Graybeard's return is "Su Shi's Visit to the Wind and Water Cave," wherein the famous eleventh–century Chinese poet is depicted crossing a footbridge (accompanied by a servant) in a landscape of plum blossoms. The "Seven Sages of the Bamboo Grove," a painting of the Kanō school, depicts third–century Taoist scholars, musicians, poets, and aesthetes (not all contemporaries and not all hermits). The historical Sages opposed the authorities and conventions of their era, but in this updated depiction they promote refined culture, eccentricity, inebriation, and pleasure.

Representative seventeenth–century aesthetic recluses include Kinoshita Choshoshi (1569–1649), Ishikawa Jozan (1563–1612), Fujiwara Seika (1561–1619), and Shokado Shojo (1584–1639).

Kinoshita Choshoshi, a samurai, could no longer reconcile the tensions of service. He recluses to a Kyoto–area hermitage, where he wrote and taught poetry. Using his wealth Kinoshita assembled a magnificent library of Chinese and Japanese books of poetry. His *Sanka no ki* ("An Account of My Hut in the Mountains") is composed in the style of Kenkō.

A war veteran, Ishikawa Jozan quit service to study Chinese philosophy. Jozan built a hut he called Shisendo ("Hall of the Poetry Immortals"), here installing portraits of three dozen Chinese poets, most of them hermits, adding *kanshi* (Chinese–language poems) to each.

Shokado Shojo was a Buddhist monk living in a hut on the grounds of a Tokyo shrine, adept in calligraphy, painting, and tea ceremony. The subjects of his paintings are modest: birds, flowers, blossoms, bamboo, and simple calligraphy.

Fujiwara Seika was a prominent advocate of neo–Confucianism, which not only provided the state with a rationalist philosophy but promoted nationalism through rejection of Chinese culture and language. Originally an adherent of Zen Buddhism, Seika contrived a rationalist *hina* or "quiet sitting" to counter Zen meditation. As with the sentiment of "The Four Admirers," Seika promoted self-cultivation, sagacity, and political legitimization, the last serving to advance centralization.

PART III

THE MODERN WESTERN WORLD: RENAISSANCE TO ROMANTICISM

CHAPTER 7

EREMITISM IN THE RENAISSANCE

39. From Hermits to Solitude in Early Modern Europe

Multiple factors caused the end of eremitism and hermits in the late medi-eval and early modern Western world. The first factor is the growing wealth of monasteries acquiring larger buildings and land holdings with increased numbers of lay workers, while monks pursued scholarly or ritual activities, excluding from their bounds influence of the spiritual movements of the era. This factor has been mentioned in prior sections.

A second factor is the increased consolidation of power by monarchy and ecclesiastical authority. A third factor is the vast social displacement, poverty, and homelessness in the economic shift from agriculture to urban and mercantile life, from the late medieval through the sixteenth century and beyond. Highlights of these disruptions include the Crusades, the Black Plague, the Hundred Years War, and the religious wars of the Protestant and Counter Reformations.

Among the changes brought about by historical circumstances in the late Middle Ages is a new search for spiritual solace outside conventional religion—seen in the rise of mysticism and new spiritual orders (such as the Franciscan Spirituals)—plus a growing anticlericalism directly or indirectly impugning monks and hermits. In medieval times, solitude was associated with forests, islands, and anchorholds where hermits resided, but these refuges were gone, as were the hermits.

An important effect of the decline of eremitism is the revised perception of solitude. Where individuation in the Middle Ages complements labor and daily life (including monastic and eremitic living), the social chaos of the last medieval centuries challenged the concept of solitude. Where the desert and early medieval hermits saw *eremos* as a spiritually nurturing if harsh physical remoteness, they nevertheless were supported by a sense of community within creed, contrasted to a corrupt and worldly society.

With the decline of moral example in monasteries and churches, solitude as virtue was no longer identified with monks. Church and state had always encountered severe moral critics during the Middle Ages, such as Abelard and John of Salisbury, themselves neither hermits nor monks. Ignatius of Loyola (1491–1555), founder of the Society of Jesus (Jesuits), shifted solitude from eremitic ends to modern means. After months of austerity living in isolation in a cave near Manresa, Catalonia (Spain), Ignatius emerged with the core of his book, *Spiritual Exercises*. The book is a manual of devotions and mental exercises for lay and religious with worldly duties. For Ignatius, solitude is a device for dispelling distraction from duty. The regime cultivates a streamlined alternative to eremitism.

The Protestant and Catholic Reformations in sixteenth–century Europe fostered a genre of literature satirizing hermits, in part because real hermits had disappeared.

Early sixteenth–century Spanish playwrights Bartolomé de Torres Naharro and Juan Timoneda, and Portuguese playwright Gil Vicente, put fraud hermits into love triangles. The play *El Condenado por Desconfiado* by the Spanish monk and dramatist Tirso de Molina (1579–1648) weaves a complex scenario wherein a hermit prays to learn his counterpart in virtue, but is answered by the devil, who recommends a certain criminal who happens to cares for his aging father, a presumed act of mercy. The perplexed hermit becomes a robber, soon leading a band of robbers. One day, the criminal flees the city on murder charges. He encounters the hermit–turned–robber and joins his band, but returning to the city to care for his father, is captured, and condemned to death. His father persuades him to confess, so that he may go to heaven upon execution. Meanwhile, the hermit–robber, mortally wounded in a fight, learns of his exemplar's confession, but doubts God's grace. He dies, and goes to hell.

The anonymous Spanish picaresque novel *Lazarillo de Tormes* (1554) features a subplot in which young Lazarillo takes the identity of a corrupt deceased hermit in order to enjoy his livelihood. Lazarillo soon discovers that the late hermit was married and his wife and family are pursuing Lazarillo, his imposter.

French vagabond poet François Villon (1431–1463) was a picaresque counterpart, his life featuring flights from murder charges involving his attacks on several fellow rakes who happened to be priests. The epic poem *Orlando Furioso* by Italian poet Ludovico Ariosto (1474-1533) includes among its myriad characters and plots a lecherous old hermit "skilled in sorcery." French writer and fabulist Jean de La Fontaine (1621–1695) composed fables and stories featuring ribald caricatures of priests, monks, and hermits. In one fable, a rat–hermit lives in a cheese and dismisses the petitions of troubled fellow rats by telling them he has renounced the world. But in another fable, an arbitrator (lawyer) and an almoner (physician) solicit a hermit's advice about the best path to follow in life:

> Let me ask you, have you found
> This knowledge where vast crowds abound?
> No; trust me, it can only be
> The fruit of sweet tranquillity.
> Shake but the water in your vase,
> And you no longer see your face;
> But let it once more still remain,
> And straight your likeness comes again.
> Midst worldly scenes you'll never learn
> The love for which we all should yearn.
> Believe me, friends, the desert's best
> For him who'd study his own breast.
> To each the Hermit's words seemed good,
> And, henceforth, each one sought the wood.

A century later, a protagonist of the famous novel *Ivanhoe* by Walter Scott (1771–1832) is the character Friar Tuck, called a hermit. Among the novel's anachronisms: friars did not exist as early as the story's historical setting, and Tuck carries rosary beads not in existence then. Tuck dines on venison, not pulses and water, as belied by his weight. The narrative suggests that he was expelled from a monastery and defrocked. One character pointedly calls Tuck a "lusty hypocrite."

An indirect critique of eremitism comes from the English poet William Cowper (1731–1800), who helped popularize the story of sailor Alexander

Selkirk (1676–1721). Selkirk quit the privateer ship on which he was a second mate to live on a deserted island off Chile. He regrets his decision almost at once, but spends four years on the island, ingenious in surviving, before another British ship happens to anchor there. Cowper's poem, titled "The Solitude of Alexander Selkirk," extrapolates its subject to fit the sentiment of his age:

> O Solitude! Where are the charms
> That sages have seen in thy face?
> Better dwell in the midst of alarms,
> Than reign in this horrible place.

Selkirk's experience inspired Daniel Defoe's 1719 novel *Adventures of Robinson Crusoe*. Defoe maintained that solitude in wilderness is reprehensible and that proper Christian life is within society. This solitude begs of purpose because the fictional Crusoe goes so far as to wonder whether all people are at base selfish in wanting others to service their own interests.

The pinnacle of British attacks on eremitism in the age of rationalism and Enlightenment is historian Edward Gibbon's *History of the Decline and Fall of the Roman Empire* (1776), discussed in section 7. Ironically, Gibbon is widely known for his quotation of Scipio Africanus: "I was never less alone than when by myself," although he may have better quoted Seneca: "I am never more in action than when I am alone in my study."

40. Roger Crab: Early Modern Hermit

Perhaps the last medieval and first modern hermit in England was Roger Crab (1621–1680), eccentric author of the biographical pamphlets *The English Hermite* and *Dagons-Downfall*.

At the age of twenty Crab made twin vows of celibacy and vegetarianism, based on religious and ethical motives. He joined Oliver Cromwell's nonconformist Puritans in revolting against the Catholic monarch Charles I in 1642 and actively fought with Cromwell's army. In 1648, however, Crab is sentenced for indiscipline—not battlefield disobedience but likely for joining the Levelers, who espoused radical egalitarian land reform and opposed authority. Released from prison two years later, Crab settled in the village of Chesham outside London as a small merchant, a "haberdasher of hats." His trade proved lucrative enough that a few years later he sold the business, gave his money to the poor, and became a hermit.

Crab then moved to Ickenham (also near London), devoting himself to asceticism, mysticism, astrology, and health (then called "physick"). He devised a diet based on Scripture, condemning flesh and alcohol, eating only bread, bran, herbs, and roots, drinking only water. He advised over a hundred patients. Crab's abstinence from flesh was not only motivated by religion and health but was a form of social protest against the wealth and corruption of (as he enumerates) "Priests, Councellors, Lawyers, and the rude multitude instructed by them, ... King, Bishops, Parliament, Army, Trades, Sects, Gentlemen and Farmers."

Such sentiment made public was bound to spur resentment. Crab was arrested four times for "Sabbath–breaking," that is, suspicion of being a wizard. Upon each arrest, Crab railed against the magistrate about freedom and tyranny. Crab was cudgeled, put in stocks, whipped, and imprisoned. He finally moved to a cottage outside London, spending the last twenty years of his life in quiet solitude.

Roger Crab could have been the model for the Mad Hatter of Lewis Carroll's *Alice in Wonderland*—but there is no evidence that Carroll knew of him. Crab's abstinence and his political and social views project him into a long eremitic tradition, however little he may have realized.

41. In Defense of Solitude: Petrarch to Rousseau

In the late Middle Ages, the realization that institutional eremitism would not last pointed some observers toward an individual option. Thus the sentiment of French poet Eustache Deschamps (1346–1406): "If the times remain so, I shall become a hermit. / For I see nothing but grief and torment."

The Renaissance Italian poet Francesco Petrarch (1304–1374), known chiefly for his lyric poetry, penned a notable essay titled *De Vita Solitaria* ("On the Life of Solitude" or "On the Solitary Life"), begun in1346 and finished ten years later. Petrarch dwelt in the whirlwind of literary life versus ecclesiastical politics, himself a minor cleric (though not a priest). For a period of years he longed to escape his personal moral entanglements. He established a "fair transalpine solitude" in the town of Vaucluse, outside of Avignon, France, where he retreated to avoid the papal court that employed him.

Petrarch's essay on solitude extols the saints who embraced solitude: Ambrose, Augustine, Remigius, Peter Damian, Francis of Assisi. He mentions "orators who loved the life of solitude": Cicero, Seneca, Demosthenes. His identifications are overstated. The essay returns to arguments favoring solitude, compatible with ancient civic virtues as much as Christian spirituality. The theme of active versus contemplative life was an old topic dominated by religious writers, but Petrarch rejects the attempts to balance the two, preferring a humanist and philosophical point of view—plus a serene rural setting and a composed mind. Still, Petrarch's stays in Vaucluse were sporadic, always lured away by his worldly ambitions.

In 1347, Petrarch wrote *De otio religioso* ("On Religious Leisure" or "Repose of the Cloister") to his beloved brother Gherardo, who had entered a Carthusian monastery. In this work Petrarch extols spiritual quietude and condemns worldliness, ruing the very life he had been pursuing. Petrarch eventually retired to the Padua town of Arquà, now called Arquà Petrarca.

The Spaniard courtier and bishop Antonio de Guevara's 1539 *Menosprecio de corte y alabanza de aldrea* ("Contempt for Court and Praise of the Village") strikes a picaresque tone to his clear criticisms of court, safeguarded by the positions the author held. The French poet Maurice Sceve's 1547 *Saulsaye: eglogue de la vie solitaire* ("Willow Run: Ecologue of the Solitary Life") helped revive the Roman writers Cicero and Seneca on the subject of solitude. Sceve composed *Saulsaye* after entering country retirement.

Michel de Montaigne (1533–1592), French lawyer and civil servant of the monarchy, crafted a consummate literary style in his *Essays*, at once a Latin classicist and a modern, a fideist, a Stoic, and a skeptic, allied to no extreme, marked by melancholy and resignation. His essay, "On Solitude," is a stoic acceptance of the folly of society and the wisdom of living a life of imagination and virtue. Montaigne's solitude entails separation from the crowd, disdain for ambition, aloofness in the heat of conflict, and a tragic sense of life.

Like Petrarch, Montaigne rejects the religious dichotomy between contemplative and active lives, instead construing the contemplative as the solitary. Montaigne recommends that the wise person flee the vicious crowd and its contagion. We have not gotten rid of our own vices in order to have to contend with the vices of others, he argues. Solitude brings leisure and ease for the pursuit of virtue. But fleeing the crowd is not enough, he avers; one must root out gregarious instincts in the self, in order to repossess the self, to assure contentment with the self. While Seneca may have said that we are all chained to fortune, Montaigne would say (not quoting Seneca) that the chains are of our own making. Even the worldly householder, with wife, children, possessions, and good health, must not depend on them for happiness. Wisdom does not shirk loyalty or duty, but reserves "a back shop" all one's own, to establish true liberty, a retreat to solitude.

Montaigne represents the paradox of solitude, wherein his solitude is a moral protest against society, while the act of becoming solitary itself provokes social fragmentation. The retreat to solitude is itself an expression of the new individualism of the early modern era. The aristocratic humanist tradition of maintaining a country retreat, hearkening to Roman times, conceives of rural solitude as a means to retreat into self. But rural solitude is both a privilege for the well-born and a path negating the communitarian recovery of society. For Montaigne, the solitary is a community itself, the solitary communing with his ideas, thoughts, and readings.

In Petrarch, and less so in Montaigne, the life of the solitary aspires to parallel the life of the hermit. Whereas the hermit communes with God through private meditation in his retreat from monastic life, the solitary enjoys privacy as a secondary retreat from renouncing the social.

A peculiar twist in the rise of solitude is evidenced in the French-born philosopher and scientist René Descartes (1596–1650). Weary of crowded Paris for pursuing writing and research, Descartes moved to Amsterdam, boasting of being able to "live without being deprived of any of the conveniences to be had in the most populous cities, and yet as solitary and as retired as in the midst of the most remote deserts." Descartes embraced the ancient sentiment from Strabo to Erasmus to Francis Bacon that "a great city is a great solitude." However, Descartes did not fully comprehend the paradox of his desired solitude—urban access to goods and services versus rural quiet, isolation, and nature. Rather, Descartes valued a circle of close intellectual friends and like-minded colleagues always at hand. His philosophical views countenanced an aristocratic retirement versus an eremitic or ascetic motive.

This paradox of solitude was observed by French writer Jean de La Bruyere (1645–1696) in his posthumous *Dialogues sur le Quiétism* ("Dialogues on Quietism"). The essay is a product of Le Bruyere's friendship with Cardinal Bossuet, both authors supporting a restrictive traditional theological interpretation of solitude. Quietism arose in France as a challenge to traditional theology. The Jansenist movement commended an inward spirituality marked by a pessimistic view of human nature that clashed with

Jesuit activism. Quietism was based on contemplation, personal piety, and private austerities, and did not solicit ecclesiastical or doctrinal approbation. These preferences were cautiously reflected in the personal asceticism of the philosopher Blaise Pascal (1623–1662), whose quietude is reflected in his disapprobation of "*divertissement*," saying that the people's unhappiness is the result of being unable to stay quietly in own's room.

La Bruyere criticized contemporary adherents of quietism as having no personal obligations yet having no self either, essentially solitaries. The term La Bruyere uses is "isole"—the solitary is isolated, though not quite alienated in the modern sense. La Bruyere opposed the desire for physical solitude that is not inspired by religion but is a self-constructed philosophy. The controversy highlights the transition of solitude in this era.

François Fénelon (1651–1715), an archbishop and poet, sympathized with quietism, though with cautious deference to tradition. In his 1697 *Maxims of the Saints* ("*Explication des maximes des Saints sur la vie interieure*"), Fénelon emphasizes the spiritual values of austerity and silent prayer over the external pieties favored by the ecclesiastical authorities of the era. "Christ Himself," Fénelon writes suggestively, "Whose retirement to solitary places... [is] not to be forgotten, has given us the pattern which it is proper for us to follow..." In 1699, the papacy condemned quietism, proscribing and suppressing Fénelon's *Maxims*. Fénelon quietly assented.

In the same year 1697 when *Maxims* appeared, Fénelon's novel *Adventures of Telemachus* was published, presenting an unambiguous eremitic theme. In the novel, the king's advisor witnesses the treachery around the throne and quietly recluses to the isle of Samos to live as a hermit in a cave, later returning to the Greek mainland to live in solitude on his own rural estate. The novel explores the ethical dilemma of service versus withdrawal in a version of the classic Confucian dilemma, updated for the intellectuals of early modern Europe contemplating revolt not merely against wealth and power but against an entire ethical system. Rural solitude represented a moral dimension that contrasted sharply with the corruption of court and city.

Jean-Jacques Rousseau (1712–1778) is primarily identified with his *Social Contract* (1762). But that work, in turn, proposes a solution to more fundamental questions about the nature of society addressed in two earlier key writings of Rousseau. Despite his chronological status as an Enlightenment era thinker, Rousseau proposed a social and philosophical system opposed to the momentum of the rationalist age, one built on the notion that human nature is essentially solitary.

Where Enlightenment philosophers optimistically argued for reason, science, and progress, Rousseau's first discourse, *Discourse on the Sciences and Arts* (1750) announced the radically contrary notion that Western civilization was now experiencing social and ethical regression. According to Rousseau, government and law arose to secure order, and the arts and sciences consolidate this authority in order to protect and justify a decadent facade. Luxury dissipates morality. Economic disparity of class reduces the value of the individual to the measure of his consumption.

In his second discourse, *Discourse on the Origin and Foundations of Inequality Among Mankind* (1754), Rousseau identifies two species of inequality, that based on nature and that based on social and political inequality. Natural or physical inequality refers to bodily constitution, health, and mental capacities. Political and social inequality is deliberate, based on law, authority, power, prejudice, culture, convention, and subjugation. The latter are detrimental accompaniments to the advantages gained by the development of society and its transformation from an animal–like existence.

Describing this transition from a primitive to civilized state, Rousseau anticipates modern findings of anthropology and paleontology. He is not far off in his description, while himself acknowledging that his sketch is conjectural and hypothetical.

Human pursuit of survival irrevocably transformed into associations between humans, the foundation of social groups. Chronologically this transformation led from hunting and gathering to clans and tribes, to viability of larger populations, then to territoriality, competition, and the development of hierarchy and power. In the primitive era, humans largely resided in nature, had simple appetites, were tolerant of weather, enjoyed keen eyesight, and slept well. Unlike the view of Hobbes, humans are not intrinsically evil or vicious, Rousseau maintains. A natural empathy emerged from their common life. In the state of nature, each person was his own master, without bonds of constraint, and enjoyed a solitary nature.

Will and consciousness transformed the state of nature and redirected it towards the path to civilization. Animals choose, humans will. Consciousness provokes the capacity to select and to will. Will promotes a sense of potential or perfectibility. External accidents radically shift primitive human behavior, making humans sociable, therefore (says Rousseau) "wicked." As Rousseau puts it, the first man to enclose property and announce that it is his (and found others to believe him) was the true founder of society. This was the source of many crimes, war, murders, and horrors, pitting the ego against others, violating the ethos of the solitary state of nature. Thus, Rousseau sees property as the source of societal problems, and in ethical terms the source of greed, pride, covetousness, and egoism. Property engenders the mentality of civilization.

Rousseau elaborates on the impact of his premises. The disappearance of equality leads to property, wealth of the few leads to servitude of the many. Society emerges, with oppression destroying empathy. Institutions emerge to safeguard the new order. The end of the original state of nature is the end of solitude. Rousseau cites two ancient philosophical exemplars of solitude: Diogenes and Stoicism. Of Diogenes, Rousseau states that the Greek solitary could not find a wise man because such men were of a bygone era.

Rousseau's essential anthropology of solitude and human nature is expressed in the two discourses, yet his *Social Contract* receives the most critical interest today, primarily because it intended to resolve a necessary or inevitably corrupted human condition given the premises of the discourses. In the *Social Contract*, Rousseau attempts to address the issue of society as a contemporary given; there can no longer be a system that recovers original human nature. Hence his famous opening declaration that "Man was born free, and is everywhere in chains" refers to social man, contemporary people in contemporary society.

Rousseau was proscribed and exiled by both church and state for his radical writings advocating a freedom and individual autonomy untenable in his day. He unwittingly collected many enemies among the elite of France and Switzerland until he was literally fleeing for his life. The philosopher David Hume invited him to England but they soon fell out, Hume indignant at Rousseau's penchant for solitude. Rousseau safely returned to Paris under a wealthy patron's protection. Out of the experience of persecution and exile came the collection of essays posthumously published in 1782 as *Reveries of a Solitary Walker* ("Les reveries du promeneur solitaire").

The *Reveries* are sketchy essays Rousseau composed in his seventies for his own perusal and solace. In the "First Walk," Rousseau acknowledges that his work emulates the style of Montaigne, noting that while Montaigne wrote his essays for public consumption and therefore discretely held back deeper feelings, Rousseau writes only for himself, holding back nothing.

While the *Reveries* can be counted significant among writings on solitude, Rousseau was understandably brought to the work in bitterness. From the opening lines he describes himself as "alone on the earth." Of his critics and foes, he says:

I am a thousand times happier in my solitude than I could possibly be living amongst them. … Whatever they may do, my contemporaries shall ever be nothing to me.

And in "Sixth Walk" Rousseau notes:

The conclusion I am able to draw from all these reflections is that I was never truly adapted to society, where all is constraint, obligation, duties; and that my independent disposition always rendered me incapable of a subjection necessary to him who wishes to be something in the world.

42. Hermits in Renaissance Art

With the near disappearance of hermits from the late Middle Ages, through the Renaissance, and through the Protestant and Catholic Reformations, hermits became an object of nostalgia, antiquarianism, or eccentric interest. These sentiments are reflected in the art of the era.

Among popular subjects of Italian and Northern Renaissance art are saintly hermits: Paul of Thebes, Anthony, Jerome, and the temptation of St. Anthony described by his biographer St. Athanasius. Hermits are depicted in works of varied artists and traditions: Matthias Grunewald (1470–1528) in Germany, Hieronymus Bosch (1450–1516) in Dutch Netherlands, Pieter Bruegel (1525–1569) in Flemish Netherlands, Jusepe (or José) de Ribera (1591–1652) in Spain, and Michelangelo Merisi da Caravaggio (1571–1610) in Italy.

Among their many engravings, the Flemish Sadeler brothers Jan (1550–1600) and Raphael (1560–1628) produced several sets of engravings depicting historical hermits: *Oraculum Anchoreticum: Requiem animae* (twenty–five hermits), *Solitudo sive vitae patrum eremicolarum* (twenty–nine hermits), *Trophaeum vitae solitariae* (twenty–four hermits), *Sylvae sacra: Monumenta sanctiorus philosophie quam severa anachoretarum* (thirty hermits), and *Solitudo sive Vitae feminarum anachoritarum* (twenty–four women hermits).

The variety of artists in this era testifies to the popular interest in a curious and eccentric historical subject. At the same time, the highly stylized presentation o hermits reveals enthusiasm but not historical accuracy.

43. Eremitism in Eighteenth Century Britain

The demise of eremitism in England after King Henry VIII's suppression
of monasteries, monks, nuns, and hermits, left a void in English culture and
imagination after so many centuries of cultivating the imagery and inspiration of the hermit. A reversal of early modern hostility toward hermits
can be seen in scattered poets anticipating Romanticism. Their works are
stylized, even maudlin.

In 1668, the English poet Abraham Cowley (1618–1687) published an
essay "Of Solitude" and an accompanying poem "Solitude," both rich in
classical allusions, the poem composed in Latin. The essay sets out the merits
of solitude in society, being "well fitted and set right but upon a very few
persons," for theses few must know the world enough to see through its
vanities, yet possess enough virtue to despise them. Short of this, "a man had
better be in a fair than in a wood alone." Cowley's poem alludes to Genesis:

> Oh Solitude, first state of Human–kind!
> Which blest remain'd till man did find
> Even his own helpers Company.
> As soon as two (alas!)
> together joyn'd, …

Irish poet Thomas Parnell (1679–1718) composed "The Hermit," published posthumously by Alexander Pope. The lengthy, stylized poem tells
of a hermit who ventures from his isolated dwelling to go wandering, to
encounter the world and himself. Alexander Pope (1688–1774) himself
composed his famous "Ode to (or, Ode on) Solitude" at the precocious age
of twelve, masterfully capturing the sentiment of solitude in its narrator's
self–effacement.

> Happy the man, whose wish and care
> A few paternal acres bound,
> Content to breathe his native air,
> In his own ground.
> Whose herds with milk, whose fields with bread,
> Whose flocks supply him with attire,
> Whose trees in summer yield him shade,
> In winter fire.

Blest, who can unconcernedly find
Hours, days, and years slide soft away,
In health of body, peace of mind,
Quiet by day,
Sound sleep by night; study and ease,
Together mixed; sweet recreation;
And innocence, which most does please,
With meditation.
Thus let me live, unseen, unknown;
Thus unlamented let me die;
Steal from the world, and not a stone
Tell where I lie.

Among dozens of poems on solitude in this period are "Hymn to Solitude" by James Thomson (1700–1748), "Ode to Solitude" by Joseph Warton (1722–1800), "Ode to Solitude" by Joseph Cockfield (1740–1816), and "The Pleasures of Solitude," by Peter L. Courtier (1776–1847). In chapter 8 of his only famous novel *The Vicar of Wakefield*, Anglo–Irish writer Oliver Goldsmith (1730–1774) inserts a poem sometimes called "Edwin and Angelina" after its main characters. The poem reflects nostalgically on eremitism, now ended in England. In Goldsmith, the hermit is sensitively, if romantically, portrayed as a balance of solitude and gentleness, without a tinge of misanthropy.

Another example of nostalgia for hermits among pre–Romantic poets is Scottish poet James Beattie (1735–1803) in his poem "The Hermit." Beattie was a professor of philosophy, opposed to the rationalism of Thomas Hobbes. The stylized poem features the narrator reflecting on the priority of nature over society as teacher and moral exemplar.

Anglican bishop Thomas Percy (1729-1811) dabbled in old Northumbrian ballads, and created an historical tale set during the fourteenth–century wars of England and Scotland. The protagonist in Percy's 1771 poem, "The Hermit of Warkworth: A Northumberland Ballad," is a nobleman who early in life becomes a repentant hermit after accidentally slaying his beloved. The ballad also popularized an existing Warkworth hermitage by providing it with an origins story.

Finally, too, may be counted Mary Robinson (1758–1800), a prolific poet of elegant, reflective style, whose poem "Anselmo, the Hermit of the Alps" describes a man still haunted by his beloved's death, and now in older age a hermit and wanderer.

Hermits attract Romantics, but the Romantics realized that hermits could no longer be depicted as contemplative medievals; once projected into the contemporary world hermits would have to be molded by other forces. Hence the wild and tortuous path of the involuntary hermit Samuel Taylor Coleridge (1772–1834) portrays in his 1800 poem "The Mad Monk," his version of Mary Robinson's poem. Coleridge recasts romanticism to emphasize its gothic, exotic, and preternatural dispositions. In Coleridge the presumed monk is the jealous murderer of his beloved, now crazed in his haunted wanderings. The mad monk is no mere sentimentalist but reminiscent of eccentric hermit–penitents and "fools" of the early Christian centuries of Asia Minor.

1. Hermits in didactic children's literature

A genre of late eighteenth and early nineteenth–century English literature is the didactic tale for children featuring an idealized hermit, not quite medieval nor romantic, safely presented within a stylized contemporary narrative.

Among such works is the 1807 *The Hermit of the Forest, or, Wandering Infants: a Rural Tale* by Richard Johnson (1733–1793) and Thomas Bewick (1753–1828). The hermit motive in the story is melancholy, presented constructively within eremitic virtues such as harmony with nature and high morals. (The "celebrated" hermit is named Honestus.) The "wandering infants" motif borrows from traditional fairy tale characters such as Hansel and Gretel, but here the details are presented less disturbingly.

Honestus has lost his family to raiders and goes deep into the forest to dwell as a hermit. After ten years, a pair of infants appear at his door. Astonished, he takes care of them, though they sigh for their father. One day a fox hunter comes through the forest and up to the hermit's hut. The children recognize their father. The circumstances of their lot is explained—a wicked brother of the hunter had left the children to die hoping to inherit the wealthy man's goods. Honestus refuses the celebratory gifts of the rich man and soon leaves the estate to which the rich man had invited and feted him. The hermit returns to the woods only to discover that his own lost children have discovered his dwelling and dutifully await him.

John Bewick, co–author of the story above, provided woodcut illustrations of a hermit for a children's chap book (or "toy" book) using Banbury blocks, engraved woodcuts often illustrating such works at the time, named after the Oxfordshire town of Banbury.

The Hermit; or, The Unparalleled Sufferings, and Surprising Adventures, of Philip Quarll, an Englishman is a 1727 children's version of Defoe's classic *Robinson Crusoe*. The author Edward Dorrington is purportedly a merchant who discovers the shipwrecked Quarll on an uninhabited Pacific island off of Mexico. Bewick's woodcuts for the book show Quarll in various venues, in his hut, fishing, the object of the sailors' search, and his rescue.

Another didactic children's book of the era featuring a hermit is the 1819 *Fairburn's Cabinet of Instruction and Amusement*, by John Fairburn. The section titled "The Hermit" in this collection is representative of the genre, intent to moralize rather than entertain. The hermit represents the child–reader as the innocent or naive wonderer who questions human suffering, evil, and God's permission. Presenting a simple, unattached adult (a hermit) to ask these questions substitutes a child character in the role, relieving the child–reader of troublesome quandaries.

> A hermit, who had passed the greatest part of his life in the middle of a lonely desert, remote from all mankind, whose food was the fruits of the earth, whose drink was the crystal fountain, who might, had not one single doubt arisen, have ended his days in devotion and happiness. This doubt was, whether Providence guided the actions of men or not; for, said he, if heaven does really interest itself in the concerns of mortals, how happens it, that we so often see vice triumphing over virtue, and the good man suffering great injuries from the hands of the wicked? In order to clear the matter up, he determined, even in his old age, to leave his humble cell, and to visit the world.

The hermit befriends a well–mannered man and travels with him, but the fellow turns out to be an immoral wretch, a robber and murderer. The hermit flees him in confusion and despair. An angel visits the hermit and tells him that the evil man and his actions were just a test of the hermit's virtue and patience. All ends well, mercifully sparing the child–reader of doubts through the vicariousness of the didactic and contrived tale.

2. Almanac hermits

An ambiguous mix of popular facts, poems, seasonal trivia—plus eccentric hermits and unintentional irony—the English almanac of Edward Hone titled *Every–Day Book and Table Book*, subtitled *Everlasting Calendar of Popular Amusement*, appeared annually from 1825 to 1830, frequently reprinted thereafter, usually in two or three volumes. The tone of the almanac reflects eighteenth–century English values and styles. Its entries on religious hermits are cribbed from Alban Butler's famous 1756 *Lives of the Saints* (distinguished in Hone's subsection "Index of Romish Saints"). Hone renders the more eccentric details. He records entries for Paul of Thebes, Anthony the Great, Simeon Stylites, Piran of Cornwall, John of Egypt, and John Climacus, among a few others. Among Hone's entries:

> A hermit owned a cat, his constant companion. In a petition praying God to reveal his model saint, the hermit is told that his model is to be St. Gregory, "wherefore the hermit sighed" because Gregory had so many riches and the hermit was intentionally simple. But the divine voice "commanded him to be quiet because he had more pleasure stroking and playing with his cat" than Gregory in his riches.

> St. John of Egypt was a hermit, inured to obedience by an ancient holy anchoret, 'who made him water a dry stick for a whole year, as if it were a live plant. He walled himself up at the top of a rock, from the fortieth or forty–second to the ninetieth year of his age, and drew the admiration of the whole world on him.'

> Of St. Martin of Tours, Hone writes that "turning hermit, he lived on roots and wild herbs, and unawares ate a quantity of hellebore sufficient to kill an unprivileged person." Martin suffered no ill but a disciple who ate the herb he had to bring back to life.

> Ulrick learned in "a prophecy that he should become a saint, whereupon he starved and hermitized …" The skin stuck to his bones, he rarely slept, wore a hair shirt under iron mail, and daily immersed himself in cold water during winter.

Of a certain St. Thalilaeus, the almanac notes: "This saint was a weeper in Syria. He hermitized on a mountain during sixty years, wept almost without intermission for his sins, and lived for ten years in a wooden cage."

Hone offers much lore about eccentric secular hermits, too. Under the category of "conjurers" he describes Francis Kimberley of Birmingham, "a hermit in a crowd" whose dark shuttered house was filled with objects and bric–a–brac from lumber to thousands of unread books, though spiders outnumbered the latter. Hermit Kimberley "did not cultivate the acquaintance of the human species," and died in1756, "unlamented."

Another such hermit, living in Glodwick Lows, near Manchester, in 1826, was Billy Butterworth, noted for "melancholy appearance, which is increased by an immensely long black beard which makes him an object of terror to the neighbouring children." His makeshift hut, assembled from wood, stone, and metal, without nail or fastener, held extensive rooms, grottos, chapel, and a garden, snug in all weather conditions. Butterworth happily entertained visitors in conversation as long as they did not pry into his life story.

Hone prints an anonymous poem, "A Hermit's Meditation," which begins: "In lonesome cave / of noise and interruption void, / of thoughtful solitude / a hermit thus enjoy'd..."

3. Ornamental hermits

A curious and short–lived affectation arose in eighteenth–century England. Men of means and eccentric taste took up the practice of installing on the grounds of their estates an "ornamental hermit." An ornamental hermit was not a real hermit but a man employed by the estate–owner to reside in a contrived hermitage for a period of time, making scheduled appearances on the grounds to the pleasure of the employer and the marvel of guests. In her 1933 book *English Eccentrics*, Edith Sitwell relates her discovery of an 1886 book by a certain John Timbs that describes solicitations for ornamental hermits.

The employer Charles Hamilton, near Pains Hall, Surrey, advertised for a hermit for a seven–year term at seven–hundred pounds, who must not leave the grounds or speak to the servants, to be provided a Bible, reading glasses, a mat and hassock, hourglass, and a camlet robe. He was never "under any circumstances" to cut his hair, beard, or nails. The first applicant lasted three weeks, later spotted in the village pub. No successor is known.

John Timbs himself advertised for an ornamental hermit, offering remuneration of fifty pounds a year for seven years of service if the applicant would live underground, sight unseen. A hired ornamental hermit did reside at the site for four years.

Two aspirants to positions as ornamental hermits include one in 1810 advertising in a local newspaper in Plymouth. An 1830 aspirant boasted fourteen years experience in a cave on a certain baronet's grounds, describing himself as having a long beard and strolling about with an hourglass.

Gordon Campbell, author of the 2013 book *The Hermit in the Garden*, notes that the revolution in garden design in eighteenth–century Georgian England brought "follies" into landscape gardens, aesthetic structures often including hermitages, which in turn might include a hermit hired to live in one, secular figures in a droll landscape.

The ornamental hermit represented several themes of contemporary interest: horticultural, antiquarian, philosophical, literary, and architectural. The decline of genuine religious hermits also coincided with cultivation of melancholy and the rise of romanticism. But even in its heyday, the demand for ornamental hermits engaged only a handful of eccentrics.

Representative of the ornamental hermit was an ancient "Father Francis" at Richard Hill's Hawkstone, a model ornamental hermitage. A *momento mori* ("Remember that you must die") is inscribed on a wall in Latin; a table displays a skull and eyeglasses. Another Father Francis resided at Woodhouse, while an ornamental hermit Carolus resided at Tong Castle, Shropshire. An estate at Shelbourne boasted a hermit to entertain at summer garden parties, where guests were in on the ruse. Vauxhall Gardens also boasted a live hermit. Hermitages appeared on estates in Northern Ireland and Scotland as well.

Campbell himself believes that Charles Hamilton's solicitation for an ornamental hermit is apocryphal. He concludes with the interesting speculation that garden gnomes are descendants of ornamental hermits. Though Campbell does not mention it, perhaps the St. Francis of Assisi statues in gardens today echo ornamental hermits as well, or less popularly, the *jizo* in Japanese gardens.

CHAPTER 8

EREMITISM IN THE ROMANTIC ERA

Romanticism is the expression of feeling, emotion, and sentiment, identification with idealized pastoral or wild nature, and nostalgia for a lost historical ethos, in Europe a mythologized Middle Ages. Romanticism dominates European aesthetics from 1750–1850.

But Romantic writers and artists also revolted against contemporary society and conditions brought about by social disruption, technology, and economic capital: urbanization, factories, poverty, homelessness, degradation of nature, centralizing power of authorities, abuse by elites and the wealthy. Romantic assertions of social revolt were often muted and politically naive. Expectation that the French Revolution, for example, would alleviate social and economic conditions was quickly thwarted. Thus, the solitude expressed by Romantics is both individual and social, foreseen by Rousseau and directly experienced in the late eighteenth and early nineteenth centuries.

44. Eremitism and Romanticism: England

English writers highlight the many themes of Romanticism. While women writers largely address the social and political side of Romantic concerns, in essays on abolition of slavery, the plight of factory workers, suffrage, and women's rights, male writers are chiefly literati.

Perhaps the most representative Romantic English poet is William Wordsworth (1770–1850). Wordsworth's famous 1798 poem "Lines Written a Few Miles above Tintern Abbey," the setting of which centuries before was a thriving monastery, evokes forest ruins and the poet's imagined last resident, with whom he identifies, a hermit:

> … wreaths of smoke
> Sent up, in silence, from among the trees!
> With some uncertain notice, as might seem
> Of vagrant dwellers in the houseless woods,
> Or of some Hermit's cave, where by his fir
> The Hermit sits alone.

The image of the solitary hermit provokes deeper reflection on both society and self. Wordsworth's contemporaries would know that the setting of Tinturn Abbey in the Wye Valley typified the worst of the industrial revolution: noise and pollution from factories, surrounding forest clear–cut to stoke the foundries and provide raw materials for the area's tanneries, entire hillsides quarried for coal, and workers and residents living in squalor and ill health. Society is irredeemable, the poet suggests. Remnants of the past provoke nostalgia but also melancholy about the present and the future's bleak prospects.

In Wordsworth's 1805 poem "The Solitary Reaper" is a woman, "yon solitary highland lass," swinging her scythe, which the poet, despite the industrial sounds of the valley, hears rising above all sounds.

In more blithe mood, his 1807 "I Wandered Lonely as a Cloud" places the poet strolling beloved hills and valleys "When all at once I saw a crowd, A host, of golden daffodils …." The poet is clearly relieved that the crowd is not of people!

Wordsworth's 1814 grand project, a lengthy multi–part poem called "The Excursion," features characters called The Wanderer and The Solitary, with The Solitary referring to his cottage as "my domain, my cell, my hermitage, my cabin, what you will—I love it better than a snail his house." The poem assesses a lost world remembered and advocates for an alternative to irreconcilable modernity. And in "The Prelude" (from Book 4, "Summer Vacation"), published posthumously, Wordsworth celebrates solitude:

When from our better selves we have too long
Been parted by the hurrying world, and droop,
Sick of its business, of its pleasures tired,
How gracious, how benign, is Solitude …

Other major English poets underscore solitude as a Romantic theme. In his 1797 poem "This Lime–Tree Bower My Prison," Samuel Coleridge (1772–1834) identifies with "the solitary humble bee" that is never deserted by Nature, ever awake to Love and Beauty. In his 1798 "Rime of the Ancient Mariner," the character of "The Hermit" appears at the end of the poem, when the accursed Mariner pleads for the forest hermit to shrive him, though the hermit is not necessarily a priest or monk. As in "The Mad Monk," the poem sustains a melancholic and dark Romanticism.

Lord (George Gordon) Byron (1788–1834) presents the Romantic hero wandering in nature through forest, mountain, and by waterfalls, in his poem "Solitude," part of his famous "Childe Harold's Pilgrimage." Byron argues that this path is not a baneful solitude but is "to hold / Converse with Nature's charms, and view her stores unrolled." He contrasts the poet with the crowd, with the "tired denizen" of the world who is "flattered, followed, sought and sued" and concludes that this lonely state of individuals in the crowd is what the world wrongly calls solitude.

In the same larger poem, Byron speaks of the stirrings of

the feeling infinite, so felt
In solitude, where we are least alone;
A truth, which through our being then doth melt,
And purifies from self …

And elsewhere in the same poem:

There is a pleasure in the pathless woods;
There is a rapture on the lonely shore;
There is society where none intrudes.

Less literal is the solitude of Percy Bysshe Shelley (1792–1822) when he echoes the Romantic concept of the solitary wanderer pursuing numinal surety in Shelley's lengthy "Alastor, or The Spirit of Solitude" (1816). Similarly, John Keats (1795–1821) pursues the nature solitude of Byron in his 1815 poem "O Solitude!" He admits that solitude among flowery slopes, rivers, and trees "is my soul's pleasure" but would be best when to nature "two kindred spirits flee." Two solitaries? The context reveals the facts. At the time the twenty–five year old Keats wrote this poem, he worked in the busy pharmacy of a dreary urban hospital surrounded by a poor neighborhood, where he also resided. Thus Keats's hope for a companion ("kindred spirit") to accompany him to a distant, benign setting.

The 1818 novel *Frankenstein, or, The New Prometheus*, by Mary Wollstonecraft Shelley (1797–1851) reflects Gothic Romanticism while pioneering several genres: science fiction, horror, perhaps mystery. The story is dark, tragic, and movingly effective, a story exploring alienation, solitude, and the modern crisis of thought, nevertheless written within what Shelley herself described as "elementary principles of human nature." The plot is forecast in chapter one by Victor Frankenstein's own self-realization: "I shunned the face of man; all sound of joy or complacency was torture to me; solitude was my only consolation—deep, dark, death–like solitude."

The unnamed monster reflects the alienation and suffering of the unwanted, the ugly, the misbegotten of God. His angry murder sprees mingle with heartfelt desire for tolerance, sympathy, understanding, and reconciliation, especially when he discovers the tranquil domestic life of the cottagers, such a contrast to himself as miserable, wretched, "an imperfect and solitary being." Shelley created an imaginative fiction but also related a moving parable of the era's consciousness.

Often overlooked as a significant poet of solitude is Emily Bronte (1818–1848), whose only popular work is the novel *Wuthering Heights*. As a youth on the solitary moors, isolated from neighbors and schooled in the comfortable leisure of home and books, Emily and her sister Charlotte imagined a romantic fantasy realm called Gondal. Emily's earliest poems reflect this ideal land of liberty and solitude.

Emily decried the world in strong terms: where "Men knelt to God and worshipped crime, / And crushed the helpless …" Emily Bronte's romantic themes of solitude, melancholy, and disdain for society extend the Romantic spirit in British literature.

45. Eremitism and Romanticism: France

The Romantic movement in France is foreshadowed by Rousseau's social themes. Two novels transport solitude—and their protagonists—from ancient deserts and medieval wildernesses to contemporary settings. François René de Chateaubriand's novel *René* (1802) sends its protagonist to the American South; Étienne Senancour's novel *Obermann* (1804) sends its protagonist to social reclusion in Switzerland.

In poetry, Alphonse de Lamartine's *Meditations* (1820) captured the melancholy aspect of Romantic sensibility—the first poem of his collection is titled "L'Isolement" ("Isolation" or "Loneliness"), evoking nature contrasted with the poet's disaffection with society and the world: "Why on earth an exile I must stay? / There is no sympathy between earth and me."

Though an aristocrat and military officer, Alfred de Vigny (1797–1863) grew disillusioned with war, politics, and worldly affairs, as reflected in his novels. In *Stello* (1832), the character of Doctor Noir counsels the poet in a paean to solitude: "[The poet must] follow the conditions of his being, freed from the influence of associations, even the most beautiful, because Solitude alone is the source of inspiration. Solitude is holy." He adds, "All associations suffer from the vices of the convent." The poet must become not a monk seeking community (that is, "the convent") but become a hermit, a secular hermit given the times. His hermitage will be within the desert of the city and modernity. Nature and wilderness are too cold and hostile, as Vigny shows in the later novel *Chatterton* (1836), where the protagonist cannot tolerate city life, finds rural life petty and oppressively unintelligent, and fears wilderness.

A literal note to eremitism in Romantic era France is in the remark by Victor Hugo in Book 6, Chapter 2 of his famous 1831 novel *Notre Dame de Paris* ("The Hunchback of Notre Dame") set in the Middle Ages. Hugo describes the anchorhold of Mme. Rolande of the Tour–Roland. Grieving the death of her father in the Crusades, she is walled up in her "premature tomb," "making her bed on the cold ground without even a stone for a pillow, clothed in sackcloth, and living only upon such bread and water as the compassionate might deposit on the ledge of her window—thus receiving charity after bestowing it." Engraved over the window is the Latin phrase "Tu, ora," meaning "Pray, now," which passers–by pronounce as "Trou–aux–rats," meaning "rat hole." Hugo remarks disingenuously that the new saying is "a rendering less sublime perhaps than the original; but, on the other hand, decidedly more picturesque."

French poet and essayist Charles Baudelaire (1821–1867) subsisted on the cusp of Romanticism transitioning to the Decadents. His life of dis-affection and disdain for society engendered a solitude at once aesthetic, philosophical, but also deeply psychological, approaching social alienation were he not an artist. In a prose poem titled "Solitude," Baudelaire dismisses the "journalist" and the "babbler" always jabbering to the public about trivia. They would uphold solitude as a Christian virtue but not, of course, for themselves. They represent "the frantic ones who seek happiness in animation, and in a prostitution which I could call fraternary..." Baudelaire accepted his own miserable bouts of solitude as the necessary concomitant to artistic freedom.

46. Eremitism and Romanticism: Germany

Two German literary classics prior to the eighteenth century are the basis of later positive views of eremitism. The first is the medieval poem "Parzifal" by Wolfram von Eschenbach (1160–1220), mentioned in section 16. The poem highlights the hermit Trevrizent as a bridge between the values of fallen humanity and religious aspiration. Once a chivalrous knight, Trevri-zent renounced knighthood and became a hermit to atone for the crimes of his brother.

The second classic is set in the tumultuous Thirty Years War of 1618 to 1648. In the lengthy picaresque novel *Simplicissimus* by Johann Grimmels-hausen (1621–1676), an impoverished orphan boy is raised and tutored by a forest hermit, who is in fact the governor's brother–in–law. The hermit dies, and the boy grows up in the governor's court. He spends his life pursuing travels and adventures in the midst of war and social chaos, a picaresque thief, soldier, "vagabond, quack, and cheat," peddler, fool, and palmer. At novel's end, Simplicissimus renounces the corrupt and evil world to become a hermit.

Two literary authors of German Romanticism attempt works with the traditional theme of the medieval wandering artist: Wilhelm Heinrich Wackenroder (1773–1798) and Ludwig Tieck (1773–1853). Wackenroder's 1787 *Confessions of an Art–Loving Friar* ("Herzensergiessungen eines kunstliebenden Klosterbruders") celebrates the poignancy of medieval and renaissance art versus Enlightenment celebration of ancient Greek art as an extension of reason and logic. Tieck's 1788 novel *Franz Sternbald's Wanderings* ("Franz Sternbalds Wanderungen") evokes a medieval artist's travels and reflections.

Novalis (1772–1801) addresses the reconciliation of medieval and modern society and sensibilities in his posthumous 1802 novel, *Heinrich von Ofterdingen*, which chronicles a romanticized medieval poet's life, and in his 1799 essay "Christendom or Europe" ("Die Christenheit oder Europa"), reflecting what one scholar calls "Romantic cosmopolitanism."

The hermit is central to a significant number of eighteenth–century German writers, perhaps because the hermit is such a central character of German folklore. The extant works depict hermits from different perspectives: 1) religious, 2) critical, and 3) romantic—from requited love, to disillusion with society and the world, to embrace of solitude and nature, to 4) the grotesque, where madness is the hermit's motive. The Sturm und Drang ("Storm and Stress") literary movement anticipated the Romantic movement centered on individuality, subjective feeling, and social estrangement.

1. Religious

Johann Wolfgang von Goethe's 1773 poetic drama "Satyros, or the Idolized Demon of the Woods" contrasts two views of nature. The hermit and the satyr vie with one another to claim the forest (representing nature and the universe) as complementary to their virtues. The hermit pursues a deep spiritual insight, while the satyr tries to seduce people to his level.

Goethe inserts four spirits or anchorites in the last scene of *Faust* (1832), part one. The hermits spiritualize nature (Naturvergesitigling) as Pater ecstaticus (ever in motion), Pater profundus (the deep motivating force of nature which is divine love), Pater seraphicus (nearly transcendent), and Doctor Marianus (the loftiest spiritual state). For Goethe, the hermit stands between earthly and spiritual worlds.

Christoph Martin Weiland (1733–1813) published the epic poem "Oberon" in 1780. The poem evolves a plot and setting of the Robinsonade genre, a tale of a shipwrecked solitary. The Spanish knight Alonso shipwrecks on a deserted island. His wife, children, and friends have perished. The vanities of society are revealed. Supernatural elements pervade the tale: angelic voices, a magic portal, elf rulers, a sacred grotto. A mysterious couple, Huon and Amanda, seek out Alonso's advice to reconcile with king Oberon. Eremitism is presented as a last stage before wisdom, and a reconciliation with nature.

In the 1801 novel *Heinrich von Ofterdingen* by Novalis (1772–1801), the character Friedrich von Hohenzollern is an old hermit with a lifetime of experiences, now at peace with himself. He reflects to visitors on the necessary individualism of youth and the appropriateness of solitude in old age. Once a knight, with family now dead, Heinrich dwells in a cave, reading and contemplating.

Konig Eginhard (1809) is a dramatic fragment about a forest hermit, an old legend found in Grimm, recreated by Ludwig Uhland (1787–1862). The hermit senses timelessness in events around him. When King Eginhard and his abducted bride Adelheit escape to a forest castle, they encounter the hermit Paul, who discourses to them about the forest and nature's reflection of the divine and the timeless.

In the 1811 tale *Die Heimatlosen* by Justinus Kerner (1786–1862), the hermit is called a Waldvater or nature spirit, the fatherly spirit presiding over nature. The theme is "Todessehnsucht" or "longing for reunion" (with the spirit of nature). The protagonist is a sailor returning home after a prolonged voyage only to learn that his wife has remarried, convinced of his death at sea after such a lengthy absence. Saddened, he retreats to a mountain forest to live out his long years. At death, the mountain folk bury him in a stalactite cavern, where his body is preserved. This tale presents the hermit as a symbol and literal personification of nature.

In his eponymous 1813 novel, Adelbert von Chamisso (1781–1838) explores his romantic hero Peter Schlemihl's eremitic motive to be the loss of his shadow, an intriguing projection of the individual in society. Despite his wealth and status, Schlemihl cannot break into society or develop relationships. On a trip to Egypt, he suddenly decides to renounce his former life. Imitating the early Christian desert hermits, he disappears from society.

Joseph Eichendorff (1788–1857) wrote the novel *Eine Meerfahrt* ("The Sea Voyage") in 1835. The hermit is Don Diego, once a knightly adventurer who sought El Dorado, overcame shipwreck, and resisted the plaudits of the queen of a deserted island on which Diego established safe haven for the ship's survivors. He returns alone to Spain, becoming a hermit. The story is a metaphor for the storms of life that part to reveal a strong spiritual tranquility rescuing the buffeted but conscious soul.

2. Critiques of Eremitism

Several German writers were critical of eremitism. The 1749 poem "Der Eremit" by Gotthold Lessing (1729–1781) attacks sham piety, depicting a charlatan who pretends to be a forest hermit in order to attract attention and deceive women. When accused and brought before a judge who insists on knowing the names of the seduced women (the judge's motive being to embarrass the families), the sham hermit names the judge's wife.

In Lessing's *Nathan der Weise* (1779), the protagonist Nathan the Jew argues the superiority of a humane and social life versus eremitism. His Muslim friend Al–Hafi, Saladin's treasurer, has witnessed worldly corruption, and now rejects society. He plans to flee to solitude in India. A third character, a Christian lay brother, serves a patriarch conspiring with the Templars to assassinate Saladin. Like Al–Hafi, the Christian wishes to flee the world, a motive which Lessing professes to respect as an ideal but criticizes as renouncing moral responsibility within the life sphere of Nathan's acquaintances.

Jakob Lenz's 1775 drama *Die Kleiner* ("The Younger") remained unfinished but sufficiently reveals the author's intended critique of eremitism. The central character Engelbrecht discovers a hermit who withdrew from the world to allow his worldly–minded brother to reach courtly office unrivaled. But the hermit despairs at the news of the political struggle consuming his brother. He doubts his own motive and wonders if he should have assumed worldly responsibility after all.

Lenz's unfinished novel *Die Walderbruder* (1776) features protagonist Herz who becomes a hermit in a forest to preserve his idealistic image of a woman he knows only through correspondence. Herz is an idealist obsessed with his imagined object of purity but comfortable in his hermitage, oblivious to the gossip in the society to which his friend Roth pleas that Herz return. On a freezing winter night, Herz must abandon his hut. In town he crosses paths with his idealized woman. But the novel, as mentioned, was left unfinished.

Friedrich Maximilian Klinger (1752–1831) wrote several relevant works re hermits. His 1776 drama *Sturm und Drang* features the protagonist Blasius, disillusioned by the world, witnessing the conflicts of his friends and their failed relations with women. He rejects society to pursue a spiritual life in harmony with nature. In Klinger's 1776 tragic drama *Die Zwillinge* ("The Twins"), protagonist Grimaldi suffers from the death of his beloved Juliette and longs to become a hermit, but is weighed down by melancholy. His friend Fernando constantly belittles him. Only Juliette's brother Guelfo understands him. Grimaldi evolves an inner solitude.

Klingor's 1791 novel *Fausts Leben, Thaten und Hollenfahrt* ("Faust's Life, Deeds, and Descent into Hell") revives the theme of the devil's challenge (to Faust), intending to expose the hypocrisy of a supposedly–virtuous man. In this case the man is a hermit; the novel parallels the temptation of St. Anthony. Faust is impressed by the hermit's lack of moral pride and presumption. But ultimately the hermit is made to fall and plunges into madness; death consumes all of the story's characters. Klingor's intent (like the devil's) is ultimately to besmirch the hermit.

3. Eremitism & Requited Love

Wolfgang Goethe (1749–1832) composed two versions of "Erwin und Elmire," based on the ballad of "Angelica and Edwin" in Oliver Goldsmith's 1766 *The Vicar of Wakefield*. Goethe's 1775 version is a light opera emphasizing the emotional turns of the characters. Erwin disappears into mountain solitude and a hermit's hut because Elmire has scorned his professions of love, yet he remains haunted by her. Bernardo visits Erwin and persuades him to return and reveal his feelings to Elmire. Erwin returns in hermit's disguise. Elmire confesses her bad behavior towards Erwin, professing her love for him. The hermit reveals himself as Erwin. A joyful reconciliation ensues. Bernardo sings lyrics opposing eremitism and praising the responsible citizen and dutiful householder.

Goethe's 1787 prose version of "Erwin und Elmire" reveals a slightly new plot. A reflective, mature Erwin is inspired in his reclusion by the spirit of a wise old hermit he did not come to meet, now deceased. Though occasionally pained by Elmire's memory, Erwin recalls the old hermit's tranquil mien and is at peace. In this version, another couple is introduced: Valerio and Rosa. Valerio is upset by Rosa's petty jealousies and visits Erwin for advice. Then the two young women, Rosa and Elmire, appear at the hut, contrite. Reconciliations ensue. A grateful departure from the hermitage that has imbued all with its peace ensues. The hero of this version of the story is the invisible character of the old hermit, whose values embrace all to appreciate nature, tranquility, and the spiritual.

4. Eremitism & Madness

In the 1800 novel *Godwi* by Clemens Brentano (1778–1842), the hermit Werdo Senne suffers the fate of Klinger's Grimaldi. The novel narrates the circumstances of the past: courtship and engagement, Werdo's business voyage, the unscrupulous Godwi's falsification of the Werdo's death in order to marry the young Marie, Werdo's beloved, and have her bear his child. Werdo returns. Marie commits suicide with her child. Werdo becomes a hermit, his only consolation his harp, sad songs, and the solace of nature and God. Brentano outlines the literary trope connecting art, melancholy, and madness.

Paralleling Brentano's Werdo is Walter, the protagonist of the eponymous novel by Annette von Droste–Hulshoff (1797–1848). *Walter* is an 1818 story of suffering, the triumph of evil, and a tortuous eremitism. Walter is born of the frail angelic Theatilde and Alhard, a rogue–knight prone to restlessness and melancholy. As a knight, Alhard befriends the hermit Balduin—a man once wealthy but who has now discarded his possessions—and his beautiful daughter Alba, with whom Walter falls in love. But Walter is obliged to go on crusade, with marriage to a society maiden Caecilia promised as reward on his return—and his heart is divided. Upon Walter's return, many have died: Alhard, Balduin, and Alba. In sorrow, Walter seeks out the hermit Verenus, who warns him against eremitism because of Walter's disposition. Walter insists. Where Balduin's motive is moral consciousness, and that of Verenus is wise experience, Walter's motive is regret and flight.

The 1799 poem "Hyperion, or The Hermit in Greece" by Friedrich Hölderlin (1770–1843) describes Hyperion's search for wisdom in nature after suffering life disappointments. The historical context is the Greek war for independence from the Ottoman Turks (1821–1832). Hyperion persuades himself to lead a troop of fighters, but their bestial behavior upon victory only further disillusions him. Hyperion's pursuit of solitude is motivated by pessimism towards society and an embrace of innocent nature.

Wackenroder's traditional tale of a medieval wanderer–poet contrasts with his 1799 *Ein wunderbares Marchen von einem nackten Heiligen* ("Wondrous Eastern Tale of a Naked Saint"), a tale of piety and madness set in Oriental exoticism. A cave–dwelling hermit is the only person who hears the rush of time in a noisy whirling water wheel. Driven to madness, the hermit perpetually turns the wheel. On a moonlit night overseeing the river bank, the hermit hears the music of lovers floating downstream on a boat. Their beautiful music displaces the whirling wheel of time in his mind and heart. The hermit is freed from earthly life and time itself, ascending to heaven attended by angels.

Among his famous stories of fantasy and horror, E. T. A. Hoffmann (1776–1822) wrote the 1819 story "Serapion," about a mad hermit who thinks he is the original St. Serapion, the Egyptian Christian desert father. Ironically, the hermit's intent and social relations are impeccable, the first–person narrative relates, and he refutes every objection to eremitism proposed by the narrator. Yet he is a madman.

Nikolas Lenau (1802–1850) published an 1832 horror story "Die Mario-netten" about a hermit maddened by tragic love. A dark hermitage and death symbols lend a pall to a tale retrospectively–told by the reclused Count Robert, who sorrows for his only daughter Maria. While the count was away on crusade, young Maria was seduced by a wanderer Lorenzo, and she commits suicide. As with Brentano among others, eremitism is clearly linked to madness.

A nostalgia for didacticism appears in the 1812–15 fairy tale collection of the Grimm brothers Jacob (1785–1863) and Wilhelm (1786–1856). Several Grimm tales include hermits in traditional roles of giving advice or contriving moral lessons.

In "Brother Frolick," the picaresque hero has completed a lifetime of adventures and visits a hermit for advice about getting to heaven. The hermit in "The Hut in the Forest" is an "old gray–haired man" whose "white beard fell down over the table almost as far as the ground." The tale regards the third–born sibling of a woodcutter's daughter in a familiar plot involving a prince trapped into the form of an animal by a witch's spell. The conventional plot involves familiar tropes, including the perennial dangers of enormous forests. Another tale spinning a nearly identical plot is "The Old Woman in the Wood." A representative hermit appears in "The Three Green Twigs," with elements of magic and the Christian supernatural. The designation of the pious protagonist as a "hermit" enhances the tale.

Paralleling interest in the fairy tale is folkloric legend, especially the figure of the wild huntsman, universal throughout northern and central Europe, identified in northern countries as Odin. While spectral figures have rep-resented diabolical forces, anthropologically derived from the wild winds of dark autumn forests and forbidding winter nights, the model of the wild huntsman also suggests for social Romantics the strong opprobrium of the peasant classes for the rural aristocracy. The famous fox and stag hunts are emblematic of the arrogance and cruelty of the resented lords, counts, and barons.

An example of a German version of the wild huntsman is summarized by H. A. Guerber in her 1895 book *Legends of the Rhine*, relating the legend of Lowenberg Mountain, once the daily hunting grounds of a knight so fond of the chase that he would hunt on Sundays, even pursuing his quarry into a church and to the foot of the altar where a priest celebrated mass. Outraged by the insolence of the knight, who then and there slew his game, the priest solemnly curses him. The ground opens beneath the hunter's feet, and a pack of hounds from the infernal regions falls upon him, tearing him to pieces. Ever since then, on stormy nights, this sabbath–breaker's restless ghost hunts wildly through the winds, pursued by a spectral train of huntsmen and hell hounds, for he can find no rest, though dead, condemned to lead the wild hunt forever.

This legend originates in the myth of Odin, leader of the Raging Host, and is told with slight variations of place along the Rhine, where sudden windstorms rise during the night, deemed by the credulous peasantry as the passing of a mysterious heavenly host.

The German romantic poet Gottfried August Burger (1747–1794) presents the spectral agent's diabolical character in his 1774 ballad "Der wilde Jager," replacing the traditional priest with the pivotal figure of a hermit. (In 1797, Sir Walter Scott translated the poem into English as "The Wild Huntsman.") The ballad shows the huntsman, his retinue, and his hounds, setting off at dawn just as the village bell tolls for Sunday service. Two armored knights appear, one in white, one in black, the former admonishing the huntsman not to profane the day, the latter dismissing shame to old men and children. The huntsman is dismissive of the white knight, and the party rides on to the edge of a grain field where a poor widow beseeches the huntsman not to trample through her harvest. The white knight entreats the huntsman to pity, while the black knight laughs, and the huntsman and his party trample through the field.

The hunting party rides swiftly through the forest, espying a stag, which finds shelter in the hut of an old hermit. The huntsman declares he will burn the hut down and drive out the stag. The hermit throws himself at the huntsman's knees. The white knight urges the hunter to leave the poor hermit, but the black knight cajoles the huntsman, who then strikes the

hermit a fatal blow. At that moment, the huntsman turns into a phantom,
to be chased eternally by hell's dogs.

47. Eremitism and Romanticism: United States

The nascent United States inherited no eremitic tradition. Hermits first
appear in embellished eighteenth and early nineteenth–century tales and
anecdotes. The tales represent a romanticism of wilderness, and, except for
the first historical item below, no report alludes to religion.

- In 1694, a millenarian group of German pietist men led by
  Johannes Kelpius settled near the Wissahickon Creek near Ger-
  mantown, Pennsylvania. The group believed that the Book of
  Revelation identified the imminent second coming of Christ,
  which they confirmed by astrology, numerology, and star–watching. They constructed a monastery, adopting a Rosicrucian symbol.
  Kelpius died in 1708. The group of hermits eventually disappeared.
  In 1961, near a stone hut on the property called the Cave of Kelpius,
  the Rosicrucian Society placed a commemoratory monument.

- A late eighteenth–century broadside printed in Worcester, Massachusetts, titled "An Account of the Wonderful Old Hermit's Death and
  Burial, Aged Two Hundred Twenty Eight Years," describes physician
  Dr. Brake and attendants searching for a rumored hermit in a wilderness area. They find his empty cave and await the hermit's return from
  foraging. The returning hermit greets the party and invites them into
  his cave. The hermit expresses "great satisfaction" in their visit, noting that they were "the first human beings that he had seen from the
  time that he first landed on this shore, which was about two hundred
  years." Dr. Brake records observations about the physical appearance
  of the hermit, and proffers rum. After protestations the hermit drinks
  so much that he falls comatose and dies. The next day the whole party
  helps bury him. The temperance–minded manuscript writer adds: "Poor
  old man! He lived about two hundred years in his cave, free from the
  busy scenes of the world, and enjoying all the happiness of a retired
  life! And might perhaps have lived as many more, had he not drank

that horrid draught! Cursed liquor! Thousands have fell a sacrifice to its bewitching power."

- A popular eighteenth–century pamphlet is titled "The Pennsylvania Hermit: A Narrative of the Extraordinary Life of Amos Wilson." The story: Wilson's sister Elizabeth gave birth to illegitimate twins (one child, in other versions). She could not convince the father to marry her despite her insistence. One day the exasperated father meets her and the infant(s) in the woods, kills the infant(s), and threatens her with a gun to stay silent. Elizabeth is arrested for murder, but is too intimidated to tell the truth to judge and jury. Learning of her scheduled hanging, her brother Amos rushes to the town to speak to her. She tells him the facts of the case. Amos then rushes to the judge, successfully convinces him of Elizabeth's innocence, then rushes to the Governor with exonerating documents, procures a written pardon, and rushes to the execution scene, swimming a river, losing a horse, finally arriving. Alas, he is too late. Elizabeth had been hung to death. The distraught Amos, taking the guilt upon himself, recluses from society, never to be seen in public again. Amos Wilson purportedly composed an essay, "Sweets of Solitude."

- The hermit Robert Voorhis (1769–1832) is described in an 1829 pamphlet titled "Life and Adventures of Robert, the Hermit of Massachusetts." Robert's mother was Black, and he is born into bondage in Princeton, New Jersey, and taken with his owner–family to a Maryland plantation, where he grows up. After marriage and having a child, Robert arranges with a white acquaintance to pay the family's emancipation using money Robert had saved. But the acquaintance steals the money and arranges for Robert to be captured and transported to South Carolina on a slave ship. Robert escapes to safety and stows away on a Massachusetts–bound ship. From New England, he spends years sailing merchant ships to save money. After a long absence, he returns to search for his wife and child, only to learn they are probably dead. The news sends the despondent Robert into reclusion. He finds a solitary place near Providence, Rhode Island, living most of his remaining life in a cave. Robert died in Massachusetts.

- An 1817 broadside tells the story of "The Old Hermit of Western Virginia," narrated by John Fielding and Captain James Buckland. Exploring the wilderness, the two happen upon a cave–dwelling hermit who describes his life, from his 1589 (!) birth in London, England, to various seafaring adventures, from Italy to shipwreck, to the American colonies. The hermit's rapport with wild animals is such that they dance at night for him.

- A 1788 pamphlet titled "The Hermit, or, An Account of Francis Adam Joseph Phyle" relates the story of an eighteenth–century New Jersey hermit who lived forty years in a cave on the outskirts of a farm and forest near Mount Holly. The account describes the Swiss–born Phyle's penitential wanderings and pursuit of solitude after having killed a man in a duel in Canada. Neighbors treat him well, though they do not understand his language; Phyle did not speak English. He foraged for food and would accept gifts. In the winter of 1778, a neighbor checking on him found Phyle prostrate and feverish. The hermit died the next day.

- Contemporary newspaper accounts describe the "hermitess" Sarah Bishop (1753–1810). Born and raised in Long Island, New York, her father's house was burned down by British soldiers during the American Revolution, and she was assaulted by a British officer, causing her such anguish that she became a forest solitary. Escaping to the hills near Ridgefield, Connecticut, Sarah found a cave in which to live. She held a few possessions, and cleared forest space to grow food. Only after decades did she accept the visits of others.

48. Johnny Appleseed: Americana Hermit

The historical John Chapman (1774–1845) became the folkloric hermit Johnny Appleseed even within his lifetime because he exhibits all of the characteristics of what mid–nineteenth century American culture identified in its frontier heroes, namely, that they be eccentric and colorful but innocuous.

Chapman is part wilderness hermit in his habits, appearance, and livelihood, part religious hermit in his affectation for Swedenborgianism. As a young man leaving his remarried father and step–siblings, Chapman walked from New York to Pennsylvania, then hit upon the notion of procuring apple seeds (abundant in cider mills) to grow trees in clusters on diverse properties he leased.

Chapman eventually buys disparate tracts of land in Ohio and Indiana, accommodating the markets of increasing westward populations. His interest in apple seeds contradicts modern science and marketing, wherein distinct apple trees are grafted in order to produce a predictable variety. Apples in this era, regardless of variety or quality, were used by rough–neck frontiersmen for making cider and vinegar, not for eating. Tapping this demand was a novelty. Chapman was soon dubbed "Johnny Appleseed" by contemporaries.

From Pennsylvania, Chapman visited the new settlements of Ohio in the first decades of the 1800s, shrewdly purchasing plots of several acres to grow trees. By the second and third decades, Chapman actively walked the circuit of Ohio's western border with Indiana. Evidence shows that Chapman traversed all of Indiana by the 1830s, anticipating population influx. But no evidence shows that his itinerancy was related to religious evangelism, though the Great Awakening was in full force. Indeed, his Swedenborgianism early took its own subjective course, so that even the New Church congregations ignored him. Chapman's religiosity, typically that of a hermit, was eccentric and eclectic, unrelated to congregations and doctrines.

Early nineteenth–century American society can be viewed in the context of the frontier thesis of historian Frederick Jackson Turner. Turner's thesis maintains that with each successive migration westward came a reversion to primitive living. This reversion might be reflected in crude social behavior such as the drinking and fighting ubiquitous among male settlers, but more benignly evident in Chapman's animism, animal sympathy, herbalism, and esteem for indigenous peoples.

Scholar Robert A. Ferguson (in his book *Alone in America*, 2013) sees frontier individualism more negatively—through the observations of Alexis de Tocqueville and Ralph Waldo Emerson, among others—as the product of American transcendentalism's idealization of self and as the loss of domesticity in the frontier movement, resulting in a strong need to mythologize, to create heroes, and to ignore the destructive aspects of their actions.

Both approaches explain a great deal about the conflict between American respect for and abuse of nature and the peoples they encounter. Johnny Appleseed was a last representative of the culture's chance to reconcile American values.

According to biography, Chapman ate off the land but was vegetarian, slept on the ground in the open, wore minimal clothing, even in winter, and walked everywhere barefoot. He is both Romantic hero and hermit. Descriptions of Chapman are consistent and reasonable portraits of a hermit and wanderer. Details about his itineraries and specific anecdotes begin the drift towards Chapman as Appleseed even during his lifetime. By the twentieth century, details of childhood, religious proselytizing, and wilderness feats embellish his story.

PART IV

THE MODERN WESTERN WORLD: THE NINETEENTH CENTURY

CHAPTER 9

FROM EREMITISM TO SOLITUDE:
EARLY NINETEENTH CENTURY

49. Romanticism and Solitude: United States

Social Romanticism did not directly affect the United States, but a broader intellectual movement extrapolating original European Romanticism emerged as Transcendentalism, with Ralph Waldo Emerson (1803–1882) and Henry David Thoreau (1817–1862) its chief expostulators. The literature of the nineteenth century reflected the shades of Romanticism seen in Europe, also addressing the phenomenon of solitude.

Ralph Waldo Emerson

On the topic of solitude, Ralph Waldo Emerson has been largely overshadowed by his protege Thoreau. Emerson is cerebral and technical, while Thoreau's practical experiences in nature and wilderness combine with a deep introspection to give Thoreau a rich store of material for musing and writing. Nevertheless, Emerson's command of literary sources and observational skills excel in his comprehensive works on solitude: *Nature* (1836), *Self–Reliance* (1841), and *Society and Solitude* (1857). Their argument is better demonstrated in reverse chronological order.

Society and Solitude opens with an anecdote about a solitary who leaves the city for wilderness, buys a house and plants trees, but still does not feel isolated. He adds more trees and hedges, and evergreens for year–round concealment. The solitary argues that he is only waiting to shuffle off my corporeal jacket to slip away into the back stars, and put diameters of the solar system and sidereal orbits between me and all souls—there to wear out ages in solitude, and forget memory itself, if it be possible.

Emerson does not disapprove, acknowledging that genius feels the "necessity of isolation," and can be assigned (quoting Swedenborg) the loftiness of heaven. Who sees through society has only two paths: "either habits of self–reliance" or a "religion of love."

Society and Solitude unravels a philosophy of solitude that begins in the mundane and in social relationships, and evolves into something deeper and organic. We are "clothed with society" as products of the society and culture in which we grow to adulthood, a culture conveyed to us not just in books and learning but by the people with whom we are socialized and whom we encounter in our daily lives. We are literally dressed in society, "dressed in arts and institutions," such that the majority feel whole and self–sufficient by flowing with society's standards, not by seeking their own.

Emerson concludes that in this world "solitude is impractical and society fatal." He quips: "People are to be taken in very small doses." Here are echoes of Rousseau and the Stoics.

Emerson more vigorously pursues the virtues needed to resist society in the essay *Self–Reliance*. He counsels: "Trust thyself: every heart vibrates to that iron string." Like the Stoics, Emerson finds acceptance a necessary virtue, not to wish to be other than oneself, not to wish for a different world. The motive is not complacency: "Whoso would be a man must be a nonconformist ... Nothing is at last sacred but the integrity of your own mind." Further, "What I must do is all that concerns me, not what the people think ..."

> It is easy in the world to live after the world's opinion; it is easy in solitude to live after our own; but the great man is he who in the midst of the crowd keeps with perfect sweetness the independence of solitude.

Integrity of mind determines how an individual proceeds in society. Emerson grants that "for non–conformity the world whips you with its displeasure." But the solace of knowing that society and its reactions historically conform to power, authority, and pleasure, all destructive of individual will, bolsters confidence. Those who respond to worldliness by dropping out of it psychologically, materially, or literally, follow degrees of exercising solitude. "Let us affront and reprimand the smooth mediocrity and squalid contentment of the times," writes Emerson, for ultimately, "The world has been instructed by its kings." That is, not by its sages or solitaries.

At this point, the individual is on the brink of recognizing the power of intuition, what Emerson considers wisdom. Because intuition is an individual criterion of moral rather than social judgment, the majority of people will remain unable or unwilling to develop their intuition, and will fall back on external authorities. Even sages and saints are such authorities, Emerson argues. Not the group but the individual has the responsibility to mature the will and embrace virtue.

Intuition and individual exercise of virtues are to Emerson "divine fact." Only with maturation of these virtues can our solitude be truly functional. "Your isolation must not be mechanical but spiritual, that is, must be elevation." And this is a near–definition of Transcendentalism. The individual will manifest to others a higher ethic, an eternal law, not a social conformity.

Opposed to self–reliance is discontent, regret, creeds (which Emerson calls "a disease of the intellect"), superstition (a "fool's paradise"), travel to seek enlightenment, property, or a government to protect property. Emerson counsels:

> Insist on yourself; never imitate. Your own gift you can present every moment with the cumulative force of a whole life's cultivation; but of the adopted talent of another you have only an extemporaneous half–possession.... Nothing can bring you peace but yourself. Nothing can bring you peace but the triumph of principles.

In the essay *Nature*, Emerson identifies nature as wilderness, a setting distinct from both self and society, viewing nature from the perspective of solitude.

> To go into solitude, a man needs to retire as much from his chamber as from society. I am not solitary whilst I read and write, though nobody is with me. But if a man would be alone, let him look at the stars. The rays that come from those heavenly worlds will separate between him and what he touches.

Emerson's thoughts now progress from solitude as the absence of socializing to solitude as the affirmation of the attributes identified in *Self–Reliance*.

The argument in *Self–Reliance* develops the idea of nature. In nature one feels rightfully placed, and can rightly place self and the world. But Nature does not reveal itself automatically. Harmony with nature is built upon harmony within self, with the individual's understanding of nature as order, beauty, and spiritual expression of virtue. Nature is an object of our intellect when we seek out meaning and are prompted to creativity. "Nature is a discipline of the understanding in intellectual truths," Emerson states. Rightly understood and appreciated, "Nature is made to conspire with spirit to emancipate us." Not rightly understood, nature seems hostile and violent, a projection of our own immature minds. Only a thoughtful solitude, outside of chamber and society, yields us these essential insights.

In his essay "Literary Ethics" (1838), Emerson writes:

> The poets who have lived in cities have been hermits still. Inspiration makes solitude anywhere. Pindar, Raphael, Angelo, Dryden, De Stael, dwell in crowds, it may be, but the instant thought comes, the crowd grows dim to their eye; their eye fixes on the horizon, on vacant space; they forget the bystanders; they spurn personal relations; they deal with abstractions, with verities, with ideas. They are alone with the mind.

In "Friendship" (1841), Emerson refines the solitude criteria already described, concluding simply:

> I chide society, I embrace solitude, and yet I am not so ungrateful as not to see the wise, the lovely and the noble minded, as from time to time they pass my gate.

Henry David Thoreau

Like his exemplar Emerson, Henry David Thoreau (1817–1862) comprehended solitude, and wrote about it in a deep and familiar way, temperamentally more a solitary than Emerson's more cerebral disposition, as already noted. Thoreau called himself a hermit on more than one occasion, living within a fluid realm of solitude on the one hand and intimate family and old acquaintances on the other. Emerson once noted that Thoreau, a

"Spartan–Buddhist," would have been an ideal monk in a bygone era.

One strength of Thoreau was his ability to link a transcendentalism—which parallels some philosophical aspects of Romanticism—to social and political issues, in the tradition of social Romanticism, as in *Civil Disobedience* (1849), *Slavery in Massachusetts* (1854), and several essays on John Brown. Further, Thoreau can be appreciated not only for intellectual achievements but for his pursuit of real–life experiences in living simply, in outdoor explorations of nature and wilderness, in his approximation to eremitic values in his two–year experiment at Walden, and in his nature and seasonal writings: *A Week on the Concord and Merrimack Rivers* (1849), *Walden* (1854), *Walking* (1862) and the *Journal*, posthumously published in 1906.

In his early twenties, Thoreau may have been influenced by the Swiss writer Johann Ritter von Zimmermann (1728–1795), author of the 1756 book *Betrachtungen uber die Einsamkeit*, translated into English and published in Boston in 1804 as *Solitude Considered With Respect to its Influence on the Mind and the Heart*. In addition to a mastery of Western classics, Thoreau was keenly interested in Eastern thought, one of the first American writers to pursue contemporary translations of classic texts from China and India, such as the *Bhagavad Gita*.

Thoreau's more familiar aphorisms about solitude come especially from two sources: *Walden* and *Journal*, the latter work unknown to Thoreau's contemporaries.

From *Walden* come the signature Thoreau anthems: "I never found the companion that was so companionable as solitude" and "Not till we are lost, in other words, not till we have lost the world, do we begin to find ourselves, and realize where we are and the infinite extent of our relations." Thoreau built a small cottage in the woods near Walden Pond, living self–sufficiently for a couple of years, planting vegetables, chopping firewood, building furniture, cooking for himself, observing self and villagers of Concord, and reflecting on the vicissitudes of solitude in his journal. His book *Walden* relates this period of his life.

From the *Journal*, maintained from 1837 to1846 and from 1850–1861, come deeper insights into solitude not intended for publication:

> "By my intimacy with nature I find myself withdrawn from man."
> "My interest in the sun and the moon, in the morning and the evening, compels me to solitude."
> "I thrive best on solitude. If I have had a companion only one day

in a week, unless it were one or two I could name, I find that the value of the week to me has been seriously affected. It dissipates my days, and often it takes me another week to get over it."

"I feel the necessity of deepening the stream of my life: I must cultivate privacy. It is very dissipating to be with people too much."

"I do not know if I am singular when I say that I believe there is no man with whom I can associate who will not, comparatively speaking, spoil my afternoon."

"I am tired of frivolous society, in which silence is forever the most natural and the best manners. I would fain walk on the deep waters, but my companions will only walk on shallows and pud-dles."

Equally significant to American philosophical Romanticism in this era are literary figures advancing concepts and images of solitude: Emily Dickinson, Nathaniel Hawthorne, and Herman Melville.

Emily Dickinson

American poet Emily Dickinson (1830–1886) transformed the reclusion for which she became famous—which confirmed her solitude and that of the universe in her eyes—into refreshingly sensitive and direct verse. Her literary status reflects a Romantic "art for art's sake" motif in that she never sought publication nor to influence others. She expressed to her sister Lavinia the desire to have her work burned after her death, yet meticulously collected a folio of nearly two thousand poems composed up to her death at age fifty–five.

Dickinson's preoccupation with disease and death reflects her observation of humanity around her, her own household where she dwelt in reclusion, her own maladies, physical and mental, plus her extensive reading. Lives were lost indiscriminately during this era, to typhus, tuberculosis, rheumatic fever and stroke, claiming men and women, high–born and low, children, youths, the middle–aged, and elderly. Dickinson's poems observe the ubiquitous toll of pain, suffering, and death around her.

These subjects built upon childhood images (the window of her child-hood bedroom looked out on a cemetery, for example). Dickinson extends the images and sensibilities to God, heaven, angels, afterlife, immortality, and resurrection. She variously described herself as pagan, druid, Cynic, hermetic, and possessed of "Sweet Skepticism" (one of her poem titles).

As always, solitude is a core theme:

> There is a solitude of space
> A solitude of sea
> A solitude of death,
> but these Society shall be
> Compared with that profounder site
> That polar privacy
> A soul admitted to itself—
> Finite infinity.

Further, that space within is crafted by the self:

> The Soul selects her own Society —
> Then—shuts the Door—
> To her divine Majority—
> Present no more — ...

Even in her twenties, Dickinson crafted her life to reflect self–discoveries. Early she refused her family's church–attendance, preferring her own beliefs. She refused marriage, equating relationship as "idolatry," and dreading the notion of being "yielded up." She embraced a religious sense of virtue in what her biographer summed as "abstinence, endurance, and renunciation," virtues she transformed into characteristics of a personal integrity and solitude. These virtues impressed Dickinson in her reading of *The Imitation of Christ* by Thomas à Kempis, which book confirmed her personal creed. She preferred the suffering Christ to the triumphant one, the cross to the crown, the suffering Jesus of the *Imitation* to the idealized figure of the Gospels.

> To put this World down, like a Bundle–
> And walk steady, Away,
> Requires Energy–possibly Agony–
> 'Tis the Scarlet way
> Trodden with straight renunciation
> By the Son of God–

Later, his faint Confederates
Justify the Road –

In 1882, late in life, Dickinson wrote of faith:

"Those—dying then,
Knew where they went—
They went to God's Right Hand—
That Hand is amputated now
And God cannot be found."

Despite pain and suffering, Dickinson held both a deep affection and loyalty to her many friends, evidenced in her considerable correspondence, and a deep love of nature, expressed early as an appreciation of plants and animals in her own spacious garden, which she tended avidly throughout her life. As a youth, she roamed nearby meadows, developing a keen scientific eye for flowering species, maintaining a folio of hundreds of dried flowers. Nature frequently appears in her poetry:

Growth of Man, like Growth of Nature—
Gravitates within—
Atmosphere, and Sun, endorse it—
But it stir—alone
Each—its difficult Ideal
Must achieve—Itself—
Through the solitary prowess
Of a Silent Life.

And Nature teaches small but vital lessons:

How many Flowers fail in the Wood
Or perish from the Hill—
Without the privilege to know
That they are Beautiful—...

Ultimately, Dickinson experienced a quiet mysticism akin to philosophical transcendentalism. She began with love of Nature, then reduction of self or ego, contentment with simplicity and the circumscribed routines of life.

During her most productive years in the early 1860s she reveals an ecstatic perception of the universe, within quiet resignation and solitary contentment.

> Take all away from me, but leave me Ecstasy,
> And I am richer than all my Fellow Men—
> Ill it becometh me to dwell so wealthily
> When at my very Door are those possessing more,
> In abject poverty—

and

> The Only News I know
> Is Bulletins all Day
> From Immortality
> The Only Shows I see—
> Tomorrow and Today—
> Perchance Eternity—
> The Only One I meet
> Is God—The Only Street—
> Existence—This traversed
> If Other News there be—
> Or Admirabler show—
> I'll tell it you—

Like the classic Chinese recluse who turns his hut into a universe, Emily Dickinson does the same in her equivalent quarters. When her last hour comes, she rests confident in the sentiment of this late poem, which could have been her death poem, brief but redolent:

> Sweet hours have perished here;
> This is a mighty room;
> Within its precincts hopes have played,—
> Now shadows in the tomb.

Emily Dickinson presents positive aspects of literary Romanticism's theme of solitude. The positive expression ends with her, however. Subsequent American Romantic writers Poe, Hawthorne, and Melville revisit darkness.

Poe, Hawthorne, Melville

In Edgar Allan Poe (1809–1849) darker melancholic, irrational, and grotesque elements of literary Romanticism dominate, elements refined and extended by Nathaniel Hawthorne (1804-1864) and Herman Melville (1819–1891).

Specific to the theme of solitude in Poe is his poem "Alone" expressing solitude as his childhood inheritance. "Silence" and the story "Silence, a Fable," are placed in macabre settings typifying Poe's melancholy. A hermit character described as "maliceful" appears in a story within the story "Fall of the House of Usher." Poe's dark psychology holds no interest in the Romanticism of Wordsworth and his followers.

The 1837 psychological short story "Fragments from the Journal of a Solitary Man" by Nathaniel Hawthorne is characteristically melancholic. Protagonist Oberon, disillusioned with the world and suffering elements of madness, regrets his life of reclusion. He is nostalgic for moments of human society and affection, but remains unable to identify with others. In "The Man of Adamant," published in the same year, Hawthorne tells the story of a selfish man who treks through forests to distance himself from society, finding a cave in which to live, pray, and read the Bible. The ghost of a young woman once attracted to him before his reclusion appears, seeking to soften his heart, but he responds with ire at her presence, driving her away. Years later, as settlement in the area increases, his body is discovered by settlers, who bury the remains but never again venture near the eerie spot.

The literary work of Herman Melville exemplifies American Romantic literary depiction of dark solitude. In his famous epic novel *Moby Dick*, Melville coins the word "isolatoes" to describe the crew of the ship *Pequod*: "They were nearly all Islands on the *Pequod*, Isolatoes too, I call such, not acknowledging the common continent of men, but each Isolato living on a separate continent of his own."

The novella *The Encantadas*, meaning the "Enchanted Islands," bears an intentionally ironic title, for the islands are grim wastelands frequented only briefly by sailors and pirates. "Sketch 9" of *Encantadas* depicts Oberlus, a sailor stranded on the island who consciously pursues the busy solitude of a Selkirk or Robinson Crusoe. But gradually Oberlus is driven mad by deprivation and isolation. In his mental agitation he kidnaps and enslaves visitors to his island. The story of a dark, solitary soul is complemented by its bleak natural setting.

In *Typee* the narrator scorns people; in *Mardi* he finds no one "with whom to mingle sympathies." The narrator of *Moby Dick* opens the novel declaring: "Call me Ishmael," thus identifying himself with the exiled son of the biblical Abraham, exiled into wilderness and forever cursed by circumstances. In *Pierre*, the female character Isabel is the involuntary isolato. In *Israel Potter*, the title character wanders like the Hebrews in the desert. Finally, the character of John Marr (in the late poetry collection *John Marr and Other Sailors*) finds himself unable to make sympathetic communion with others, who reject him. These hapless victims of involuntary isolation are scrutable and sympathetic.

Within a separate world but interacting afflictively with others is Captain Ahab in *Moby Dick* (1851), an arrogant egoist whose voluntary solitude is rightly circumscribed by the narrator as a sociopathy. Ahab's vision is personal but projects outward to encompass nature and the universe as his antagonist. "I'd strike the sun if it insulted me" is his famous imprecation. Ahab inverts the Romantic vision of harmony with nature into a grotesque and morbid collapse. (Melville actively criticized Emerson's optimism).

In a moment of self–reflection, Ahab laments:

> When I think of this life I have led; the desolation of solitude it has been; the masoned, walled–town of a captain's exclusiveness, which admits but small entrance to any sympathy from the green country without,—oh, weariness! heaviness! Guinea–coast of solitary command!

Melville's "isolatoes" are sketches of his own life of depression, social isolation, poverty, and eventual neglect. The character of Bartleby in the novella *Bartleby the Scrivener* (1853) comes to represent Melville's last insight (his last work of fiction penned for income). The demure Bartleby enters employment as a copyist in the narrator's law firm, but soon announces that he "prefers" not to work any more, though he refuses to leave his desk. The narrator treats Bartleby with exasperated patience and tolerance, unable to penetrate Bartleby's mind or heart. As the days pass, Bartleby takes to living day and night in his corner of the office, "preferring" not to do anything. At wit's end, the narrator vacates the firm from the building. The next tenant, not inclined to patience, has the police remove Bartleby to jail, where Bartleby quits eating and dies. The enigmatic isolato achieves a philosophical understanding that eludes the narrator, who at story's end sighs: "Ah, Bartleby! Ah, humanity!"

Melville's sympathy for isolatoes paints them in varied psychologies and depths not fully appreciated in the mid–nineteenth century, nor fully explored even today. The fiction of Melville marks the end of Romantic literature in the United States, wrecking the fate of his characters against the complex enigma of solitude.

50. Romantic Art and Solitude: Early Nineteenth Century

Romantic–era painting acutely reflects the disparate elements of social romanticism (political and nostalgic), perceptions of nature, and the Romantic hero in solitude.

The German painter Caspar David Friedrich (1774–1840) presents the solitary hero in his famous painting *Wanderer Above the Sea of Fog*. The figure's face is turned outward and away from the viewer: is the wanderer in triumph or anguish in the presence of wild nature?

The mood is more reflective in Friedrich's *Monk and Sea*, where the solitary monk or hermit is dwarfed by nature and easily merges into a natural tableau. More nostalgic are *Two Men Contemplating the Moon* and *Man and Woman Contemplating the Moon*, the latter provoking Irish playwright Samuel Beckett to note that the painting inspired him to write *Waiting for Godot*. As in the *Sea of Fog*, nature is hostile and forbidding in Friedrich's eerie *Rocky Reef on the Sea Shore* and the striking *Sea of Ice*.

In contrast, the many British landscape painters of the era (William Hodges, John Constable, J. M.W. Turner, Samuel Palmer, the Cozen brothers, among others) are irredeemably nostalgic, portraying nature contrived and benign. German painter Phillip Otto Runge (1777–1810) also embodies nostalgia in his *Days of Time* series.

More reflective of original Romanticism is *Melancholy*, a work by French painter Constance Marie Charpentier (1767–1849). Her subject includes solitude but better illustrates the contemporary school of melancholia. British painter William Blake (1757–1827) anticipates darker Romanticism in his vivid images of classic themes from grand religious and mythical sources, moving Romanticism's themes away from the subjective.

Naive Social Romanticism and political optimism are embodied in the famous *Liberty Leading the People* by the French painter Eugene Delacroix (1798–1863). Original Social Romanticism opposing modern forces is perhaps best represented by Spanish painter Francisco Goya (1746–1828), whose response to the violence and wretchedness of the Napoleonic Peninsular Wars is graphically portrayed in his *Disasters of War* series and familiar *The Third of May, 1808*. The later Goya embodies the dark Romantic preoccupation with the grotesque and morbid, his subjects including asylums, monsters, witches, and the Inquisition. Neither of these painters or trends evokes a salutary solitude found among Romantic German and French writers of the era, rather a continued descent of Romanticism into alienation.

51. Eremitism and Literature: Britain and Europe

As literary historian Robert Sayre concludes of French Romantic literature—though true of all Romanticism in this era—Romanticism and realism pursue parallel themes of solitude after the early nineteenth century.

Realism grinds the moral and aesthetic values of Romanticism into the grim dust of modern society. Romantic heroes attempt to overcome modern strictures that destroy the past, or try to attain the heights of natural wisdom and emotion, realism depicts Romantic heroes as frustrated or ruined by modern society, succumbing to morbid excess, egoism, or social failure.

Realism magnifies the failures of the Romantic heroes, reduced to involuntary solitaries. Indeed, where solitude was once the privilege of insightful souls, it now comes to embody the social alienation of the individual. The Romantic motif of "art for art's sake" withdraws the arts from even attempting any longer to influence or intersect with society.

At the same time, the European literature of the latter nineteenth century is fascinated by hermits and solitude. Fictional accounts of hermits and solitaries range from the didactic and contrived to masterful modern allegories, and to the decadent and mocking. Among nineteenth–century European writers pursuing hermit themes is a roster of famous writers: Hans Christian Andersen, Anton Chekhov, Rudyard Kipling, Guy de Maupassant, Charles Reade, Leo Tolstoy, and Oscar Wilde—to which may be added an American satirist of hermits: Mark Twain.

- Hans Christian Andersen (1805–1875): "The Silent Book" (short story, 1851). "The Silent Book," sometimes titled "The Silent Album," is a sentimental remembrance of a solitary. Off a forest road sits a lonely farmhouse, and in the yard lies an open coffin holding a dead man, his face covered with a white cloth, a book of dried flowers next to him. Someone in the house

is explaining that the man lived in a city and was once quite knowledge-
able, but something happened. Dark moods possessed the rest of his
days until he came out to the country, in poor health. He could run wildly
through the forest, but when persuaded to sit with his book of flowers
he would browse through it quietly, often tearfully. He had requested
to be buried with the book, and the men in the house will comply.
Each flower in the book reflects a stage in the man's life: an oak leaf,
water lily, lilies of the valley, honeysuckle, hothouse flowers, a blade
of grass. A swallow darts about, chirping. The men emerge from the
house. Hammer and nails are applied. The man and his silent book
are "hidden, forgotten."

- Charles Reade (1814–1884): *The Cloister and the Hearth* (novel, 1861).
  The novel is set in late medieval Holland and Europe, characteristically
  melodramatic in the nineteenth–century style of historical romance.
  A subplot of the larger novel features Gerard, who flees the evil town
  mayor, leaving his wife Margaret, who is pregnant, unbeknownst to the
  couple. Gerard's conniving brothers send him a message, purportedly
  by a friend of his wife, that she has died. After a period of mourning,
  Gerard becomes a Dominican friar. Years later, preaching throughout
  Europe, he reaches Holland and discovers that his wife is alive. Torn
  between his clerical vow and spousal love, he becomes a hermit in a
  cave. His physical and mental sufferings continue, especially haunted
  by human love. Margaret discovers him. He gives up his eremitism.
  They agree to live separately and in celibacy, Gerard raising their son.
  Margaret contracts the plague and dies. With this last sorrow, Gerard
  dies, too.

- Oscar Wilde (1854–1900): "The Teacher of Wisdom" (short story, 1879).
  Wilde's didactic fairy tale presents a man who, since childhood, is filled
  with the perfect knowledge of God. Upon reaching a certain age, he
  leaves parents and home to travel exotic lands and cities, sharing this perfect knowledge of God. One day, as his many disciples assemble around
  him to hear him preach, the man falls into tears and great sorrow that
  he himself cannot understand. His Soul tells him that he has given away
  the perfect knowledge of God and must now remain silent. His disciples
  insist on hearing his teaching, but he vows to remain silent. They fall
  away until he is alone. He walks on, finds a cave, and lives as a hermit.

One day, a young man passes by the cave entrance, in the morning with empty hands, returning in the evening with hands full of "purple and pearls." He is clearly a robber, but the hermit says nothing. One day, the man passing by glares angrily at the hermit, objecting aloud to the hermit watching him. The hermit replies that he pities the man's lacks of knowledge of God, more precious than pearls. The robber draws a sword, demanding the hermit give him this knowledge or be slain. The hermit refuses. The robber leaves, boasting of the evil pleasures his treasure will now acquire. The hermit follows, beseeching him to stop. At the city gates, the robber vows he will enter the city unless the hermit gives him the knowledge of God. The robber turns to enter. Conceding, the hermit whispers his knowledge to the robber. At that moment, the hermit falls to the ground weeping. A darkness envelopes them, and a supernatural being, of "feet of brass and hair like fine wool" raises up the hermit, telling him that once the hermit had perfect knowledge of God, but now he has the perfect love of God.

- Guy de Maupassant (1850–1893): "Solitude" (short story, 1884) and "The Hermit" (short story, 1886). "Solitude" begins after a dinner gathering, when an old friend invites the narrator for a stroll in the Champs–Élysées. The old friend is the monologist in the story, the narrator recording his friend's words until the end of the story when the two companions break off. Maupassant places in the monologue the clear sentiment of the day: solitude sought out for artistic or literary creativity no longer exists, for solitude now represents alienation from society, from others, from the universe. The monologist feels "condemned to solitude," and no longer reveals his thoughts or beliefs to anyone. At the end of their walk, the narrator cannot decide if his friend is right or has lost his mind.

- Guy de Maupassant. In "The Hermit," the narrator tells his companions about an older man he once knew who lived as a hermit on a mountainside overlooking the sea in southwestern France. The story is chiefly a monologue by the hermit. One spring, the narrator visiting the area, climbs a mountain, surprised to discover a hermit. Only after repeated visits does he enter the hermit's confidence. The man tells the narrator why he became a hermit. He had lived comfortably in Paris from inheritance, an idle life of dissipation. One night he flatters a vulnerable young woman serving drinks at a bar. They go to her flat. The next morning as he leaves money on her bureau, he stares in shock at a framed photograph of himself twenty years before. He asks the young woman about the photograph. She says it was supposed to be a photograph of her father, given to her by her mother years ago. The man makes his way out quickly. Quitting Paris he finds the isolated cave on the mountainside, where he has lived since. The narrator returns the following season, but there is no trace of the hermit on the mountainside.

- Leo Tolstoy (1828–1910). "Three Questions" (short story, 1885) and "The Three Hermits" (short story, 1886).

  In the didactic tale "Three Questions," a certain king had three concerns: 1) to know the right time to begin anything, 2) to know the right people to listen to and those to avoid, and 3) to know the most important thing to do. The king's counsellors offer contradictory advice, so the exasperated king decides to ask a hermit in the woods. The king approaches with his retinue, but leaves the horses and guards behind to walk through the woods in commoner's clothes. When the king arrives, the hermit is digging garden beds in front of his hut. He greets the visitor perfunctorily and continues his work. The king explains to the hermit the dilemma of the three questions. The frail old man continues his work, saying nothing. The king volunteers to work while the hermit rests. He repeats his question, working while the hermit rests.

  Suddenly a wounded man runs up, and the king and hermit try to bind his stomach wound. The man admits that he had tried to kill the king and was wounded by one of his guards on the road. The man was angry because his brother had been executed at the king's order. The king reveals his identity. The wounded man admits that he would have died of his wound but now that the king has saved his life, he promises to serve the king faithfully. They are reconciled. The king accepts the man's service. Meanwhile, the hermit has been watching, and returns to work in his garden. The king repeats his three questions. The king has his answers, replies the hermit. The most important time was to help bind the wounded man, the most important people were himself and the wounded man, and his most important work was digging the bed, then binding the man's wounds. The most important moment, in short, is the present one, when one sees a need and has the power to do something for the good.

- Leo Tolstoy. "Three Hermits" begins aboard a ship of pilgrims visiting shrines. They sit on deck enjoying the sun and calm sea. A bishop strolls past a group of men, one of whom has been telling a story and pointing out to sea but falls silent when the bishop approaches. The bishop asks to listen. The man had been pointing to an island where hermits live, three holy men, very old, intent upon the salvation of their souls. A telescope is procured. The bishop can detect the island as the ship passes. Suddenly determined to see the hermits, the bishop convinces the reluctant ship captain to designate that a crew member row him to the island in a boat. The ship anchors. The bishop is dutifully rowed. Three old men wait on the shore for the visitor. The bishop immediately wants to know what the hermits do for their salvation. They reply that they only pray all day: "We are three, You are three, have mercy on us!" The bishop shakes his head. He tells the hermits he will now teach them to pray the "Our Father." He announces one phrase, the others repeat. This goes on the entire day, until the three old men can recite the entire prayer. They recite even as the bishop returns to the boat at nightfall and is rowed back to the ship. The anchor is lifted. The ship sails on. The pilgrims sleep in the darkness. The bishop looks back at the receding island with satisfaction. Suddenly, he sees a glow on the water, not moonlight, not birds or fish. He points it out to the helmsman, who shouts in terror that the hermits are running after the ship on the water as if on dry land, with a glow of light surrounding them. The passengers are startled awake. The hermits have caught up. The bishop leans over the rail. "We've forgotten the prayer," shout the hermits. "We knew it as long as we recited it, but when we stopped we forgot it." The bishop shouts back that their prayer will reach God regardless and that it is not for him to teach them. He bows to the hermits. The hermits return to their island, the glow receding into daybreak.

- Anton Chekhov (1860–1904). "The Bet," (short story, 1889). Chekhov's provocative story features a modern anchorite. A once rich banker recalls events fifteen years ago. At a party of gentlemen, conversation emerges about capital punishment. Most guests consider capital punishment immoral and speculate about life imprisonment. The wealthy banker, who is the party host, says that he would personally prefer to be killed at once rather than by degrees. A young lawyer objects. The banker loses his temper, bangs his fist on a table. He taunts the lawyer, saying he would not be able to be in a cell for five years. He bets two million. The lawyer replies firmly that he could stay not five but fifteen years. The bet is confirmed before the appalled guests. Fifteen years later, the banker now rues the foolish bet. He is about to lose two million; the lawyer has lost fifteen years. The arrangement called for the young lawyer to be imprisoned in the garden wing of the banker's house, the doors sealed. The lawyer would not see or hear anyone, receive no correspondence or newspapers, but could read, write, and play a musical instrument. By leaving a note at a garden window constructed for the purpose, the lawyer could request books, wine, or other solicitation. The story recounts the lawyer's activities over the years, each year reflecting different moods, revolving around books, his reading voluminous and deeper as the years pass. On the eve of the fifteenth year, the banker is distraught because he has no money. He goes out to the garden, winter snow already blowing cold. He sees the lawyer, a thin skeletal figure, sleeping while sitting at the table strewn with books and writings. The banker quietly breaks the door seal, intending to enter the garden wing and suffocate the man, freeing himself from obligation. But he reads what the man has written and goes out in tears. The lawyer had written that he scorns all things human and will deliberately quit the garden enclosure in disdain of the banker's money. In the morning the gardener awakens the banker with news that the lawyer is gone.

• Rudyard Kipling (1865–1939). "Miracle of Purun Bhagat" (short story, 1895). Kipling's story is a sentimental and sympathetic tale from his *Second Jungle Book*. A young brahmin attains wealth and celebrity but one day renounces the world to become a *sannayasin* or hermit. He wanders, finding an empty shrine in which to live, and withdraws from the world. Nearby villagers, aware that a saint dwells within their precincts, bring him food and guard him from visitors. Monkeys and deer visit him, and he shares his blanket with them. One rainy night the animals awaken the hermit, nudging him repeatedly until he realizes that the water now pouring into his cave means that the mountainside is collapsing and that he and the villagers are in danger. The hermit is old and feeble but runs to the village, awakening all and leading their flight. A great landslide overcomes the empty village. But the villagers are safe. They laud the miracle of their timely escape. But the old hermit has succumbed to the effort and dies.

- Juliana Horatia Ewing (1842–1885). "The Trinity Flower: A Legend" (short story, 1885). The story, from Ewing's collection *Jackanape, Daddy Darwin's Dovecot, and Other Stories*, is a Victorian fairy tale and sentimental didactic children's story with a religious theme featuring the herbalism popularly associated with hermits. (The Trinity flower is the *Trillium erythrocarpum*).

A hermit "in days of yore" lived in a cave on a hillside, maintaining flower and herb gardens from which he frequently selected herbs as medicines for the villagers. From crabapples on the site he made a healing conserve. But the old hermit has nearly lost all of his sight. A village boy was stealing crabapples. One evening sitting on the hillside, the hermit overhears the boy boasting to another boy. The hermit reveals himself, and the boys run away. Meanwhile, plague had broken out in the village. The hermit takes conserve to the sick. He passes a house where a boy moans in pain; entering the house the hermit discovers that it is the boy who boasted of theft. The hermit gives the boy some of the conserve, pointedly noting that he would have had more had not someone stolen his crabapples, depriving both the hermit and the villagers. The boy tearfully admits that he is the thief. The plague subsides. The hermit returns to his cell. The contrite boy reappears, vowing to serve the hermit. The hermit is dismissive but the boy persists, cleaning, sweeping, tidying the garden, going to wild places to gather rare plants and herbs and bring them to the hermit's garden. As the hermit's sight further dims, the boy leads him to new plantings in the garden to touch and smell them. The hermit's grief over his diminishing eyesight deepens. He prays daily to recover, the boy saddened. One day the hermit dreams that he stands at the garden gate distributing herbs to a crowd of people. A pilgrim lingering in the crowd, hearing of the hermit's plight, proffers a Trinity flower. Putting it in the hermit's hand, his eyes are opened. He can see clearly. When the hermit awakens, he relates his dream to the boy, describing the flower's three leaves, three petals, three sepals, all white with streaks of red. The boy vows to find it. That autumn, a stranger passes the hut. From the garden gate he beckons the boy and gives him a tuber, the root of the Trinity flower, he explains. Take it to the hermit, says the stranger, who then slips away. When the boy brings it to the hermit, the boys describes the stranger. The hermit confirms that the passerby is the "Angel of Death."

Autumn and winter are long and try their patience, but with spring the Trinity flower begins to grow. Excitedly, the hermit and the boy kneel by the plant, praying for sun and rain that it might blossom quickly. One day, the flower is about to bloom. The boy waits in the garden at dawn. The flower blooms. He cuts the flower and rushes to the hermit, who is still sleeping. The boy doe not want to awaken him. He leaves the flower beside the hermit, stationing himself outside the old man's cell, where he falls asleep. Before sunrise the boy is awakened by the hermit's greeting. The hermit emerges from his cell, looks at him tenderly, and rushes to the gate and beyond. Startled, the boy calls to him, asking of his eyesight. The hermit assures him that he can see. The hermit passed so quickly, and did not return as hours passed. Trembling, the boy enters the cell to discover the hermit's dead body stretched on his sleeping mat, and in its hand is the Trinity flower.

- Richard Gordon Smith (1858–1918). "The Hermit's Cave" (short story, 1908) and "Chrysanthemum Hermit" (short story, 1908). A British traveler living in Japan for many years, Smith collected folk tales assembled in his *Ancient Tales and Folklore of Japan* (1918). "The Hermit's Cave" tells of the village of Nomugi, at the foot of Mount Norikuradake, where several children suffered handicaps: a girl's leg is deformed, a boy is deaf, a third blind. Doctors and medicines had proven unsuccessful, but the children play, laugh, and live as normally as they can, frequenting the grassy slope of an old dam at the end of the village. One day the children are surprised by an old man with a long white beard approaching them from the direction of the mountain. The man is friendly, and tells the three children that they will be cured of their ailments, but should not yet tell their parents. He asks them to return the next day. The children continue their play, saying nothing at home that night. The scene is repeated the next day, the old man checking the children's progress, until one day they are fully cured. That evening, news of the cures flies through the village. The adults decide that the next day two men should follow the children from a distance, to see who this magician might be. Many children from the village accompany the original three. After checking the three, the old man amuses the children with magic. From dead sticks spring blossoms, a stone thrown in the air becomes a dove, a few cryptic words summon monkeys from the hillside. The children clap in delight. One of the village men blurts to the other that the old man must be a wizard. The old man, hearing this, announces to the children that all tricks are finished for the day, that he is going home and the children should do likewise. The two hidden men and the children try to follow the old man who scrambles up toward a cave, but soon disappears. The cave is empty. Then one of the children cries out. All look up. The old man stands on a cloud at the summit of the mountain. One of the men exclaims that it is the fabled hermit of the mountain. Later, the villagers erect a shrine at the foot of the mountain named Sendokutsu Temple, or Sennin Temple, meaning Temple of the Immortal, the Sage, or the Hermit.

- Richard Gordon Smith. "Chrysanthemum Hermit" tells of an old man who lives at the foot of the mountains of Nambu, in Saitama Prefecture. The old man's name is Kikuo, meaning Chrysanthemum–Old–Man. He had long been part of the small guard that protected their lord, his castle, and his estates. One day the little guard is overthrown, and the lord and his retainers flee to the mountains, hoping one day to avenge their defeat.

Knowing his lord's love of flowers, especially chrysanthemums, Kikuo creates flower beds of chrysanthemums, which please his lord greatly. One day the lord falls sick and dies. Kikuo extends the flower beds around the lord's grave to assuage the dead man's spirit, and soon the beds of brilliant chrysanthemums are so expansive that villagers and children come to admire them. Years pass. Kikuo lives as a hermit in a cottage. He teaches the village children to read and write, and is much revered by the villagers. One day, the old man falls sick. During the day his pupils attend him but at night he is alone. Kikuo awakens one night to find his bed surrounded by children, too beautiful and noble to be village children. They are the spirits of the chrysanthemums. They have come to inform him that Heaven allots him little time, that he will die in thirty days, that they are grateful for his care but that they, too, will accompany him. They all shed tears. The old man declares that he is ready, has no regrets but to lose the flowers. The spirits disappear. As foretold, Kikuo dies thirty days later, as does every chrysanthemum in the flower beds. The old man is buried next to his lord, and the villagers plant chrysanthemums, believing it will honor and please the dead, but are puzzled because the flowers fade and die as soon as they are planted. The two graves retain their solitude, with only the wild grasses growing round them.

With his 1889 novel *A Connecticut Yankee in King Arthur's Court*, eminent American satirist Mark Twain (1835–1910) presents hermits more retrogressively than Spanish picaresque fiction or the scurrilous tales of La Fontaine. In an acerbic passage, the protagonist joins a procession to the Valley of Holiness, and narrates this encounter with hermits:

> We drifted from hermit to hermit all the afternoon. It was a most strange menagerie. The chief emulation among them seemed to be, to see which could manage to be the uncleanest and most prosperous with vermin. Their manner and attitudes were the last expression of complacent self–righteousness. It was one anchorite's pride to lie naked in the mud and let the insects bite him and blister him unmolested; it was another's to lean against a rock, all day long, conspicuous to the admiration of the throng of pilgrims and pray; it was another's to go naked and crawl around on all fours; it was another's to drag about with him, year in and year out, eighty pounds of iron; it was another's to never lie down when he slept, but to stand among the thorn–bushes and snore when there were pilgrims around to look; a woman, who had the white hair of age, and no other apparel, was black from crown to heel with forty–seven years of holy abstinence from water. Groups of gazing pilgrims stood around all and every of these strange objects, lost in reverent wonder, and envious of the feckless sanctity which these pious austerities had won for them from an exacting heaven.

52. "The Temptation of St. Anthony" in Art

Gustave Flaubert (1821–1880) published *The Temptation of Saint Anthony* in 1874, a novel begun when he first viewed Bruegel's famous painting. The novel inverts familiar Christian desert hermit hagiography, where the sedate and contemplative hermit triumphantly fends off pesky demons. Instead, the long narrative anticipates surrealism in its dizzy concoctions of scenes. Anthony is tormented and ambivalent, complaining of inertness and misery, devolving into rambling monologues, beset by voices, hallucinations, strange creations, and seductive visitors, including a Queen of Sheba and a female character named Lust.

In 1890, Anatole France (1844–1924) published *Thais*, also an intentionally scurrilous version of a desert hermit, one who enters the city to successfully convert a famous harlot but becomes obsessed with her after returning to the desert. The hermit goes back to the city, finding Thais on her deathbed in a convent, infused with faith and piety. The lustful hermit disdains her faith as illusion and professes his love for her.

Not unexpectedly, the temptations of St. Anthony described in the biography by St. Athanasius are the subject of many painters in the Western world. During the Italian Renaissance and Baroque periods, and during the Netherlandish Golden Age, painters adhered to the religious intentions of the earliest hagiography, depicting the temptations as diabolical torments, highlighted by the stalwart if nervous defense of the hermit.

The earliest illustrations of the theme were in medieval books and missals. In formal art, the earliest work is credited to German engraver Martin Schongauer (1435–1491), imitated in a painting by the then twelve year old Michelangelo (1475–1564). Among painters of the theme in the Northern schools (German, Dutch, Flemish) are Matthias Grunewald (1470–1528), Hieronymus Bosch 1450–1516), and the school of Pieter Bruegel (1525–1569).

Painters of the later nineteenth century decadent schools predominate in modern times. The temptation theme is revived, the style and motif of the early modern depictions inverted. The theme becomes an opportunity for depicting, indeed, promoting, the salacious. In his book *On Ugliness*, semiotician Umberto Eco (1932–2013) noted the reversal of roles in the depiction of Anthony's temptations after the appearance of Flaubert's novel.

The late nineteenth and early twentieth century modern school of painters of the temptation theme are decadents: French–born Henri Fantin–Latour

(1836–1904), Belgian–born Felicien Rops (1833–1898), German–born Lovis Corinth (1858–1925), and English–born John Charles Dollman (1851–1934). In the nineteenth century, only the realist French painter Jean–François Millet (1814–1875) salvages sympathy for Anthony. A transition is seen, however, in the surrealists, who echo the early modern depiction of the grotesque with new energy, among them the German painter Max Ernst (1891–1976), British–Mexican Leonora Carrington (1917–2011), the Spaniard Salvador Dalí (1904–1989), and Mexican Diego Rivera (1886–1957). The surrealists rehabilitate Anthony. The overtly religious painters, the Jewish Arthur Szyk (1894–1951) and the contemporary Irish Catholic Eugene de Leastar, are symbolists, remarkably similar to one another in theme and composition.

53. Philosophers of Solitude: Kierkegaard to Nietzsche

Four nineteenth–century philosophers transformed solitude from the hagiographic and romantic iconography of the hermit past into the existential hero of the present, bereft of faith, solace, or support.

Søren Kierkegaard

Søren Kierkegaard (1813–1855) marks the transition from traditional European thought, still infused with the influence of institutional Christianity in its metaphysics and morals, to a modern view of philosophy and psychology wherein society and its thought is adrift, wrecked against the shoals of skepticism, doubt, and loss.

Kierkegaard often used suggestive pseudonyms for his book authors: Victor Emerita in *Either/Or*, Johannes de Silencio in *Fear and Trembling*, and Johannes Climaticus in *Philosophical Fragments and Concluding Unscientific Postscript*.

Kierkegaard identifies the "single individual" as the solitary human self struggling to ascertain knowledge. "If you have never been solitary, you have never discovered that God exists," he concludes in *Works of Love*. Each person is alone in finding truth, hence a "subjective" truth in contrast to the presumptuous "objectivity" of the philosophers and theologians with their dry and lifeless abstractions. In the pursuit of truth, the "knight of faith" or "knight of hidden inwardness" works alone in anguish, indistinguishable socially from anyone else but struggling inwardly to find and embrace truth or God. Kierkegaard opposes institutional religion for its facile presentation of dogma and adherence. The Old Testament portrayals of Yahweh's suspension of morality in order to afflict Abraham and Job do not reassure but, rather, are signs of contradiction, despair, and untruth. Thus Kierkegaard is counted the precursor of existentialism.

Arthur Schopenhauer

Arthur Schopenhauer (1788–1860) is the paramount philosopher of pessimism, overturning the German idealism of Kant and Hegel to argue against the demonstrability of reason and ethics. In his three–volume *The World As Will and Representation* (issued in successive editions from 1819 to 1859), Schopenhauer criticizes the Stoics as dependent upon reason in overcoming suffering. He extols the virtues and practices of the "overcomers of the world," namely, the "voluntary penitents" of Indian philosophy and the hermits of early Christianity, adding Christian mystics like Meister Eckhart, plus those whom Schopenhauer elsewhere considers geniuses of solitude.

Schopenhauer assesses contemporary philosophy as sophism distracted by logic against daily life, the latter the strength of Greek and Roman thinkers. Schopenhauer is original in introducing Eastern thought to the West, emphasizing non–theism and emptiness, underscoring, however, his repute as droll and pessimistic, with his irascible personality abetting the perception of his philosophy.

For Schopenhauer, hermits are now lost to history, replaced for the intelligent person by solitude, espousing the disinterest in the world once occupying the social Romantics. In *Counsel and Maxims*, he writes: "A man can be himself only so long as he is alone; and if he does not love solitude, he will not love freedom; for it is only when he is alone that he is really free." And in *The Wisdom of Life*: "An intellectual man in complete solitude has excellent entertainment in his own thoughts and fancies, while no amount of diversity or social pleasure, theaters, excursions and amusements, can ward off boredom from a dullard."

Fyodor Dostoyevsky

The Russian writer Fyodor Dostoyevsky (1821–1861) captures Kierkegaard's religious sensibilities in his novels, animating fictional characters with the era's deep unease. Each character is no mere collection of personality traits but embodies a universe of belief, philosophy, and torturous spirit. The characters in his last novel *The Brothers Karamazov* (1880) exemplify the currents of the age. Dostoyevsky's Father Zosima is the ideal *starets*, beloved advisor to believers but hated by jealous fellow monks; Ivan Karamazov is a crafty intellectual and ruthless cynic; Alyosha is a heartfelt but struggling religious novice.

Two works of Dostoyevsky consciously pursue solitude: the tale of the Grand Inquisitor told by Ivan in *The Brothers Karamazov* and Dostoyevsky's early 1864 novel *Notes From Underground*.

The story within the novel is intended to explore the culmination of institutional control over a society that historically persecuted the solitary. The medieval Grand Inquisitor of Spain one day enters the cathedral grounds and spots a vaguely–familiar figure in the courtyard performing a miracle, surrounded by a breathless crowd. The Inquisitor is incensed, ordering the man seized and imprisoned. That night the Inquisitor visits the prisoner alone in the church dungeon. The arrested man is not named but the Inquisitor rails again him for returning to upset what churchmen like himself have spent fifteen–hundred years perfecting, namely, a doctrine and mental system that enables them to exercise absolute control over the minds and souls of the masses. How dare him return to contradict this structure! The Inquisitor grows irate that the prisoner says nothing, and announces that on the morrow the prisoner will be declared a dangerous heretic and be burned at the stake before jeering crowds that hours before stood in awe at the prisoner's miracle and teachings.

The 1864 *Notes From Underground* is the first existential novel, crystallizing in a single work what would become characteristic elements of existential fiction centering on an alienated protagonist given to tangled interior interlocutions and obsessively lured by the world and its destructive social entanglements. The self–described "anti–hero" and unnamed narrator in *Notes From Underground* is a restless, resentful, and involuntary solitary with no way out of the frame of mind in which he finds himself. The very first line reveals the depth of his isolation: "I am a sick man. I am an angry man. I am an unattractive man." The character anticipates protagonists in twentieth–century successors: Kafka, Hesse, Pessoa, Camus, Sartre. The narrator has trapped himself, an unnamed and faceless government clerk in a useless office from which he has resigned because of an inheritance he has already consumed. Dostoyevsky himself observed that the narrator's "tragedy lies in his consciousness of his own deformity.... I am the only one to have depicted the tragedy of the underground, made up of suffer-ing, self–torture, the consciousness of what is best and the impossibility of attaining it, and above all the firm belief of these unhappy creatures that everybody else is the same and that consequently it is not worth while trying to reform."

Dostoyevsky draws out a possible, if not unique, response to his era. He perceives the transmogrification of Romantic solitude into alienation, underscoring the effects of social dissolution on individuals. The novel is a response to the bourgeois optimism of the 1863 novel *What is to Be Done?* by Nicolay Chernyshevsky, who believed that society is improved by the blossoming of human nature through faith in the reasonableness of realized self–interest.

Dostoyevsky's narrator asserts that he is innocent, the victim of injus-tice at the hands of elites and rivals. The respectable attain their positions effortlessly, ruthlessly, calling their work reasonable and within the laws of nature. And the mass of men accept these arguments, admire this class, imitate its manners. But those in the underground refuse! The narrator will neither accept nor bend, though he suffer humiliation after humiliation. He declares: "It is best to do nothing! The best thing is conscious inertia! So long live underground!"

The dilemma of the solitary is to be too worldly–wise to trust the "normal" man or woman, yet achingly clinging to an interdependence on them. For the narrator, obsession is dysfunction, acting out his bitterness or resentment in a social circle. Dostoyevsky's protagonist highlights the experience of social intercourse as utter fiasco. The narrator concludes that solitude, underground, doing nothing in the social sense of action, is better in the long run because there isn't anything else, because there is nothing to be done. Clinging to the hope—or dream—that something will change keeps the solitary sane, even if that something will never occur.

Friedrich Nietzsche

Friedrich Nietzsche (1844–1900) is one of the most forceful writers of modern times, influencing philosophy, creative arts, literature, and politics. His understanding of solitude and his presentation of the solitary as a new thinker on the horizon of history merits his stature at the close of the nineteenth century. Influenced by Schopenhauer's defense of solitude as personal temperament, Nietzsche enriches and extends solitude into an integral aspect of psychical and creative life, not abstractly philosophical but an existential state of being. At the same time, Nietzsche utilizes literary devices and layers of creative masks or personae, complex, provocative, and easily misconstrued.

If his ideas make Nietzsche an inevitable solitary, so do his physical maladies and irritable personality. Like Schopenhauer, he is conscious of his psychological isolation, dubbing himself the "hermit of Sils–Maria" (the Swiss residence of his summers, year–round during his last ten years of lucidity). Like Schopenhauer, too, Nietzsche is a master of the aphorism. In his 1881 book *Daybreak*, he affirms: "I go into solitude so as not to drink out of everybody's cistern. When I am among the many I live as the many do, and I do not think I really think. After a time it always seems as if they want to banish my self from myself and rob me of my soul." And in *Ecce Homo* (1888, published posthumously), he writes, "One must avoid chance and outside stimuli as much as possible; a kind of walling oneself in belongs among the foremost instinctive precautions of spiritual pregnancy." Also in the same work: "I am solitude become man." Elsewhere, Nietzsche writes of his need for "absolute solitude" and of solitude as "recovery," safeguarding what Carl Jung would call one's "hidden aspect."

For Nietzsche, solitude must be the basis of a philosophy of life, neither systematic nor subjective, the adherent being not a solitary first but a "free spirit," an Übermensch, Higher Man or Overman, among what he calls (in *Beyond Good and Evil*) "born, sworn, jealous friends of solitude." The philosopher of solitude, analogous to a member of the ancient Greek Academy or Stoa, challenges traditional thought and morality, but also maintains a clear ethos. The representative of this philosophy looks inward, dismissing societal interests as the distraction of those lacking the ability or will to pursue a thorough examination of self necessary to cultivating solitude.

The solitary arouses the resentment of society, which is why society criticizes and isolates the solitary. As an example, Nietzsche points to the persecution of the Christian mystics by Church authorities. In *Thus Spoke Zarathustra* Nietzsche writes that human beings are the cruelest of animals, conjuring tragedies, bullfights, crucifixions, and hells against humanity. In contrast, he identifies characteristics of the free spirit: independence from society and fatherland, from biases, science, even detachment from one's virtues, the latter being a check on the ego and a balance to conserve oneself. Our truest virtues are courage, insight, sympathy, and solitude.

All society makes one impure, Nietzsche argues. He inveighs vigorously against authority, tyranny, society, and popular morality because society constantly attempts to destroy individual self–esteem and capture the individual for its own uses. The result is alienation and fragmentation of self. The tension between self and society is turned by society into the conflict of selves against selves, for society's own nefarious purposes. Yet Nietzsche does not consider himself "preaching" to anyone who does not already perceive solitude as wisdom towards which to work.

Nietzsche experimented with philosophies and personae in his earliest writings, as mentioned. The dramatic characters of Zarathustra and the hermit in *Thus Spoke Zarathustra* (1883) and the madman in *Joyful Wisdom* (1881, also translated as "The Gay Science") are the most representative of Nietzschean personae. They represent Nietzsche himself.

Zarathustra is not the historical Zoroaster but a counterpart, perhaps chosen by Nietzsche as the first historical founder of a religion, or because of the irony of inverting the god of morals— Zoroaster's Ahura Mazda—for the god of nature, Angra Mainyu. Or perhaps the bombastic tones of the *Avesta*, the *Gathas*, and Zoroastrian scriptures appealed to him.

Nietzsche portrays Zarathustra as a religious prophet with Biblical overtones, a Moses descending from the mountain with a new vision for humanity and a new set of tablets. With Zarathustra, Nietzsche evolves the notion of self–transcendence and transvaluation, methods of self–control and individual achievement culminating in the Übermensch or Overman. Yet Zarathustra presents a benign, productive will to power, a sparse and unassuming figure among other people, much like Nietzsche himself. The creative use of a persona or mask like Zarathustra allows Nietzsche to express his ideas at the moment. This style makes the work a monument of philosophical originality.

Zarathustra and a hermit are the characters of the "Prologue." Zarathustra renounces his solitude and descends the mountain to share his wisdom. His first encounter is with a forest hermit, who recognizes Zarathustra and comments on his changed attitude: "No stranger to me is this wanderer. He passed through here many years ago. Zarathustra, he was called, but he has changed." The hermit declares that Zarathustra once carried his ashes into the mountains but now carries fire into the valley, that he is awakened but goes to the land of the sleeping, that he has lived in the sea but now comes ashore. When Zarathustra replies that he loves humanity, the hermit answers that he himself entered solitude because he loves God, not man. He advises Zarathustra not to go to men but to animals and to stay in the forest. Zarathustra asks the hermit what he does in the forest, and the hermit replies that he makes and sings hymns before God. Zarathustra says he must hurry on, bringing humanity a gift. The hermit asks what he takes but Zarathustra demurs. They laugh and part from one another. Alone again, Zarathustra wonders to himself. "Can it be that this old saint in the forest has not yet heard? God is dead!"

The four volumes of *Thus Spoke Zarathustra* are a dramatic elaboration of Nietzsche's philosophical explorations of the late nineteen–century cultural reality that religion is no longer the animating force of society. Zarathustra reveals a philosophy of life based on "love of earth" and the vitality of life and thought. Zarathustra is confounded by the reality that society and the masses cannot receive or embrace his insights, not only because of their turpitude but because they cannot transcend themselves or identify with a meaning other than what the inherited culture and social mores give them. Zarathustra owns that when he first came to men, he committed the great folly of hermits: going to the marketplace.

In short, Zarathustra (like Nietzsche) will share his teaching with everyone, with anyone who will listen. But now Zarathustra knows better. In the marketplace, everyone believes that each is equal and rejects the suggestion of becoming a higher soul. Zarathustra warns the higher soul to flee the marketplaces: "Flee, my friend, into solitude." Solitude is wilderness, contrasted with cities where people are smug and sluggish, and the powerful exhibit the three vices of voluptuousness, passion for power, and selfishness. The higher soul calls for "the courage of hermits and eagles," a courage that is "subtle, spiritual, and intellectual." That supreme courage must be summoned in order to accept the necessity of passing through the "seven solitudes," (variously interpreted, as in the chapter titles of Ralph Harper's 1965 book *The Seven Solitudes*, as "The Night of Absolutes," "Self–Isolation," "Hidden Inwardness," "Excursion into Chaos," "The Destruction of God," "The Great Noon," and the "Journey from Paradise").

The seven solitudes, whether viewed as afflictions or challenges, constitute shame and silence before great thought, loss of all ground, searching, absence of friends, highest responsibility, the going–beyond morality to embrace the perspective of eternity, and, finally, convalescence. Such is the inheritance of any solitary, but especially the solitary embarking on a quest for truth, with convalescence as the last stage of reconciliation with that truth.

Without God or society, Nietzsche's higher soul is thrust into existential and necessary solitude, but learns to laugh and to dance. Nietzsche's prophet and hermit are presented without trace of satire, derision, or criticism. They are the only genuine ascetics among the fallen idols, and in his *Genealogy of Morals* (1887), Nietzsche affirms: "All honor to the ascetic ideal insofar as it is honest ... so long as it believes in itself and does not play tricks on us."

Self–transcendence or transvaluation is necessary because contemporary culture is not animated by religion but by power, greed, corruption, and violence. But it is not a matter of restoring what Nietzsche declares to be myth and delusion. He is keenly aware—like his Zarathustra character and unlike the people in the marketplace or the bourgeoisie of his *fin–de–siecle*—that something must replace God or the Western world will collapse morally, and take the rest of the world with it.

That set of new and necessary values will not emerge nor be comprehendible to the entire culture. Humanity teeters on the brink of this horrible realization, as the story of the madman in *Joyful Wisdom* shows. The madman combines the ancient Greek Cynic philosopher Diogenes with Nietzsche's apprehension of culture. The madman is another persona expressing Nietzsche's own ideas. The madman's message is met by the same obtuseness of the marketplace denizens experienced by Zarathustra, with dismissive arrogance and religious skepticism. Like Zarathustra, the madman realizes that his message cannot be brought to the marketplace.

One morning the madman, carrying a lit lantern, runs into the marketplace, crying out over and over that he seeks God. Those in the marketplace do not believe in God. The madman provokes their laughter. They shout and jeer, asking him if God is lost like a child or is hiding in fear, has emigrated, or is away on a voyage. The madman booms out: "Where is God? I will tell you. We have killed him, you and I. We are all murderers." He speaks of the signs of God's death: the dimming of the sun, the emptiness of space, the growing cold, the night closing in. He asks those in the market if they do not yet hear the gravediggers burying God, not yet smell the divine putrefaction, for gods, too, die and decompose. So what will the murderers do now? How will they cleanse their knives of blood, what water can do it, what atonement? Or will they become gods themselves and appear worthy of the murder?

The madman falls silent, staring back at his listeners. They gape in astonishment. Hearing no reply, the madman throws down the lantern, shattering it. He mutters that he has come too soon, that the people do not understand, that the news has not reached their ears, like light from a star not yet reaching the earth, though they have done this themselves. The reader realizes that this version of Diogenes is contemporary: the madman quits the marketplace and enters the churches, striking up the *requiem aeternam deo*, "eternal rest to God."

Thus Nietzsche addresses the inevitable link between God and morals, concluding in *Genealogy of Morals* that "Nothing is true, everything is permitted," echoing Dostoyevsky's persona in *The Brothers Karamazov* who states, "Everything is permitted." Nietzsche did not read Dostoyevsky's novel, but the two prophetic visions converge. Nietzsche is not a formal atheist or nihilist gloating about the death of God, for he is neither engaged with the details of theology nor optimistic about the liberation that science promises. The solitary Übermensch is intent to rescue wise spirits from a godless world wherein the powerful abandon the veneer of morals and society becomes more wretched.

CHAPTER 10

EREMITISM AND SOLITUDE:
EARLY TWENTIETH CENTURY

Eremitism and solitude in the early twentieth century West expand quickly throughout prominent thinking and writing in the West, inspired by romantic nostalgia in Anglo–Catholic Britain, by pessimism and thematic solitude throughout the continent during a fitful era of social crisis and war, and by a mixture of both moods in the United States.

54. Eremitism in British Literature

Anglo–Catholic nostalgia about hermits persisted into the turn of the twentieth century. In an 1893 essay titled "An Hour With the Hermits," the Irish travel writer Marybella Macaulay recounts a visit to an unnamed monastery of hermits near Corduba, Spain. She recalls the atmosphere of antiquity about the city, the ascent on donkeys up a precipitous mountain path to the monastery, and a guided tour through the novitiate building, where skulls are prominently displayed. Silence is strictly observed. Each hermit has a cell, the monks meeting only at Mass. Sleep is taken from five to midnight. Each hermit studies a practical skill, and tends a garden from which extra fruit is sold for the common purse. Macaulay visits the cemetery. The allotted hour of visiting time ends. She expresses both pity for the austere lives of the hermits and gratitude for their piety.

Just a few years later, travel writer Herbert Vivian (1865–1940) retraced
Macaulay's journey in an 1899 essay with more detail, titled "Sons of the
Wilderness: Hermit Monks of Sierra Morena, Cordoba, Spain." The tradi-
tionalist Vivian adhered to Jacobitism, a movement advocating restoration
of the line of Catholic king James II, overthrown in 1688. Though his details
echo Macauley's, down to the bishop's permission and the tinkling bell for
Mass, Vivian reveals both awe and discomfort, as when he recounts seeing
what he calls "weird scenes," such as a hermit

> praying in most absolute solitude before a skull set upon a rock…
> remaining motionless for endless minutes amid the deathless
> silence of Nature. The scene carries us back into the Dark Ages,
> and I know not which is grimmest—the mocking expression of
> the skull or the derisive gaiety of the palms and rose bushes in
> the background. A bell tinkles in the distance, and the rapt hermit
> rises slowly from his knees, with a strange, far away joy lighting up
> his rugged face. And I return to Cordoba.

In *The Spirit of Place, and Other Essays* (1899), Catholic writer Alice Meynell
(1847–1922) reflects on solitude and place, identifying the solitudes offered
by settings but often overlooked or missed as opportunities for reflection.
She anticipates the subject of *The Poetics of Space*, by Gaston Bachelard (first
published 1958), but superficially. Her essay "Solitude" drifts and wanders.

Less tolerant than the Catholic Meynell is the Congregationalist popularizer Jonathan Brierley (1843–1914), whose essay "The Solitaries" in his
1906 book *Religion and Experience* sums up solitude as rejection and isolation
before God and the world, as experienced by Pascal and Wordsworth, to
be remedied by Christian faith.

Two famous English Catholic writers of this period are Hilaire Belloc
(1870–1953) and G. K. Chesterton (1865–1936). Hilaire Belloc was a polemical apologist for the conservative Catholicism of his day, and an inveterate
traveller, as reflected in his 1908 essay "On A Hermit Who I Knew." In
the Apennines, Belloc encounters a man dwelling in a cave overlooking
a city, who receives the traveler hospitably, exchanging details of life and
thought. Belloc presses for the man's religious sentiment several times, but
the hermit demurs.

Like Belloc, Chesterton was a polemical Catholic apologist. His 1935 essay

"The Case for Hermits," mentions Diogenes and St. Jerome as solitaries craving an audience; Chesterton adds obtrusive comments about child–rearing and Communism. Both essays are throwaways for a devoted audience.

In a 1914 Father Brown short story ("The Fairy Tale of Father Brown"), Chesterton presents the hermit Heinrich at the heart of an historical mystery in a small Balkans–like principality. The hermit is one of three brothers in an assassination plot, but the reader must figure out if Heinrich became a hermit to escape the plot or out of guilt for his role in it.

In a rambling 1894 essay titled "Hermits, Ancient and Modern," Charles Dickens, Jr. (1837–1896), editor of his father's literary serial *All The Year Round: A Weekly Journal*, anticipates the mediocre essays of Belloc and Chesterton. The author is intent to confirm the continued existence of hermits from anecdotes of contemporary Londoners, foreshadowing Edith Sitwell's eccentrics with his own roster: a gentleman living in a garret, an Irish hermit found upon his death to hold significant investments, and a woman in black dubbed a "lady anchorite" and "votaress."

Arthur Conan Doyle (1859–1930) is famous for his fictional creation Sherlock Holmes, but Doyle himself hoped to be remembered for his historical fiction, including short stories set in the waning Roman Empire. The sympathetic 1911 "The Coming of the Huns," included in Doyle's 1922 collection, *The Last of the Legions and Other Tales of Long Ago*, features an old Christian hermit Simon Melas dwelling in an obscure cave on a Danubian hillside, living out his eremitic days. He happens upon a fellow–hermit Paul who is a Donatist and anti–Trinitarian, and they fall out. Simon also quarrels with an articulate Roman officer assigned to a nearby outpost, familiar with Plato, Stoicism, and Marcus Aurelius, whom the old hermit scorns. One day, strange dark forms appear on the endless plains to the east: ponied warriors on the move, a massive Hun army. The old hermit pursues decidedly unhermit–like actions in response.

British novelist John Cowper Powys (1872–1963) may best be known for unpersuasive novels revolving around characters struggling with versions of solitude. However, his 1933 nonfiction book *A Philosophy of Solitude* refreshingly draws from Stoicism, Taoism, Romanticism, and Nietzsche, with occasional references to German idealism and pessimism. Though not original, Powys explores the psychology of versions of solitude. For example, he advises couples that "True lovers are twin–hermits, carrying each other, in their separate imaginations." "What is advisable for us now," he pleads, "is to cultivate some definite substitute for the lives of hermits and hermit–saints." The book is a modest call to revive historical eremitism serving a new goal.

Theodore Francis Powys (1875–1953), the younger brother of John Cowper Powys, published his first book in 1916, *The Soliloquy of a Hermit* (*Soliloquies …* in the 1918 edition). The work is an extended collection of reflections representing Powys's pessimism—not Schopenhauer's but Nietzsche's, not that of Christianity but that of the historical Jesus. He dislikes the vengeful God of the Old Testament, and admits that sometimes he appears to be an infidel, sometimes a Christian, and sometimes a heathen. The simple life is the deeper life, Powys writes.

> I, too, for a long while, have looked round this corner and that corner for God's secret, and at last I have discovered that I can do very well if I loiter through my life without knowing any secret at all. … In the old days when I held my head in the sand of mystery, I thought that something wonderful would happen to me; and now I believe that the most wonderful thing is that nothing wonderful happens. We are, just as we are, and nothing else.

Some day, Powys says, mystics will put aside their pens speculating about God's mysteries and instead busy themselves all day long "peacefully planting cabbages."

Powys's romp appreciates life, nature, and simplicity in the stars, the fields, the trees, and the earth. He shuns society because it is always ruled by the mob, by hatred and hypocrisy, that which put Jesus to death. Of books he likes Wesley and Bunyan, but Hardy and Nietzsche were in his library early, and later influences ranged from Jacob Boehme to Pascal, Spinoza, and Simone Weil. Powys is eclectic, tapping themes not to be developed in England until decades later, only after the angst of world wars and existentialism. As a hermit Powys reflects a serene confidence in nature and in the necessity of harmonizing self with the natural world, the testament of a sensitive soul unique to the early twentieth century.

Powys followed *Soliloquy* with a number of soon–neglected short stories, novels, and fables, culminating in the writer's 1936 decision to quit writing. Powys lived alone in a rural area of Dorset, seldom venturing to the village but seen about his grounds in small tasks.

Solitude in early twentieth–century English literature is dominated by Joseph Conrad (1857–1924). Conrad's exotic settings of Africa, Asia, and the sea are compelling metaphors for social isolation from familiar Western settings. Further, the characters in his novels and short stories find themselves in these settings either already disposed to isolation or lured into painful realization of an alienating solitude haunting their ambitions. While the characters are personae of Conrad's own physical ailments and depression, they also reflect his personal philosophy.

Conrad's characters correspond to Melville's "isolatoes" (though Conrad did not read Melville). George in *The Arrow of Gold* describes himself as "the completest possible stranger in the moral region... I was as much of a stranger as the most hopeless castaway." Captain Anthony in *Chance* is described as "a hermit withdrawn from a wicked world, ... [one of the] silent, solitary men, the voluntary, passionate outcasts of their kind." Marlow (in *Lord Jim*) glimpses the depths of solitude in Jim's story, "a sense of utter solitude" so deep that "all I had lately seen, all I had heard, and the very human speech itself, seemed to have passed out of existence."

Conrad depicts an alienation with no alternative but individualism, though this insight is not a solace. As Razumov (in *Under Western Eyes*) puts it: "I am independent—and therefore perdition is my lot." In *The Nigger of the Narcissus*, the empathy of the ship's crew toward the dying Black man is a temporary breakthrough, the possibility of a true solidarity that may persist into societal existence on land, but in Conrad's view is bound to disintegrate given all the other forces of human nature. Defying their captain, the *Narcissus* crew is "lost, alone, forgetful and doomed."

In *Heart of Darkness*, the darkness is the jungle and primitive peoples, but Westerners carry their own darkness into this setting, projecting their own shadow desires, ultimately clashing with reality. Set free from Western morals, the white man in alien settings is abandoned to excess, unchecked by peers and authority, experiencing collapse and loss of self–control. Only solidarity, faith, and loyalty can rescue isolation. Yet the effort is itself difficult, obstructed by a great psychological weight, as the character Heyst in *Victory* admits, for "he had made up his mind to retire from the world in hermit fashion, yet he was irrationally moved by this sense of loneliness which had come to him in the hour of renunciation."

Conrad argues for a moral fate linking humanity, an "invincible conviction of solidarity that knits together the loneliness of innumerable hearts." Our ills are retribution from a blind fate. Like Melville, Conrad might conclude that we are all isolatoes. As he puts it (in *Heart of Darkness*): "We dream as we live—alone."

55. Eremitism in European Literature

Franz Kafka

Perhaps Franz Kafka (1883–1924) is the most representative writer of the first half of the twentieth century. Kafka projects into his fiction lives of social estrangement and profound solitude. His personal sense of monotonous diurnal loss and helplessness becomes a creative resource for the production of novels and short stories (most of which were published posthumously). This inner process drove Kafka to write incessantly. In a 1913 letter to his fiancée Felice Bauer, Kafka writes: "I need solitude for my writing; not 'like a hermit'—that wouldn't be enough—but like a dead man." In *The Trial, The Castle, Metamorphosis*, and other fiction, Kafka identifies haunting images of unrelieved alienation.

Of the many representative stories, two reflecting the depth of intractable solitude are characteristic existential fables or parables. In a fragment from "The Great Wall of China" titled "An Imperial Message," the dying emperor entrusts his faithful servant with a message. The messenger must cross interminable passageways, corridors, stairways, and courtyards, push through thick crowds, interminable multitudes, passing these through still more courtyards, stairways, steps, and multitudes. You are waiting by the window at evening for the message that will not come.

In "Before the Law," a man from the country has come to the door of the Law, seeking admittance, redress, and resolution. The doorkeeper denies admission but tells the man he may gain permission later. The door is open but there are interminable doors and doorkeepers beyond, and the doorkeeper warns him not to attempt to enter. After a while, the man petitions again, in vain. Now he waits sitting on a stool. The doorkeeper occasionally engages him in polite conversation. Days and years pass, and the man clings to his place, asking why no one else has also come like himself seeking admission to the Law. The doorkeeper replies that this door was only for him, the petitioning man, and now the doorkeeper is going to shut the door.

Rainer Maria Rilke

Austrian poet Rainer Maria Rilke (1875–1926) is a paragon of solitude on three different levels: in his personal interests, in his writings, and in his daily life. Rilke notes that his early mentor, sculptor Auguste Rodin, was a solitary before becoming famous, after which he became a solitary again. Rilke himself was a loner, wanderer, and social misfit, the hapless "poet" of Sigmund Freud's essay "On Transience," though Freud makes light of the poet's despondency by asserting that better things are in the future.

In his modest first work *The Book of Hours* (1905), Rilke laments lost religious faith, idealizing the stark Christianity of Russia in images of poverty and simplicity contrasted with European decadence. Translator Robert Hass has noted that the early Rilke saw the vast steppes of Russia as a symbol of dissipation of self, later coming to use the contrasting image of a hut as the consolidation of actualization. Early Rilke wrestled, too, with the conflict between his lack of empathy for society's masses while himself obliged to dote on the detestable wealthy class that appreciated the arts.

In the posthumously published *Letters to a Young Poet*, Rilke tries to resolve the dilemma by identifying solitude as the necessary path of creativity. "Love your solitude," he writes to the aspiring poet, advising him to craft spirit and mind around solitude, a vast solitude in which the self can walk for hours without meeting anyone. With time, "your solitude will be a hold and home for you even amid very unfamiliar conditions," a solitude to which one must cling, then cultivate. "The necessary thing is after all but this: solitude, great inner solitude." If the poet has nothing to share with others, he should share the things of nature: night, winds, streets, trees, animals, things full of being.

With *The Book of Images* [or *Pictures*] (1906), Rilke elaborates on images of solitude as a symbolist: weary angels wandering silently, children who know their rooms intimately, lonely travelers, a solitary tree silhouetted against the sky. Among images are moving portraits of social alienation: a blind man, an idiot, a dwarf, a waif, all in a pall of melancholy. The poem "Lament" adds more striking images of solitude: a dead star, a stopped clock, a passing voice full of tears. "All things are long past and far," writes Rilke. In "Autumn," solitude is irrevocable, not involuntary, not imposed but recognized; in "Solitude," it is palpable. The solitary is like a stranger returning to a disremembered place, not recognizing anyone.

With *New Poems* (1907) comes a tactile sensibility influenced by his years as secretary for Rodin. Rilke now writes of things felt rather than of feelings, objects such as panthers, swans, flowers, paintings, and statues, exploring his responses, sifting them, returning to the poetic muse for meaning. In "Let This Darkness Be A Bell Tower," (in *Sonnets to Orpheus*) Rilke projects a tower representing darkness, annihilation, and the possibility of transcendence from suffering. "The Buddha in Glory" openly conveys a luminous mystical sense of transcendence.

Rilke's grand vision is in his last work, a set of ten poems comprising the 1923 *Duino Elegies*. The premise of the *Duino Elegies* is foreshadowed in Rilke's earlier concern about the aloneness of human beings in a god–forsaken universe, where memory and patterns of intuition raise the sensitive consciousness to a realization of solitude. The earlier elegies evoke the presence of angels as surrogates for the absence of God. Rilke centers death and alienating solitude on our will to live. The fulfilled angels are those who die young, without consciousness of fate: the child and the hero, but also those who bear intimate relationship as two solitudes, mutually respectful. Ultimately, says Rilke, we belong to the earth and must love it—not belong to the contrived world of society, not (to use a series of his images) to the street jugglers, billboards, and carnivals, but to the blue and yellow gentians, the startled bird, the catkins hanging from the hazel trees, the raindrops falling on dark earth.

Hermann Hesse

The earliest works of German–born writer Hermann Hesse (1887–1962) reflect the individual's search for meaning: aesthetic, ethical, and psychological. This theme is particularly vivid in Hesse's youthful fairy tales, written in the first two decades of the twentieth century.

In "The Forest–Dweller," a young man defies the prevarications of elders to venture outside of tribal boundaries; discovering that he can survive after all, he never returns. In "The Painter," a man takes up painting as an avocation. Away from his apartment, he returns to discover crowds eagerly milling about to see the work of the now–famous artist. The crowd misinterprets the paintings, misunderstands their themes, even misidentifies depicted objects, but they avidly buy and trade the works. The painter quits the place in disgust and does not return.

In "Faldum," a stranger appears at the village fair performing magic that grants anyone whatever they wish, first arousing vanity but progressively stirring malice, greed, and violence among the townspeople who demand their desire be fulfilled. A deeply affected young observer wishes to be far away and as lofty as a mountain. He becomes exactly that, arising just outside the old town, dispassionately watching it grow and decline over the years, watching the forests and their denizens, watching the river and clouds from his welcomed solitude and disengagement. Finally, he senses his consciousness wane in the grand course of the sun, moon, and stars overhead.

A story from Hesse's early period, titled "The Wolf," (1907), presents the plight of a small group of misfits, a hated pack of wolves, eking out existence in a harsh wintry mountain with the whole of (human) society set against them, eager to exterminate them. A solitary wolf survives the pack as long as possible. In his 1908 story "The Field Devil," Hesse recreates the story of the hermits St. Paul of Thebes and St. Anthony, the latter plagued by the Devil and his minions, satyrs, centaurs, and other beasts pressed to serve evil. The little field devil, a small satyr, secretly admires Paul, who rejects the little satyr's inquiries because of his appearance. After witnessing the inner joy of the hermits despite their worldly deprivations, the little satyr decides to join Paul in his recent death, stops eating, and quickly weakens. The raven that fed Paul brings him bread, and the little field devil dies happy. Far later, when other hermits come to inhabit the area, they find the robed little corpse and are about to bury it properly when they recoil and flee, noticing the little horns and cloven feet.

Hesse's 1920 book *Wandering: Notes and Sketches* ("Wanderung: Aufzeichnungen") is written as fiction but reads like autobiography. The wanderer passes houses, trees, farms, skies, his pithy thoughts revelatory of a solitary's soul. Wandering is a type of eremitism, a solitary effort, indeed, an avocation, no mere amusement. In a mountain pass, the narrator reveals that wandering renews his vigor for life, that though he is alone he does not suffer from loneliness. Nostalgia and romanticism hover. The wanderer, like a *sadhu*, or more like a dreamer or sleepwalker, dissolves temptations of the world and the senses. At each crossroad, encountering a bridge, a farm, a lake, a mountain, the wanderer's reflections deepen. At one point he makes a telling distinction between the historical hermit and the romantic stereotype of literature, averring that real hermits are solitary, not stealing away from life out of weakness. To the narrator, Beethoven and Nietzsche are hermit exemplars. Hermits, too, possess an insight lacking to conventional believers, for they pray in natural settings. To wander is to be solitary, to be restless. Yet the mind is not alone but full of sights, sounds, and haunting memories.

Published in 1926, *Siddhartha* falls between Hesse's major novels, each depicting the search for understanding through experience, a solitary and archetypal Western quest. The search is resolved tenuously in *Siddhartha*, the story of a young man's enlightenment quest parallel and juxtaposed to the historical Gautama. Like Gautama, Siddhartha partakes of a worldly life and vices typical of Western society, struggling to resolve his entrapment. The novel's true model of enlightenment, more than the fictionalized Gautama, is the character Vasudeva, the ferryman–hermit. Siddhartha is on the cusp of world–weariness (Hesse uses the word "nausea"), what the character calls *maya*, or illusion. But Vasudeva prevails, with his absolute attachment to nothing worldly, with his profound silence and eremitic example. Vasudeva is a widower–hermit living alone in the forest. He becomes to Siddhartha as a god, a bodhisattva, a savior.

Hesse returned to eremitic themes in his last novel *The Glass Bead Game*, published in 1943. The protagonist Joseph Knecht lives in the utopian secular monastery of Castalia, its male scholars absorbed in abstract intellectual pursuits encompassing universal knowledge expressed in the glass bead game. Joseph is impressed by an old scholar called "Elder Brother" who left Castalia to dwell in Bamboo Grove and pursue Chinese philosophy and *I Ching*. Later in the novel, Joseph reflects on his time with Elder Brother, feeling himself "surrounded by the hermit's atmosphere," thrilling to past memories of the hermit's hut, his yarrow stalks, his meticulous garden, absorbing the hermit's "neat, pedantic and wise Sinicism."

Joseph becomes disenchanted with the parochialism of Castalia but is simultaneously lured by the world, where he thinks his intellect can be of value. The novel ends with his ignominious death almost as soon as he enters the world. Herein lies the novel's eremitic lesson.

Hesse also presents his protagonist as an ancient desert hermit in an included addenda, a short story of a previous life, titled "The Father Confessor," set in the city of Gaza in the days of St. Hilarion. A seasoned old hermit and a young hermit Joseph meet in the byways of the desert, the young scrupulous hermit learning wisdom from the wise and practical old man.

Fernando Pessoa

Portuguese writer Fernando Pessoa (1888–1935) was a prominent modernist literary figure in early twentieth–century Europe. His poetry associates him with avant–garde literary circles. But Pessoa is best revealed in prose, specifically *The Book of Disquiet*, written in the 1910s and 1920s, left in thousands of literary fragments published posthumously, thus a book not influencing contemporaries but uniquely reflective of the era and the theme of solitude.

Like Kafka a bureaucrat, Pessoa, too, reflects a radical introspection, alienation, solitude, and estrangement characterized by a droll sense of tedium and lethargy, all written in scintillating prose. From the opening pages, Pessoa tells us that he writes alone in his quiet room, ever alone but voicing the solitude of the thousands who ache for self-expression, an affirmation beyond mere hopes and dreams. Pessoa echoes the ancient skeptics, adding a decidedly existential slant. He is no Romantic, disparaging the impulsiveness, the excessive emotionalism, the naive clinging to the possible, the confusion between need and desire, ultimately, the turning inside out of the privacy and solitude of the soul promoted by Romanticism. Consciousness tolerates no illusion. Metaphysics is exhausted.

Pessoa asserts that he has always sought how not to act, holding in scorn the aspirant to action and even the aspirant to transcend action. Only abdicating action altogether is best. Renunciation, doing without, is the mystics' path. Denying absolute reality is the Buddha's path. Denying relative reality is Christ's path.

Pessoa advocates inaction and withdrawal not as equivocation but as the greatest option available to human beings. Freedom to withdraw from others is freedom from money, society, love, glory, curiosity. "To be born free is the greatest splendor of man, making the humble hermit superior to kings, even to the gods, who are self–sufficient by their power but not by scorning it."

Acting in the world requires having no sensibilities, no feelings, no sympathy, ruthlessness and precision, the very attributes of the successful and worldly: captains of business, industry, and politics, religious idealists, even poets and artists. Pessoa admits that he is not bold enough to embrace bohemianism; in his case the results would be absurd or impossible.

Pessoa's psychology of disengagement and solitude consists of dreaming, imagining a childhood of farms, rural paths, groves of trees, clear skies. But dreams are not transformative. Dreams offer no solace. But dreams do constitute the landscapes of solitude, the paradigms of understanding. "All I asked of life is what Diogenes asked of Alexander: not to stand in the way of the sun." Pessoa admits "there were things I wanted, but I was denied any reason for wanting them. As for what I found, it would have been better to have found it in real life."

Ultimately Pessoa admits he cannot assuage the deep emotional distress, the "disquiet," that plagues him. In lucid moments, he recognizes himself in stark terms: that throughout life, he had been viewed by others as an intruder or stranger, more colorfully as an overturned bucket, a wheelless cart, something forgotten by some god or other, nothing but Destiny's ripped–up papers, his life a tragedy booed off stage by the gods.

Perhaps Pessoa is not a solitary personality destined to reconcile the creative forces he held with the inheritance of self and circumstances. Or perhaps his very situation and expression, unflinchingly open, is his intended bequest to anonymous future readers. Or, again, perhaps for Pessoa, life could be nothing more than, as he put it in a letter, a deep and calm depression.

The Decadents

The trajectory of several French writers after Flaubert leads to the designation of Decadents. Their focus was on an aesthetics of self, with divergent results. Anticipated by Baudelaire—still a Romantic, strong–willed and asser-tive—the decadents include Jors–Karl Huysman (1848-1907), Paul Valery (1871-1945), Henri Barbusse (1873-1935), and Marcel Proust (1871-1922).

In Huysman's *A rebours* ("Against Nature" or "Against the Grain," 1884), the protagonist Jean De Esseintes, born of impoverished noble parents, sells his inherited rural estate to live in a shabby Paris flat where he can pursue aesthetic pleasures in solitude, like a modern Thebaid. Benignity of nature and wilderness is now banished as too frightening, inverting the historical and romantic's solitary quest. But banished, too, is participation in the city and modern life, the bane of historical solitaries.

Paul Valery's eponymous character in *Monsieur Teste* (1896) similarly with-draws to his room, refusing to deal with society, though he continues to ruin others through the stock exchange, becoming a "monster" of arrogance and self–centered solitude, insisting that money is the animating spirit of society.

The narrator of Henri Barbusse's *L'Enfer* (1908) parallels Huysman's Des Esseintes. A young man from the country comes to the city, becomes a faceless bureaucrat, and lives in a hotel where he spies on the couple in the next room through a hole in the wall, coming to conceive a solipsistic world in his circumscribed consciousness.

Finally, in Marcel Proust's languid and lengthy seven–volume *A la recherche du temps perdu* ("Remembrance of Things Past" or "In Search of Lost Time," 1913–1927), the atmosphere hovers around individuals' incapability to communicate, and the narrator's meticulous recording of life events that ever requires "an inviolable solitude; reading or dreaming, secret tears or paroxysms of desire." No reasonable interpretation of solitude is capable any longer within the decadent's aesthetics of self.

William Butler Yeats

Irish poet William Butler Yeats (1865–1939) composed four poems with hermit themes. The earliest is the familiar "The Lake Isle of Innisfree," published in his 1893 collection *The Rose*. The opening lines announce withdrawal, reclusion:

> I will arise and go now, and go to Innisfree,
> And a small cabin build there, of clay and wattles made;
> Nine bean-rows will I have there, a hive for the honey-bee,
> And live alone in the bee-loud glade ...

The lapping water of the lake, concludes the poem, is the rhythm of the universe, heard within the "heart's deep core."

"Three Hermits" was published in the 1914 collection *Responsibilities and Other Poems*. Quiet humor underlies the situation of the three hermits, sitting together seaside. The first hermit regrets falling asleep in prayer, bemoaning the failure of holy men destined for rebirth, but the second replies that their love of God is sufficient to save them, destined to return as a poet, king, or a "witty, lovely lady." The third hermit, "giddy" at a hundred years of age, merely "sang unnoticed like a bird."

"Symbols" was published in 1933, part of *The Winding Stair*. The poem evokes images of the Tarot:

> A storm–beaten old watch–tower,
> A blind hermit rings the hour.
> All–destroying sword–blade still
> Carried by the wandering fool.
> Gold–sewn silk on the sword–blade,
> Beauty and fool together laid.

The burning watch–tower of tarot card 17 is an ancient symbol of destruction. The swords of the minor arcana are not flaming here but nevertheless abet annihilation; a flaming sword is that which drove humanity out of

paradise. The wandering fool of tarot card 1 carries a walking stick, but the
poem assigns a sword to him: the fool wandering into danger with a horrible
weapon. The hermit prophesies destruction given the flaming tower. Is the
hermit blind in the sense of unwise, wrong, or physically unaware? In the
tarot card 9, the hermit is Diogenes seeking a wise person, never finding
one. With Yeats, a blind hermit is the psychological self prophesying a
greater doom, and a personal one.

Commentators have considered the poem as part of Yeats's larger
depiction of the fate of post–colonial Ireland, but the Tarot here is used
skillfully as an historical and mythographic tool. As a member of the occultist
Golden Dawn, Yeats held an abiding interest in the esoteric.

The poem "Meru" was published in 1935 in *A Full Moon in March*, as
part of "Supernatural Songs." Meru refers to the sacred mountain of India;
the poem conjures the insight of hermit wisdom over the passage of time:

> Civilisation is hooped together, brought
> Under a rule, under the semblance of peace
> By manifold illusion; but man's life is thought,
> And he, despite his terror, cannot cease
> Ravening through century after century,
> Ravening, raging, and uprooting that he may come
> Into the desolation of reality:
> Egypt and Greece, good-bye, and good-bye, Rome!
> Hermits upon Mount Meru or Everest,
> Caverned in night under the drifted snow,
> Or where that snow and winter's dreadful blast
> Beat down upon their naked bodies, know
> That day bring round the night, that before dawn
> His glory and his monuments are gone.

From destruction to rebirth to destruction again is the fate of humanity.
The poem's sentiment is reminiscent of the first Christian hermit Paul's
fateful questions: "How fares the human race? Are new roofs raised in the
ancient cities? Whose empire it is that now holds sway in the world? Do
any still survive, snared in the error of demons?"

Kahlil Gibran

Lebanese–born writer Kahlil Gibran (1883–1931) lived in the United States much of his life, but his work does not build on American influences, working in the form of tales and parables. Gibran's upbringing informs him of both Christian and Muslim cultures, updated by modern philosophy and psychology. While best known for *The Prophet* and other larger works, Gibran's short fiction reveals the breadth of his insight. Five tales specifically center on hermits.

In "The Two Hermits" (from *The Madman*, 1918), the hermits live together in a skete. An earthen bowl is their only common possession. An evil spirit enters the older hermit. He goes to the younger hermit demanding that the two part. The demand saddens the young man. Seeing the old hermit's determination, however, he brings out the earthen bowl and proffers it to the old man since it cannot be divided. The latter angrily refuses it, insisting that the bowl must be divided. The young hermit accedes. The old hermit cries out angrily that the younger man will not fight.

In "The King–Hermit" (from The *Forerunner*, 1920), the narrator tells of a young man living in solitude in a mountainous forest. He had been a king but quit his throne to live in wilderness. The narrator intends to learn wisdom from this man. He ventures to the place and soon finds the solitary. They exchange greetings. The narrator asks the solitary for his story, and he obliges, recounting: One day, at the window of his palace, his chamberlain was walking with an envoy. He tells the envoy that he himself is like the king, strong-tempered, enjoying robust wine and games of chance. After a turn in the garden, the pair return, the chamberlain saying that the king is like himself, a good marksman, a lover of music, one who bathes three times a day. On that day, relates the young man, he left the palace. The forest and nature are the great kingdom of fellowship and beauty. Go now to the city, the solitary tells his visitor. Watch there the people. Observe who is a king without a kingdom, who is a slave among subjects. And with that the young solitary rises and leaves.

In "Finding God" (from *The Wanderer*, 1932), two men walk in a valley. One points sympathetically to a mountainside hermitage, saying of the hermit residing there that he seeks only God, nothing of the world. The other man replies that the hermit will not find God unless he comes down and shares the joys and sorrows of the people. The first man assents politely but replies that the hermit is a good man, and that one good man's absence does better than the seeming goodness of the many.

In "The Hermit Prophet" (from *The Wanderer*, 1932), a hermit regularly goes down to the city and preaches eloquently, becoming famous. One day three men visit his hermitage. They speak of the hermit's fame, which has surely brought him much wealth. Will you not give us of your riches, they ask, for we have little. The hermit replies that he had nothing but a mat and jug of water, which they can take if they wish, but of gold or silver or anything else he had none. The three men look at the hermit with disgust. They berate him as a cheat and fraud who teaches what he himself does not do. They leave.

"The Hermit and the Beasts" (from *The Wanderer*, 1932) tells of a hermit in the hills so pure of spirit that the birds and animals visit him regularly and he speaks to them. One evening, he speaks of the virtue of love. A leopard notes to the hermit that though he speaks of love, where is his mate? The hermit says he has none, upon which the animals utter a cry, rise, and leave, wondering how the hermit could speak of what he did not know. That night the hermit wept bitterly.

"The Tempest" is an early work published posthumously in the 1947 collection *Secrets of the Heart* and represents Gibran's early conviction about the primacy of solitude. The narrator is curious about a well–born young man who left the village for a hermitage in the hills. One day, strolling the woods, a strong tempest drenches him and he happens across the hermitage. The narrator knocks and is let in by the man, who is reserved, even disdainful at the visitor's plea for shelter. They exchange few words until the man perceives his visitor's respectfulness. He lights a fire and politely brings out food and drink. Conversation is cautious. The solitary pursues the topic of solitude with measured but passionate explication about "spiritual awakening." Hours later, the hermit leaves the hut in the raging storm, telling his guest to stay the night if he wishes, while he will be away all night, unafraid of the tempest.

A bold view of solitude is *The Madman*, a collection of short stories on a single theme published in 1918 but derived from earlier uncollected writings in Arabic. The theme reflects the influence of Nietzsche, Jung, Tagore, and Blake, masterfully incorporated. The narrator has become a madman, he owns, because he no longer uses a mask in society. In "The Friend," he announces:

> The I in me, my friend, dwells in the house of silence, and therein
> it shall remain for ever more, unperceived,

unapproachable. I would not have you believe in what I say
nor trust in what I do—for my words are naught but your own
thoughts in sound and my deeds your own hopes in action. When
you say, 'The wind blows eastward'; I say, 'Yes, it does blow
eastward;' for I would not have you know that my mind does not
dwell upon the wind but upon the sea. You cannot understand my
seafaring thoughts, nor would I have you understand. I would be
at sea alone.

In "The Great Sea," Gibran artfully discloses the nature of philosophy built
upon by the personalities who would salvage the world: the pessimist who
throws salt into the sea, the optimist who throws sugar, the philanthropist
who puts dead fish back into the sea, the mystic who traces his shadow on
the sand even as the waves obliterate it, the idealist who scoops up sea–foam
to carry away in a precious jar, the realist who listens by the shore to the
roar of the sea from a shell put to his ear, and the puritan whose head is
buried in the sand. There is none who can be trusted, none to whom one
can disclose any secret. The poet and his soul, witnessing these examples,
"left that sea to seek the Greater Sea."

In "The Pomegranate," the narrator lives within this fruit but the many
seeds begin jabbering their views on life and the universe until a cacophony
is raised and the narrator happily goes to live in a quince, "where the seeds
are few, and almost silent." The cacophony may be in our own heads from
listening to others or from listening to ourselves. The society of others is
as bad as the society of an undisciplined mind. There is no alternative but
to seek silence.

"On Talking" is a short chapter on silence in Gibran's famous *The Prophet*
(1923), wherein the Prophet is asked to address various topics. Talk constitutes lack of peace with thought, inability to "dwell in the solitude of your
heart," such that in much talking, "thinking is half murdered."

Eugene Ionesco

We jump from the early twentieth–century to Romanian–French writer
Eugene Ionesco (1909–1994) and his 1973 novel *Le Solitaire* ("The Solitary"
or "The Hermit"). This chronological leap caps the century's solitude themes.
Ionesco inhabits the vague literary realm between existential absurdist on
the one hand and post–modern on the other, within a political realm at

home both before and after World War II, dangling between precipitant social decline on the one hand and authoritarian collectivism on the other. The novel could have been written at *any* time in the twentieth century; compared to Ionesco's plays "The Hermit" may be more realistic.

In his 1959 absurdist drama *Rhinoceros*, Ionesco anticipates his later theme when a character tells another, "Solitude seems to oppress me. So does the company of other people."

The unnamed protagonist of *The Hermit* is adrift in modern urban society as a spectator not in control of his spirit. Unlike the existentialism of earlier writers, here is modern alienation that is at the root of late twentieth–century technological society. The hermit never studied, is no rebel. He is just a bored office worker—the occupation of Kafka, Pessoa, and Dostoyevsky's underground protagonist—afflicted by thoughts and daydreams, who quits his job after getting an inheritance. "What are my desires? That people leave me alone; that other people's desires leave me alone and don't involve me in their repercussions. What I desire most of all is not to have any desires." Still, he espies everything vigilantly, watching crowds and passers–by from a restaurant window is his amusement. He admits a sadness, dejection, weariness, even disgust with life and the world. He is afflicted by the idea that he is going to die, and jumps out of bed in the morning frightened out of his wits. He cannot stand crowds, but he cannot stand being alone. Nor can he construct relationships with others. He starts drinking to ease his panic attacks and despair, oppressed by the brunt of fear and anxiety unless he can numb himself.

Suddenly a revolution breaks out. Is it 1789? 1848? 1968?—or sometime in the future? Gunfire is heard in the city, red flashes in the night, the noise of crowds and barricades. Nearer and nearer to his apartment building comes the agitation, until the whole district is in an uproar and our protagonist is nearly wounded walking in the street. He rushes indoors, stocked up with food and drink, and pulls mattresses against the windows of his fourth–floor apartment. The revolution outside sweeps on. But within the safety of his cell grows an intimacy with solitude. "Time went by. Months went by. Years maybe.... It was rare that I had any outside contact. And then came a time when I saw no one at all." This sudden isolation brings him tranquility.

The apartment becomes a universe, a niche in a prison, a speck within galaxies. Strange mystical experiences begin, luminous skies, stars in daylight, and brilliant light, events that seem to bring the hermit purpose and meaning. For the first time he experiences happiness. "I was billions of centuries for cosmic systems. I was billions and billions of miles for people I didn't even know, for billions of people who consorted within me, who became indignant and revolted, who fought one another, loved one another, who loathed one another. Yes, all that was in me."

The revolution ends. He reenters the world. The ruins have been rebuilt. He does not recognize anyone, but it does not matter. Life returns to routine. Memories linger like a residue. He admits that if he had tried, he may have made something of life. But what would he have wanted? Suddenly a tree burgeons forth before his window, and from it a great flower rises right up to where he can reach it. Birds chirp happily. The walls fall away to reveal an endless vista of gardens, forests, a cool breeze and strong sunlight. The narrator speaks of a light within, a light that remains.

Perhaps, after all the speculation about madness, this is what people suspect is the private vision of the true hermit, this light that enters into the self and remains and justifies everything. Ionesco sketches a possibility for not just solitaries but anyone at all.

56. Philosophers of Solitude: Wittgenstein to Berdyaev

The philosophers of solitude in the twentieth century do not set out to extol solitude but are identified here based on themes of their writing. Solitude had become an intrinsic condition of the era, however, as social alienation, as modern individualism, and as potential rediscovery of a key element of philosophical thought. Reflection on solitude prepared a new basis for eremitism.

Ludwig Wittgenstein

Austrian–born philosopher Ludwig Wittgenstein (1889–1951) entered into prominence in the whirlwind academic circles of Vienna and London with his 1922 publication of *Tractatus Logico–Philosophicus*, hailed by logical positivists. The book argues that knowledge is impossible and that the self does not exist in the psychological sense, only as a logical or linguistic proposition. Critic Ernest Gellner calls the work a "poem to solitude," not the solitude of the poets but the mind–stripped atomistic individualism promoted by technology and industry in the early twentieth century.

Yet beginning in 1914 and throughout his life, as often as possible, Wittgenstein lived alone in summer in a hut in Norway, explaining his decision to Bertrand Russell that hitherto he had prostituted his time talking to intelligent people. The first years in Norway proved his most productive, culminating in the *Tractatus*.

Wittgenstein's posthumously published *Philosophical Investigations* (1953) overturned the basic assumptions of the *Tractatus*, arguing that though knowledge is attainable it is ineffable, even mystical. Did solitude time contribute to this reversal? Gellner views Wittgenstein's reversal sociologically. The solitude of the atomistic is replaced by the solitude of culture, thus reflecting the inexorable triumph of modern life.

Albert Camus & Jean–Paul Sartre

The French writers Albert Camus (1913–1960) and Jean–Paul Sartre (1905–1980) are often identified together because of their parallel existentialist themes, breakthrough literary works, and their political activism.

Camus's 1942 novel *L'etranger* (translated as "The Outsider" or "The Stranger") presents an alienated protagonist indifferent to society and overwhelmed by circumstances beyond his comprehension. Camus's first major essay, *The Myth of Sisyphus*, also published in 1942, maintained that the human search for meaning is fruitless and absurd, hence the philosophy of absurdism. Camus argues that integrity, not mere ethics, must drive individuals, wherein is to be found personal freedom and freedom from the pernicious ideologies of the era.

Camus is conscious of the role of solitude in the formation of self, applying an appreciation of solitude to the creative and intellectual potential of the individual. In an early 1939 essay describing formative physical settings, Camus writes:

> There are no more deserts. There are no more islands. Yet there is a need for them. In order to understand the world, one has to turn away from it on occasion; in order to serve men better, one has to hold them at a distance for a time. But where can one find the solitude necessary to vigor, the deep breath in which the mind collects itself and courage gauges its strength?

The theme of the absurd is explored on a larger social scale in Camus' 1947 novel *The Plague*. Plague is an event but also the very condition of existence, the only universal, according to Camus. We are obliged to identify with the plight of others, returning to the motif of integrity. The nonfiction counterpart of *The Plague*, the 1951 essay *The Rebel*, advocates not political or social revolution but a perpetual state of individual rebellion in the search for humanistic values. Has this not been the hermit's quest since antiquity?

Sartre emerged into the literary world with his 1938 novel *Nausea* (originally titled "Melancholia") wherein a young solitary cannot assign meaning to his life or work, doubting the correspondence of consciousness and the world. The insight is highlighted by a revelation occurring as he looks upon a chestnut tree—though not an allusion to the Buddha's Bodhi tree experience. The novel's decidedly cerebral phenomenological ideas reflect Sartre's intense study of the German philosopher Edmund Husserl (1859–1938).

Sartre elaborates his existentialism in nonfiction works such as *Being and Nothingness* (1943) and *Existentialism and Humanism* (1946). In a famous play *No Exit* (1944), wherein three strangers are trapped in the same hotel room from which they cannot escape, one character concludes: "Hell is other people."

The hallmark notions of authenticity, bad faith, and intentionality underlie Sartre's works, both philosophical and literary. Like Camus, Sartre engaged in political work in World War II, especially with the French resistance movement, but the two famously clashed over ideology, and both backed away from the descriptive term "existentialism" after establishing archetypal figures of alienated solitaries in their influential fiction.

Martin Heidegger

The German philosopher Martin Heidegger (1889–1976) focused not on beings and their history but on the phenomenon of being itself. His 1927 *Being and Time*, though unfinished, explores the sense of time in respect to consciousness. Heidegger criticized philosophy for historically concentrating on rational and mental constructions rather than consciousness of being. A second part of *Being and Time* would have explored this history of philosophy, but Heidegger instead concentrated work on exploring the phenomenon of being and developing a vocabulary for how it functions in human expression, such as literature, poetry, and technology.

Heidegger coined the German term "Dasein" to describe that being which is human. The concern is not so much psychology but phenomenology, what actually happens when that being functions, consciously or not.

What happens is both will and intentionality (Nietzsche) but also anguish (Kierkegaard). Ultimately, Heidegger sees human beings uncritically following a pre–worn path to collective action and self–destruction, especially with regard to technology.

The discovery of self requires a different and conscious set of actions. The prerequisite, however, is "Gelessenheit" (meaning "releasement"), a term Heidegger adopts from Meister Eckhart. Releasement requires solitude, openness, and abandonment of mind–content. Heidegger further qualifies the idea of openness, using the term "Befindlichkeit" to mean "disposed to," that state of mind that is open–to or open–for, not just a mind that is open.

In his 1929–1930 lectures, *The Fundamental Concepts of Metaphysics*, Heidegger explored two integral human characteristics: our predilection for lack of "attunement" (or *Stimmung*) with the world and environment, and our constant awareness of the passage of time. These lectures are an extension and resolution of issues presented in *Being and Time*. We usually personalize our lack of attunement negatively as melancholy, alienation, or isolation, but in fact attunement is a cultural and societal experience. In contrast, solitude is a condition of being and consciousness, and is positive when one begins to re–engage with nature and a harmonious universe. All traditions know that human beings are forever restless, conscious of impermanence and of their own individual finitude. Individuation reconciles the phenomenon of alienation.

Individuation is the process of becoming aware of being. The subtitle of Heidegger's *Fundamental Concepts of Metaphysics* was originally "World, Finitude, Individuation." But Heidegger specifically considers individuation to be the process of discovering one's solitariness. Hence Heidegger's final subtitle was "World, Finitude, Solitude." Individuation is "that *solitariness* [emphasis in the original] in which each human being first of all enters into a nearness to what is essential in all things, a nearness to world."

Nikolai Berdyaev

The Russian philosopher and religious thinker Nikolai Berdyaev (1874–1948) described himself as a Christian existentialist. His book *Solitude and Society*, published 1934, applies solitude to society as part of philosophical thought. He begins with several premises.

Philosophy has two enemies, religion and science. The chief error of religion is that it objectifies itself, making itself revealed truth, external to human consciousness. Religion intervenes into the natural spiritual responses of the human community, supplanting them with its own notion of truth, its own flawed philosophies, attempting to objectify its base of authority.

On the other hand, science dismissively identifies philosophy with religion. Throughout the Middle Ages, philosophy is the handmaiden of religion and could not extricate itself from the attacks of science until philosophers themselves renounced philosophy's objectivity. A philosophy of existence thus emerges. The philosopher's tragic situation is that the objectifying criterion of both religion and science excludes the true knowledge that springs from the personal, individual experience of the mystery of Being.

Because of the personal, even subjective, foundation of knowledge, philosophy cannot accept only traditionally–defined objectivity. It must purify anthropological nature to reveal original nature, transcendental nature, which is personalist—not egoist, subjectivist, individualist, empirical, or nominalist. But the result is spiritual sterility.

Berdyaev then surveys Western philosophy. Objectification, the making of spiritual or mysterious phenomenon into objects, begins with Plato and Aristotle. Philosophy denies the subjective, denies the mystery of existence, denies creative or subjective knowledge. German idealists like Kant and Hegel objectify the subjective, while Kierkegaard, Dostoyevsky, Nietzsche, and Heidegger make the existential breakthrough on the perception of knowledge, though they are pessimists regarding human nature.

Berdyaev holds that existential understanding illuminates Being to some degree. God cannot be objectified without taking into account a given culture and its experience of religion and theology as a social experience, the given society's experience, and its social expressions. Religion is a social and cultural expression that became institutional, an organ of objectification, overriding or suppressing truths only revealed subjectively.

The pursuit of knowledge attempts to overcome solitude as negative isolation. But true solitude transcends the facile ways of society, the incapability of transcending, the failure of communion with Being. In solitude, past and future have no ontological existence: states of Heaven and Hell are revealed as false objectifications. Each of us confronts the mystery of personality alone, in solitude, or in communion with others also directing themselves to this mystery. Though Berdyaev sees original solitude as a failure to transcend, the most mature personality will be conscious of a necessary solitude as an apartness from both nature and society, even when a sense of communion assuages what he calls the "nostalgia of solitude."

As a Christian existentialist, Berdyaev understood Christian symbolism as human expressions of fundamental questions about Being, which thus constitute revelations. Nothing in the world—certainly not institutionalizations of the questioning spirit—will satisfy because they are objectifications. All existential philosophy, beginning with Kierkegaard and Nietzsche, reveal the false objectification of God. No political or social thought, Berdyaev avers, can substitute for the individual search for communion: the search for heartfelt love and the overcoming of alienation from society and the world.

57. Simone Weil, Philosopher of Solitude

French philosopher Simone Weil (1909–1943) was a teacher, scholar, thinker, writer, laborer, and, ultimately, mystic. Weil's radical analysis of the social, economic, and political issues of her era constitutes a grand critique of modern civilization. In her essay "Sketch of Contemporary Social Life" (1934), for example, Weil develops the theme of authoritarian power as the trajectory of modern culture, arguing that blind collectivity has subordinated actions and thoughts. Weil does not defend the individual as *laissez–faire* atom but as the organic and cooperative foundation of decentralized communities, attacked by inimical modern forces, by "production and consumption," abetted by modern science, technology, labor, and money. Institutions represent the perennial historical flaw: when good they expect conformity, when odious they extend their oppressiveness.

Weil analyzes the relationship between economics and the state, with militarism as an adjunct in extending economic control and social behaviors that are goals of the powerful. Productivity, progress, consumption, and limitless expansion of desire and power are all aspects of modern culture. And yet society revolts not against its own oppressors but against nature.

Weil's phrase "The Great Beast," describing the collective state, its elites, and its apparatus, derives from Plato as much as from the Book of Revelation. The Great Beast has existed throughout history. "The Great Beast" is the title of an essay in which Weil transitions from social ills to antidote. As an example, she states, referring to ancient history: "Rome is the Great Beast of atheism and materialism, adoring nothing but itself. Israel is the Great Beast of religion. Neither one nor the other is likeable." She extends her critique to the modern Church: "A society like the Church, which claims to be Divine is perhaps more dangerous on account of the *ersatz* good which it contains than on account of the evil which sullies it. "Something of the social labelled divine: an intoxicating mixture which carries with it every sort of license." The Great Beast is always repulsive. Society is a project of individual relationships, not a reductionism to the fictional collective. Individuals as authorities contrive symbols, ploys, and coercive social structures. Anthropology calls these "totems" (not Weil's term), which define God, religion, and the norms of society via the power of institutions to interpret and sanction.

Weil maintains that individual's accession to society, and therefore renunciation of values to the collective, is based on ignorance and fear, fear that without society people will collapse into crime and evil. The social collective, represented as state—corporatist or institutional—is made to transcend individuals, as if the state is a supernatural entity from which nationalism and war are as normal as science, progress, and consumption. All of these evils occur simultaneously in a social context. The individual has probably never reflected on these issues at all, never acknowledged his or her degree of complicity in this system. Apologists for the Great Beast argue that, indeed, the individual need have no direct responsibility.

But society itself *is* the Great Beast, Weil tells us, not some particular product of society, not even the state, the mode of production, the elite class, or any social product. Nietzsche had pointed out that the contrived dichotomy of good and evil traps individuals in fear. Weil's solution is not Nietzsche's transcendence of morality but renewal of the idea of relationship. "Relationship breaks its way out of the social. It is the monopoly of the individual. Society is the cave. The way out is solitude."

Weil continues:

> Meditation on the social mechanism is in this respect a purification of the first importance. To contemplate the social is as good a way of detachment as to retire from the world. That is why I have not been wrong to rub shoulders with politics or society.

Weil's activism championing a just society took her in the 1930s from France to Spain, from teaching to factory work, from farm labor to labor unions, and as eyewitness to war fronts, atrocities, and the revulsion of war. In the 1940s she fled with her family to England and actively pursued resistance work.

The sources of Weil's thoughts on solitude are two: first, her analysis of the nature of society, using modern sociological and psychological tools,

and, secondly, her religious philosophy, wherein Weil focuses her same keen
thinking on spiritual themes. Weil discusses Christianity and Catholicism
with a solid grasp of the literature, vocabulary and doctrine. At the same
time, she holds strong reservations and criticisms about the same collectivist
tendencies of the Church she critiques (as in her statement above). Weil
never converted to Catholicism despite her great affinity for Jesus, sanctity,
and the moral virtues of traditional Catholic thinking. Thus Weil's solitude is
not based on specific examples of saintly hermits, nor romantic or aesthetic
sources, but is entirely philosophical and experiential.

In "La personne et le sacré" (translated as "Human Personality"), Weil
develops the notion that art is essentially anonymous. The realm of the
impersonal genius created "Gregorian chant, Romanesque architecture, the
Iliad, the invention of geometry." In quintessentially Platonic expressions,
Weil writes, "What is sacred in science is truth; what is sacred in art is
beauty. Truth and beauty are impersonal." "Impersonality is only reached
by the practice of a form of attention which is rare in itself and impossible
except in solitude, and not only physical but mental solitude." This level of
solitude is never achieved by those who think of themselves as members
of a collectivity, as part of something which says "We." Solitude is thus
a separation for the sake of productivity or individual self–expression.
More importantly, solitude is permanent enough to both sever that sense
of subordination to social groups and constructive enough to achieve a
renunciation of ego, what Weil calls "impersonality."

Solitude has a moral and ethical component that the collectivity or group
lacks, or, more specifically, cannot claim. To desire absolute good but then
seek it in the world of externals fails because the world of externals is the
realm of merely relative goods. Weil extrapolates her concept of solitude
into the realm of the sacred, concluding that just as everything sacred in
the individual is impersonal, so society is its opposite: profane, idolatrous,
the realm of falsity. Yet human beings live and work in this realm. Avarice,
gold, ambition, even science and art, are of the social world. Only love "is
more or less an exception: that is why we can go to God through love, not
through avarice or ambition." One cannot truly go to God through the
social, through institutions, which refine and redefine God according to
culture, always in an idolatrous way.

In the essays "Decreation" and "Love," Weil works out a concept of
suffering, renunciation, purity, gratitude, joy, and being, which is the process
of approaching God. The approaching to God is the state of selfless love

that rejects "pseudo–immortality," that false clinging to a prolongation of earthly social identity rather than a transcendent presence in the impersonal. Along the way, solitude is necessary but is no long a matter of aloneness or alienation. It has very concrete application to daily life. "Do not allow yourself to be imprisoned by any affection," Weil warns.

> Keep your solitude. The day, if it ever comes, when you are given true affection there will be no opposition between interior solitude and friendship, quite the reverse.

Again, in the posthumous *Gravity and Grace*, Weil remarks:

> Solitude. Where does its value lie? For in solitude we are in the presence of mere matter (even the sky, the stars, the moon, trees in blossom), things of less value (perhaps) than a human spirit. Its value lies in the greater possibility of attention. If we could be attentive to the same degree in the presence of a human being.

Weil died of tuberculosis in England, her life a brief thirty–six years. Her spiritual goal, the insight that saturates her writing, is aptly summarized by the poem that concludes "Decreation," where she sees her life as uprooted but necessarily remaining "rooted in the absence of a place," exiled from "every earthly country," an uprooted self that "seeks greater reality." "It is necessary to uproot oneself. To cut down the tree and make of it a cross, and then to carry it every day."

58. Romantic Eremitism in American Literature

Early twentieth–century literature in the United States largely remained under the benign spell of romantic eremitism.

Naturalist and essayist John Burroughs (1837–1921) specifically lauds Wordsworth and Cowley as models of solitude poetry. Burroughs includes his essay "Solitude" in Section 5 of Chapter 8 of his *Brief Essays* (1895). He reflects a continuity of solitude thinking exemplified by Emerson and expanded by direct acquaintance with the natural world. The essay extols the virtue of solitude contrasted to urban life and fellowship, cities representing a "dark side" of life. "Hermits generally have a fine streak in them, which preserves them in solitude," notes Burroughs. "We readily attribute some extra virtue to those persons who voluntarily embrace solitude, who live alone in the country or in the woods, or in the mountains, and find life sweet."

This "fine streak" or "extra virtue" is insight into vanities and the capacity to reject them. Writes Burroughs, "The more simple and refined taste loves the seriousness and sobriety of the country." Despite the preeminence of Wordsworth and Cowley, however, Burroughs confesses, like Keats, that he himself would appreciate a friend who would understand and share his motives for solitude.

The Maine author Sarah Orne Jewett (1849–1909) describes the fictional "Joanna, a woman hermit" in her 1910 novel *The Country of the Pointed Firs*. Two chapters highlight the story of Joanna, "a nun or hermit person" who lived on an island. "There was something mediaeval in the behavior of poor Joanna Todd under a disappointment of the heart." One character remarks of Joanna that she was "crossed in love" and doomed to melancholy, retiring from the world, to "get away from folks."

O. Henry (1862–1910) presents a "hermit of the Hudson" in his amusing satirical short story "To Him Who Waits," published in his collection *Options* in 1909. Suffering unrequited love, a man of thirty moves from worldly New York City to a Catskills cave for ten years. He is attracted to a young woman who visits him occasionally. One night, the hermit "threw down his Marcus Aurelius and threw off his gunny–sack toga." He shaves his beard, retrieves his old clothes, and saunters into town—only to discover an upsetting surprise about the young woman.

American poet and philosopher George Santayana (1863–1952) was born in Spain, grew up in Boston, studied and taught philosophy at Harvard University, and retired to Europe after World War II. Santayana presents an antiquarian, classical view of the hermit in his 1901 poem "A Hermit of Carmel." The poem opens as the sun sets over medieval Mount Carmel. The hermit reflects on the struggle against temptation in the wilderness. A crusader–knight passes and they converse. The knight is in service to gain the hand of his benefactor's daughter. Though he says nothing, the hermit recognizes the knight as a lost brother from his family's childhood escape from marauders who had attacked their village. Accepting his solitary contentment, the hermit's life parallels the happiness that the knight will find in his homecoming. The poem is a tableau, a scene, a moment of historical nostalgia. (In a sequel poem, "A Knight's Return," the knight goes back to Europe to marry; the hermit is not mentioned.)

Edith Wharton (1862–1937), a society matron of the Gilded Age, enjoyed a great talent for narration. She settled in Paris after 1908 and drew inspiration from travels in France and Italy. "The Hermit and the Wild Woman" is from her 1908 collection *The Hermit and the Wild Woman and Other Stories*. The Renaissance Italian setting features an orphaned boy who escapes raiding marauders by hiding in a forest. He becomes a cave–dwelling hermit. On one occasion, hearing of an old austere hermit, he ventures across mountain heights to reach the old man, who scorns the young man's motives. Years later, a young woman fleeing a stifling cloister encounters the protagonist, who after long coaxing fails to persuade the "wild woman" to return to the convent, she being intent on the freedom of solitude and nature, crafting herbs and caring for animals. The story is a mild version of *Thais*, but with no moral treachery impugned to the hermit.

Wharton's 1909 poem "Ogrin the Hermit" is based on the Tristan and Iseult tale, with the fleeing adulterers coming across an old hermit's hut. Ogrin shields them from their pursuers, and convinces Iseult to return to her life station (Tristan is absent from the dialogue).

59. Realist Eremitism in American Literature

Three American writers of the first half of the twentieth century dispel the remnants of romantic eremitism while retaining fierce solitude: Robert Frost, Robinson Jeffers, and Ralph Ellison.

Robert Frost

The most creative period of American poet Robert Frost (1874–1963) was his earliest. His more celebrated poems—"Mending Wall" (1914), "The Road Not Taken" (1916), "Stopping By the Woods on a Snowy Evening" and "Fire and Ice" (1923)—reflect a richness of language, sensation, observation, psychological insight, and poetics. The poems considered in this section appeared in the early collections: *A Boy's Will* (1913), *North of Boston* (1914), *Mountain Interval* (1916), and *New Hampshire* (1923).

Nearly all the Frost poems on themes of solitude are early, heartfelt poems arising from deep and volatile experience and emotion, employing the cadence and language of the classics. They reflect an experience of nature grounded in the land, mountains, and dark forests of New England

and its (perhaps stereotyped) culture. In a 1916 letter, Frost himself notes that a poem evolves not from thought but from "a lump in the throat, a sense of wrong, a homesickness. It is never thought to begin with. It is at its best when it is tantalizing vagueness."

A Boy's Will, Frost's first published collection, appeared in 1913 in England (he was unknown in the United States). The collection is not merely about youth but about unresolved hauntings and psychological specters. The very first poem, "Into My Own," establishes the mood of introspection with the theme of disappearance, of leaving the world behind to enter an infinite forest. Of anyone who would search for him: "They would not find me changed of from him they knew— / Only more sure of all I thought was true." "Ghost House" presents a lonely dwelling inhabited by a "slow and sad" lad and lass, perhaps Frost and his wife. Depression is the poet's "November Guest," called "my Sorrow," which wanders the withered pasture and the "desolate, deserted trees." Though "Storm Fear" is raw emotional reaction to winter isolation, Frost deftly weaves themes of contagious claustrophobia with introversion. The fantastic images of nature are well grasped in the picture "To the Thawing Wind" of late winter rain melting the ice on the window: "Melt the glass and leave the sticks / Like a hermit's crucifix. …"

Nature intersects with emotion. After a quarrel with his wife, the poet dreams of withdrawing to the forest ("A Dream Pang"), watching clandestinely as his wife looks for him, but hesitates as if to go no further and appear to relent. "My Butterfly" reveals the poet's strong sense of identity and empathy. The butterfly is the trembling soul, abandoned by sun and flowers and gentle breezes, alone to face the coming of fatal winter and death. *A Boy's Will* culminates with the world–weary "Reluctance," the poet returning home when the land is bleak in winter, flowers gone, and dead leaves huddled, all things quiet and resigned. The return is reluctant, from what sad journey the reader only senses.

North of Boston, published in 1914, also in England, announces themes of New England character: stoic, frugal, rooted, without worldly aspiration or severance from nature, detecting truths in the cycle of the seasons, the precariousness of social existence clinging to cooperation with nature, themes explored descriptively as narrative, not as subjectively and expressively as in *A Boy's Will*.

The collection opens with the famous "Mending Wall." The poet must lay down principles for encountering the world, society, and others frequently hostile. A successive poem, "The Mountain," enlarges the wall into a mountain whose looming presence circumscribes the village and its pastures and waters, especially affecting the human inhabitants, who like the character in the poem speak tersely and move on.

Each poem in *North of Boston* is a vignette of social encounters establishing boundaries of self. "Home Burial" conjures murder, adultery, burial, and haunting, a radical set of circumstances with the chilling matter–of–factness of style informed by the classics but modern in expression and cadence. "The Black Cottage" and "A Servant to Servants," the latter with gothic twists, are narratives, not poems. "The Wood–Pile" evokes the stillness of winter. The narrator is alone and "walking on the frozen swamp one gray day" when he encounters a neat cord of maples, "cut and split and poled"— mysteriously neglected, evidently for years, forgotten by someone easily turned to "fresh tasks," forgotten past efforts, or simply gone, leaving the remnants of memory and time to fade away.

Mountain Interval (1916) is highlighted by "The Road Not Taken," which establishes the individual with a fundamental decision from which there is no alternative—and for which there is no social input or companionable advice. The domestic poem "Birches" recalls the memory of boyhood: "Whose only play was what he found himself, / Summer or winter, and could play alone." Tragic themes become common–place and cruel. "The Hill Wife" describes interior solitude and mental deterioration. A woman in loneliness and unspoken fear of shadows, strangers, and imagined stalkers one day disappears into the forest and never returns, bearing a great burden she had been unable to communicate to her husband, who never found her. In "Out, Out," a boy happily wielding a buzzing chain saw is briefly distracted by his sister's call to supper, and the mad saw slips and cuts deep into his hand. A doctor cannot save him, and the boy dies. "And they, since they / Were not the one dead, turned to their affairs."

In 1917, Frost published "A Way Out" in an obscure literary magazine as a one-act play. The story features a hermit living in a remote farmhouse in humble conditions. A man comes to the door and invites himself in, demanding food and acting belligerently. The hermit tries to put up with him, unsure of the stranger's motives. The stranger finally reveals that he is a fugitive murderer and needs a place to stay. He sizes up the hermit in appearance, and remarks on his isolation, his lack of human contacts. After a brief struggle, the fugitive kills the hermit, puts on his clothes, and imitates his appearance. He conceals the body just as a search party of police arrive at the farmhouse door, as had the fugitive just hours before. They know of an old hermit resident there and assume that the murderer is the hermit. They ask him if he has seen a stranger. The fugitive deftly points away, to the woods, where he thinks he saw a man flee—and the story ends. The tale evokes Frost's own despairing moments seeking to change his identity (but to what?) and find "a way out," but at what cost?

With *New Hampshire* (1923) came Frost's two final signature poems: "Fire and Ice" and "Stopping By Woods on a Snowy Evening," both representative poems of insight, with the familiar theme of decision. Lesser known poems in this collection consolidate the concept of solitude and explore it creatively. The book distends again, like its predecessor, to encompass social exchanges.

"Two Witches" introduces the solitude of women, called witches because they are "old–believers" or simply because they perceive what men do not. "The Witch of Coos" alludes to the female protagonist of "Home Burial." "The Pauper Witch of Grafton" refers to the magic powers of the feminine: her husband "got more out of me / By having me a witch." In "The Lockless Door," the narrative's metaphor is the solitary's private self. After many years, a knock comes at the door of a dwelling. The narrator turns out the light, tiptoes to the window, and climbs out, from there bidding the knocker enter: "so at a knock / I emptied my cage / To hide in the world / And alter with age." Finally, "The Need of Being Versed in Country Things" presents a forlorn house gutted by fire long ago, leaving but the now–abandoned barn, spared by a shift in the wind. Birds fly in and out of the house through its broken windows. The murmur of birds is like a human sigh over a sad forgotten past, but to the birds themselves, unconscious of past damage or present forlornness, there is really nothing sad "about the abandoned house's fate."

> But though they rejoiced in the nest they kept,
> One had to be versed in country things
> Not to believe the phoebes wept.

In these early poems, Frost underscores the sense of solitude and isolation, even in the presence of others, who after all do not constitute a community. His theme of separateness is not new in American literature, reflecting Thoreau, Hawthorne, Melville, and Dickinson. Frost ignores the optimism of nature and self in Walt Whitman and later American poets such as Carl Sandburg.

Robert Frost once wrote to his daughter Lesley that sorrow "overcasts my poetry if read aright. No matter how humorous I am, I am sad. I am a jester about sorrow." To editor and friend Louis Untermeyer, Frost later in life candidly described his disposition as a disease: "My disease I guess is accidia (Fr. Acede).... a loss of faith, undue retreat into one's self, a sense of futility and a paralyzing estrangement from God and man." Frost definitively realigned the American literary trajectory of the solitary in the early twentieth century.

Robinson Jeffers

American poet Robinson Jeffers (1887–1962) described his philosophy of solitude as "inhumanism," the displacing of the centrality of human beings by nature. His poetry collections of the 1920s—*Tamar* (1924), *Roan Stallion* (1925), *The Women at Sur Point* (1927), and *Cawdor* (1928)—are long narrative verse deftly handling themes of incest, violence, and madness against the wild backdrop of churning sea, endless sky, copious forests, and isolated homesteaders, the settings reflecting Jeffers' own residence in Carmel, California. Shorter lyric poems hone his insights and images. Jeffers' work is based on elements reflecting classical influences from Aeschylus to Shakespeare, Calvinism to Nietzsche, Freud and Jung, anthropology and mythology.

In *Tamar and Other Poems*, Jeffers expands a view of nature as flux into a more visionary view of nature as continuum. Human beings are made of the stuff of nature: the rhythm of the sea and the primordial intensity of fire. Jeffers describes moments of intense revelation, of insights into reality and nature. Nature reveals "the excesses of God" and offers "divinely superfluous beauty" (both phrases are poem titles). In "Point Joe," the poet writes that "one must forgive nature a thousand graceful subtleties," in contrast to the human world choked with desire, aggression, and maledictions. In "Fog," Jeffers exposes human vanity in its "gluttonous" dream of God, believing that humans can achieve a longed–for unity, whether the folly of Caesar and Napoleon "in the throes of worldly ambition," or Christ and Gautama pursuing "sacred hungers." They are all dreamers, Jeffers avers, "worshippers of oneness," dreamers of a unity of human nature equivalent to the unity of nature itself.

Jeffers assesses the flaw to be not in wicked human nature but in ambition. Daily life and society embody the flaw that does not taint nature. In

"Boats in a Fog," Jeffers conjoins the flight of birds and the flight of planets wherein all human activity is necessarily cut off from this unity. In "People and a Heron," the poet sees shellfish–gatherers on a twilight beach and a solitary heron off to the side, and muses as to "why a lone bird was nearer to me than many people." Watching the stars at night, the poet reflects (in "Autumn Evening") that "No matter / what happens to men... the world's well made through." A vast difference separates humans and nature, but not from any superiority of consciousness on the part of humans. In "The Broken Balance" the poet avers that he has "paid my birth–dues; am quits with the people." Jeffers' pessimism is clearest in another passage of the poem:

> Men moulding themselves to the anthill have choked
> Their natures until the souls die in them; ...
> The world's turned upside down;
> The good do evil, the hopes in criminals; in vice
> That dissolves the cities and war to destroy them.
> Through wars and corruptions the house will fall.
> Mourn whom it falls on. Be glad: the house is mined, it will fall.

While eschewing romantic nostalgia, Jeffers also scoffs at modernism and the notion of human progress. Despite his realist style, Jeffers shares the anguished outrage of his post–World War I generation of intellectuals and artists appalled by the mass slaughter and purposelessness of the war, a generation pessimistic about a collective redirection averting future catastrophes. At this point, however, unlike his European counterparts, Jeffers discovers an inkling of a solution in eremitism.

In "An Artist" (1928), Jeffers writes about a hermit. The poem represents a new application of insights, a reconciliation of ideas with a form of daily life. The narrator encounters a once–famous sculptor now reclused in the desert mountains. The sculptor has renounced not only the world but even marble and bronze, working now a vein of stone. The hermit elaborates on his life: he lives eight miles from town, from where he fetches food. He has a cave, water, and no lack of material. "I need, therefore, nothing. As to companions, I make them," the sculptor tells the poet. "What more? Sympathy? Praise? I have never desired them and also I have never deserved them." The hermit–sculptor lives only to form some ideal of humanity in stone, he says. But his sculptures are laughable to God, for they reflect only what the sculptor's sad eyes have seen of the world. Still, the hermit tells his visitor, his sad eyes have peace, for they have seen sunrises and stars. And, he concludes: "I hope ... that when I grow old and the chisel drops, I may crawl out on a ledge of the rock and die like a wolf."

The narrator tells us that he will not reveal the whereabouts of the hermit. Nor has he ever returned to visit him. "While he lives," the poet states, "let him alone."

With the creation of a hermit character, Jeffers begins reflecting on other radical forms of life, on the apocalyptic roles of prophets and saviors, in part, perhaps, to clarify the role of the poet. The poet shows reality, but the prophet applies an insight to this showing. The prophet does not prescribe but interprets. Is prophecy a new role Jeffers conceives for his artistry in this period? He contrasts the savior, who takes up the additional role of showing, applying, prescribing, and saving—the added burden of a vision of self as meritorious enough to claim divine grace. The savior is not an example but an avatar, if not divinity itself. But to desire to save a people is to misconstrue the vision of the poet and the prophet, to project the vision outward, to lose the self to madness.

The savior's role, projecting the vision outward and assigning authority to it, is the opposite of Jeffers' artist–hermit. Salvation is an individual path for one's self, a path that only inner insight will lay out for pursuit. The savior's mistake is to see good and evil residing in a meritorious people, and to desire to obliterate the evil. But the people are neither good nor evil. What drives the savior beyond the prophet's role of mere observation, Jeffers argues, is a madness of desire. These thoughts from "Meditation on Saviors" show a new stage for Jeffers.

The seeker after God will only encounter himself and, worse, the true horror of God's indifference. Jeffers' poem "Dear Judas" further explores the theme of prophet versus savior, contrasting the disillusion of Judas with the misdirected desire of Jesus to expend himself for the masses.

Throughout the 1930s, Jeffers crafted a reconciliation between human and natural worlds. Anger yields to philosophical reflection. The conventional God is "hardly a friend of humanity," but, like Spinoza, Jeffers identifies God with Nature, in which case God is "very beautiful." In "Signpost," Jeffers offers advice to those who want to know how to be human again. He writes:

> Turn outward, love things, not men, turn right away from human-
> ity ... if you like how the lilies grow, lean on the silent rock until
> you feel its divinity. Make your veins cold, look at the silent stars

> ... For what we love, we grow to it, we share its nature... Now
> you are free to become human. But born of the rock and the air,
> not of a woman.

In "Flight of Swans," Jeffers warns that a follower of such reflections "will not wind himself into hopes nor sicken with despairs." Such a person will realize the vanity of hope but not a meaninglessness of life and death.

In "Nova," Jeffers writes that the "invulnerable beauty of things" is itself the face of God, and living in that presence is sufficient. And in "The Answer" the poet tells us that integrity and wholeness should be our objects of love: "Love that, not man."

Although he had clearly profited from a close reading of sages, in "Theory of Truth" Jeffers refers negatively to Lao–tzu, Buddha, and Jesus. They embarked on the pursuit of truth but mingled, as he puts it, their own "impurities" with their visions of what is. This is an inevitability of which Jeffers, too, is guilty, but the important point is to be conscious of that personal quest and its desires. The sages Jeffers names produced thoughts and reflections that the world would deem insane, Jeffers acknowledges, for who but "tormented persons want truth."

But this torment, this private agony, reflects Jeffers, "muddles the finding." The named sages would annul the universe to "annul the suffering." Is the search for truth, therefore, doomed to frustration and the fragmentation of wisdom? Yes, Jeffers concludes, "until the mind has turned its love from itself / and man, from parts to the whole."

The preface to the 1948 *The Double–Axe and Other Poems* elaborates on "inhumanism," though the meaning by then is implicit to long–time readers. All of his previous work, Jeffers points out, has been nothing less than "the rejection of human solipsism and recognition of the transhuman magnificence." Inhumanism, he argues, is "the devaluation of human–centered illusions, the turning outward from man to what is boundlessly greater. The attitude is neither misanthropic nor pessimistic, nor irreligious," Jeffers argues, offering a reasonable detachment as rule of conduct, instead of love, hate, and envy. While a guide, not a rule, says Jeffers, inhumanism nevertheless bids us to "Turn away from each other."

The late poems of Jeffers do not surpass his early work. He echoes Lucretius with the poem "De Rerum Virtute," and lauds the ancient Chinese nature poets, who "loved landscapes and solitude," in his "On An Anthology of Chinese Poems."

Robinson Jeffers evolved a philosophy of life confronting deep psychological issues and the problems of society and civilization. Through his poetry, and with years of observation and reflection from what scholar Robert Zaller calls (and titles one of his books) "the cliffs of solitude," Jeffers pursued a complex search for consolation.

Ralph Ellison

Ralph Ellison (1914–1994) published one novel, his 1951 book *Invisible Man*, widely esteemed a classic expression of African American literature, its themes reaching universal concern with alienation, society, self, and solitude. Ellison acknowledges that the structure of his novel was influenced by Dostoyevsky's *Notes From Underground*, an association revealed not only in structure, especially the prologue and ending, but in the persona of the novel's protagonist.

Notes From Underground opens with the narrator's self-description:

> I am a sick man. I am an angry man. I am an unattractive man.... I couldn't make myself anything: neither good nor bad, neither a scoundrel nor an honest man, neither a hero nor an insect. Now I go on living in my corner and irritating myself with a spiteful and worthless consolation that a wise man can't seriously make himself anything, only a fool makes himself anything.

The prologue of *Invisible Man* opens similarly:

> I am an invisible man. No, I am not a spook like those who haunted Edgar Allan Poe; nor am I one of your Hollywood-movie ectoplasms. I am a man of substance, of flesh and bone, fiber and liquids—and I might even be said to possess a mind. I am invisible, understand, simply because people refuse to see me.... I am not complaining, nor am I protesting either. It is sometimes advantageous to be unseen, although it is most often rather wearing on the nerves.... You wonder whether you aren't simply a phantom in other people's minds. Say, a figure in a nightmare which the sleeper tries with all his strength to destroy.... You ache with the need to convince yourself that you do exist in the real world, that you're a part of all the sound and anguish, and you strike out with

your fists, you curse and you swear to make them recognize you. And, alas, it's seldom successful.

Like Dostoyevsky's narrator, Ellison's is unnamed, and also relates the end of the story in the beginning, telling us that he has gotten nowhere in the world except to suffer its rejection, at least revealing its nature to him. Dostoyevsky's protagonist responds directly to the naive idealism of contemporary social reformers in nineteenth–century Russia, who maintain that hard work and effort will bring equality and justice. Ellison's protagonist knows that assumption as the philosophy of Booker T. Washington. In a telling opening chapter, the narrator recites a speech by Washington (though not attributed to him) to the white elite of the town. He chokes on the phrase "social responsibility" and instead says "social equality," bringing down the wrath of his listeners, to whom the narrator must apologize for his mistake.

The novel details the protagonist's life as a Black man in the contemporary (1930s and 1940s) United States, the course of his experiences revealing the nature of society and social illusion. The insight is of a Black man, but fundamentally that of an invisible human being, a solitary.

The narrator is underground, in what he calls "hibernation, … a covert preparation for a more overt action." He thinks he may reenter the world because "not all sickness is unto death, neither is invisibility." But by the end of the story, we know that, psychologically, at least, he will remain underground.

The novel tumbles from one illusion and hope to another: from college prospects to expulsion, from factory employment to dismissal due to hostile white workers and a mistrustful old Black supervisor, from embrace by the Brotherhood—a thinly–veiled Communist Party—to being driven out into the street over the group's hypocrisy, authoritarianism, and racism. The narrator learns of Ras the Exhorter, a Black nationalist espousing separation. He finds himself in the midst of a riot in Harlem—the 1942 Harlem Riot being the clear historical precedent for Ellison. In the midst of night, of burning buildings and roaming mobs, a horsebacked Ras, looking like a surreal African king, appears suddenly. With police moving inexorably into the burning Harlem streets, the narrator falls through an uncovered manhole.

Everything has betrayed him, everything is tainted beyond redemption. He replaces the manhole cover. Eventually he will make his way to where he began the narrative. "So I would stay here until I was chased out. Here, at least, I could try to think things out in peace, or, if not in peace, in quiet. I would take up residence underground." The end is in the beginning.

Ellison's breakthrough in *Invisible Man* is to touch upon the universality of solitude as a cultural and racial experience, and to catalog the insights of a solitary sufferer thrown into history, a Black man made universal, yet doomed to invisibility.

CHAPTER 11

EREMITISM IN EASTERN THOUGHT
AND INFLUENCE

60. West Meets East: Eremitic Journeys

The Western interest in Eastern religion and philosophy arose as soon as translations were published. Emerson and Thoreau read the 1785 English translation of the *Bhagavad–Gita* of Charles Wilkins (1749–1836). Schopenhauer read the *Upanishads* in an 1801 Latin translation by the French scholar Anquetil Duperron (1731–1805), who also translated key Persian texts, including the *Zend–Avesta* and the *Life of Zoroaster*, published in 1771. Whether Nietzsche read these French translations is unclear. By the time Max Muller began assembling the fifty volumes of his monumental English–language translations compiled as *Sacred Books of the East* in 1879 (completed in 1910), the Eastern classics had influenced every corner of Western intellectual interest, including the formulation of philosophies based on the newly–available Chinese, Persian, Hindu, Buddhist, and other texts.

Helena Blavatsky (1831–1891), a Russian emigre to the United States, published *Isis Unveiled* in 1877, a founding text of Theosophy, wherein she describes the hidden sources of a forgotten common world religion or esotericism. Subsequent expository books include *The Secret Doctrine: the Synthesis of Science, Religion and Philosophy* (1888), and *The Key to Theosophy* (1889).

George Gurdjieff (1866–1949), Greek–Armenian philosopher and teacher, proffered an alternative to Blavatsky's theosophy in his "Fourth

Way," a spiritual path additional to or transcending the three historical categories of mind, heart, and body which he associated with the ways of yogis, monks, and fakirs. Gurdjieff's Fourth Way was intended to be an alternative and new method of self–development, derived from eclectic sources, from Sufi to Tibetan Buddhist to Eastern Christian to secular occultism such as freemasonry. He published nothing during his lifetime, all ascribed works being published posthumously. Importantly, however, Gurdjieff rejected eremitism.

The best indication of Gurdjieff's intentions may be his pre–1912 purported travels throughout Asia described in the posthumous book *Meetings with Remarkable Men*, written in Russian and not translated in the West until the 1960s. Here Gurdjieff tells of encountering mysterious sages, culminating in a journey to the secret Sarmoung Brotherhood (to which monastery he was led blindfolded). The Brotherhood gives him what become his major insights. Gurdjieff's travels, like his Fourth Way, may have been metaphoric after all.

In *Magic and Mystery in Tibet* (1929), the French explorer Alexandra David–Neel (1868–1969) relates sites and insights into Tibetan culture not previously seen by Westerners. Unlike Gurdjieff, her details are reliable. Also unlike Gurdjieff, she professes herself a Buddhist, not a Theosophist, nor someone contriving her own philosophy. Her book describes psychic phenomena, telepathy, *tummo* ("inner fire"), plus mystical theories, spiritual beliefs, lamas, and *gomchen* (hermits).

David–Neel tells of an old lama hermit who insists that he would accept death from a murderer rather than have the murderer condemned to death. She describes the mountainous crags "often chosen as dwelling–places by Tibetan hermits. Firstly they deem them a suitable ground for spiritual training. Secondly they think that they find there the opportunity of using their magic powers for the good of men and animals, either by converting malignant evil spirits or by forcibly preventing their harmful activity—at least, simple people ascribe that charitable desire to these 'holy ones'."

David–Neel tells of a famous cave lama "whom the mountaineers called Jowo gomchen (Lord contemplative hermit)." He lived in complete seclusion, receiving provisions from villagers and herdsmen. Three or four months a year snow blocked the paths to the cave. David–Neel spends a week in a nearby cave, "visiting the gomchen each day. Though his conversation was full of interest, I was still far more interested in watching the daily life of a Tibetan anchorite."

David–Neel notes that while other Westerners have visited lamaist monasteries, none had visited the gomchens "about whom so many fantastic stories are told," and none had observed their contemplative life. During her travels, she encounters two wild hermits on the Nepal frontier who flee at the approach of her party. On another occasion she encounters a hermit and inquires from a translator about him. "This lama is a peripatetic ascetic from Bhutan," she is told. "He lives here and there in caves, empty houses, or under the trees. He has been stopping for several days in a small monastery near here." In her enthusiastic manner, David–Neel notes: "I had no definite plan for the afternoon, why should I not go to the gompa (monastery) where he was staying, and persuade him to talk?" In another anecdote, visiting a mountain hermitage and staying in a cave at night, she looks out on the myriad stars in the night sky and paraphrases Milarepa: "I feel that the hermit's life, free of what we call 'the goods and pleasures of the world,' is the most wonderful of all lives."

In her 1927 *My Journey to Lhasa*, David–Neel describes highlights of her 1923 visit to the region. She encounters two hermits who had never left a cave and never spoken. When she approaches them they merely smile. Many such cells appear as she travels, dotting a precipitous trail as her party passes, with the hermits living in them stretching out their hands for alms. These hermits had taken vows of silence and austerity.

British–born esotericist and popularizer Paul Brunton (1898–1981) professed himself a theosophist with an interest in Hinduism. His 1936 book, *A Hermit in the Himalayas*, relates his travels to the Indian Himalayas and a solitary respite in a mountain bungalow.

Brunton is a comfortable Westerner describing himself as "an idler" and "do–nothing," "useless to society and unprofitable to myself." His eremitism is a sham one, joking that while he does not appear before his servant in a "starched uncomfortable shirt for dinner" he does shave daily. "A beard … would be quite fitting to a hermit, but I fear to go as far as that." The mail–carrier is invaluable to "a twentieth–century hermit like myself. … Modern habits for modern hermits is my slogan."

On solitude, Brunton tells us: "Use solitude but do not abuse it.... I believe in rhythm, in withdrawal only if followed by activity, in solitude only if followed by society, in self–centered development only if social service is its later complement, in spirituality only if nicely balanced by materiality. … Asceticism is not attractive to the modern man. My belief is that it is also not essential." Thus does Brunton glibly injects himself into Eastern eremitism.

A similar British dabbler into Eastern exoticism is W. Somerset Maugham (1874–1965). His 1944 novel *The Razor's Edge*, set in the 1920s and 1930s, traces the intimate lives of typical British and American upper class, focusing on an American who rejects the society of the rich to embrace a vagabond quest for spirituality that ultimately takes him to India. But the protagonist is completely overshadowed by the novel's other characters, and the author won't put articulate words into the character's justification for disdaining the values of the West.

The work (the title is from the *Upanishads*) contrives to be curious about what it reduces to exotic fakirs and mysterious powers. For example, the protagonist has learned from a swami a technique of hypnosis that conveniently cures migraines. Absurdly, the high–minded protagonist refuses alcohol for tea upon first reuniting with his American friends, but a few chapters later he is gulping down bacon and eggs with a beer for breakfast!

Maugham's protagonist encounters (told third–hand) an unnamed but influential holy man in India—not the hypnotist swami but clearly Ramana Maharshi, whom Maugham himself visited in Ramana's ashram on a journey to India in 1938. From this trip Maugham derived the flimsy identification with the novel's protagonist, in an era when many British and Americans trekked to India, anticipating what one book reviewer calls the "commodification of Eastern spirituality."

Harold Musson (1920–1965) was the scion of a wealthy British military family, a World War II veteran, a captain, and a graduate in languages from Cambridge University. Musson became Nanavira Thera, a Theravada Buddhist monk and hermit in a Sri Lankan jungle. His writing attempted to meld Buddhist thought—drawing from the content of the Pali canon and the historical Buddha's authentic suttas—and Western existentialism and phenomenology. Nanavira sought to stimulate modern Western intellectuals to reexamine the thought of the historical Buddha, applying Western ideas (he mentions, Kierkegaard, Dostoyevsky, Kafka, Joyce, Heidegger, Marcel, Sartre, and Camus) to forward unorthodox but more palatable conclusions about Buddhism. However, Nanvira's ideas provoked controversy among orthodox–minded Buddhists, for his ideas reject the primacy of commentarial texts such as the famous *Visuddhimagga* of Buddhaghosa.

Nanavira described his hermit life to several visitors over the years. He first tried living on a mountain but had difficulty procuring food, then tried living in a cave but was soon displaced by nearby industry. He found the jungle of Bundala congenial, and describes in detail his one–room hut or *kuti*: eight by twelve feet, concrete floor, mud or straw mat, a shelf of Pali and Western books. Outside is a latrine and a protected water source.

In a letter, Nanavira described himself as "something of a solitary by nature, sadly lacking in warmth of feeling either for or against other people." In another, he refers to "The Artist at Work," a short story by Camus, in declaring himself "solitaire" not "solidaire."

Buddhist authorities in the city (Colombo) and the monasteries not only resented his philosophizing but also his eremitism, considering his hermit life arrogant. In turn, Nanavira believed that his eremitism scandalized authorities because it contrasted with their complacent beliefs and comfortable lives.

Nanavira's daily food was brought to him by villagers, as is traditional, but this became the unfortunate source of amoebiasis, a gastrointestinal parasitic disease he contracted towards the last years of his life, a disease with uncontrollable effects which no local medical expert could resolve. In 1962 Nanvira began writing to trusted correspondents about the justifiable efficacy of suicide for an advanced practitioner (*sotapanna* or "stream–enterer") such as himself, whose body frustrates all attempts at practice and meditation. By 1963 he developed arrhythmia. Nanavira took his life in 1965.

Henri Le Saux

Henri Le Saux (1910–1973) spent twenty years as a Benedictine monk in his native France, at Kergonan monastery famed for its cultivation of Gregorian chant. In 1944, Le Saux professed an interest in India and Hinduism, writing—through a French priest Jules Monchanin, residing in India—to the bishop of Tiruchirapalli, who responded enthusiastically to Le Saux's inquiries. Le Saux indicated to Monchanin a mutual desire to pursue Hindu religious expression, study the Tamil and Sanskrit languages, and adopt the physical lifestyle of the common people. He reached India in 1948 and spent the rest of his life there as a Hindu–inspired sannyasi (holy man), hermit, traveler, and writer.

Charmed by all he encountered upon arrival, Le Saux immediately adopted the life of a sannyasi or holy man, wearing robes, eating dahl and rice, learning customs and languages with alacrity, incorporating Hindu chants, prayers, readings, and practices into his daily monastic routines. At first, he still echoed Western missionary rhetoric, however, speaking of a desire to help Christianize Hindus. But this does not last long.

Jules Monchanin (1895–1957) lived a semi–eremitic life in Bhakti Ashram. Thoughtful and retiring, he preferred the quiet life of a parish priest. Henri and Jules found a Christian ashram, Shantivanam. They visited Hindu counterpart monks from the order of Ramakrishna, attended the *darshan* or public presentations of Aurobindo, and mingled with followers of Ramana Maharshi at the holy mountain of Arunachala.

Hermits and holy men dwelt for extended periods in the many caves of Arunachala. Ramana's presence there, followed by eager reading of Ramana's teachings on *advaita* or non–dualism, silence, and solitude, deeply impress Le Saux. He takes up the name of Abhishiktananda. For three years he lives as a wandering sadhu among the caves of Arunachala. Abhishktananda maintained that advaita revealed to him a truth more profound than anything he had known in Christianity. But he wavered between renouncing Christianity and adhering to Hindu advaita.

Abhishiktananda learns from Ramana the depths of advaita as not aspiration but truth. The guru Gnanananda confirms this confidence to him with Hindu ceremony and ritual, simple parables, direct discourses on solitude and self, and through the use of long periods of silence. Abhishiktananda writes the book *Guru and Disciple* on his experiences with Gnanananda but also a long essay titled "Esseulement" or "Total Solitude." He enters retreat (1956) at the Chola temple at Tamal Nadu with its Mauna Mandir or Temple of Silence, experiencing "awakening" to the Absolute, the Alone. In his diary Abhishiiktananda composes a poem:

> In serene solitude, in sovereign solitude,
> In serene fullness, in sovereign fullness,
> In blessedness,
> In the solitude of my fullness,
> In the fullness of my solitude,
> In the solitude of my blessedness,
> In the blessedness of my fullness.

In another diary passage, Abhishiktananda tries to identify the emptying of self: "Living alone with oneself, not with one's books, not with one's thoughts, not with one's daydreams, not with the emanations of one's subconscious, but alone with oneself, in the nakedness, 'as it were,' of one's spiritual substance."

While the paradox of maintaining Christianity and Hindu advaita continued unresolved, other paradoxes shadow Abhishiktananda's life. He loses interest in Shantivanam, especially after the 1957 death of Jules Monchanin, and now embarks on incessant travel. He craved solitude and silence but travel brought new friends, colleagues, admirers, and reluctant celebrity at conferences and forums. He published several books promoting Christian–Hindu dialogue, but always tried to separate himself to pursue solitude. In his final years, he took up an interest in Zen.

In a 1962 diary entry, Abhishiktanada writes of himself in the third person, that "The solitary is all alone face to face with himself, all alone face to face with God, in the depth of himself..." God has withdrawn all signs, symbols, and images. There is no conceptualization left. All that is left is *kevala,* the solitude that has no name, what Abhishiktananda called "the totally blank page in the Ten Pictures of Zen."

Note must be made of British–born Benedictine priest Bede Griffiths (1906–1993), who came to Shantivanam in 1968 when Abhishiktanada had decided to pursue solitude. With two other monks he assumed stewardship of the ashram. Not unlike Abhisiktanada, Griffiths pursued popularization of Hindu–Christian dialogue, but with greater emphasis on Christianity, and less interest in eremitic spirituality or solitude.

Crook & Low

John H. Crook (1930–2011) became a leading British sociologist specifically interested in the northern Himalayas, where in the 1980s he pursued an expedition accompanied by psychotherapist James Low, a Tibetan Buddhist dzogchen meditation teacher and translator. The resulting collaboration was the 1997 book, *The Yogins of Ladakh: A Pilgrimage Among the Hermits of the Buddhist Himalayas.* The work documents the practices of lamas and hermits in northwestern India on the Himalayan boundary of Tibet, describing visits to yogins in monasteries, villages, and caves. Crook acknowledges the work of ambitious travelers before him, beginning with Alexandra David–Neel, placing his own effort in the same tradition, balancing travel writing and scholarship.

In Tibetan Buddhism, a yogin is an advanced practitioner, in contrast to the monk whose practice is circumscribed by the exigencies of monastic life. The Buddha's insight can be seen as the realization that the individual could achieve enlightenment through his or her own efforts, without the intervention of priests, a realization having a profound effect on individual practice (in Hindu India and beyond) but also on social structure, rejecting the authority of the Hindu Brahmins.

Further, Gautama's individual model was the wanderer, the casteless yogic practitioner, who, together with the mutual aid of the envisioned sangha, becomes the alternative to prevalent orthodoxy, avoiding Hindu caste but also the extreme asceticism of Jainism, a contemporary alternative to Hindu orthodoxy. Hence the Buddha's model is similar to Tantric non–priestly Hinduism in its physical rituals (such as meditation) but evolving away from sadhu asceticism as well. The result is a holistic and thorough–going method of transforming the self.

The remnants of Hindu Tantrism—the aura of rituals, offerings (*puja*), demons, and mystic powers—cling to the evolved Tibetan Buddhist yogins. To this aura must be added similar remnants derived from the Bon religion and the influence of the harsh landscape of Tibet and the Himalayas, plus the evolution of a largely isolated monastic culture. The yogin is unique even within the Buddhist tradition.

Crook and Low contrast the "wild yogins" versus the "scholarly monks" of monasteries, whether Hindu or Buddhist, focusing on the established legacy of yogins projecting into the present, although cultural, political, and technological changes to Ladakh have virtually abolished the tenuous link to the living past.

From initial contacts with yogins, Crook and Low learned of yogins hidden in the mountains, pursuing meditation, achieving psychological ease, assurance, and confidence. Integral to yogin belief is karmic responsibility, liberation in one lifetime, and the Bodhisattva vow to liberate all sentient beings. The authors discover that despite isolation, the yogins are well read, for example, recommending Chandrakirti (successor to Nagarjuna) to the authors, one Rinpoche explaining that Chagchen and Dzogchen are two methods to the same end. Yogin training includes evocation of a protector, advanced meditation, and esoteric practices (visualized channels of breathing, *tummo*, dream meditation, Illusory Body, Clear Light, and Intermediate State, the last being meditation on the *bardo*). After completing training in a year and a half, a yogin chooses to live in community or as a hermit.

Crook and Low observed the popular high esteem for hermits—they have "gone beyond." To live year–round in a mountain cave requires the "Four Jewels of the Kadampas," namely, to be unafraid to meditate alone in a cave, to have little food, to risk illness, and to die with no one knowing your circumstances.

In a small village of Drakung, the authors discover a small hut once occupied by a famous hermit who had died fifteen years earlier. No further occupants use the hut; it contains four small chambers: a kitchen, shrine room, toilet, and sleeping area. In the Zangskar valley, the authors come upon a hermitage in the craggy slopes, a cavity in the cliff face built up with block and boulders. A monk beckons them inside. Past a small entrance chamber is a dark staircase leading to an upper story. Here are two small rooms; in one sits a second monk, smiling at the visitors over a gas stove with a boiling pot of tea. The little hermitage includes a window with a view of sky, and an aperture in the face of another room through which trickles a spring of fresh water. Finally, too, they encounter a gray–bearded hermit living on the grounds of a cemetery, dressed raggedly, of calm and peaceful disposition, a practitioner of Mahamudra. His eyesight is failing, he tells them, acknowledging that when he is blind he will die.

Crook and Low learn that an English woman is in the very mountains of their travels, in a cave, pursuing a retreat. It turns out that she is Tenzin Palmo, about whom more below.

While all the hermits have chosen not to be monks in the ecclesiastical sense, some learn advanced practices and continue them even while marrying and pursuing the life of a lay person, such as a farmer or herder. They are no longer strictly hermits but they further confound the yogin model—let alone the monastic one. Yogins who are hermits, and those who have learned the discipline (and now pursue it as lay people), have transcended a strictly ascetic path to master the "Sutra path" of philosophy and intellect, pursuing the tantric path, the path toward attainment of "Buddhahood in one lifetime." This is the Bodhisattva vow that the yogins find compatible with different lifestyles. This characteristic thought has its counterpart in ancient Chinese Taoist practices, with its farmer hermits and eremitic married couples. Yogins are "cloud wanderers" akin to Zen monks who drift from monastery to monastery with no premeditated plans. Here is a unique model of general lay society, embodying virtues both personal and practical.

Augusthy Keemattam

The city of Rishikesh, India, is mentioned in many ancient Hindu sources, and reappears as a significant site of religious activity in the late nineteenth century. Rishikesh is situated near the Himalayas in northern India, on the banks of the Ganges headwaters, surrounded by lush forests and countryside. The area is the site of many temples, shrines, and ashrams. Modern Westerners may have first heard of Rishikesh when the Beatles visited in early 1968.

Augusthy Keemattam published the 1997 book *The Hermits of Rishikesh: A Sociological Survey*, a survey of the religious character and institutions of the area. The hermits of the title include sadhus, swamis, *sants* (saints), and *yatins* (ascetics). The author defines "hermit" as one withdrawn from ordinary social life, living in solitude, not necessarily adhering to a sect, tradition, or common rule. The hermit is occupied entirely with spiritual pursuits, as reflected in lifestyle. The author identifies individuals fitting this definition, studies hermits living variously in or near Rishikesh, and develops a socio-logical breakdown of their backgrounds and ascetic practices.

Keemattam observes that most of the hermits follow the traditional Hindu *vanaprastha* or third stage of life, that of renouncing family for solitary forest–dwelling. Thus the hermits are literate, familiar with Hindu scripture and spiritual writings. They originate as middle class, half of whom maintain modest bank accounts, living from the small interest, having largely severed financial ties to family and relatives. The hermits live in huts of thatch or concrete, some in caves or tents, a third with electricity or running water. They are not wanderers. The (few) women hermits live in ashrams. Half of the hermits depend on ashrams and other institutions for food.

The hermits are all celibate (*brahmacarya*), practice silence (*mauna*), and regularly read spiritual sources (*svadhyaya*). Many do not adhere to a specific devotional practice, and include non–theistic hermits practicing meditation. Practitioners of devotional worship (*bhakti*) adhere to a personal deity as the object of mystical devotion, and carry distinct marks, such as ochre–colored clothes, malas, forehead markings per sect, or matted hair. Most of these hermits identify with the Saivite (Shiva) or Vaisnavitae (Vishnu) tradition. They likely followed a guru and had lived as a sadhu for about ten years before becoming hermits; few hold a negative motive (such as orphanhood or unrequited love) for their eremitism.

Tenzin Palmo

British–born Diane Perry (b. 1943) attributes her mother's spiritism as a source for seeking alternative religious inspiration. At eighteen years of age she considered herself a Buddhist. Perry worked as a librarian in London for several years, saving funds to travel to India, departing at twenty–one to teach at a school for young Tibetan exiled lamas. That year, the school was visited by Khamtrul Rinpoche, a prominent Drukpa Kagyu lama whom Diane immediately perceived would be her guru and teacher. She received a limited ordination from him and the name Tenzin Palmo, thereafter associating with his community, although she subsequently attained other levels of ordination (Tibetan Buddhism having no ordination for women).

Perry then spent six years at an area monastery in Himachal Pradesh and, at the behest of Khamtrul Rinpoche, another six years advanced practice in a monastery in the Himalayan valley of Lahaul. During this time, she developed a strong interest in the eremitic tradition exemplified by Milarepa and continued by the contemporary Togdens, the latter an isolated community of ascetics possessing para–normal powers. She learned of Togden female counterparts, called Togdenmas. Discovering them to be nearly extinct, she resolved to one day re–establish their lineage. In 1976, at the age of thirty–three, Tenzin entered a mountain cave retreat for preparation.

The cave was an overhang on a natural ledge of the mountain, open on three sides but walled by Tenzin's associates, who added a door and double–glazed window. Ten feet by six feet, the cave had a magnificent view of the mountains and Lahoul Valley below, a nearby source of spring water, and profound silence and isolation. Her possessions included an old wood–burning stove piped outside, and two wooden boxes, one for a table, the second for meditation and sleeping. A wall depression housed books. All provisions were brought in. Tenzin Palma ate once a day, at noon, in keeping with monastic tradition. Winter cold often reached minus 35 degrees F., but she only used the stove for her midday meal.

Perry relates to her biographer Vicki MacKenzie, in the 1998 book *A Cave in the Snow*, that she was never lonely, and was completely happy not seeing anyone. She kept no diary or notes, emerging after twelve years, and has thereafter downplayed her solitude retreat to actively promote Buddhist women and nuns and to champion vegetarianism among Buddhists. In 2000, she founded Dongyu Gatsal Ling Nunnery in Himachal Pradesh, India, as her original teacher Khamtrul Rimpoche had urged her to do.

Bill Porter

American author and translator Bill Porter (b. 1943) has translated Chinese poets (writing as Red Pine) and Buddhist texts, coming to prominence in 1993 with his book *Road to Heaven: Encounters with Chinese Hermits*. The opening paragraph of the book, on page one, succinctly introduces the persona of the Chinese hermit: living in mountains, wearing simple clothes, eating simple foods, "out of touch with the times but not with the seasons."

After living and studying in East Asia many years, Porter penned the travelog from his 1989 search for hermits in contemporary China: Taoist and Buddhist, the latter variously Pure Land, Chan, or Tantric. Porter displays great empathy for his favorite land and personalities, offering quick, relevant, and interesting historical and biographical anecdotes to give his readers context in every chapter and locale he visits.

The focus of Porter's search for hermits was the Chungnan (Zhongnan) Mountains, the historic refuge of ancient hermits. Porter's journeys pursued steep and dangerous cliffs, past isolated farms and villages, and into neglected temples and shrines refurbished only lately for tourists and manned by tight-lipped monks who occasionally direct Porter to the right places with a wink and a silent nod. The hermits are reserved, philosophical, plain, with a sense of humor. One old hermit tells Porter about his few planted vegetables, of gathering wild plants, of coming down off the mountain once every couple of years. Why do you live there? asks the author. For the quiet, comes the answer. How do Taoists and Buddhists commingle in these mountains? One hermit replies simply that both follow the same path but simply dream different dreams.

Porter's book inspired the 2005 documentary film *Amongst White Clouds*, by Edward Burger, seeking out Buddhist hermits in the same Chungnan Mountains; Porter himself revisited the region for the 2015 documentary film *Hermits*, directed by Shiping He and Peng Fu. Porter has published travelogs of further China travel, revisiting historical hermits in his 2016 book *Finding Them Gone: Visiting China's Poets of the Past*, and offering lectures on Chinese eremitism. Porter is today more popular and more widely read in China than in the West.

The interest in hermits among Chinese youth today may be piqued, in turn, by interest among Westerner observers, but also reflects a renewed concern—in an era of social complexity, urbanization, and technology—for the culture's historical roots, its original cultural philosophies of life: Taoism and Buddhism. A short documentary video by Max Dun and Ellen Xu titled "Summoning the Recluse" addresses the question directly in its tagline: "Why some Chinese millennials are taking up the hermit's life in the mountains."

61. Charles de Foucauld: Hermit of Contradiction

The last romantic hermit of the West did not encounter the East but rather Africa. The French hermit Charles de Foucauld (1858–1916) remains a sign of contradiction.

Sympathetic observers place Foucauld among the saintly whose religious vision grew with intimate knowledge of a different faith. His literal practice of moral virtues places him among the poor and oppressed as a solitary and a precursor to modern inter–religious dialog and understanding. On the other hand, critics view Foucauld as an unconscious agent of Western cultural imperialism who could not escape or transcend the nefarious role of superior–minded evangelizer and apologist.

Foucauld was born of an ancient aristocratic family originating in the Middle Ages, playing key roles in the religious history of France in the Crusades and through centuries of service to the French crown. The weight of this tradition slipped from him as an orphan, a declared agnostic, and an indifferent student. The mediocre military cadet inherited the family fortune when shipped to French North Africa for service. Unexpectedly, he was fascinated with religion, witnessing the fervor of Muslims and Jews in Morocco intently pursuing their traditions. After army service Foucauld returned to North Africa in 1882 disguised as a rabbi, traveling, taking notes, making pencil drawings, and returning to Paris to publish a breakthrough geography book.

Foucauld then makes a pilgrimage to monasteries and churches in Palestine, returning to France as a convert, then a monk, joining the Trappist order. Finding monastic life in France too boring, he transfers to a poor Trappist monastery in Syria, surrounded by woodland, cavernous rock, and wildlife. His spiritual disposition blossoms; he disavows interest in theology or in becoming a priest, but is attracted to solitude. Requests to become a hermit are denied, so Foucauld quits the Trappists, moves to Nazareth, and becomes a beggar, working as a caretaker for a convent.

From Syria Foucauld writes that he lives like a hermit, embracing humility, poverty, abjection, solitude, and suffering. He longed to found an order of hermits, but that would oblige him to become a priest, but in 1901 he returns to Paris to pursue the idea, then gives it up and goes to Beni Abbes in western Algeria to found an order of lay brothers, not hermits. His writing in this period reveals a strong interest in mysticism but does not mention historical hermits. Foucauld describes his "solitary little house" on the border of the town—"a delightful and perfectly solitary hermitage."

In 1905, Foucauld moved near a mountain range from which French soldiers had withdrawn. He enjoyed a spectacular view, and built a mud hermitage among the native Berbers. Foucauld is alone, and remains so for many years, describing his desert solitude as quiet and wholesome, confessing his reluctance to depart from it. He helps the peoples around him, laboring in their projects and sharing his supplies, but has no converts. On one occasion Foucauld returns to France to recruit a companion, but can find no one.

With the outbreak of World War I, German ally Turkey promoted attacks on French outposts in Africa, arousing tension between Algeria and Morocco. Despite bouts of anemia, scurvy, and fever, Foucauld constructed a fort, with Tuareg help, to protect the surrounding population in the event of attack, the fort also serving the French military as a stockpile of arms and ammunition for Tuareg allies. In 1916, he writes patriotic sentiments in his diary, referring to the civilizing function of France among the colonies, and the need to make the populations both French and Christian. To the prioress of the Nazareth nuns who had once employed him, Foucauld writes to commend the France of Charlemagne, St. Louis, and Joan of Arc. Late in 1916, Arab raiders reached Foucauld's desert outpost, seized him for ransom and took the French army stockpile of weapons and food. A Berber guard accidentally shot and killed him.

Too early in history to say that he successfully fostered Christian–Muslim dialog, Charles Foucauld did influence the Catholic worker–priest movement in the twentieth century, and inspired several fraternities of the Little Brothers of Jesus and Little Sisters of Jesus, a legacy of his founding and a model of work and life with the poor.

NOTE: In May 2020, the Catholic Church announced forthcoming canonization of Charles Foucauld as a saint.

62. The Renaissance of Eremitism in Hindu India

Ramakrishna & Vivekananda

Ramakrishna (1836–1886) popularized many manifestations of modern Hinduism, from bhakti to advaita, with a mix of religious edification and spiritual advice. His closest disciple Vivekananda (1863–1902) founded the Ramakrishna Mission as a religious society, bringing Hinduism to increased Western attention, especially through his attendance at the Parliament of the World's Religions in Chicago in 1893. Western awareness of both Ramakrishna and Vivekananda increased with biographies by the French writer and Nobel laureate Romain Rolland (1866–1942).

Ramakrishna placed solitude into the context of spiritual tools used to promote consciousness and the attainment of enlightenment, though solitude is a modest part of his established thought. Among Ramakrishna's sayings in the compilation *Gospel of Sri Ramakrishna* are two hermit stories:

> A forest hermit in meditation is distracted when a crow on a nearby tree caws loudly. The hermit glares at the bird and it falls dead. The hermit thinks, "My spiritual progress must be great for this to happen." He sets out begging and comes to a house. The housewife is dutifully serving her husband when the begging hermit knocks on the door. She calls out for the door–knocker to wait. The hermit knocks again. The woman replies, "Please be patient. I will attend you in a moment. I am not your crow." The hermit realizes that his spiritual progress is not so much after all.
>
> A forest hermit receives many visitors but he has no money for food to feed them. He decides to go directly to the king to beg for money for this purpose. At the palace, the king is busy with other guests, and the hermit is ushered into a line to wait. The king prays loudly, "Lord, God, give me money. Give me money!" Hearing this, the hermit turns to leave. The king stops his prayer and calls to the hermit: "Why are you leaving if you have come to request something of me?" The hermit replies, "I came to beg money from you to feed my guests. But I see now that you are begging for money though you have a palace and rich friends. So why should I beg from a beggar? Better that I beg from God." And with that the hermit turns and leaves.

Vivekananda's prolific work explicates what he considers a "practical spirituality" and a "practical Vedanta" to a wider audience. Solitude as a tool is assumed, as noted in his essay "Karma-Yoga." He writes that "The ideal man is he who, in the midst of the greatest silence and solitude, finds the intensest activity, and in the midst of the intensest activity finds the silence and solitude of the desert." His example of self-restraint is that the "ideal man" should pass through crowded streets of a bustling city as calmly as if in a cave.

Rabindranath Tagore

The shift from eremitic solitude to solitude as a sense of equilibrium and tranquility, suggested in Vivekananda, is instanced in India's celebrated poet Rabindranath Tagore (1861–1941). An early work highlighting his own life direction is his 1884 play *Prakritir Pratisodh* ("Nature's Revenge"), wherein a sanyasi, or hermit, renounces his isolation to embrace nature and a life of moderation and affection. Such was the path Tagore followed in his personal life.

Still, the hermit remains a source of practical wisdom. In Tagore's 1900 poem "Deeno Daan" ("Destitute Donation"), an arrogant king has consecrated a golden temple to god. A crowd of devotees linger there, but a hermit sitting beneath a tree cries out that no god dwells in the temple. Informed of the scene, the outraged king approaches the hermit to denounce him. The hermit reminds the king that in a recent fire, when thousands lost their homes and became destitute and hungry, the king used his money to build the temple, not to help the poor. Not a god but the king's vanity fills the temple. God's house is the infinite sky and stars, the hermit says, yet the king thinks to build a house for God?

Aurobindo Ghose

Sri Aurobindo (1871–1950) renounced politics for religion and philosophy, deeming the redemption of Indian culture against British occupation to depend on the continuity of Hindu tradition. He significantly advanced Hindu thought by emphasizing awareness of its foundation in Yoga as principle and method.

For Aurobindo, solitude is an integral aspect of traditional Hindu practice. "We must not make life a waiting for renunciation, but renunciation a preparation for life; instead of running from God in the town to God in the forest, we must rather plunge into the mountain solitude in our own souls for knowledge and joy and spiritual energy ..."

In "Essays on the Gita" (in his *Essays Human and Divine*), Aurobindo identifies the spiritual goal of "a meditative mind turned towards solitude and away from the vain noise of crowds and the assemblies of men." In "Self–Consecration" (in his *The Yoga of Divine Works*) he writes that "The endless difficulties that arise from the environing world," are dispelled by erecting firmly against them a defense of outer physical and inner spiritual solitude, safe behind a wall of inner silence. Here the practitioner remains impassive, untouched by the world and by others. "To be alone with oneself or alone with the Divine" is the path of "Godward passion of the heart."

Ramana Maharshi

The Indian sage Ramana Maharshi (1879–1950), teacher of Advaita Vedanta, is known for his practice of mauna, or silence. He spent years in solitude in the caves of Arunachala Mountain, and when later pressed for a public presence (darshan), Ramana spent hours in public silence, not as eccentricity but as historically–recognized and conscious expression of spiritual teaching. The Hindu tradition of mauna refers to silence as a practitioner's vow in undertaking an austerity or *tapa*, but also to a condition and product of deep meditation and quietude. Silence is not the absence of communication but a positive state of mind.

Ramana frequently defined solitude as a preparation for silence. He defines "dwelling in solitude" as "the state of being free from mental concepts." As with predecessors in the Hindu tradition, Ramana sees solitude as a tool, not end: "Restraint of speech, not accepting anything from others, conquest of desire, renunciation of action, continence, and Solitude are all aids in the early stages of this samadhi yoga." Part of the goal is to achieve "the perfection of Solitude." For Ramana, sagacity is possible when solitude is perfected as a state of mind and body, pointing to that which "the sage who has inner and outer senses controlled, in Solitude and equanimity..."

Solitude is context or precondition, while silence is the goal. Ramana notes that "the Self is that where there is absolutely no I–thought. That is called Silence...." Silence is the qualitative aspect of the state of solitude. Silence is the most powerful practice for breaking through maya (delusion, ignorance) to a perfect state of mind. Thus, in part explaining his public sittings, Ramana states that "Silence is the highest and most perfect form of instruction which the guru can give, for by its nature it is the closest to the essential object of such instruction, which is the realization by the disciple of the incommunicable and inexpressible Absolute."

J. Krishnamurti

Jiddu Krishnamurti (1895–1986) was an Indian–born philosopher whose
engaging teaching style and non–adherence to a specific religion or school
strengthened his trenchant observations. He advocates a radical rejection
of accepted social expectations in favor of greater independent thinking.

Krishnamurti's father was a theosophist, employed by Anne Besant
and Charles Leadbeater at the Theosophy Society headquarters in Adyar,
India. Under the tutelage of Besant and Leadbeater, the young Jiddu was
groomed to become the next World Teacher, establishing the Order of the
Star in the East as an organization to support the effort. Jiddu was taken on
world–wide travels to give speeches. In 1922 (at age twenty–seven), he and
his younger brother visited Ojai, California, where a trust had been established for their residence. Here Krishnamurti reported mystical experiences
(which recurred throughout his lifetime). The content of the experiences is
significantly independent of Theosophical thought. In 1929, Krishnamurti
announced his refusal to be Theosophy's World Teacher. He dissolves the
Order of the Star in the East, rebuffing Theosophy for an independent path.

In a sense, however, Krishnamurti was to continue to function as a "world
teacher," pursuing the quest for an ethical order fundamental to the human
mind. Solitude is a key concept in his thinking. Here are two examples:

> In a 1955 public talk in Bombay, Krishnamurti echoes Rousseau in
> identifying dependence of human thought on society and sociali-
> zation, even in eremitism. He asks whether truth can ever be iden-
> tified without breaking from the content of the very society within
> which a person depends for vocabulary, thought, the mechanics
> of reflection. "The sannyasi, the monk, the hermit renounces the
> world, renounces society, but his whole pattern of thinking is still
> conditioned by society; he is still a Christian or a Hindu, pursuing
> the ideal of Christianity or of Hinduism." Thought and practice
> remains "essentially conditioned" because society's function limits
> the individual within social bounds as much as psychological ones.

An entry in Krishnamurti's *Notebooks* addresses the necessity of solitude,
or aloneness:

> The hermit and the monk are never alone in their cell, in their
> retreat; they have still the burden of the past, their traditions,

their gods, their experiences and knowledge; they are never alone, they are full of thought, determinations and creating visions, disciplines. They have changed their names and their clothes but aloneness is not near them. But yet you must be alone ...

This aloneness is solitude:

> For the total development of the human being, solitude as a means of cultivating sensitivity becomes a necessity. One has to know what it is to be alone, what it is to meditate, what it is to die; and the implications of solitude, of meditation, of death, can be known only by seeking them out. These implications cannot be taught, they must be learned.

This learning is not passive receiving of thought or tradition but is actively animated by a "state of inquiry." To learn solitude means to inquire into and actively experience solitude, otherwise one remains dependent on second-hand resources and past socialization. In Krishnamurti, philosophy clears the way for self–knowledge. The method adopts a frank and dogged Socratic–like questioning, a non–religious Buddhist psychology, and pursuit of a fundamental order underlying human existence.

63. The Hermit in the Tarot

The tarot originated in the Renaissance as a tool of divination, but was popularized as ancient Egyptian occultism in eighteenth–century France and beyond by Antoine Court de Gébelin (1725–1784) and Jean-Baptiste Alliette (1738-1791), the latter calling himself Etteilla. Belief in the Egypt connection lingers. With the advent of modern psychology, the universality of the images of the tarot are now perceived as representations of powerful archetypes of the subconscious (in the style of Carl Jung).

The hermit is the ninth card of the Major Arcana. The hermit represents a universal stirring of feelings and emotions with respect to society and human interaction. In the popular mind, the hermit represents solitude and self–determination in a positive sense, but negatively (reversing the card) holds a misanthropic and anti–social attitude. The tarot taps this paradox.

The striking image commissioned for the Rider–Waite set of tarot cards

and Arthur Edward Waite's 1911 publication of *Pictorial History of the Tarot*
present the full accoutrement of symbolism in the hermit. The hermit in
Waite is not garbed like a beggar but like a friar, a Capuchin. He is not a
wanderer but projects a mission with his lantern and staff. Waite does not
mention it, but the lantern clearly suggests Diogenes the Cynic, the Greek
precursor of the Western hermit, who searches for a wise person among a
world of fools. Not being a beggar, the hermit does not represent isolation,
idleness, or inability. His long white beard, habit, and walking stick remind
Waite of the Ancient of Days (William Blake's depiction), and his lantern
is the Light of the World, shed for enlightenment of others. Hence, the
hermit is not Diogenes the miscreant, the mischievous, the misanthrope.
The hermit is a sage, not simply searching for truth and justice but bringing
them to others. He stands at a precipice, like the Fool (card 1), but knows
when to stop. He is not, like the Fool, on a quest or an adventure. The
hermit seeks to bring light to others.

The mystery and motive of the solitary in Western history has always
proven unsettling to the common person. The image of the hermit outside
the context of daily life or subordination to authority has perplexed many. In
Mary Rotha Clay's classic *The Hermits and Anchorites of England* (1914), and in
later research, we see glimpses of hermits in medieval England categorized by
dwelling–place: island, fen, cave, lighthouse, forest, hillside, highway, bridge,
town, and cloister, demonstrating by their independence why ecclesiastical
authorities preferred for them the anchorhold. In the history of the Tarot,
this antipathy is carried over; the hermit has represented negative values:
circumspection, dissimulation, roguery, and corruption at worse. Reversed,
the card came to represent disguise, concealment, fear.

To which Waite replies that the negative characteristics are "artificial and
arbitrary." Waite rehabilitates the hermit based on its universal archetype,
going so far as to reject the concept of prudence assigned to the hermit by
some, for this card is not mere temperance but enlightenment. The Hermit
has attained enlightenment and now offers it to those who emulate his path.

The other image in the Tarot associated with the path of solitude is the
Four of Swords, effectively rendered in Rider–Waite as a knight or effigy
of a knight lying on a tomb in an empty church. A stained glass window in
the background depicts a mother and child. The image of the knight and
swords projects finality, whether triumphant or failed. The silence of the
church is either serenity or abandonment. But the image of the Madonna
and Child is so universal a portrait of nurture, protection, and refuge, that

the viewer concludes that the solitude represented in this card suggests continuity, rebirth, and transformation.

The archetype affirms the putting away of the vanities of the old self, of resting in contemplation before marking the clean and innocent slate of a new life. The Four of Swords signifies the need to experience the solitude of the knight, and the embrace of the Universe.

The Hermit in the Tarot represents introspection, spiritual maturity, discipline or control, protection of the reservoir of wisdom versus dissipation of energy, active cultivation of sagacity, equilibrium between reality and wisdom and between authority and self–confidence, self–enrichment by all that contribute to wisdom, prudence associated with silence and measure, love as the protection of universal balance, creativity as the life force preserving wisdom and harmony, with its ability to offer these virtues as renunciation and as humaneness.

Russian–born P. D. Ouspensky (1878–1947) popularized interest in the occult and the ideas of G. I. Gurdjieff. In 1913, Ouspensky penned *The Symbolism of the Tarot*, a short work on the images of the tarot, using the recently issued Rider–Waite pictorial deck as his basis. Ouspensky (incorrectly) interprets the hermit as Hermes Trismegistus, and his accoutrement as an occult or gnostic symbol. Here is his rumination on the symbolism of the hermit:

> After long wanderings over a sandy, waterless desert where only serpents lived, I met the Hermit. He was wrapped in a long cloak, a hood thrown over his head. He held a long staff in one hand and in the other a lighted lantern, though it was broad daylight and the sun was shining.
>
> "The lantern of Hermes Trismegistus," said the voice, "this is higher knowledge, that inner knowledge which illuminates in a new way even what appears to be already clearly known. This lantern lights up the past, the present and the future for the Hermit, and opens the souls of people and the most intimate recesses of their hearts.
>
> "The cloak of Apollonius is the faculty of the wise man by which he isolates himself, even amidst a noisy crowd; it is his skill in hiding his mysteries, even while expressing them, his capacity for silence and his power to act in stillness.

"The staff of the patriarchs is his inner authority, his power, his self–confidence.

"The lantern, the cloak and the staff are the three symbols of initiation. They are needed to guide souls past the temptation of illusory fires by the roadside, so that they may go straight to the higher goal. He who receives these three symbols or aspires to obtain them, strives to enrich himself with all he can acquire, not for himself, but, like God, to delight in the joy of giving.

"The giving virtue is the basis of an initiate's life. His soul is transformed into 'a spoiler of all treasures,' so said Zarathustra.

"Initiation unites the human mind with the higher mind by a chain of analogies. This chain is the ladder leading to heaven, dreamed of by the patriarch."

CHAPTER 12

HERMITS AND SOLITARIES:
LATER TWENTIETH CENTURY TO THE PRESENT

64. The Rehabilitation of Hermits in the West

The image of the historical hermit was rehabilitated by a motley assembly of creative and religious figures in the twentieth century. They are not traditional figures dependent on old definitions. Having observed the experience of centuries and embracing the rehabilitation of solitude, they crafted wider universal principles for eremitism.

Jean Giono – France

Jean Giono (1895–1970) is best known to English–language readers for his 1953 tale *The Man Who Planted Trees*, about a solitary who reforests a barren region of the Provence Alps. The story is a late work for a writer first published twenty years before. Giono established a strong reputation in Europe as a craftsman of stories thriving on the sketch or incident, beginning with his first short story collection in 1932, titled *The Solitude of Compassion*.

In Giono's work, the virtue of compassion is often solitary not because it goes unrewarded but because it militates against social instinct. Human beings functioning in society are often cruel, indifferent, and rapacious. Removed from the conventions and contrivances of society, especially (or specifically) when returned to a relationship with nature, human beings can recover their inherent potential for sympathy, compassion, and balance.

This capacity is portrayed in eloquent understatement in *The Man Who Planted Trees*, which Giono wrote simply to persuade people to plant trees and to love planting trees. The story is far larger than even this ambitious desire. Giono creates a hermit as a model of human creativity and happiness, a figure whose accomplishments he praises as godlike, whose character he describes as pure virtue.

The narrator of the story is a young man traveling by foot through a deserted area of Provence (southern France) near the Alps. The region is marked by high winds and lack of water that have turned the region bare and scruffy, leaving the ruins of sad and abandoned villages. The year is 1913. In this setting, the narrator encounters a hermit.

The hermit is a shepherd, the only person living in this desolate land. He lives alone with his sheep and a dog. The narrator is surprised because the shepherd does not conform to the hermit type. The man lives in a house, not a hut, is clean, groomed, the house orderly, the food good. This is no garrulous and grumpy recluse but a thoughtful and purposeful man, he reflects. The next day, the narrator witnesses the hermit's occupation, his passion: the planting of acorns that will one day become oak trees, thousands of them. In answering the narrator's insistent questions, the shepherd (he is not called a hermit, and is called by name after he reveals it to the narrator) notes only that he plants trees because he has no other urgency, his wife and son having died. The shepherd had withdrawn into solitude, and noticed that the land was dying for lack of trees.

The two men part. A world war follows. After the war the narrator takes to the road again, himself a solitary. He recalls the ten thousand oaks that Elzéard Bouffier had hoped to see, and sets out in that direction. The narrator finds the hermit and, speechless, witnesses thousands of thriving trees over miles and miles. The parallel momentum of creation and anonymity continues to unfold over the years. The forest grows healthier. Water, flora, fauna, and human residents return. Government officials are attracted by the "natural" growth of this new forest, but the anonymity of Bouffier is just as "natural." The narrator notes that Bouffier worked in solitude, and towards the end of his life lost the habit of speech—or saw no need for it. The story concludes with a forest ranger visiting the forest and helping secure pubic protection for it, telling the narrator that Bouffier knows more about trees than anyone, that he had discovered a way to happiness.

Basili Girbau – Spain

The Benedictine monastery of Montserrat in Catalonia (Spain) is over a thousand years old, famed throughout Europe for its hermits and twelve hermitages. But its last hermits—Father Estanislau and Father Basili—died in 2003 and have not been succeeded. In the late 1990s, the hermit Basili Girbau granted an interview published in *Integral* magazine (since rebranded, the interview no longer available) titled "Disillusionment is Positive."

Fr. Basili lived in the historic Santa Creu hermitage, a cave with enclosing glass wall, containing a bed, table, chairs, gas stove, books, and a cross. On the wall are a pair of pictures of Ramana Maharshi. Basili notes that he has spent half of his life traveling the world like the protagonist of Ramon Lull's medieval romance *Blanquerna*, in search of knowledge and spiritual understanding. He was sixty–six years old at the time of the interviews. Here is a summary:

> To be a hermit today is possible with the help of God. A grace, a love if you will, gives me this strength. This grace, call it a love, gives me the strength to live happily without so many needs. It is not a matter of philosophizing or discoursing…. The one thing I want to do is to deepen my consciousness, and I believe my work helps all of humanity. I am apart from others, but I coexist with them, therefore I feel close to them.
>
> Solitude is what someone feels who lives in an anonymous city surrounded by thousands of other people, living a terribly lonely life. But I do not live in that notion of solitude, which is external. That misery would be the absence of God, the absence of this plentitude, this point of transcendence. In my hermitage I have found peace, joy, interior silence, release or detachment from things that happen, and I see how faith, love, prayer, really take effect and become useful. My goal is to deepen this interior life and cultivate a spiritual life beyond the material.
>
> There are many points in common between contemplation, Christian mysticism, and the various Eastern religious currents that have created a new spirituality in the second half of this century. The medieval book *The Cloud of Unknowing* is a beautiful treatise with many points in common with the practice of Zen meditation. St. John of the Cross recommended spiritual exercises towards union with the divine and emptying of the mind that are

basically the same as those of transcendental meditation. I discovered Ramana Maharshi through a book in1963; he spoke of
jivan mukti or "man without mind," which is parallel to Christian
practice.

Basili argued that religiosity in the West has declined due to the value
placed on material comforts, but also to the emphasis on rational discourse
and the products of technology that do not benefit humanity but are
"instead evoking overarching fear, as in the manufacture of nuclear weapons
and the arming of nations to the teeth. We live without interior, without
depth, unclear of proportion, rationality, or clarity." Religion coexists and
is lived at this superficial level, even perpetuating barbarities in its name.
The only alternative is for a profound change in society, where people must
first "disillusion themselves. Disillusionment is positive, it is liberation, it
prepares a person for enlightenment. Disillusionment rids us of illusion,
so that what remains is real."

Maronite Hermits – Lebanon; Coptic Hermit – Egypt

The Maronite Church evolved a rite within the Antiochan Syriac tradition
in union with the Catholic Church. Historically, the church or ecclesiastical
structure emerged from a monastic founding by the fourth–century hermit
Maron. The Syriac hermit tradition is sustained by hermits, not by monks nor
by hermits attached to monasteries as cenobites. Thus St. Maron recovered
the Syriac eremitic tradition and adapted it to his own spirituality. Thus, too,
the hermit is distinguished from the anchorite, shut away in a hermitage. The
Maronite hermit is unique, however, in intersecting with the community, as
the original sociological observation of the historian of late antiquity Peter
Brown notes (section 7). The reputation of the hermit and the eremitic
tradition is a constructive and positive one in the Maronite Church.

The last major hermit canonized by the Catholic Church is the Lebanese Maronite priest Sharbel, or Charbel (1828–1898), who wrote nothing,
of whom no collections of sayings is compiled, and about whom little is
known. His fame in the twentieth century and thereafter derives from the
posthumous miracles attributed to him and to his intercession culminating
in his canonization in 1977.

Sharbel was born in northern Lebanon near cedar forests. He entered a
monastery at twenty–two years of age, and divided his time between work

in the fields and religious duties. He likely requested permission to live in greater solitude, permission likely granted based on his conduct of life. The Maronite order followed the Eastern practice of maintaining a skete or small hermitage of two hermits, so that Sharbel was able to enter a nearby hermitage when he was forty–seven, where he remained the rest of his life.

Not surprisingly, several religious hermits have been active in Lebanon in the latter twentieth century and thereafter, despite the Second Vatican Council abolition of the status of hermit. The four hermits are: Antonios Chayna (d. 2009), a priest, monk, and university professor who retired to a mountain hermitage in 1982; Sister Mary–Jesus Abboud, who lives in a hermitage on the grounds of an ancient convent (as of 2004); Youhanna Khawand, a priest, monk, and teacher, who started a hermitage in 1998 on the grounds of a 1673 monastery; and 4) Dario Escobar Montanya Sanchez, born in Colombia, studied and ordained in the United States, and a teacher for many years. Rejected by his bishop in his bid to become a hermit, Escobar traveled to Lebanon to become a Maronite monk, eventually occupying an abandoned hermitage. He is 87 years of age in 2021.

Though a Coptic Orthodox priest and not Maronite, Fr. Lazarus El–Anthony has popularized Middle Eastern eremitism. Formerly a teacher in his native Australia, Fr. Lazarus converted to Christianity after reading Thomas Merton's *The Seven Storey Mountain*. He became a Coptic desert hermit in southern Egypt, where he lives in a cave, regularly greeting pilgrims.

Thomas Merton – United States

The American Trappist monk Thomas Merton (1915–1968) was a prolific writer on a variety of religious subjects, known especially for his popularization of the monastic life and for his advocacy of eremitism, even among lay readers.

A Trappist monk since 1941, Merton leaped to fame as a writer with his autobiographical *The Seven Storey Mountain* (1948). He was to publish over sixty books and pamphlets, over five hundred articles and contributions to books, plus translations and poetry. (After his death, with publication of private journals and correspondence, a more controversial, contradictory, and iconoclastic figure emerged.)

The public life and writings of Merton reflect several phases: 1) traditional defense of monasticism in the modern world, 2) defense of monasticism using existential concepts, and introducing eremitism, 3) social and political concerns and a philosophical defense of solitude, 4) mysticism, transcendence, and Eastern thought.

Even in his early years of conversion and the decision to enter monastic life, Merton expressed an interest in the Carthusian order, which has an official status for hermits. Because he became a monk in 1941, access to the Carthusian order headquartered in France was not possible. In 1953 Merton floated to his abbot the suggestion of transfer but was politely refused. Merton was early attracted to eremitism and solitude. He found the Gethsemani monastery overcrowded, busy, highly ritualized, and noisy—the opposite of an atmosphere conducive to contemplation.

With 1948 publication of *The Seven Storey Mountain* and ordination to priesthood, Merton was afforded a reclusive corner of the monastery library for writing. Despite the popularity of his first books, some critics viewed them as a romanticized portrait of monastic life. By 1951, when he became Master of Scholastics at Gethsemani, Merton realized that his definitions of contemplation and spirituality were abstract and even cold, not serving his new sensibilities nor effectively communicating to his popular audience.

At the outset of his second phase, Merton was introduced to Christian existentialism by Max Picard's 1948 book *The World of Silence*. In 1953–54, Merton writes *Thoughts in Solitude* (not published until 1958), and a preface to Jean Leclerq's book on the Renaissance hermit Paul Giustiniani, signaling Merton's definitive defense of hermits within the monastic tradition, arguing that the "the exigencies of Christian life demand that there be hermits." In 1955, Merton writes *Dans la desert de Dieu*, a work on solitude privately printed only in French and Italian. Again Merton considers transferring to the Camaldolese, but the Trappist Order and his abbot quash the idea.

Merton dug in. He believed that contemporary monasticism revealed the weakness of its attempted modern–day spirituality. He begins developing the theme of solitude as a basis for monks to separate from society, but also for the spiritual development of individual monks for whom eremitism ought to be an option. Further, he advocates that lay people need more silence and solitude in their lives to develop a spiritual life.

Merton begins employing a new existential vocabulary: alienation, the absurd, the stranger, mass man, and the need for psychological integration. He distinguishes the individual from the person, criticizes socialization's transformation into materialism, and responses to hostility towards solitude. His compassion for suffering humanity is joined by the prescription of solitude, unmasking the false self built up by the contrivances of society against the true self. The true self is discovered only in the solitude of self and the solitude of God.

Published in his 1960 book *Disputed Questions*, Merton's "Notes for a Philosophy of Solitude" (retitled "Philosophy of Solitude" in later reprints), is his best essay on the topic. The premise of the essay is that everyone is a solitary in the existential sense, never fully conscious of aloneness because they allow society to fill their minds and hearts with "diversion, systematic distraction, borrowing Pascal's term, *'divertissement'*."

The tyranny of diversion channels the individual towards a solitude that is alienation from self and values. True solitude is not withdrawing from society but transcending it, becoming fully awake, withdrawing therefore from the false and the absurd of contrived social life towards true community. The hermit, says Merton, is a witness to a profound truth about human nature and about God the transcendent. The desert hermits of ancient Christianity are remembered not only for their asceticism but also for their charity. Their contemplation was not intellectual but the awareness of divine mercy transforming and elevating one's emptiness and turning it into the presence of perfect love. To the argument that one cannot withdraw from others, Merton replies that the hermit points not to others but to God "out of pity for the universe, out of loyalty to mankind, and without a spirit of bitterness or of resentment."

Merton concludes that "The life of the hermit is a life of material and physical poverty without visible support." The hermit is not automatically a more spiritual person, a person without worries, cares, frustrations, or insecurities. The image of Robinson Crusoe is "the myth not of eremitical solitude but pragmatic individualism," which has a secure and clever reply to every practical dilemma. The hermit is not so convinced. The hermit experiences (and this is not Merton's analogy but could have been) not the paradisiacal oasis of Crusoe but the arid desert and dryness of soul described by St. John of the Cross, though more modestly, if more ridden with angst.

Merton indicates the paradoxes of solitude: solitude is peace, but not as the world understands it; the solitary is happy but not in the worldly sense; solitude is richness, not of possessions but of emptiness; solitude is closeness to God, without perspective, without separation.

Merton's explicit praise of eremitism in the "Notes" offended ecclesiastical censors, who demanded three revisions, eliminating the words "monk" and "hermit" for "solitary"— ironically serving to broaden the theme of solitude for readers of every station in life. Having done so introduces the next phase of Merton's thinking in the first half of the 1960s.

Merton now addresses social and political issues such as war, racism, poverty, and violence. He increases his output by writing articles and essays more timely and critical in perspective than leisurely and reflective books. His increasing respites of solitude help, frequenting an empty cottage on the monastery grounds as a hermitage. In 1964 he circulates an essay to an international meeting of Cistercian abbots on provisioning solitude in monasteries, detailing creation of lauras and how they would work.

Shortly afterwards, Merton receives permission to move into the cottage on the Gethsemani grounds as full–time hermit. Living here is his preference, he writes to Dorothy Day in 1965, admitting that he could not adequately be both an activist and a hermit. In his last years, Merton decidedly pursues eremitism, writing elsewhere: "You will never find interior solitude unless you make some conscious effort to deliver yourself from the desires and the cares and the attachments of an existence in time and in the world."

The writings from 1965–68 present a new emphasis on the historical Christian mystics and on Taoist and Buddhist thought, seeing solitude in the context of enlightenment. Correspondence with a variety of spiritual figures and scholars from Sufism to Zen proves invaluable. Merton's vocabulary now includes terms like "emptying," "transcendence," "Christ–consciousness." But the clear indifference, even hostility, of the Gethsemani monks towards eremitism, and the growing lack of privacy surrounding his daily life, take their toll. Merton was sensitive to and hurt by the former, but ambivalent about the latter, at once thriving on personal contacts but regretting the disruptions to his solitude. In 1968, he considers relocating to a Trappist monastery in California, or even Alaska, being given permission for the first time to travel.

That spring, Merton lectures at the monastery of Our Lady of the Redwoods in California, finding the experience invigorating. That fall, he accepts the invitation to speak at a conference of Asian monastic leaders in Bangkok, Thailand. He considers the conference an opportunity to explore other venues for solitude and to deepen his concept of the monastic life. From his posthumous journals, for example, we know that he was enthusiastic about the Dalai Lama's advice to him to read the metaphysics of the Vajrayana school. Merton died in Bangkok, electrocuted by a faulty fan in his room.

In a frontispiece poem to *The Solitary Life*, Merton wrote:

> Follow my ways and I will lead you
> To golden–haired suns,
> Logos and music, blameless joys,
> Innocent of questions
> And beyond answers.
> For I, Solitude, am thine own Self:
> I, Nothingness, am thy All.
> I, Silence, am thy Amen.

Thomas Merton published *The Wisdom of the Desert* in 1960, a collection of favorite sayings of the Christian desert hermits. The Preface to the little ensemble surprisingly emerges as a clear, precise and useful introduction to eremitism as a whole.

In entering the desert, Merton asserts, the hermits abandoned the city for solitude—not just abandoned the pagan character of urban life but also abandoned their presumably increasing Christian presence, which did not transform society because Christianity was ideally extra–mundane. The hermits were ahead of their time, not behind it, not pragmatic, not individualistic, not even rebels against society. They simply believed that their values were sufficient for governing themselves and for providing humane fellowship.

The hermits needed no false social front or self. While they accepted dogmatic formulas of the Christian faith, in their simplest and most elemental forms, the hermits nevertheless concentrated on pursuing the transcendent will of God, which might differ from cell to cell, citing St. Anthony's dictum: "Whatever you see your soul to desire according to God, do that thing, and you shall keep your heart safe." This formula works because the desert hermits are sensitive, mature, and detached, working toward a transcendent and mysterious inner reality. Their simplicity, compunction, solitude, labor, poverty, and charity are quiet, humble, and sensible, based on *quies*, "rest" or "tranquility." Yet this virtue is never discussed or analyzed by the hermits. Merton declares that the desert hermits "had much more in common with Indian Yogis and with Zen Buddhist monks of China and Japan."

Disclosed by their sayings, the desert hermits strike readers as humble, quiet, and sensible, clearly conscious of themselves and of human nature. They are not the fanatic ascetics that hostile historians and novelists have portrayed. By the end of the fifth century, the monasteries of Scete and Nitria, so close to the desert, had become as worldly (to the hermits) as the cities, with their draconian laws and punishments. Merton notes that whips hung outside a Scete church to punish delinquent monks, thieves, and vagrants. To this the desert hermits would have profoundly demurred, for they represent, in Merton's view, the "primitive 'anarchic' desert ideal" of spirituality and enlightenment. Merton concludes *The Wisdom of the Desert* by repeating a telling reality as true as in 1960: that while the times are right for solitaries and hermits, reproducing the past is not sufficient for transcending it and all worldly limits. For this, each solitary must find his or her own way, discover his or her own strength, faith, and virtue.

With *The Way of Chuang Tzu*, published in 1965, Merton accelerated his trajectory toward compatible traditions. Most of the book presents traditional sayings attributed to Chuang–tzu, but Merton's preliminary note indicates his new appreciation for the vocabulary of Eastern thought. He writes that "Chuang Tzu is not concerned with words and formulas about reality, but with the direct existential grasp of reality in itself." And with *Mystics and Zen Masters*, published in 1967, Merton elatedly discovered the universality of eremitic thought in the Zen figures who "regard sparsity and moderation in all things as the most important matter and as being beneficial to the hermit. This they combine with the greatest equanimity and tranquility of mind and outer modesty...." The book compares and contrasts Zen masters and Christian saints and sages, searching out the commonality between Buddhist and Catholic thought.

Merton's last book, the 1968 *Zen and the Birds of Appetite*, extends the reflections of the previous book. He compiled his own recent diverse essays, lectures, and book reviews of Zen topics, and explored the thought of D. T. Suzuki and Kitarō Nishida, reflecting a fresh discovery of deeper Zen thought.

Robert Lax – United States

Robert Lax (1915–2000) is largely overshadowed by his association with the Trappist monk and fellow convert Thomas Merton, and with their circle of Columbia University friends of the 1930s and 1940s. In *The Seven Storey Mountain*, Merton characterized Lax as a prophet "without rage," referring to Lax's personality: intense, engaged, but also detached. Lax was the schemer, the dreamer, sometimes the clown. His droll manner and long face suggested to Merton that Lax "meditated on some incomprehensible woe." What woe Lax never let on.

Lax vagabonded across North America and Europe, becoming a solitary on the Greek island of Patmos from 1964 up to his death, occasionally writing poetry, but always demurring to discuss himself or his motives. Even to interviewer Peter France, who wrote of him in the 1996 book *Hermits: The Insights of Solitude*, Lax refused the title of "hermit," objecting that it sounded too self-conscious. Besides, he was not self-sufficient, like a hermit, not even handy, he owned. Lax was attracted to solitude because it was necessary to creativity and equanimity.

65. Rehabilitation of Hermits in the United States

Jack Kerouac

American writer Jack Kerouac (1922–1969) was an unlikely candidate for an experiment in solitude, but he undertook a sixty-three day stint as a fire look-out on Desolation Peak, in the Cascade Mountains of Washington State. For years his life had been a zigzag from aloneness to social frenzy. At the time of his solitude experiment, the famous books that were to confirm his place in American literature epitomizing the Beat Generation of the 1950s were not yet written. The winding trail of drugs, alcohol, sex, homelessness, vagabonding, in-group, and incessant reading and writing was beginning to unravel into despair.

In 1954, Kerouac took up the study of Buddhism as a possible solace. On the advice of poet-scholar-translator-roughneck Gary Snyder, who had worked as a fire look-out himself, Kerouac applied for the lookout job and was accepted to work during the summer of 1956. He spent sixty-three days on Desolation Peak with, as he put it, "no characters, alone, isolated." The record of this period is the first part of his novel *Desolation Angels* (1965), entitled "Desolation in Solitude," plus a little of the second part. Since all of Kerouac's fiction is literal autobiography, these passages testify to his frantic search for solace, highlighted by Kerouac's jocular, cynical, compulsive, subjective persona.

Kerouac passed most of his fire tower days conjuring memories, fantasizing, and counting the days until he could return to San Francisco, return to normalcy, return to dissipating avoidance of self. Occasionally he evokes

without insight the famous Chinese mountain hermit Hanshan, icon of the
Beat circle. "Desolation Adventure finds me finding at the bottom of myself
abysmal nothingness worse than that no illusion even——my mind's in rags."

Back in San Francisco, Kerouac noted: "The vision of the freedom of
eternity which I saw and which all wilderness hermitage saints have seen, is
of little use in cities and warring societies such as we have." The following
year (1957) Kerouac finally publishes *On the Road*, and *Dharma Bums* the
year after that—and so the legendary chronicler of the Beat Generation is
established in history. But though he published regularly thereafter, Kerouac's
self–destruction spun unchecked and in growing solitude until his death in
1969 at the age of forty–seven.

Buddhism scholar Robert Thurman remarks in his introduction to Jack
Kerouac's posthumously published book *Wake Up: A Life of the Buddha* that
Kerouac's Catholicism was a decisive factor in whether Kerouac sided with
the Beat Generation's Zen or with the orientation of Tibetan Mahayana
and its closer analogies to Christianity. As Kerouac himself acknowledged,
Mahayana Buddhism was for him "the word and the way I was looking for,"
a clear allusion to his original Catholicism. In the contrast of Mahayana
Buddhism's angels, saints, and demons to Zen's dry, hard disciple and
emphasis on meditation, Kerouac leaned toward the former, so superficially
as to further underscore Kerouac's inability to control the direction of his
life. He called Gautama "the blessed hermit."

Kerouac found model secular hermits in hobos. In 1960 he published
an article titled "The Vanishing American Hobo," in *Holiday Magazine*.
Kerouac laments the demise of the true hobos, the vagabonding pack rats
who founded California, brought down by ubiquitous police from their
"idealist lope to freedom" in "hills of holy silence and holy privacy" and
out of their cardboard jerrybuilt huts and flying boxcars.

The "footwalking freedom" of mountain man Jim Bridger or of Johnny
Appleseed is peculiarly American, notes Kerouac, comparing their lives to
Japan's mountain hermits, "waiting for Supreme Enlightenment which is
only obtainable through occasional complete solitude." In the United States,
camping is healthy but a crime for those who make it a vocation. Poverty
is a virtue among monks but vagrancy is a crime. The hobo in Brueghel
is an innocuous figure, but today a potential criminal, especially the Black
hobo, "the last of the Brueghel bums." "John Muir was a hobo who went
off into the mountains …"

Kerouac enumerates other "hobos" fulfilling his notion of nonconformist, iconoclast, perhaps solitary: Jean Valjean, Beethoven, Li Po, Jesus, Buddha, Chief Rain–In–The–Face. Like a sadhu, the hobo walks the back-roads for a meal, not needing to beg. The contemporary hobo ends up in the city, populating the poorer districts, such as New York's Bowery. Paris is friendly to hobos. Most European countries do not understand them, but "America is the motherland of bumdom."

Kerouac relates that he was a hobo himself once, until around 1956, when bad publicity about hobos scared the public. Kerouac was once in Tucson walking to the desert with his backpack at 2 a.m., intending to find a place to sleep, when police stopped him. They wanted to know where he was going. Kerouac explained that he'd spent the summer in the Forest Service. Asked if he had money why he didn't stay in a hotel, he replied that he likes the open air and, besides, it is free. Why? he is asked. Kerouac replies that he is studying hobo. "There's something strange going on, you can't even be alone any more in the primitive wilderness ..."

Edward Abbey

Edward Abbey (1927-1989) was a boisterous environmental activist noted for novels and radical politics, but recalls a year retreating into reflective solitude in his 1968 book *Desert Solitaire: A Season in the Wilderness*. The book represents the author's chronicle of a year's stint as park ranger in Arches National Park near Moab, Utah, as caretaker of what Abbey called a "33,000–acre garden." His chronicle interweaves nuance of personality with the magnificent environment Abbey encountered, displaying an ency-clopedic knowledge of plants, rocks, animal life, and meteorological lore. Abbey's unabashed love of wilderness and its preservation rivals that of his heroes Muir, Thoreau, and Audubon. Abbey was opinionated, garrulous, and sardonic, as his tempestuous life shows, but he could be sensitive and easily awed by isolation, solitude, and silence.

Of his solitary desert pursuit, Abbey wrote that he wanted to avoid "the clamor and filth and confusion of the cultural" and discover "the bare bones of existence, the elemental and fundamental." The year (minus winter) includes rich first–hand accounts of desert flora, snakes, water, rocks, heat, rivers, and a feral horse. Abbey spent the hours alone, often pursuing daredevil adventuring. He offers splendid polemics against anything threatening nature and wilderness. His is no desert spirituality or eremitic journal–keeping, though. Abbey is too ornery, too rough. For all his bravado and exploits, he keeps his sentiments close. He wonders if the one thing better than solitude is society, by which he means not cities but (perhaps echoing Keats)—a friend.

Eccentric American Solitaires

The November 21, 1938 issue of *LIFE Magazine* titled "Cuckooland" ("Screwy California" in the table of contents) profiled eccentrics of Hollywood, California in the 1930s, among them several hermits: Peter Howard, called "Peter the Hermit," a Dr. Newman, and Harry Hermann, called "Herman the Hermit." Peter Howard played bit parts in silent films, usually as a "biblical" character given his eccentric appearance: long beard, robe, and staff. He often posed for photos with tourists. Howard lived in a wooden shack on the outskirt hills of Hollywood, with a burro, a goat, and a dozen greyhounds.

Nothing else is known of the other hermits except what the magazine captions tell us: "Dr. Newman" is the sole member of his own religious cult and lives in a tree. Not unlike Peter Howard in appearance, Harry Hermann ("Herman the Hermit") frequently walked the streets of Hollywood dressed in robe and long beard.

Noah John Rondeau (1883–1967) was born and grew up in the High Peaks region of the Adirondack Mountains of New York State. He worked as a handyman, hunter, trapper, and wilderness guide, moving to the Cold River forest wilderness out of disgust for modern society. He lived between two cabins from 1913 to 1950. Rondeau accepted visitors as early as the 1920s, who came to name his residence Cold River City (he was dubbed "mayor" of the town, "Population: 1"). In 1950, at the age of sixty–seven, Rondeau was forced from his Cold River forest residence when the state's conservation department closed the forest after a major windstorm. Rondeau subsequently lived in several Adirondack locales, but no longer self–sufficiently. In old age he moved to a retirement home. Much of what is known of Rondeau's daily life as a hermit comes from his extensive journals, which he wrote encrypted.

Ray Phillips (1892–1975), born in New York City, was a World War I veteran, achieving the rank of captain. He worked as a food inspector during the 1920s before moving to Maine to live first on Monhegan Island, then on Manana Island, where he built a twelve by fifteen–foot home of local driftwood, without electricity, using battery–run television and radio.

Philips sailed and fished, entertained visitors, and made regular visits to the mainland for supplies and library books. He became known as "The Hermit of Manana Island."

Robert E. Harrill (1893–1972), born and raised in North Carolina, was committed to a psychiatric hospital at the age of sixty–two, after unsuccessful employment and failed marriage. He escaped, making his way to Fort Fisher State Recreation Area. Harrill discovered an abandoned war bunker near Cape Fear River, in which he lived thereafter, gathering seafood, growing vegetables, and subsisting as a hermit. Revealed to nearby residents, a steady stream of curious visitors come from afar, some leaving donations, others posing for photos with him for a small fee. Harrill was dubbed "The Fort Fisher Hermit" and became a popular tourist attraction in the state.

In the 1950s, hermits and misfits descended on the Everglades, Florida's southwest coast. Among them were Arthur Darwin, Martha Frock, Robert Ozmer, Leon Whilden, Foster Atkinson, and Al Seely.

Arthur Leslie Darwin (1879–1977) lived on the island of Possum Key from 1945 until his death, allowed to stay on the island after designated part of the National Park System in the early 1950s. He constructed a one–room concrete block house fourteen by sixteen–feet, without electricity, catching rainwater in a cistern. He grew fruit and vegetables to sell in Everglades City, until encroaching mangroves and their tannic acid altered the island soil and forced him to abandon growing. Darwin kept a radio, had no books, and avoided visitors.

Martha Frock (b. 1919?) lived on swampland in the Everglades six miles from the nearest road, in a house made of wood resting on concrete blocks. She lacked electricity, using a hand pump for water, and because she had no vehicle, relied on neighbors for supplies.

The most literate Everglades hermit was Robert Roy Ozmer (1899–1969), former newspaperman, actor, sailor, and artisan. Photos show him in a jaunty beret. Ozmer was well read and traveled extensively. He came to Pelican Key Island to live alone, hoping to cure his alcoholism.

Danish-born Leon Whilden moved to the Everglades in 1949 to live in what became Big Cypress National Preserve. He lived alone on Orchid Isles, at his multi–acre nursery, selling orchids and tropical plants.

Al Seely was a machinist, musician, surveyor, and military veteran. One day in 1969, diagnosed with six months to live, he moved to Ten Thousand Islands, living first in a fishing hut on Panther Key, then on Dismal Key in the two–room house of former resident and hermit Foster Atkinson (about which below). Seely painted, sold his art, read widely with a full bookshelf, and worked his sixty–five acres growing food. He left copious notes published posthumously in 2010 as a book titled *The Phony Hermit.*

Foster Atkinson resided on Dismal Key during the time Seely lived on Panther Key. Seely moved to Atkinson's house after the latter's death at seventy-two. According to Seely, the alcoholic Atkinson failed at everything he pursued. Atkinson had traveled the rails as a hobo and quarreled with every employer. He was selling sea shells while living in a tent on a main-land beach when he became caretaker of the Dismal Key house, where he lived the rest of his life.

Willard Kitchener MacDonald (1916–2004), a World War II military deserter who fled to Canada to avoid conscription, lived in isolation near Gully Lake, Nova Scotia. He became known as "The Hermit of Gully Lake." In 2003, when he lost his hut in a forest fire, local authorities moved him to a new cabin. Facing health problems and fearing institutionalization, Willard fled to the forest, later found dead.

Bernard Wheatley (1919–1991) was an African American physician who quit his career and moved to Hawaii to become a hermit. He graduated from medical school in 1945, becoming a surgeon in New York and Sweden. One day Wheatley walked away from his profession, family, and friends, wandering Europe and America, and settling into a cave in the Kalalau Valley on Hawaii's Kauai Island, accessible only by boat or over rigorous mountain terrain.

A 1959 issue of *Ebony Magazine* describes Dr. Wheatley as persuasive and articulate, able to quote Freud, Jung, Schopenhauer, Kant, and Tolstoy, deeply read in the New Testament, Eastern religions, and esoteric thought. Wheatley cited Jesus and Buddha as his heroes. He quit the world, he explained to his interviewer, because he viewed all institutions as corrupt and spiritually void. On his island, Wheatley inevitably attracted visitors, but had little patience for entertaining insincerity. He lived uninterruptedly as a hermit, and *Ebony* noted that he would have gone unnoticed had he lived in India.

Richard Proenneke (1916–2003) lived thirty years of solitude in the remote Twin Peaks region of Alaska. Mechanically adept and an amateur naturalist, Proenneke was eminently qualified for the survivalist undertaking. He was eventually employed by the National Park Service for his knowledge and wilderness experience. Proenneke built a log cabin from hand tools, explored mountains and rivers on foot and by canoe, and meticulously observed animal behavior and habitat, recording thoughts with sympathetic attachment to wilderness.

Proenneke maintained a diary, regularly corresponded with family and friends, and enjoyed increased personal contacts during visits away from the cabin. From the beginning, an old pilot–friend flew in food and supplies on a regular basis over the years, permitting Proenneke to perfect his wilderness situation and stay in his beloved cabin year–round. Eventually his stay extended to thirty years. After films about his isolated wilderness life popularized his fame in the 1980s, Proenneke lamented losing his earlier years of solitude, which better revealed the degree of self–sufficiency that he had attained. He began his pursuit of wilderness life late at age fifty–one; at eighty–one he entrusted his cabin to the National Park Service, maintained for visitors ever since.

66. Contemporary Men Hermits Around The World

Historical hermits have often reflected a religious motive, as have modern counterparts. Here are six religious men hermits, followed by non-religious.

Benedictine monk and hermit Dunstan Morrissey (1923–2009) founded Sky Farm Hermitage in 1977, in Sonoma, California. Sky Farm served as his dwelling, adding several cottages for retreatants over the years. After his death, two hermits have managed Sky Farm and continue to offer retreats.

Richard Withers (b. 1955) is a canonical hermit living modestly in a poor Philadelphia neighborhood. He adheres to a religious schedule but also engages in social and charitable work in his neighborhood.

Priest and hermit Charles Brandt (1923–2020) resided within old–growth forest on Vancouver Island, British Columbia, in Canada. Once an ornithologist, Trappist monk, and active book conservator, Brandt remained an avid photographer and naturalist, offering meditation retreats at his cabin. He is author of *Meditations From The Wilderness: A Collection of Profound Writing on Nature as the Source of Inspiration* (1997).

Daniel Bourguet (b. 1946) is a French Protestant hermit of the Reform sect, a former pastor and university professor, author of over two dozen books on Christian topics, none particular to eremitism. When studying as a youth,

Bourguet felt a desire for solitude, discovering that his superiors approved of his aspiration. He spent time at a Trappist monastery and Dominican community before undertaking solitude at his own hermitage in a wooded area of Cevennes, southern France. Bourguet lives in a single–room log cabin completely off grid, including the absence of media, yet like a *starets*, visitors seeking his counsel are numerous and regular. Bourguet has served as prior of the Order of Watchers, a virtual network of spiritually–minded hermits.

Maxime Qavtaradze (b. 1954) can be counted a modern stylite. The Georgian Orthodox priest lived alone atop Katskhi pillar, in a cottage adjacent to a chapel, 130 feet high (forty meters), from 1993 to 2015. Maxime would lift by pulley supplies prepared by fellow monks, though he descended the pillar twice a week. The pillar and chapel date from the tenth century; accessing the top of the pillar was forbidden by Patriarch Ilia II to preserve the site.

Norman Davies is a Jewish contemplative living in Malaga (Spain) as a hermit. He describes his daily life as "the practice of a dedicated and intentional prayerful lifestyle akin to solitary monasticism or eremitism. This is decided rarety in Jewish history and in twenty–first century Jewish practice it is virtually non–existent." Davies, a former music teacher in the UK, cites Philo of Alexandria and the Essenes as ancient models, acknowledging the influence of his pre–conversion life as a Carmelite monk.

Motives among solitaries may converge around creativity, as Anthony Storr noted in his book *Solitude: A Return to the Self*. Two examples of creative hermits are Valerio Ricetti (1898–1952) and Manfred Gnädinger (1936-2002).

Ricetti, an Italian immigrant to Australia, arrived as an adolescent. He found work on steamboats. One day chancing upon a series of caves he decided to dwell in one. Over time he enhanced the caves via galleries into adjoining rock to create finished masonry passages and rooms, adding a water well, ample gardens, and wall iconography. Ricetti lived like a hermit. Injured one day, he was discovered by a passer–by, taken to hospital, and his dwelling-place revealed. Visitors praised his creation and he discovered the Italian community around Griffith, New South Wales, where he lived. Ricetti was interned with other Italians during World War II, put on road maintenance crews, where he shared his building skills, and returned to dwell in his cave after the war. In 1952, beset by mental illness, Ricetti returned to Italy, where he died shortly afterwards. The cave is today called "Hermit's Cave," maintained on the provincial registry for historic architecture.

Born in Germany, Manfred Gnädinger settled in Camelle on the coast of Galicia (Spain) in his twenties. He took up residence in a seaside hut, sculpting rock and driftwood in Gaudi–like configurations, dubbing the coast that displayed his works his museum. Man, as he was called, tall, long-bearded, and gaunt, lived a simple hermit life, with a small garden and neither electricity nor running water. He sculpted scores of figures and filled hundreds of notebooks with thousands of artistic sketches. Thirty years later, a horrific oil spill from the off–shore British tanker ship Prestige destroyed all of his work, bringing down all the sculptures and coating the beach and shoreline past his hut in thick black oil. Man was distraught. He died a month later. His "museum" has since been partially recovered by the village and preserved in commemoration of the hermit–artist.

If not creativity or overt belief, other contemporary hermit men are motivated by a personal response to the world.

Scottish–born Jake Williams has been a sailor, musician, handyman, and hermit. Williams lives in the Scottish Highlands, in the middle of a forest, where he contrives everything from tools to gardens using found objects recovered during expeditions to distant urban areas. He is the subject of the 2011 documentary film *Two Years at Sea* and continued media attention.

Sometimes the lure of escape overcomes the potential hermit, as in the example of Masafumi Nagasaki (b. 1936), who once worked in a factory in Osaka, Japan, dreaming of living on a deserted island. One day in 1989 he left civilization behind to live alone on the deserted Japanese island of Sotobanari (Okinawa Prefecture). He lived without electricity, water (except rainfall), animal food—or clothing, given that no one ever visited the deserted island. Nagasaki is the subject of several news reports and films, wherein he would insist he wanted to live out his life on the island. But in 2018, a passing boater noticed him and notified authorities. Nagasaki was involuntarily removed from the island, placed in public housing, and refused permission to return to the island.

Italian–born Pietro Lentini sought to escape years of dissipation, becoming a hermit in the Umbrian region of the Apennines, on Mt. Aspra, in Valnerina. He found a ruined dwelling, furbished it—acquaintances later helping in the task— and lives there in silence and solitude, lacking running water and electricity, now with a solar-charged mobile phone gifted to him for emergencies. Occasionally Lentini descends to the town for provisions. He pursues a makeshift Christianity of his own crafting and frequently plays a worn flute. Lentini is seventy years old.

Since 1965, Chilean–born Faustino Barrientos lives alone on the shores of Lake O'Higgins in Patagonia, southernmost Chile. His dwelling is the remnant of a boat cabin. He lives from herds, livestock, and supplies from a boat that passes every ten days. He has no electricity, but uses battery–powered short wave and ham radios. Barrientos visits the nearest town every few years, riding by horse the twenty–five miles over mountains to exchange his animals for food and batteries. The inhabitants think he is crazy. He expresses no spiritual or other motive for his hermit lifestyle.

In 2001, Canadian researcher Robert Kull journeyed to a tiny deserted island in southern Chile to begin a year–long experiment in solitude wilderness. Kull had recently earned degrees in biology and psychology, and was scheduled to pursue a fellowship in behavioral studies in British Columbia, specifically interested in the effects of deep wilderness solitude. He convinced his doctoral faculty to accept his project, assembled food, clothes, supplies, and tools, and embarked. While pursuing observations and notes, Kull developed a routine of meditation; in his last months on the island, he quit reading and writing to concentrate on meditation, listening, stillness, and observation. Kull attributes the gradual realization that the self and all of nature is sufficient and sacred to the simplification undergone by the self–sufficiency and solitude he was able to experience. Kull recounts his year in his book *Solitude: Seeking Wisdom In Extremes* (2008).

Neil Ansell lived alone in Penlan Cottage in the rural isolation of Wales for five years, without car, phone, clock, or fossil fuel. In 2011, Ansell published a book on his solitude years, *Deep Country: Five Years in the Welsh Hills*, imminently observant while self–effacing about his routines and the wild creatures that shared his forest. Ansell observed birds, grew food, and foraged. The silence outside reflected a growing silence within. Interior monologue quieted to a whisper, then fading away entirely. While he had not practiced meditation beforehand, Ansell notes that he came to understand the Buddhist concept of no–mind. The self becomes as much a part of the landscape as a stone. Ansell's five years were cut short by a virus he contracted, perhaps carried by bats or mice.

David Glasheen (b. 1943) enjoyed an elite and privileged life as a millionaire stock broker in Australia until the 1987 stock market crash wiped out his wealth. Glasheen decided to quit society, eventually moving to deserted Restoration Island, where he learned to fish, cook, and survive with a poor solar–powered internet connection and an annual boat trip to buy supplies. He was frequently visited by journalists and old acquaintances;

his wife divorced him as soon as he fell into poverty. Seventy–seven year old Glasheen has published a memoir titled *Millionaire Castaway* celebrating over twenty years of solitary life.

Since 1989, Mauro Morandi (b. 1939) has lived alone on the Italian island of Budelli, near Sardinia, a national park. Morandi has assembled solar panels, collects rainwater, makes furniture out of driftwood, and takes photographs of the island, enough to fill a book. Morandi gives occasional interviews, displaying a confident and relaxed perspective on solitude and self–sufficiency. A gentle skeptic, he nevertheless keeps up with family, acquaintances, and the world via mobile phone and social media. Pressured by national park authorities, Morandi quit the island April 2021.

Many other men have pursued a hermit life, in a variety of places around the world: British–born Brendon Grimshaw (1925–2012) moved to an island of Seychelles, East Africa. Pedro Luca (b. 1937) has lived in a cave in Argentina for the last forty years. New Zealander Tom Neale (1902-1977) spent sixteen years alone on a South Pacific island, more a survivalist than hermit. "Pete" has lived in a cave off the Kaikoura coast of New Zealand for over thirty years.

Russia counts many hermits beside the media–famous Agafia Lykova. For reasons suggesting a criminal past, "Viktor" moved to Siberia sixteen years ago to live in solitude, while Nikolai Gromov (b. 1947) presents the strange case of having left to the Siberian taiga in fear and remorse that he had slain his wife in a pique of drunkenness. Twenty–four years later, Gromov returned to his old dwelling. His wife had not been killed after all, but had died in an accident during Gromov's self–exile. Gromov remains alone with the burden of his history.

Some apparent or aspiring hermits reveal pathological motives. Carlos Sanchez Ortiz, a young medical doctor, disappeared from his home in Spain, to be found twenty years later in a Tuscany forest in Italy. Mushroom pickers who crossed his path passed information on to a European missing persons organization. His family was contacted, describing then twenty–six year old Carlos as severely depressed. They prepared to visit him, if only for a short meeting, but the forest hermit had disappeared again.

A similar motive may have impelled Filipino Mang Emigdio. He took off suddenly, abandoning wife and children, when a typhoon destroyed their home in 1987. Emigdio was found living in a mountain cave, refusing to leave, his pitying family and villagers helping him eke out a solitary life with regular visits.

Wilderness solitude is not equated to survivalism by hermits. The case of Chris McCandless (1968–1992) remains perplexing and elusive. McCandless may have grown up suffering childhood trauma, but its effect was, typically, unnoticeable to others. He expressed an enthusiasm for nature, outdoors, and wilderness when young, also demonstrating a strong empathy for homeless people with whom he sometimes mingled in Washington, D.C., offering them food, clothing, and comfort, in the shadow of the comfortable suburban home where he grew up with his parents. Over the years, his favorite reading was Tolstoy and Thoreau.

Upon college graduation, McCandless announced to family and friends a planned road trip. He had just given away his savings of $24,000 to charity, and disappeared, traversing the United States to end up in Alaskan wilderness. McCandless was intent upon plunging into wilderness survival, though he carried no food or gear, nor had acquired survival skills, only an expanded idealism. At first he attended to an evocative journal paralleling Thoreau's, but the late entries change tone. His successes had waned in just four months. He foresaw a fast–approaching fate.

As McCandless biographer Jon Krakauer notes, McCandless had a copy of Louis L'Amour's memoir *Education of a Wandering Man*, a page quoting from Robinson Jeffers's poem "Wise Men in Their Bad Hours":

> Death's a fierce meadowlark: but to die having made
> Something more equal to the centuries
> Than muscle and bone, is mostly to shed weakness.

On the other side of the page, which was blank, McCandless penned a brief farewell: "I have had a happy life and thank the Lord. Goodbye and may God bless all!"

McCandless died from starvation or food poisoning, at the age of twenty–four.

The case of Christopher Knight (b. 1965) is described in Michael Finkel's 2017 book *The Stranger in the Woods: The Extraordinary Story of the Last True Hermit*. Knight spent twenty–seven years in a wooded camp in Maine close to tourist and visitor cabins, from which Knight stole food and provisions with great deftness. The biographer's dogged interviews and identification of details reveal Knight to be a classic recluse (versus hermit). Knight was eventually caught, publicly rued his thievery, and has slipped into obscurity.

67. Contemporary Women Solitaries Around The World

Women hermits have traditionally been religious, with their existence in convents and anchorholds assumed, seldom seen or verified. This phenomenon has spanned geography, cultures, and historical eras. In recent decades, awareness of hermit nuns has increased. Similarly, non-religious motives for solitude and forms of eremitism among women have also emerged. Here are several modern religious women hermits, followed by non-religious.

The pseudonymous Pinions was an Englishwoman who became an anchorite in the Anglican tradition. She published the autobiographical *Wind on the Sand: The Hidden Life of an Anchoress* in 1980. Influenced by Christian spiritual classics (such as *The Cloud of Unknowing*, John of the Cross, and Ruysbroeck) Pinions became a nun, entering a community she eventually left because it was too busy and not sufficiently spiritual. She became a hermit, using the *Ancrene Wisse* and *Rule* of St. Benedict as guides; a local bishop approved of her residing in a small cottage as a hermit.

British–born Rachel Denton, once a teacher who spent a year with Carmelite nuns in seclusion, became a canonical Catholic hermit in Lincolnshire, where she strives to be food self–sufficient, sells her calligraphy, and adeptly uses social media.

Hermit–nun Mother Thekla (1918-2011) is famous as librettist to the composer John Tavener. She founded the Orthodox Monastery of the Assumption in 1966, moving it to Yorkshire in 1971. She outlived several nun–residents over the years. The nuns lived in separate cells and only came together for meals. The last recruitant–resident hermit–nun was American–born Mother Hilda, once a Byzantine scholar. One day, Mother Hilda took the elderly Mother Thekla to a nearby Anglican Abbey and left her there, subsequently selling the original monastery. Mother Hilda died in 2010. Mother Thekla had no successors to her monastery.

London–born Julia Bolton Holloway (b. 1937) holds a doctorate in medieval studies, and lives as a hermit in Florence, Italy. She works as a librarian and cemetery caretaker, and pursues social work with Roma immigrants. Once married, divorced, then an Anglican nun, Holloway maintained a busy career of scholarship in medieval studies, retiring from the faculty of the University of Colorado. She then moved to Italy, converting to Catholicism. Her focus is late medieval Europe and Italy, with books on Julian of Norwich and St. Brigit of Sweden. She maintains two websites, one on medieval Florence and another on medieval women mystics.

Perhaps the most famous recent British hermit–nun is Sister Wendy Beckett (1930–2018), an adept art historian, prolific writer, and recognized television personality known for nearly sixty books, video documentaries, and audio presentations on art. Less known is Sister Wendy's status as a Carmelite nun living as a hermit when not in the public limelight.

Among representative American women with canonical status as a hermit is a theologian and spiritual director Sister Laurel O'Neal of California, who blogs at "Notes from Stillsong Hermitage."

British–born Sara Maitland (b. 1950) is a convert to Catholicism, long a writer of religious themes and fantasy fiction. She published *A Book of Silence* (2008) to aptly describe her various experiments in living a solitary life based on the virtue of silence. Geographically, Maitland centers on several places: her original home on a moor in Northumbria, on the mountainous Scottish isle of Skye, with its natural grandeur and intimidating silence, on Mount Sinai, which she visits as part of a pilgrimage group, and in Galloway, Scotland, where she settles in a shepherd's cottage, practicing silence and contemplation. Maitland's themes interweave solitude, silence, *accidie* (the spiritual lethargy that attacks hermits), creation myths as grand metaphors, and the psychology of fairy and folk tales. A recurring theme in Maitland's work compares the Eastern and desert hermit's desire for emptiness versus the Western Romantic literati's desire to write and to fill themselves with nature.

Jane Dobisz spent a winter of solitude in an isolated log cabin as a Zen novice. From the experience, she wrote *One Hundred Days of Solitude: Losing Myself and Finding Grace on a Zen Retreat* (2004), originally titled *The Wisdom of Solitude: a Zen Retreat in the Woods*. Dobisz describes the cabin, the food, the sensations of winter, the abiding solitude—and her regimen of sitting, walking, ritual bowing, and wood–chopping, following the guidance of a Korean Zen master. Twenty–five years later, Dobisz became Zen master Bon Yeon and remains an active Zen teacher in the Boston area.

Michaela Ozelsel (1949–2011) was born in Germany, grew up in Turkey, and become a professional psychotherapist and lecturer in the United States. As a Muslim woman well versed in Sufi and Islamic texts, Ozelsel was uniquely qualified to provide a first–hand account of a Sufi *halvet* or retreat, offering psychological insight as well as apt citations from Islamic commentaries. The account is her 1996 book *Forty Days: The Diary of a Traditional Solitary Sufi Retreat.*

Secular American women have pursued solitude through literary reflections, as well as direct encounters in wilderness, as in these examples.

May Sarton (1912–1995) was an important figure among American women writers and feminists. Her *Journal of a Solitude* (1973) represents a turning point both in her career and in the book's influence on feminism. Sarton's notion of solitude was deliberately polemical, arguing that women are solitaries, marginalized in society and culture. Always having lived in a whirlwind of company, visiting Europe and residing in Cambridge, Massachusetts, Sarton finds life in a small New Hampshire town droll, a "vacuum of boredom," yet at her age she feels exhausted and "scattered" by visitors. Sarton reveals a failed resolution about solitude, a harsh view of solitude as loneliness.

Doris Grumbach (b. 1918) was a long–established writer at seventy-five years old when she had the opportunity one Maine winter to find herself alone in a small town for fifty days, a time she recounts in *Fifty Days of Solitude* (1995). Solitude is never absolute but she elects to exchange a minimum of words and to deliberately not relate with anyone. Rather than boring minutiae, Grumbach's record of these days reveals a sharp mind attentive to detail and introspection.

Living alone in rural Virginia, writer Annie Dillard (b.1945) reflects an inquisitive interest in nature in her book *Pilgrim at Tinker Creek* (1974). Her background is theology, lightly summoned to wrestle with or reconcile extremes of the natural world. Passages reflect Thoreau's literary style, circumscribed by a studied distance from nature and from transcendentalism. Solitude is a cautious ambiguity in the natural world.

Wildlife ecologist, writer, and photographer Anne LaBastille (1933–2011) published the autobiographical *Woodswoman: Living Alone in the Adirondack Wilderness* in 1976, chronicling her life as an avid naturalist. LaBastille built her own off–grid log cabin in the Adirondack forest next to a lake, away from roads and human habitation. The cabin becomes her physical and psychological sustenance, the embodiment of her solitude, as she records nature, silence, and occasional disruptive events, dismissing the notion of being a hermit or philosopher, at ease with wind, trees, and snow, eschewing traffic, noise, and pollution.

Stephanie Mills is an environmental writer and lecturer. The theme of her *Epicurean Simplicity* (2002) is reconciliation of simple living with a philosophy deriving pleasure from nature, based on Epicurus and Lucretius as much as Thoreau. Her autobiographical account records off–grid life on thirty–five acres of northern Michigan woods.

At seventeen years of age, Jane Carter (b. 1954) left her family home in Melbourne, Australia, to spend a year alone on uninhabited De Witt Island off Tasmania. A fishing vessel dropped her off, and she soon learned to fish, forage, cook, garden, and shelter. Government authorities opposed her presence on the island, but she refused to leave; local fishermen defended her presence there, occasionally bringing her supplies. The year was 1971, and Jane Cooper's motives for her experiment in solitude fit the mood of the times: she wanted to find her true self in a chaotic world full of war and violence. Jane became a media curiosity; a year later, she left the island, returning to obscurity.

An emblematic woman hermit living in wilderness today is the British–born Emma Orbach (b. 1955), born to privilege, daughter of a successful musician, educated in boarding schools, an Oxford graduate specializing in Chinese. Orbach had moved to an intentional community with her reluctant husband and children, then decided to live alone in an isolated setting after divorce. For over two decades she has lived in rural western Wales in a round mud structure similar to a yurt, without electricity, fossil fuel, or running water. She chops wood, grows vegetables, and shares her land with chickens, goats, horses, and cats.

Tamsin Calidas left London with her husband for a Scottish Hebrides island, an experiment in wilderness living for the young professional urbanites. A series of painful and emotional setbacks, including divorce leaving her to fend alone, physical injury, and financial destitution, challenge her willful attempts to make a viable solitude. Calidas addresses each threat to sheer survival by reconciling herself to the wild natural setting, learning to forage, to make ocean, flora, and fauna companionable, and confirming to herself her resilience, even in the face of social criticism and hostility. Calidas relates her quest for survival and solitude in a book–length memoir, *I Am An Island*, published in 2020.

APPENDIX

HERMIT DWELLING–PLACES: CELL, HUT, AND CABIN

In the Introduction to this book, we gathered speculations about the origins of eremitism–"speculations" because no social science identifies evidence of origins. But the universality and central role of the hermit's dwelling–place, attested by historical hermits through the centuries, suggests another useful dimension to the question of origins. Hermit remarks about hut, cell, and cottage, immediately project a physical dimension of space into the phenomenology of the hermit, a psychological dimension of eremitism fundamental to understanding the hermit experience.

Joseph Rykwert (b. 1926) was the first architectural historian to recognize the concept of the primitive hut as universally motivated by a sense of recapturing a lost spiritual state of being. The hut recreates the cave or womb, evoking simplicity and primordial nature before a decline or fall.

Rykwert was primarily interested in the link made by ancient Roman architect Vitruvius (and European successors) between home or dwelling–place and occurrences of the topic in ancient mythology. The myths concur in identifying the cosmogenic function of the hut. The only exception to this identification in antiquity is in the biblical Genesis, which maintains an anomalous creation myth wherein paradise lacks a house.

In Roman times, let alone throughout history, the virtuous occupant of the primitive hut imparts a holiness that transforms the hut into a shrine or temple, as in Ovid's famous story of Baucis and Philomon, the humble old couple apotheosized by the gods, their modest hut transformed into a temple (*Metamorphoses*, Book 8). Does the occupant transform the hut or does the hut transform the occupant?

Architectural historian Kazi K. Ashraf describes the hermit dwelling presented in early Indian Hindu and Buddhist traditions, where ascetic configurations of the hermit life shape the idea of the hermit hut. In Hindu culture, the third asrama or class is the hermit as forest ascetic. The forest hermit's hut complements his spiritual aspirations. The fourth asrama is the wandering ascetic or sadhu, who renounces any dwelling–place whatsoever, to identify absolutely with transcendence. In Buddhist India of the third century, the hut or *kuti* is distinctly for the solitary monk, a dwelling evolving from the cave or tree as place of habitation, distinct, too, from the larger building that represents multiple monks: the monastery.

While presenting the monastery as central to practitioners' lives, the Theravada tradition of Sri Lanka nevertheless celebrates the *Samannaphala Sutta* (called "The Fruit of the Homeless Life") because it asserts that the ascetic is free to achieve the perfected life of detachment and mental purity precisely because of his homelessness. Thus, the tension between dweller and wanderer is present in both Hindu and Buddhist traditions from the outset, and dwelling–place reflects this contrast.

The base of a tree, Buddhism's first hermit dwelling, evolved from the presence of a tree spirit, according to Vedic sources. The Buddha's post–enlightenment wanderings show him frequenting gardens, then hermit huts. The hut becomes a projection of self and purpose, evolving with the evolution of eremitism. The primitive appearance of the Vedic wild man is echoed by the fourth–century Jain digambara and the famous Gymno-sophists or naked philosophers contemporary with Alexander the Great, of which Diogenes the Cynic is a Western counterpart.

Historian Ashraf notes the relationship of famous solitaries and their dwelling–places. The rough temporary appearance of the fictional Robinson Crusoe's hut inevitably reflects the character's own dissatisfied and invol-untary state. Crusoe is not an ascetic or renunciate. In the case of Henry David Thoreau, his cabin at Walden is likewise temporary, but Thoreau lives there voluntarily, using the cabin to advance his intellectual interests. With the Japanese hermit–monk Kamo no Chōmei, the hut is permanent and intentional, his purpose of self–transformation entirely voluntary, thus the ideal relationship of hermit to hermit–dwelling. The dwelling is not transitional to a serious asceticism but the terminal setting completely identified with the person.

Two views of the hermit's hut contrast West and East. Where the West looked for the divine to enter the simple, the East looks from within the mind (and hut) outward. Heidegger cites Aristotle's reference to a fragment of Heraclitus, wherein Heraclitus is visited by guests who display their disdain for his small, modest dwelling, Heraclitus warming himself before a stove. Perceiving their disdain, Heraclitus tells them: "Here, too, the gods are present." The divine comes to the humble. In the poem "The Valley Wind" by Chinese poet Lu Yun (262–303), the hermit–poet's experience dwelling in his hut begins "initiating cosmic changes" and culminates: "My cottage becomes a Universe." The enlightened mind ascends to the cosmic.

In the Christian West, the "cell" designates the living quarters or individual room of the monk within a monastery. For the Christian desert hermits, the "cell" is the hut itself. The hut is the resolution of a search for an essential physical or geographic location for seeking God. The hut defines and reinforces behaviors while presenting visitors with a protocol, for the desert hermits, while not living in monasteries, did establish laura and sketes as well as individual dwellings. While shrines, churches, and temples establish immediate sacred spaces for the public, huts take on a similar sacred function for their occupants. Thus desert hermit Moses the Black can advise a monk to "Go, sit in your cell, and your cell will teach you everything" (section 8). The physical cell is transformed into the very heart and mind of the hermit.

Athanasius's *Life of Anthony* established the spiritual progression of the hermit: from withdrawal from secular life and conventional settings, to withdrawal into solitude and into desert. The process would initially involve work with a teacher or elder, confrontation with solitude and demons, followed by a breakthrough in establishing a spiritual solitude and a sacred space. These necessary stages suggest that the hermit's search for asceticism was not sustained by ecclesiastical structure or ritual but was anchored in the cell or hut. In theWest, wandering was discouraged. Leaving the cell could be dangerous. Visitors, too, could threatened the sacred character of the cell, and its occupant's work. In the East, only the adept became wanderers.

The identification of occupant with dwelling is a theme of Gaston Bachelard's 1958 book *The Poetics of Space*. While parts of the conventional house suggest subjects for psychoanalysis—basement, attic, inside versus outside, verticality, light and shadow, shapes of objects—Bachelard underscores the hermit's conscious identification with dwelling–place. The hermit masters the entire dwelling because the dwelling is the self, whole and conscious. The hermit hut embodies solitude, and in appearance necessarily—and radically—rejects embellishments. Bachelard puts it succinctly:

The hermit is before God. His hut, therefore, is just the opposite of the monastery. And there radiates about this centralized solitude a universe of meditation and prayer, a universe outside the universe.

Bachelard notes that the hut cannot receive input from the world, its riches, artifacts, or presumed enhancements, certainly not idle visitors. Poverty, or simplicity, is the source of the hut's atmosphere of harmony, the foundation of its function as a refuge.

The resolution of the hermit, the hut dweller, is often reduced to practical advice among the Christian desert hermits, as in Evagrios the Solitary (in his "Outline Teaching on Asceticism and Stillness in the Solitary Life" quoted in *Philokalia*, 1, 34–35):

> Do not pass your time with people engaged in worldly affairs or share their table, in case they involve you in their illusions and draw you away from the science of stillness. For this is what they want to do. Do not listen to their words or accept the thoughts of their hearts, for they are indeed harmful. If someone who lives in accordance with the love of God comes to you and invites you to eat, go if you wish, but return quickly to your cell. If possible, never sleep outside your cell, so that the gift of stillness may always be with you. Then you will be unhindered on your chosen path... If you find yourself continually invited outside your cell, decline the invitations. For continual absence from your cell is harmful. It deprives you of the grace of stillness, darkens your mind, withers your longing for God...

Of the hermits of Christian antiquity, therefore, the function of the cell is abstracted. The physical cell is seldom described. In China and Japan, however, several hermits offer outstanding descriptions of their huts and environs, among them Po Chu–ī (Bai Juyi), Shiwu (Stonehouse), Yoshishige no Yasutane, Saigyō, Kamo no Chōmei, Matsuo Bashō, and Ryōkan. All but Yoshishige no Yasutane are mentioned above.

Chinese Writers

Bai Juyi never became a recluse. He exemplifies a dilemma of ancient Chinese philosophy: the Confucian ideal of devoting one's intellect and skills to state and society, versus the Taoist ideal of seeking self–integration and wisdom, necessarily away and apart from the worldly "red dust" of state and society.

Bai Juyi was a respected government bureaucrat but also its perpetual critic. One day, he tells us, he was demoted and sent to Kiangsu province as marshal. Here he discovered Mount Lu.

Though he was always lured by the political and social controversies of the times, Bai remained a Buddhist "householder" with wife and children. Having immediately felt at home on Mount Lu, Bai dreamed of retiring to a small house in a wonderful landscape. He set about building a grass–thatched house of about a hundred square feet and was finished by the following spring.

Bai describes his house in detail: three spans in width, two rooms and four windows, a north door for cool breezes and a southern one of high rafters to catch sunlight, bamboo blinds, hemp curtains, wooden benches, screen partitions, and a spot for treasured objects: a *ch'in* (or lute) and books, Confucian, Taoist, and Buddhist.

Bai tells us that in the following spring he will work on the side room to the east, and fit it with paper panels and reed blinds, "for my Meng Guang." (As mentioned in section 32, Meng Guang was the wife of a Han dynasty recluse Liang Hung, the couple considered a model of marital happiness).

In front of the house are some hundred square feet of level ground. A terrace covers half, with a pond of lotus and fish, banked by bamboo and wildflowers. Nearby runs a stream among rocks, pines, and cedars, many of the trees of enormous width and height. The vines and underbrush beneath the pines block the sun from the forest floor.

On the northern side of the hall the cliff rises quickly, covered by trees and vines. A stream flows here and some tea plants grow. To the east is a modest waterfall. And to the west, where the cliff continues, Bai constructs a bamboo trough to carry water to the hut. It is an ideal setting: the mountains and valleys reveal splendors of the four seasons, "undergoing a thousand changes, assuming ten thousand forms…"

Bai Juyi's dwelling–place is a projection of self, the wonderful scenery around it displaying the myriad forms of the universe. His presence imparts a serenity unattainable in any social setting. But he is still young, still a functionary. He cannot retire, yet. Bai can daydream of retirement and the welcome life of Mount Lu. He composes "Record of the Thatched Hall on Mount Lu" upon the hut's completion. But soon he was assigned to a distant post, and never returned to live on Mount Lu.

The *Shan–shih* ("Mountain Poems") of Shiwu (Stonehouse) shares many similarities with the poems of other Chinese and Japanese Zen–monk hermits, but Stonehouse reveals many details of a hermit's daily life and his hut. He was not a wanderer, artist, or formal poet, nor a recluse official or fugitive but a monk, educated and well–studied in Buddhism under several masters. For a while he served as a meditation master and monastery abbot, acquiring an excellent reputation. But nothing suited him like the freedom of the mountains—in this case the Zhongnan in eastern China—where he composed one–hundred eighty–four verses he called "Mountain Poems," among other writings.

Stonehouse wrote in a burst of inspiration, fired with memory and insight. In the preface to his poems, he indicates that some monks had asked him to record what he had found interesting in his mountain life. "I sat here quietly and let my brush fly," he notes. "Suddenly this volume is full."

Stonehouse moved to his hermit hut in spring of 1312, on "Red Curtain Mountain and Sky Lake Spring," the latter a clear spring of water beside which he built his hut. Stonehouse's thatch hut lay "deep in the clouds... perched above a thousand peaks," in a place where, he says, "nothing but mountains meet my eyes."

Weather at his elevation is unpredictable. When rain falls the hut gets soaked, but dries well in sunshine. A heavy gust of wind rips out windows of oiled, translucent paper that serve as shutters. The dimensions of the hut are about three mats wide (about ten feet), looking cramp from outside, he admits, but he owns so little that he does not mind. Stonehouse mentions an occasional new fragrant grass mattress. His pillow is a slab of wood. He has a gilt statue of the Buddha (and three clay ones fashioned by his own hand). He moves his bookstand to read sutras by moonlight and maintains wild flowers in a vase before the statues. Among his belongings are an oil lamp, incense, a gong, and a bell. He mentions a tea stove "black with soot," a "broken–legged" cooking pot on a pile of dry leaves, a strainer with holes that doesn't strain rice, and a broken bowl he uses to mash fresh ginger.

Daily work is hard. He plows and hoes several terraced fields much of the day, and acquires a few skills: channeling a spring, using rocks to start a flame, hulling rice, chopping wood. He sometimes hauls wood to the village market for grain, his only contact with people except for occasional visits of monk acquaintances, friendly farmers, or wood–gatherers. One year he ran out of rice before spring, but another year had so much he did not know what to do with it all. Everyday is busy.

Stonehouse grew rice, millet, wheat, and perhaps soy. His garden provided vegetables; he mentions eggplants, cucumbers, yams, plus melons, hibiscus, gardenias, pawlonias, and chrysanthemums. The orchard boasts peach, plum, pear. On the mountain he gathers edible thistles and herbs such as pigweed, wormwood, and Solomon–seal, plus vine buds, chestnuts, pine nuts, pollen, and tea leaves. A typical meal mixes bamboo, rice, mushrooms, and pickled ginger.

Stonehouse's garb was as simple as his food: a patched robe made of whatever was available, depending on the season. In summer he wore short–lived mulberry paper or lotus–leaves, at other times a robe of sturdy hemp, which grew in wild abundance, braided bamboo around his waist. The patchwork he would accomplish with willow thread using a pine needle. Working, he often wore a cloth coat of coir (coconut fiber) and a leaf hat, shod in grass shoes and carrying a bamboo staff.

With the approach of cold, Stonehouse gathered a store of pine and mulberry logs but by winter's end he was burning leaves and pine needles. This meager source was his warmth by the stove, his paper quilt now replaced by an unspecified equivalent of cotton.

In his mountain hut, Stonehouse lived in the midst of wild nature, telling of the howl of gibbons, the laughter of tigers, and the usual deer, squirrels, rabbits, and birds from cranes to crows. Often he read the *Lankavatara* sutra, Tao Chien, and Hanshan (or at least remembers the latter two), but he regrets that his books have become home for silverfish.

At all times, the eremitic experience and the hut itself are the center of Stonehouse's life. "I built my hut on a lonely peak," he writes, "and pass my days in karma's wake." He wonders if he is a fool or a sage, a life of forty years as a hermit out of touch with the world. In his hut he is free from care, with nothing to change. The hut symbolizes this consciousness: "the worlds of the universe are there."

Japanese Writers

The obscure *Record of the Pond Pavilion* by Yoshishige no Yasutane (933–1002) represents an early work celebrating a solitary's dwelling. Yoshishige no Yasutane was a Confucian government bureaucrat with wife and children, retiring to become a Buddhist monk. He enjoyed books and writing in Chinese characters, and admired Chinese culture, as did many educated Japanese in the Heian era.

The short *Record* opens with a lament about the environs of the capital, Kyoto. A grand project to channel the direction of the Kamo River had split the city into a poor western quarter, flood–prone, rocky, and no longer arable, and a better–off eastern sector dominated by the wealthy. After years of saving, Yoshishige no Yasutane purchased a plot of land to move with his wife and children to a hospitable spot in the east. Here he built a small house consisting of several buildings surrounding a pond: quarters for his family, a library and study for himself, a small building housing a Buddha statue and effects, plus a little boat and oars for his children.

Within his little house, Yoshishige no Yasutane feels comfortable at last, "like a snail at peace in its shell, like a louse happy in the seam of a garment." To continue his analogies: like a quail in its nest with no interest in the vast forest, like a frog at the bottom of a well with no interest in the vast seas. Yoshishige no Yasutane sums up the balance he has attained: not bending the knee to high officials, but not shunning the faces of others by burying himself in the mountains or in a dark valley. In his study, Yoshishige no Yasutane reads the lives of past sage rulers, poets, and teachers (reminiscent of Tao Chien's reading), and writes poems after his favorite poet Po Chu-ī (Bai Juyi).

Saigyō (1118-1190) is not only the first significant figure in Japan's literary transition to the tanka and waka poetic styles, but also introduces the hermit-poet genre in his poetic collection *Sankashu* ("Mountain Home"). He does not describe his hut in detail, as do his successors, describing it as merely "a hut of sticks, flimsy as the world itself" and a "ramshackle grass hut, where no one but the wind comes to call." Instead, Saigyō expresses the inspiration derived from his hermit life in the mountains and in nature into seasonal images and sounds, important influences on later poets.

A Buddhist monk, a traveling mendicant, and a hermit, Saigyō spent much of his life without a permanent dwelling. However, his final mountain home was a hut; often in his travels Saigyō had built makeshift huts or lived in unoccupied abandoned ones for months or years at a time. His haunts included remote mountainous areas, sometimes near the sea, visiting temples and shrines, staying with friends or acquaintances garnered from family, religious, or literary ties. He returned to a monastery temple to reside shortly before his death. Saigyō's biography anticipates the travels and versifying of Bashō and the kindness, sentimentality, and simplicity of Ryōkan.

Saigyō's poetic strength derives from his identification with the nature that surrounds him in his mountain hut. He expresses his solitude by evoking sounds and images: a bush warbler sings, concealed in forest haze; a gentle spring rain trickles from the eaves of his dwelling, where its occupant is "idle, idle, unknown to others." As unknowable as the warbler. Other evocations: in spring, the beauty of the cherry blossoms prompts him to blossom-viewing all day; he wishes he could see every cherry tree, visit all ten—thousand mountains, like an omniscient Buddha. Azaleas, violets, and kerria roses are spring travel companions.

In autumn, Saigyō's melancholy nature overtakes his mood. Autumn images and sounds include falling leaves, a monkey chattering, infrequent bird song, chestnuts plopping down from the trees when fetching water from the mountain stream, deer walking right up to him, fearless of a human. Add now familiar images: crickets, chrysanthemums, pampas grass, snipes flying up from a marsh, the cry of a stag in the woods, marsh birds. The silent moonlight through his window provokes poignant contrast of image and sound: the nighttime sound of *shishi-odoshi* or *sōzu* (clackers) in a distant rice field. In contrast to spring, Saigyō sleeps during the day to spend the night moon-gazing. At the end of autumn come the blasts of icy wind.

Autumn dominates Saigyō's poems, using what would become *kigo*, seasonal words in haiku, centuries later. As in all cultures, winter is the universal metaphor for death. The lessons of solitude prepared Saigyō. In a late poem, he asks himself if it is time for a peaceful death, and replies, "Oh, yes!"

As mentioned, Kamo no Chōmei (1155–1216) lived through a chaotic and violent era in medieval Japan, applying his insights to *Hojoki*, an account of his times and of his last dwelling—place, a ten—foot square hut. While the previous section reviewed the tenor and depth of Kamo's sense of poignancy and impermanence in his writings, here we pursue details of his hermit life and hut.

At the age of fifty, having long since lost his ancestral home and livelihood, without family, rank, or stipend, Kamo became a monk–hermit, renouncing the world. At age sixty, he built his hut.

The hut was ten feet square, with foundation and thatched roof, a lean-to on the south and a bamboo porch. The interior was simple. A wall for a Buddha image, several baskets containing books of poetry and sacred writings, and a koto and lute. On the east wall is a straw mat for sleeping, next to a window, desk, and brazier.

Outside, Kamo has constructed a fenced garden and a rock pool with a bamboo pipe to drain water. The forest is close for brush–wood. From his retreat, he witnesses the change of seasons: wisteria blossoms in spring, summer cuckoos, autumn insect chirping, and snow in winter. Depending on the season Kamo picks fruits, nuts, or greens, gathers flowers or rice husks to weave. On a day trip to the mountains, he may visit an ancient temple or a famous gravesite. He writes that, given old age, he sometimes awakens in the middle of the night, whence he stirs "the buried embers and make[s] them companions in solitude."

Kamo no Chōmei sums up his hermit way of life: "Knowing myself and the world, I have no ambitions and do not mix in the world. I seek only tranquility; I rejoice in the absence of grief."

The Japanese Zen master Dōgen (1200–1253), founder of the Zen Sōtō school, sprinkled his masterpiece *Shōbōgenzō* with references to the perfection represented by the hermit's thatched hut and its exemplary occupant. In speaking of Hōjō, for example, who became enlightened when his master Baso told him that mind is the Buddha, Dōgen notes that Hōjō immediately climbed a mountain to separate himself from society:

> Living alone in a hermit's thatched hut, he survived on pine nuts and wore clothing he made from lotus leaves. ... For more than thirty years he pursued the Way by doing seated meditation. He neither met anyone nor heard about any human affairs whatsoever, and he forgot about the passing years, seeing only the mountains around him turning now green, now yellow. You can imagine how wretched the winds and frosts were.

Elsewhere, Dōgen mentions Kyōgen Chikan, who "built a thatched hermit's hut and, casting everything aside, he lived tranquilly and apart from human society" the rest of his life. Indeed, Dōgen concludes: "Thatched hermitages and cottages were where the saintly ones of old dwelt; they are residences esteemed by the saintly ones of the past."

An obscure work by a "medieval recluse memoirist," as one editor puts it, is the anonymous "Account of a Journey to the East" (*Tōkan kikō*), written circa 1242. The work is not an inspired eremitic journey nor an account of a hermit hut, but a jumble of derived literary and historical sources, the narrator–traveler noting landmarks by reciting every literary reference plucked from memory–then adding his own poem for the occasion. This instance of the travel genre may have influenced Bashō, at least in structure and style, though not in eremitism.

As already described, Matsuo Bashō (1644–1694) is best known for standardizing the formula and art of the haiku in Japanese poetry. Bashō's haiku was written in the context of several wry and personable travel journals as an itinerant Buddhist: *Journals of a Weather–Beaten Skeleton, Notes in My Knapsack,* and *Narrow Road to the Far North.* But perhaps his most famous travel piece is a brief narrative of his last dwelling place, *Genjuan no Fu,* translated by Burton Watson as "Record of the Hut of the Phantom," and by Donald Keene as "The Unreal Dwelling."

Like Kamo no Chōmei before him, Bashō's piece is the work of a world–weary observer of vanity, pretension, and human folly. He is sensitive to nature and the cycle of the seasons, honest and content with himself. There is no hint of a tumultuous life or a bitter maturity, neither Saigyō's qualms nor Kamo's pessimism.

Bashō's thatched hut is a single uncluttered room perched on a mountainside next to an old shrine, a setting reminding him of a Chinese painting.

Bashō declares himself a hermit, without visitors, not consciously pursuing solitude but just weary of the world in his old age. At fifty years of age, Bashō already counts himself old, like an old tree bearing bitter fruit, like a snail that has lost its shell, like a bagworm separated from it bag, drifting with the wind and clouds, without destination.

This formulaic modesty, necessary to the cultivator of solitude, opens the narrative of his hut. Bashō describes the mountainside setting as purifying, cleansing him of the dust of the world. The hut stands abandoned "at the crossroads of unreality," in an idyllic setting between two mountains.

From the south, the mountains exude a fragrant wind; the northern wind is steeped in the sea, cool and refreshing. Bashō came to the hut when azaleas were blossoming, wisteria hanging from the pines, cuckoos and swallows flying about. He can see a lofty pine forest shrouded in mist and glimpse a castle. One mountain reminds him of Fuji and an old cottage in which he once lived. On the other mountain, Bashō constructs a look–out he calls a monkey perch, where he can spread out a straw mat, enjoy a spectacular view—and pick lice!

Having lived an itinerant life in the company of other like–minded poets, Bashō still enjoys some socializing. But the villagers are farmers, not poets. They talk of rice planting and rabbits in their plots, and a noisome boar. When more sophisticated guests visit him night is passed in quiet conversation while moon–watching.

Bashō has no regrets for past mistakes: having chased after government office in his youth, not having become a formal Zen monk when he had the chance, or thinking that he could match the two great Chinese poets, Po Chu–ī and Tu Fu, who shaped his own sensibilities. But Bashō does not want to be misrepresented as one devoted to solitude and seeking only to hide in wilderness. "Rather, I am like a sick man weary of people, or someone who is tired of the world." Half of autumn (his life) is over, every morning and evening is new. Perhaps, Bashō wonders, this is what is meant by dwelling in unreality.

The hut is the setting and context of life and practice in the poetry of the celebrated Japanese poet and Zen monk Ryōkan Taigu (1758–1831). Within his hut, Ryōkan sits quietly, listening to falling leaves. The hut is lonely, a hut of sticks, flimsy as the world, he tells us.

Ryōkan's father was a merchant and village elder, who passed on to his son a love of poetry. The son's quiet childhood included both literature and religion, and his reticent nature rebelled at the notion of succeeding his father in business and politics. Instead, he became a Buddhist monk at the local Zen temple, and left it to train for twelve years with a Zen master, also cultivating the study of Chinese poetry and calligraphy. After the death of his master, Ryōkan traveled as a pilgrim for five years, returning to his native village after his father's death, settling himself in a nearby mountain hermitage at the age of forty.

Ryōkan called his hermitage "Gogo–an." A *gogo* is half a *sho*, the amount of rice necessary for daily sustenance. The word *an* means hermitage. The poverty of his hut is a projection of Ryōkan's own voluntary station in life. His poems describe himself, his huts, and his surroundings. The location of the hut is deep in a thick green forest, where no one can find the place except those who have lost their way. "A thousand peaks, ten thousand mountain streams yet no signs of anyone," he writes.

The path to the hut is covered with thick weeds. From the foot of the mountain rise white peaks. Ice, snow, and clouds isolate the hut all winter. The village river and a waterfall can be heard in summer, not far from the village's rice fields. A nearby spring provides Ryōkan with fresh water. In spring and summer the willows next to his vegetable garden are green; water plants float in his pond. Chrysanthemums line the fence; wisteria and ivy border the path from the heights of the hut down to the mountainside. The house is surrounded by bamboo groves. Sage covers the door.

As autumn comes, Ryōkan grows reflective. He gathers more firewood, burning dried leaves in the hearth to economize, and listens to the wind and rain. In isolation, the moon, flowers, and maple trees become friends; dense grass conceals his door; the evening rain brings tranquility. In the silence of night, he reads poems of the ancients, a few wood chips burning slowly to cast light on his books.

Winter is inevitably harsh. The mountain path to the village becomes impassible. Ryōkan depends upon his fixed stock of food. Sometimes the firewood is exhausted. There is no light from the lamp or fireplace. He lies in bed, listening to the sound pof freezing rain, lying in his bed unable to sleep.

In his reflectiveness, Ryōkan reveals potential for sociability. On quiet fall evenings he admits that he wants to share his feels "but there is no one." In several poems addressing his imagined interlocutor he asks: "please come and visit." Loneliness is not only dispelled by his reassertion that he truly loves the life of seclusion, but by his embrace of the universal sentiment of the Bodhisattva, stating that when he thinks of the sadness of the people in this world, their sadness becomes his own, and he wishes that his priest's robes were wide enough to "gather up all the suffering people in this floating world."

In one poem, Ryōkan describes his hut as a three–mat hut, in another passage
as four–mat. The hut consists of four bare walls, one window, no niche or
divider, a few poems written on a wall, while books of poetry lie on the bed
and are strewn on the floor. Ryōkan's possessions include a robe, a walking
stick, books, a lamp, and a hearth for burning firewood or charcoal. He has
a kettle, rice steamer, and a bowl. His food was procured from begging and
he had a weakness for sake proffered to him. Guests could expect little more
than "weak tea and thin soup"—and the cool breeze through his window.

As with other hermit–poets, the hermit hut is for Ryōkan a microcosm
of life and the universe. It is the setting for the cycle of being which Ryōkan
so sensitively portrays in his poetry. "My life is like an old run–down hermitage," he concludes.

The hermit hut is a symbol in pilgrimage narratives of Japanese Buddhism,
specifically in medieval to eighteenth–century Pure Land Buddhism, wherein
eremitic *hijiri* or wandering holy men promoted the use of pilgrimage by
identifying sacred places. But other Buddhist medieval tradition maintained
that pilgrimage had no value because ultimately there is no "place" or
"space" that is free of suffering in the cycle of karma, a sentiment poignantly
expressed both by Pure Land *hijiri* Ippen and by the more tradition–minded
writer Kamo no Chōmei in his description (in *Hojoki*) of Tokyo disasters.
Kamo's hut, like that of other hermits, is a response to impermanence,
and an identification of a sacred space. But Pure Land takes a specifically
sectarian trajectory.

For example, Pure Land tales present the wandering hermit Shoku fed and
kept warm in winter in his hut by miracles emanating from the Bodhisattva
Kannon. Hermits established a temple to Kannon on Mount Shosha, which
became a source of miracles in folk literature of the eighteenth century. Pure
Land pilgrimage tales depict the holy man moving beyond impermanence,
and the hermit's hut as standing outside of impermanence. Pure Land holy
men and hermits are not wanderers but seek a suitable setting for a temple
promoting Kannon. The sacred space is denoted by signs: miraculous clouds,
wonderful fragrance, celestial music, beautiful nature sounds, and mystical
light. The eremitic experience is thus secondary to the Kannon devotion
in Pure Land Buddhism.

The hermit hut as state of mind in Japanese Zen tradition is aptly pointed
out by Ashraf as the origin of the Japanese tea house, originally a tea hut.

Though *chanoyu*, the tea ceremony, was conducted in a social and ceremonial setting, the architectural concept reproduced the hut in the context of an urban rather than a mountain setting. Thus the hut reproduced a symbolic eremitism. This sensibility is represented by a short verse by a non-hermit: the court musician Toyohara Sumiaki (1450-1524), who writes:

> A place to escape to
> When one cannot ease one's cares in the mountains.
> The hut beneath the pines within the city.

Western writers

Identification of dwelling and dweller in the modern Western world is more complex, as eremitism became an anachronism, transformed into sentiment and solitude. Eremitism was the object of attritional social and economic forces, surviving in imagination and transformative literature and philosophy. It is no coincident that while literati expressed solitude, philosophers found ways of incorporating the symbol of eremitism: the hermit's hut.

The modern shift from eremitism to solitude could not properly celebrate the dwelling–place. Solitude was not the entire motive of the ancient and medieval hermits. Petrarch's Vaucluse, Montaigne's chateau, and Wordsworth's Dove Cottage were amicable homes for writers but likely hosted busy social circles. Descartes suggested Amsterdam versus Paris for the urban recluse, while Rousseau's solitary walks to the outskirts of Paris, far from people, compensated for a comfortable dwelling–place. The eighteenth–century British affectation for ornamental hermits reflects nostalgia for a lost mode of living not clearly understood by moderns, hence the contrived hermitages recreating imagined hermit cells or huts, however ahistorical the products.

A modern breakthrough is Thoreau's cabin, described in his 1854 book *Walden, or Life in the Woods*, chronicling his two year stint in a cabin in the woods of Concord, Massachusetts. "I went to the woods because I wished to live deliberately." Thoreau tells us that there, his days punctuated by reveries "in undisturbed solitude and stillness," he came to understand "what the Orientals mean by contemplation." His details about his cabin reveal the importance Thoreau placed in the construction, by his own hand, and what the cabin represented.

Thoreau built the cabin in 1845 on wooded land owned by his mentor Emerson. He hewed pine trees for the cabin. It was ten by fifteen feet with eight–foot posts, reserving unused parts of the trees, chiefly stumps, for firewood. He bought an old shanty for its sideboards, even retaining the nails, and put up siding with some help, adding the roof and floor. He meticulously itemized expenses for everything else from shingles to windows, bricks to lime. "My furniture, part of which I made myself—and the rest cost me nothing of which I have not rendered an account"—consisted of a bed, a table, a desk, three chairs, a looking–glass, a pair of tongs and irons, a kettle, a skillet, and a frying–pan, a dipper, a wash–bowl, two knives and forks, three plates, one cup, one spoon, a jug for oil, a jug for molasses, and a japanned lamp. As to the adequacy of his furniture, he quips: "I had three chairs in my house: one for solitude, two for friendship, three for society." He dug out a root cellar. Not until the approach of winter did he collect stones and bricks for the fireplace, and plaster the inside walls.

Thoreau drew water from the pond, even in winter when required to break the surface ice. He was especially pleased with his garden. He grew two and a half acres of green beans, most for market (a chapter in *Walden* is titled "Beanfields"), plus potatoes, corn, and peas. He mentions making a dish of wild purslane. Other foodstuffs he purchased: rice, molasses, rye meal, Indian meal (that is, corn meal), flour, sugar, pork, lard, apples, sweet potatoes, and pumpkin.

Although observers insist Thoreau went to his Walden cabin to write, his motive was deeper, his desire for solitude more thoroughgoing. At Walden, Thoreau states, "I experienced sometimes that the most sweet and tender, the most innocent and encouraging society may be found in any natural object, even for the poor misanthrope and most melancholy man." Yet Thoreau quit his cabin a bare two years after building it.

At the end of *Walden*, Thoreau anticipates the question of why he left. "I left the woods for as good a reason as I went there. Perhaps it seemed to me that I had several more lives to live, and could not spare any more time for that one." But in his *Journal*, an 1852 entry is more candidly regretful: "Why I left the woods? I do not think that I can tell. I have often wished myself back .... Perhaps if I lived there much longer, I might live there forever."

Even this admission belies the fact that Emerson prompted Thoreau's departure. In the summer of 1847, Emerson planned a year in England and Europe lecturing on transcendentalism and promoting his books. His wife was to stay with relatives, but at the last moment Emerson asked Thoreau to reside in the Emerson house serving as family caretaker in his absence. Thoreau obligingly left the cabin–which Emerson technically owned. The cabin was soon rented to Emerson's gardener and eventually dismantled. Thoreau recorded nothing about this set of events.

As noted in section 52, Friedrich Nietzsche more than once described himself as the hermit of Sils Maria in correspondence. During the summers of 1881 and in 1883 through 1888, Nietzsche stayed in the town of Sils Maria, Switzerland. He stayed in the same lodging, a converted farmhouse maintained by a family letting out a few rooms, providing meals, and selling a few goods. Nietzsche bought such items regularly (English biscuits, corned beef, tea, soap). At Sils Maria, Nietzsche adhered to the same meticulous routines, ate the same meals, walked the hills and mountains for hours at a time, wrote incessantly at night during bouts of insomnia, and shunned people as much as possible. And here he wrote *Thus Spoke Zarathustra*, *Beyond Good and Evil*, *On the Genealogy of Morals*, *Twilight of the Idols*, and *The Antichrist*. To a friend (in 1883) he wrote of his wish to have a small hut on the lake that would cost little given his financial straits:

> I should like to have enough money to build myself a sort of ideal dog-kennel—I mean, a wooden hut with two rooms, on a peninsula jutting out into the Silser Lake, where a Roman castle once stood. Living in these peasants cottages, as I have done hitherto, has in the end become unendurable. The rooms are low and confined, and there is always a good deal of noise. Otherwise the people of Sils-Maria are very kindly disposed to me and I think well of them. I board at the Edelweiss Hotel, an excellent hostelry. Of course I take my meals alone there at a price which is not altogether out of keeping with my slender means. I brought a large basketful of books with me to this place, so I am once more fixed up for a spell of three months.

Austrian poet Rilke, lost in cities and the disagreeable search for patrons, understood the refuge of the hut. As noted above, Rilke's translator Robert Hass notes that the early Rilke conceived of the image of the vast steppes of Russia as a symbol of the dissipation of self, while the mature Rilke used the image of a hut as the consolidation of actualization.

Austrian–born philosopher Ludwig Wittgenstein (1889–1951) built a hut in rural Skjolden, Norway, living in it occasionally throughout his life. In his 1951 obituary, the *Times* (of London) noted that "Throughout his life Wittgenstein showed the characteristics of a religious contemplative of the hermit type."

The hut was a two–story house constructed in 1913 by local workers, on the slope of a mountain overlooking a lake, considered a magnificent view by villagers. Access from the mountainside was difficult. Wittgenstein's usual itinerary was rowing a boat across the waters of Lake Eidsvatnets to the town, visiting Skjolden for supplies and gossip.

Why Wittgenstein wanted the hut remains conjecture. He was the progeny of a wealthy and cultured Vienna family, troubled by psychological problems and Austria's anti–Semitism. He taught at Cambridge University but found the clubbish atmosphere uncomfortable. Given the paucity of published output, Wittgenstein may have intended to spend more solitary time in Norway, working on logic and philosophy. Neither the furniture, food, nor his routines (other than details of some visits to the town and bits of conversations) are known.

Living in a hut in near wilderness may have suggested to Wittgenstein the landscape of philosophy itself. In his *Philosophical Investigations*, Wittgenstein mentions "signposts" suggestive of what informs philosophy versus actual logic or rules (85), and suggests that the destructive role of philosophy is like clearing rubble to build something new (118). Elsewhere in the same work he mentions that the purpose of philosophy is "to shew the fly the way out of the flybottle" (309). Getting to his hut, guests had to notice signposts, as the mountainous path had few navigational clues. Jan Estey, who attempted to identify the location of Wittgenstein's hut in person one early summer, noted the thickness of black flies on the route.

A modest solitary life reflects the limitations of expression that Wittgenstein contrasted to the grandiose designs of his colleagues. Who can know how much his hut prompted such minimalism in Wittgenstein's own philosophizing? After his death, Wittgenstein's hut was dismantled, leaving only the stone foundation and rubble. Subsequent trail markers to his house remain.

Another philosopher conceiving that philosophy presents markers, not rules, was the German–born Martin Heidegger (1889–1976), who among representative works compiled early essays under the title *Holzwege* ("Paths in Woods") and whose last collection of essays is titled *Wegmarken* ("Path-marks"). The titles suggest Heidegger's philosophical method, pursuing pathways in forests that may disappear or open new vistas, or suggest new pathways altogether, but only markers, not resolutions or definitive arrivals. The theme may have been inspired in part by his direct experience of for-ests, mountains, and open places around his own "*Hutte.*" Many observers have seen the convergence of "path" as method with Eastern thought, especially Taoism.

Heidegger's hut lies in the mountainous Black Forest of southern Ger-many, near the village of Todtnauberg, about twelve miles from Freiberg, where Heidegger lived. The hut sits on a slope overlooking a valley and within view of the Alps. Because of elevation and microclimates, the area presents varied weather patterns.

The hut is six by seven meters, specifically 236 by 278 feet, just over six–hundred square feet, better described as a cabin. The cabin is built entirely of wood, including timber shingles on the gabled roof. The exterior is painted gray, with bright yellow, blue, and green shutters and door. Inside are three rooms: from the storm porch one enters the dining and kitchen area with its heating stove, cooking stove, and bed. Beyond is an earth closet and a drying room for wood. The second room is a bedroom, taken up by beds and a wash table. From the bedroom is a third room, Heidegger's study, with a table, bed, and a desk looking out over the valley. Outside was a running stream and well. Originally the hut had neither electricity nor running water. Today the hut is unoccupied and closed.

The cabin was built in 1922 and visited during summers when Heidegger and his family lived in Marburg, where he taught. After appointment to the University of Freiberg in 1927, Heidegger often walked to the hut on weekends.

In a short 1934 article titled "Why Do I Stay in the Provinces?" Heidegger wrote that urbanites often wonder if living in mountains gets lonely and monotonous. Heidegger replies that it isn't loneliness, it is solitude:

Solitude has the peculiar and original power not of isolating us but of projecting our whole existence out into the vast nearness of the presence ["Wesen"] of all things.

Heidegger linked his work to that of his peasant neighbors: farmers, herders, woodcutters, not acting condescendingly toward them but respecting their rootedness in the soil. "My work is of the same sort. It is intimately rooted in and related to the life of the peasants."

On a deep winter's night when a wild, pounding snowstorm rages around the cabin and veils and covers everything, that is the perfect time for philosophy.

Adam Sharr, author of *Heidegger's Hut*, notes that for Heidegger the "philosophy of Todtnauberg" was the natural environs themselves, the forests, meadows, streams, and heights. These were aspects of an elemental motion—the core of philosophy reflected in its heights, versus the mundane irrelevancies occupying those who lived below. The hut and its environs complemented Heidegger's philosophizing. As it did so many others in history, regardless of era, geography, or tradition.

If—to paraphrase T. S. Eliot—to end is to make a beginning, then we end here where we began, we begin where we want to be. We end with the epigraphic poem of the ancient Chinese poet Lu Yun, "Valley Wind":

Living in retirement beyond the World,
Silently enjoying isolation,
I pull the rope of my door tighter
And stuff my window with roots and ferns.
My spirit is tuned to the Spring-season:
At the fall of the year there is autumn in my heart.
Thus imitating cosmic changes
My cottage becomes a Universe.

AFTERWORD

One goal of this book has been to show that hermits are universal in culture, geography, and historical time, diverse in belief, philosophy, and motive, yet singularly devoted to the project of self–development and solitary identity. At the same time, eremitism and its solitude themes have influenced realms of thought and living in many fields of human endeavor and achievement, from religion and philosophy, from literature to art, from culture to psychology.

At the beginning of this book, I made reference to the Hermitary website that I have maintained since 2002. I refer to it again, now that we have reached the last pages of our journey. But, indeed, the journey continues!

Want to keep up on news about more contemporary hermits and solitaries? Want to view historical hermits in art, photographs, and documentary films and videos about hermits and related themes? Even listen to music about hermits? Visit the Hermitary website (hermitary.com) to keep up on all things hermit!

BIBLIOGRAPHICAL REFERENCES

References to topics, works, and quotations are arranged by sections and appear sequentially as mentioned in the section.

Epigraph

From *Translations from the Chinese*, by Arthur Waley. New York: Knopf, 1941, p. 79.

Preface

These are representative titles; any number of scattered books about Christian hermits can be cited, though these two are among the most interesting and popular: *The Desert Fathers*, by Helen Waddell. Ann Arbor, MI: University of Michigan Press, 1983, and *The Sayings of the Desert Fathers*, by Benedicta Ward. London: Mowbrays, 1975 and Kalamazoo, MI: Cistercian Publications, 1984; *Road to Heaven: Encounters with Chinese Hermits*, by Bill Porter. San Francisco: Mercury House, 1993 and Berkeley, CA: Counterpoint, 2009 reprint; *Hermits: The Insights of Solitude*, by Peter France. New York: St. Martin's, 1996; *Solitude: A Return to the Self*, by Anthony Storr. New York: Free Press, 1988; *Solitude: A Philosophical Encounter*, by Philip Koch. La Salle, IL: Open Court, 1994.

Introduction

Gibran quote: *Sand and Foam: A Book of Aphorisms*, by Kahlil Gibran. New York: Knopf, 1926, p. 64; etymology of "eremos": entry ἐρῆμος in *Etymological Dictionary of Greek*, by Robert S. Beekes. Leiden and Boston: Brill, 2010, p. 456-457. The first modern psychological insight useful to constructing an eremitic psychology is the 1921 essay "Psychological Types," by Carl Jung. Jung not only identifies extraversion and introversion with behavioral examples but cites representative moments in Western intellectual history to identify expressions in cultures and individuals. Jung added other papers on typology and theory of types. The works are over four–hundred pages in length: *Psychological Types*, by C. G. Jung, translated by H. G. Baynes, revised by F. Hull. Princeton, NJ: Princeton University Press, Bollingen Series, 20, v. 6 of Jung's *Collected Works*), 1971. In his book *Hero With A Thousand Faces* (Princeton, NJ: Princeton University Press, Bollingen Foundation, 1949) Jungian mythographer Joseph Campbell argues that the refusal to heed the call of the heroic quest leads to either infantilism or to unique creativity. Psychoanalyst Otto Rank (1884-1939) proposed a similar idea in identifying the inspiration of the artist in his *Art and Artist: Creative Urge and Personality Development*, translated by Charles Francis Atkinson. New York: Knopf, 1943. Anthropologist Ernest Becker, in his book *The Denial of Death* (New York: Simon and Schuster, 1973), agrees with this dichotomy but holds, with post-Freudian thought, that the entire heroic quest is a denial of death, a failed search for immortality. *Shamanism: Archaic Techniques of Ecstasy*, by Mircea Eliade, translated by Willard R. Trask. Princeton: Princeton University Press, Bollingen Foundation, 2004 (first published 1951); on solitude: *The Life of the Mind*, by Hannah Arendt. New York: Harcourt Brace Jovanovich, 1978; *Authority*, by Richard Sennett. New York: Norton, 1980; Sennett had long promised a companion volume on solitude; *Solitude in Society: A Sociological Study in French Literature*, by Robert Sayre. Cambridge, MA: Harvard University Press, 1978; *Road to Heaven: Encounters with Chinese Hermits*, by Bill Porter. Mercury House: San Francisco, 1993 and Berkeley, CA: Counterpoint, 2009. Re terminology: William Hone used the term "hermitized" in his *The Everyday Book and Table Book*. London: Tegg, 1825 (v.1, p. 286), referring to St. Ulrich, who "starved and hermitized at Hessleborough." Herman Charles Merivale uses "hermitry" facetiously in his ponderous novel *Faucit of Balliol*. London: Chapman & Hall, 1882 (v. 1, p. 294): "Hermitry must be such a bore..." Perhaps "hermitry" is coined on the model of words with –ry suffix, such as wizardry or druidry.

1. Diogenes of Sinope

The life of Diogenes is recorded by Diogenes Laertius in *Lives of the Eminent Philosophers* Book 6, Chapter 2, Sections 20-71, p. 23-85, translated by Robert Drew Hicks. London: Heinemann, 1925 and https://archive.org/details/livesofeminentph02dioguoft. The quote: "A homeless exile...," is section 38, p. 39; about the lamp, section 41, p. 43; about blocking the sun, section 38, p. 39; another source of the sun anecdote is Plutarch's "Life of Alexander," book 7, section 14.3, p. 259, from *Plutarch's Lives*, translated by Bernadotte Perrin. London: Heinemann, 1919 and https://archive.org/details/plutarchslives07plut. On Diogenes: article "From Nature to Culture? Diogenes and Philosophical Anthropology," by Christian Lotz in *Human Studies*, v. 28, no. 1, 2005, p. 41-56; the life of Heraclitus is recorded by Diogenes Laertius in *Lives of the Eminent Philosophers*, Chapter 1, Sections 1-17, p. 408-425, translated by Robert Drew Hicks. London: Heinemann, 1925 and https://archive.org/details/livesofeminentph02dioguoft.

2. Stoics and Epicureans

On Stoicism: *The Cambridge Companion to the Stoics*, edited by B. Inwood. Cambridge: Cambridge University Press, 2003; on Epicureanism: *The Cambridge Companion to Epicureanism*, edited by James Warren. Cambridge: Cambridge University Press, 2009. In Book 3, chapter 13, of his *Discourses*, titled "What Solitude is and What Kind of Person the Solitary is," Epictetus refutes the notion that solitude is helplessness, insisting always on a mind in peace and tranquility regardless of the turmoil around us. When one considers the philosophical ideals, "sees the sun, the moon and the stars, enjoys earth and sea, he is not solitary, nor even helpless," p. 230-231. *The Discourses of Epictetus, with the Enchiridion and Fragments*, translated by George Long. London: Bell, 1887. The ideal of Marcus Aurelius was to desire "neither solitude nor company…," (Book 3, section 8) *Meditations by Marcus Aurelius*, translated by Meric Casaubon. London: Dent; New York: Dutton, 1906, p. 48 and https://archive.org/details/meditations00marcuoft/. In Appendix Three, titled "Solitude," of his biography of Marcus Aurelius, author Frank McLynn notes that Marcus occasionally expressed the wish to be a hermit rather than an emperor, and observes that the reflections of Henry David Thoreau's *Walden* frequently echo the *Meditations*. *Marcus Aurelius: A Life*, by Frank McLynn. New York: Da Capo Press, 2009, p. 565-586.

3. Early Judaism

For Judaism in this period: *The Cambridge History of Judaism, vol. 2: The Hellenistic Age*, edited by W. D. Davies and Louis Finkelstein. Cambridge: Cambridge University Press, 1989 and *Dictionary of Judaism in the Biblical Period: 450 B.C.E. to 600 C.E.*, edited by Jacob Neusner and William Scott Green. Peabody, MA: Hendrickson, 1999.

4. Early Christianity

For early Christianity: *The Christian Tradition: The Emergence of the Catholic Tradition (100-600)*, by Jaroslav Jan Pelikan. Chicago: University of Chicago Press, 1975; *The Cambridge History of Christianity, vol. 1: Origins to Constantine*, edited by Margaret M. Mitchell and Frances M. Young. Cambridge: Cambridge University Press, 2006; *The Cambridge History of Christianity, vol. 2: Constantine to c. 600*, edited by Augustine Casiday and Frederick W. Norris. Cambridge: Cambridge University Press, 2007; *Ascetics, Authority, and the Church in the Age of Jerome and Cassian*, by Philip Rousseau. Notre Dame, IN:

University of Notre Dame Press, 2010 (2nd ed.). For Jesus as Cynic, "Jesus and the Cynics: Survey and Analysis of a Hypothesis," by Hans Dieter Betz, in *The Journal of Religion*, v. 74, no. 4 (Oct. 1994), p. 453-475 and *Jesus, A Revolutionary Life*, by John Dominic Crossan. New York: HarperOne, 2009. A classic popularizing history of hermits of this period is *The Hermits*, by Charles Kingsley. London and New York: Macmillan, 1868 plus reprints and https://archive.org/details/hermits00kinggoog.

5. Paul of Thebes, First Christian Hermit

Jerome complains of his harsh hermit life in the desert in his letter to Eustochium (22.7), *Nicene and Post-Nicene Fathers: Series II, vol. 6*, compiled by Philip Schaff, and in *Christian Classics Ethereal Library*: https://ccel.org/ccel/schaff/npnf206/npnf206.v.XXII.html. Jerome refers to his "life of Paul" as attached in his letter to Paul, an Old Man of Concordia: https://ccel.org/ccel/schaff/npnf206/npnf206.v.X.html; "The Life of St. Paul the First Hermit" in https://ccel.org/ccel/schaff/npnf206/npnf206.vi.i.html and in *The Desert Fathers*, translations from the Latin by Helen Waddell. London: Constable, 1936 and reprints, p. 26-39; quote: "Tell me…," p. 35; "The Life of St. Paul, the first hermit," in *The Golden Legend* of Jacobus de Varagine (1230–1298) is translated as *The Golden Legend, or, Lives of the Saints*, as Englished by William Caxton. London: Dent, 1900, v. 2, p. 204–209.

6. Anthony the Great

Among many versions of the *Vita S. Antoni* or *Life of Anthony the Great* by *St. Athanasius: The Life of St. Anthony*, translated by Robert T. Meyer. New York: Paulist Press, 1978, "Athanasius, Select Works and Letters" in *Nicene and Post-Nicene Fathers: Series II, vol. 4,* and https://ccel.org/ccel/schaff/npnf204/npnf204.xvi.ii.i.html.

7. Christian Desert Hermits &
8. Sayings of the Christian Desert Hermits

Among books about the desert hermits and their sayings are *The Word in the Desert: Scripture and the Quest for Holiness in Early Christian Monasticism*, by Douglas Burton-Christie. New York: Oxford University Press, 1993; *Desert Christians: An Introduction to the Literature of Early Monasticism*, by William Harmless. Oxford: Oxford University Press, 2004; *Oasis of Wisdom: The Worlds of the Desert Fathers and Mothers*, by David G. R. Keller. Collegeville,

MN: Liturgical Press, 2005; *An Introduction to the Desert Fathers*, by John
Wortley. Cambridge and New York: Cambridge University Press, 2019.
On women hermits specifically: *The Forgotten Desert Mothers: Sayings, Lives,
and Stories of Early Christian Women,* by Laura Swan. Mahwah, NJ: Paulist
Press, 2000 and *Harlots of the Desert: A Study of Repentance in Early Monastic
Sources,* by Benedicta Ward. Kalamazoo, MI: Cistercian Publications, 1987.
Among older favorites chiefly primary sources are *Wisdom of the Desert,* by
Thomas Merton. New York: New Directions, 1970; *The Desert Fathers,* by
Helen Waddell. London: Constable, 1936 and Ann Arbor, MI: University
of Michigan Press, 1957 reprint; and *The Sayings of the Desert Fathers: The
Alphabetical Collection,* edited by Benedicta Ward. (rev. ed.). Kalamazoo, MI:
Cistercian Publications, 1984, reprinted as *The Desert Fathers: Sayings of the
Early Christian Monks.* New York: Penguin, 2003; more recent translations
are three by John Wortley: *The Anonymous Sayings of the Desert Fathers: A Select
Edition and Complete English Translation.* Cambridge and New York: Cambridge
University Press, 2013 and https://archive.org/details/TheAnonymous-
SayingsOfTheDWortleyJohn5090; *The Book of Elders: Sayings of the Desert
Fathers: The Systematic Collection.* Collegeville, MN: Cistercian Publications,
2018; and *More Sayings of the Desert Fathers: An English Translation and Notes.*
Cambridge and New York: Cambridge University Press, 2019. Translations
of key figures: *Conferences,* by John Cassian, translated by Colm Luibhéid.
New York: Paulist Press, 1985 and http://www.ccel.org/ccel/cassian/
conferences.i.html; *The Institutes,* by John Cassian, translated by Boniface
Ramsey. New York: Paulist Press, 2000 and http://www.ccel.org/ccel/
schaff/npnf211.iv.iii.html?institutes,john,cassian; *The Spiritual Meadow,* by
John Moschos, translated by John Wortley. Collegeville, MN: Cistercian
Publications, 1992 and https://web.archive.org/web/20120330220223/
and http://www.monachos.net/content/patristics/patristictexts/173-mo-
schus-meadow; *The Lausiac History,* by Palladius of Aspuna, translated by
John Wortley. Collegeville, MN: Cistercian Publications, 2015 and https://
archive.org/details/lausiachistoryof01pall/. An important study on the
social role of hermits in this era is the article by Peter Brown "The Rise and
Function of the Holy Man in Late Antiquity," in *Journal of Roman Studies* v.
61, 1971, p. 80–101. Compare the story of Moses giving directions to the
story of eighth–century Chinese Zen master Nansen (told by Dōgen in his
Shobogenzo): Nansen was on the mountainside using a sickle to cut flowers
and herbs when a traveler approached him and asked the way to Nansen's
monastery. Without looking up or stopping his work, Nansen said, "I paid

very little for this sickle." "I don't care about your sickle," huffed the traveler, "I asked you if you know where I can find Nansen's monastery." Still not looking up, Nansen continued, "And I know how to use this sickle well." With that the traveler turned and left.

9. Simon Stylites: Pillar Hermit

A life of Simeon Stylites was first written by Antonius, a monk-disciple of Saint Simon, whose Syriac manuscript was published by the nineteenth–century orientalist Paul Bedjan in his *Acta Martyrum Sanctorum*, translated by Frederick Lent as "The Life of St. Simeon Stylites: A Translation of the Syriac Text in Bedjan's Acta Martyrum et Sanctorum, volume 4," in *Journal of the American Oriental Society*, v. 35, 1915, p. 103–111, available at https://archive.org/details/jstor-592644 and http://www.tertullian.org/fathers/simeon_stylites_vita_01_trans.htm. A second source is the fifth–century historian Theodoret of Cyrrhus in his *Ecclesiastical History*. Both Antonius and Theodoret are included in *The Lives of Simeon Stylites*, translated by Robert Doran. Kalamazoo, MI: Cistercian Publications, 1992. Luis Buñuel's *Simon del desierto* premiered 1965 and was produced in Mexico by Sindicato de Trabajadores de la Producción Cinematográfica (STPC). The archeological remains of the monastery and church of St. Simeon Stylites, including the pillar, located thirty miles outside Aleppo, Syria, was largely destroyed by Russian or Syrian aerial bombing in May 2016. Re damage to relics: https://www.telegraph.co.uk/news/2016/05/13/syrian-monastery-where-st-simeon-sat-on-a-pillar-for-four-decade/.

10. Eremitism Comes to the West

The Donatists maintained that membership in the church was restricted to the elect and not open to sinners. *The Donatist Church: A Movement of Protest in Roman North Africa,* by W. H. C. Frend. Oxford: Oxford University Press, 1952. Rules: *The Rule of the Master: Regula Magistri*, translated from the Latin by Luke Eberle. Collegeville, MN: Cistercian Publications, 1977; *St. Benedict's Rule for Monasteries*, translated from the Latin by Leonard J. Doyle. Collegeville, MN: Liturgical Press, 1948 and http://www.gutenberg.org/files/50040/50040-h/50040-h.html; *Grimlaicus: Rule for Solitaries*, translated by Andrew Thornton. Collegeville, MN: Cistercian Publications, 2011; *Guigo: The Consuetudine or Customs*, translated by Ugo-Maria Ginex. Hermitage, Berkshire, UK: Hermits of St. Bruno, 2018 and https://archive.org/details/TheConsuetudineOfGuigoI5thPriorOfTheCarthusianOrder; quote: "Our chief purpose…," p. 27; *Meditations: The Meditations of Guigo I, Prior of the Charterhouse*, translated by A. Gordon Mursell. Collegeville, MN: Cistercian Publications, 1995.

11. Early Medieval Hermits of Britain

Wisdom of the Desert, by Thomas Merton. New York: New Directions, 1960, p. 5: "Of course, they acknowledged the benevolent, hierarchical authority of their bishops, but the bishops were far away and said little about what went on in the desert…" The Anglo-Saxon poems are collected in *Anglo-Saxon Poetry*, selected and translated by R. K. Gordon. London: Dent and New York: Dutton (Everyman's Library), 1954; *Anglo-Saxon Poetry*, translated and edited by S. A. J. Bradley. London: Dent and Rutland, VT: Tuttle (Everyman's Library), 1987 and at *Anglo–Saxon Narrative Poetry Project* by various translators: https://anglosaxonpoetry.camden.rutgers.edu. The Old Irish poems are translated into English and collected in *A Celtic Psaltery* by Alfred Perceval Graves. London: Society for Promoting Christian Knowledge and New York: Stokes, 1917 and http://www.gutenberg.org/ebooks/14232; *King and Hermit: A Colloquy Between King Guaire of Aidne and His Brother Marban. Being an Irish Poem of the 10th Century*, edited and translated by Kuno Meyer. London: David Nutt, 1901, and https://archive.org/details/kingandhermitac00meyegoog/; on St. Cuthbert: *Two Lives of Saint Cuthbert: A Life by an Anonymous Monk of Lindisfarne and Bede's Prose Life*, translated and edited by Bertram Colgrave. Cambridge: Cambridge University Press, 1940; *Felix's Life of Saint Guthlac*, edited and translated by Bertram Colgrave. Cambridge: Cambridge University Press, 1956; "Guthlac A" and "Guthlac B" are translated from Old English in *Anglo-Saxon Poetry*, translated by R. K. Gordon. London: Dent and New York: Dutton (Everymans Library), rev. ed., 1957, p. 256-279. The life of Godric of Finchale was popularized by the twelfth–century monk Reginald of Durham's "Life of St. Goderic," published as *Libellus de vita et miraculis: S. Godrici, heremitae de finchale,* by Reginald, Monk of Durham. London: Nicholas, 1847 and full text in Latin: https://archive.org/stream/libellusdevitaet20surtuoft/libellusdevitaet20surtuoft; translated excerpt in *Social Life in Britain from the Conquest to the Reformation*, edited by G. G. Coulton. Cambridge: Cambridge University Press, 1918 and Fordham University's *Internet Medieval Sourcebook*: https://sourcebooks.fordham.edu/source/goderic.asp; secondary sources: *The Hermit in English Literature From the Beginnings to 1660*, by Charles Preston Weaver. Nashville, TN: George Peabody College for Teachers, 1927, reprint by Norwood, PA: Norwood Editions, 1973; *The Vitae Patrum in Old and Middle English Literature*, by Constance L. Rosenthal. Folcroft, PA: Folcroft Library Editions, 1974 (reprint of 1936 ed.).

12. Hermit Revival in the Central Middle Ages

General histories of medieval European monasticism include *Medieval Monasticism*, by Giles Constable. London and New York: Routledge, Taylor & Francis Group, 2017; *The World of Medieval Monasticism: its History and Forms of Life*, by Gert Melville, James D. Mixson, and Giles Constable. Collegeville, MN: Cistercian Publications, 2016; *Medieval Monasticism: Forms of Religious Life in Western Europe in the Middle Ages*, by Clifford Hugh Lawrence. 4th ed. London and New York: Routledge, 2015; and *The Gateway to the Middle Ages: Monasticism*, by Eleanor Shipley Duckett. Ann Arbor, MI: University of Michigan Press, 1961. On specific historical figures: *Saint Peter Damian's Vita Beati Romualdi*, translated by Colin Ralph Phipps. London: King's College, 1988; *St. Peter Damian: Selected Writings on the Spiritual Life*, edited by Patricia McNulty. New York: Harper, 1959 and https://archive.org/details/stpeterdamiansel012952mbp; *Stephen of Muret: Maxims*, translated by Deborah van Doel, edited by Maureen M. O'Brien. Kalamazoo, MI: Cistercian Publications, 2002 and https://archive.org/details/maxims0000step, and *The Hermit Monks of Grandmont,* by Carole Hutchison. Kalamazoo, MI: Cistercian Publications, 1989; *Robert of Arbrissel: A Medieval Religious Life*, by Bruce L. Venarde. Washington, DC: Catholic University of America, 2003; *Saint Bruno, the Carthusian*, by André Ravier. San Francisco: Ignatius Press, 1995; *St. Robert, Abbot of Molesme, Founder of the Cistercians*, by Guy, Robert's abbot successor, in *The Lives of the Saints*, by Alban Butler. London: Burns & Oates, 1956: entry for April 29 and https://www.bartleby.com/210/4/292.html; *John Gualbert [Giovanni Guilberto], Abbot*, by Blaise Melanisius, in *Lives of the Saints*: July 12, and https://www.bartleby.com/210/7/121.html; on eremitism specifically is *The Golden Epistle: a Letter (of William of St. Thierry) to the Brethren at Mont Dieu*, translated by T. Berkeley, edited by J. M. Déchanet. Kalamazoo, MI: Cistercian Publications,1976.

13. Women Hermits in the Central Middle Ages

General works include *Anchoritism in the Middle Ages: Texts and Traditions*, edited by Catherine Innes-Parker and Naoe Kukita Yoshikawa. Cardiff: University of Wales Press, 2013; *Anchoritic Traditions of Medieval Europe*, by Liz Herbert McAvoy. Woodbridge, England and Rochester, NY: Boydell, 2010; *Rhetoric of the Anchorhold: Space, Place and Body Within the Discourses of Enclosure*, by Liz Herbert McAvoy. Cardiff: University of Wales Press, 2008; *Hermits and the New Monasticism: A Study of Religious Communities in Western Europe, 1000-1150*, by Henrietta Leyser. London: Macmillan, 1984; on women hermits: *Medieval Women in Their Communities*, by Diane Watt. Toronto: University of Toronto Press, 1997; *The Desert Mothers: a Survey of the Feminine Anchoretic Tradition in Western Europe*, by Margot H. King. Saskaton, Canada: Peregrina Publications, 1984; on specific women: Euphrosyna and Sophronia are described in Laura Swan, ibid., p. 83-84 and p. 137; Jerome alludes to Sophronia in his "Letter to Principia" (Letter 127 in *NPNF2-06: The Principal Works of St. Jerome* https://ccel.org/ccel/schaff/npnf206/npnf206.v.CXXVII.html); Hermelindis (Ermelinda) is mentioned in *Forgetful of Their Sex: Female Sanctity and Society, ca. 500-1100*, by Jane Tibbetts Schulenburg. Chicago: University of Chicago Press, 2018, p. 157. *The Plays of Roswitha*, translated by Christopher St. John. London: Chatto & Windus, 1923 and https://archive.org/details/playsofroswitha00hrotuoft/; *Consolation of the Blessed*, by Elizabeth Petroff. New York: Alta Gaia Society, 1979, which includes works by Umiltà; *Living Saints of the Thirteenth Century: the Lives of Yvette, Anchoress of Huy; Juliana of Cornillon, Author of the Corpus Christi Feast; and Margaret the Lame, Anchoress of Magdeburg*, by Anneke B. Mulder-Bakker. Turnhout: Brepols, 2011; *The Life of Christina of Markyate: a Twelfth Century Recluse*, edited by C. H. Talbot. Oxford: Clarendon Press, 1987; *Christina of Markyate*, edited by Samuel Fanous and Henrietta Leyser. London and New York: Routledge, 2004; on rules and guides: *The Book of Encouragement and Consolation*, by Goscelin of St. Bertin, edited by Monika Otter. Cambridge: D.S. Brewer, 2004; *Aelred of Rievaulx's De institutione inclusarum: two English versions*, edited by John Ayto and Alexandra Barratt. London and New York: Oxford University Press, 1984; *Ancrene Wisse*, edited by Robert J. Hasenfratz. Kalamazoo, MI: Western Michigan University Press, 2000; *The Solitary Self: Individuality in the Ancrene Wisse*, by Linda Georgianna. Cambridge, MA: Harvard University Press, 1981; *Speculum inclusorum: a Mirror for Recluses: a Late–Medieval Guide for Anchorites and its Middle English Translation*, translated and edited by E. A. Jones. Liverpool: Liverpool University Press, 2013, p. 93; Ralph Hanna III cites a letter of Bernard that "discredits hermits by arguing that a solitary 'so long as he is subject to no one, always does what his own desires teach him, and thus does not learn the merits of the splendid virtue of obedience'" in "Will's Work," p. 23-66, *Written Work: Langland, Labor, and Authorship*, edited by Steven Justice and Kathryn Kerby-Fulton. Philadelphia: University of

Pennsylvania Press, 2015, p. 27; Thomas Aquinas expresses his ambiguous view of eremitism in *Summa Theologica, Second Part of the Second Part, Question 188, Article 8*, translated by Fathers of the English Dominican Province. New York: Benziger, 1947 and http://www.newadvent.org/summa/3188. htm#article8 and https://www.ccel.org/a/aquinas/summa/SS/SS188. html#SSQ188A8THEP1); Aquinas quote: "A man may lead a solitary life for two motives. One is because he is unable, as it were, to bear with human fellowship on account of his uncouthness of mind; and this is beast–like. The other is with a view to adhering wholly to divine things; and this is superhuman. Hence the Philosopher [i.e., Aristotle] says [in *Politics*. i, 1] that 'he who associates not with others is either a beast or a god,' that is, a godly man."

14. Hermit Mystics of England

General works on hermits in Britain include the classic *The Hermits and Anchorites of England*, by Rotha Mary Clay. London: Methuen, 1914 and https://archive.org/details/hermitsanchorite00clay/; and *The English Medieval Recluse*, by Francis D. S. Darwin. London: Society for Promoting Christian Knowledge, 1944. Clay and Darwin are both still useful; more recent works: *Anchorites and Their Patrons in Medieval England*, by Ann K. Warren. Berkeley: University of California Press, 1985; *Hermits and Recluses in English Society, 950–1200*, by Tom Licence. Oxford and New York: Oxford University Press, 2013. Primary source collections include *The Medieval Mystics of England*, edited by Eric Colledge. London: Murray, 1962 and New York: Scribner, 1972, *English Mystics of the Middle Ages*, edited by Barry Windeatt. Cambridge: Cambridge University Press, 1995, and *Hermits and Anchorites in England, 1200-1550*, edited by E. A. Jones. Manchester: Manchester University Press, 2019. Among commentaries are *The Secret Within: Hermits, Recluses, and Spiritual Outsiders in Medieval England*, by Wolfgang Riehle, translated by Charity Scott-Stokes. Ithaca, NY: Cornell University Press, 2016 (the quote is the title of chapter 3, p. 40); *The Cambridge Companion to Medieval English Mysticism*, by Samuel Fanous. New York: Cambridge University Press 2011, and *Mysticism and Spirituality in Medieval England*, by William F. Pollard and Robert Boenig. Woodbridge, UK and Rochester, NY: D. S. Brewer, 1997. Quote: "I bid you…" (modernized from "I bid thee…,") in *The Cloud of Unknowing*, edited by Evelyn Underhill. London: Watkins, 1922, p. 28–29. *Revelations of Divine Love, recorded by Julian, Anchoress at Norwich*, edited by Grace Warrack. London: Methuen, 1901 and https://www.gutenberg.org/

files/52958/52958-h/52958-h.htm; *Revelations of Divine Love, shewed to Mother Juliana of Norwich*, preface by George Tyrrell. London: Kegan, Paul, Trench, Trüber, 1902 and https://archive.org/details/revelationsofdiv00juliuoft/; *The Book of Margery Kempe*, translated by Anthony Bale. Oxford: Oxford University Press, 2015 and https://archive.org/details/in.ernet.dli.2015.186348/.

15. Beguines and Brethren: Hermits of the Later Middle Ages

On the Beguines: *The Wisdom of the Beguines: the Forgotten Story of a Medieval Women's Movement*, by Laura Swan. New York: BlueBridge, 2014; *Vulgariter Beghinae: Eight Centuries of Beguine History in the Low Countries*, by Hans Geybels. Turnhout: Brepols, 2004; *The Beguines and Beghards in Medidval Culture, With Special Emphasis on the Belgian Scene*, by Ernest W. McDonnell. New Brunswick, NJ: Rutgers University Press, 1954, reprint: New York: Octagon Books, 1969; *Meister Eckhart and Beguine Mystics: Hadewijch of Brabant, Mechtild of Magdeburg and Marguerite Porete*, edited by Bernard McGinn. New York: Continuum International, 2001; *New Trends in Feminine Spirituality: the Holy Women of Liege and Their Impact*, by Juliette Dor, Lesley Johnson, and Jocelyn Wogan-Browne. Turnhout: Brepols, 1999. *Medieval Women's Visionary Literature*, by Elizabeth Petroff. New York: Oxford University Press, 1986; *Beguine Spirituality: Mystical Writings of Mechthild of Magdeburg, Beatrice of Nazareth, and Hadewijch of Brabant*, edited by Fiona Bowie, translated by Oliver Davies. New York: Crossroad, 1990; *The Flowing Light of the Godhead*, by Mechthild of Magdeburg, translated by Frank Tobin. New York: Paulist Press, 1998; *Agnes Blannbekin, Viennese Beguine: Life and Revelations*, by Ulrike Wiethaus. Cambridge: D. S. Brewer, 2002; *Marguerite Porete: Mirror of Simple Souls*, translated by Ellen Babinsky. New York: Paulist Press,1993; *Hadewijch: The Complete Works*, translated by Mother Columba Hart. New York: Paulist Press,1981; on Modern Devotion: *Sisters and Brothers of the Common Life: The Devotion Moderna and the World of the Later Middle Ages*, by John Van Engen. Philadelphia: University of Pennsylvania Press, 2008; *Devotio Moderna: Basic Writings*, translated and edited by John H. Van Engen. Mahwah, NJ: Paulist Press, 1998; Thomas a Kempis quote (modernized): *The Imitation of Christ*, by Thomas a Kempis, edited and translated by Brother Leo. New York: Macmillan, 1910, p. 43 and https://www.gutenberg.org/ebooks/1653.

16. Hermits in Medieval Arthurian Lore

The British History of Geoffrey of Monmouth, translated by A. Thompson, revised by J. A. Giles. London: Bohn, 1842 and https://archive.org/details/british-historyg01geofgoog/; quote re Dubricius, p. 195-96; *Arthurian Romances*, by Chrétien, de Troyes, translated by William W. Kibler and CarletonW. Carroll. London and New York: Penguin, 1991; quote: "I don't have…," p. 248; hermit feeds Yvain, p. 331; Perceval seeks out a "holy hermit," p. 458-459; *Parzival, A Knightly Epic*, by Wolfram von Eschenbach, translated by Jessie L. Weston. London: Nutt, 1894; quote: "Poor was his fare…," p. 261 and https://archive.org/details/ParzifalAKnightlyEpicVol1/; *Le morte D'Arthur*, by Thomas Malory, edited byP. J. C. Field. Cambridge: D. S. Brewer, 2017; *Le morte DArthur*, edited by Edward Stratchey. London: Macmillan, 1919 and https://archive.org/details/lemortedarthursi00malorich/; quote: "tasted none…," p. 379; quote: "For from hence…," p. 481.

17. Langland's Piers Plowman

The Vision of Piers Plowman, by William Langland: A Critical Edition of the B-text, edited by A. V. C. Schmidt. London: Dent, 2011; *Piers Plowman*, by William Langland, translated by E. Talbot Donaldson, edited by Elizabeth Robertson and Stephen H. A. Shepherd. New York: Norton, 2006; *The Vision of Piers the Plowman, by William Langland*, done into modern English by Walter W. Skeat. London: Moring, 1905 and https://archive.org/details/visionofpiersplo00languoft/; "Chaucer Reading Langland: The House of Fame," by Frank Grady in *Studies in the Age of Chaucer*, v. 18, 1996, p. 3–23; *Chaucer and Langland: The Antagonistic Tradition*, by John M. Bowers. Notre Dame, IN: Notre Dame University Press, 2007; quote: "In a summer season…," and thereafter, from Prologue, p. 3-5 in *Written Work: Langland, Labor, and Authorship*, edited by Steven Justice and Kathryn Kerby-Fulton. Philadelphia: University of Pennsylvania Press, 2015.

18. The Last Hermits of Medieval Europe

Hermits and Anchorites in England, 1200–1500, edited by E. A. Jones, op. cit.; on Pietro Morrone (Pope Celestine V): *The Pope Who Quit: a True Medieval Tale of Mystery, Death, and Salvation*, by Jon M. Sweeney. New York: Image Books, 2012; *Church and Sanctity: the Hagiographical Dossier of Peter of Morrone*, by George Piero Ferzoco. Monteal: CERES, 1990. The Aquila church (later

basilica) of Santa Maria di Collemaggio, founded by Pietro Murrone and
the site of his coronation as Pope Celestine V, was severely damaged by
an earthquake in April 2009. The basilica houses the hermit–pope's relics,
which were unscathed. The earthquake occurred on the 500th anniversary
of Pietro Murrone's death. On Nikolaus von der Flue: *Brother Nicholas*,
by G. R. Lamb. New York: Sheed and Ward, 1955; Jungian psychologist
Maria-Louise von Franz's *Die Visionen des Niklaus von Flüe* has not been
translated into English (original German: Zurich, Rascher, 1959), but she
remarks about Nicholas of Flue in Chapter 3, "The Transformed Berserker:
The Union of Psychic Opposites" of her book *Archetypal Dimensions of the
Psyche*. Boston: Shambhala, 1997, p. 36-57; quote: "compared to such…," p.
55; *The Actes and Monumentes of the churche, by John Foxe*. The case of Thomas
Parkinson is described in the 1563 ed., Book 5, no.205, p. 1680, modern
p.1761: https://www.dhi.ac.uk/foxe/index.php?realm=text&gototype=-
modern&edition=1563&pageid=1761; article: "Thomas Parkinson the
Hermit of Thirsk," by Frank Bottomley in *Historian*, Summer 2002, issue
74, p. 11-16.

19. Orthodox Christian Hermits: Greece

Monasteries of Greece, by Chris Hellier. London: Tauris Parke and New York:
St. Martin's Press, 1996; *Mount Athos, the Sacred Bridge: the Spirituality of the Holy
Mountain*, edited by Dimitri E. Conomas and Gregory Speake. Oxford and
New York: Lang, 2005; *Lives of the Monks of Palestine*, by Cyril of Scythopolis,
edited by John Binns, translated by R. M. Price. Collegeville, MN: Cister-
cian Publications, 1992; *St. Gregory Palamas: Holy Hesychia, the Stillness That
Knows God*, edited by Robin Amis. Southover, Wells, UK: Pleroma, 2016;
John Climacus: The Ladder of Divine Ascent, translated by Colm Luibhéid and
Norman Russell, introduction by Kallistos Ware. New York: Paulist Press,
1982; *The Philokalia, the Complete Text*, compiled by St. Nikodimos of the
Holy Mountain and St. Makarios of Corinth, translated from the Greek
and edited by G. E. H. Palmer, Philip Sherrard, and Kallistos Ware. London
and Boston: Faber and Faber, 1982-1999. Four volumes.

20. Orthodox Christian Hermits: Russia

*Russian Monastic Culture: "Josephism" and the Josifo-Volokolamsk Monastery,
1479-1607*, by Tom E. Dykstra. Munich: Sagner, 2006; *Russian Hesychasm:
the Spirituality of Nil Sorskij*, by George A. Maloney. The Hague: Mouton,
1973; *Nil Sorsky: the Authentic Writings*, edited and translated by David M.

Goldfrank. Kalamazoo, MI: Cistercian Publications, 2008; *Nil Sorsky: The Complete Writings*, edited and translated by George A. Maloney. New York: Paulist Press, 2003.

21. Hermits in Russia: Pilgrim & Old Believer

The Way of a Pilgrim and The Pilgrim Continues His Way, translated by R. M. French. Various editions: London: Society for Promoting Christian Knowledge, 2012, San Francisco: HarperSanFrancisco, 1992 and New York: Quality, 1981, New York: Seabury Press, 1965, and New York: Harper, 1954; Huston Smith quote: "Western mantra if I ever heard one," p. ix of Quality ed.; *The Way of a Pilgrim and A Pilgrim Continues His Way*, translated by Olga Savin. Boston: Shambhala, 2001; *The Pilgrim's Tale*, edited by Aleksei Pentkovsky, translated by T. Allan Smith. New York: Paulist Press, 1999; *The Way of a Pilgrim and The Pilgrim Continues His Way*, translated by Helen Bacovcin. Garden City, NY: Image Books, 1978. On Agafia Lykova (also Agafya Lykov): *Lost in the Taiga: One Russian Family's Fifty-year Struggle for Survival and Religious Freedom in the Siberian Wilderness*, by Vasilij Michajlovic Peskov. New York: Doubleday, 1994; article: https://www.smithsonianmag.com/history/for-40-years-this-russian-family-was-cut-off-from-all-human-contact-unaware-of-world-war-ii-7354256/; video: "Surviving in the Siberian Wilderness for 70 Years," Vice Media, 2013: https://youtu.be/tt2AYafET68.

22. Orthodox Christian Hermits: Ethiopia

The Orthodox Church of Ethiopia: a History, by John Binns. London and New York: I. B. Tauris, 2018; *The Monastic Holy Man and the Christianization of Early Solomonic Ethiopia*, by Steven Kaplan. Weisbaden: F. Steiner, 1984.

23. Hermits in Medieval and Later Judaism

General histories include *The Cambridge History of Judaism, v. 6: The Middle Ages, The Christian World*, edited by Robert Chazan. Cambridge and New York: Cambridge University Press, 2018 and *The Cambridge History of Judaism, v. 7: The Early Modern World, 1500-1815*, edited by Jonathan Karp and Adam Sutcliffe. Cambridge and New York: Cambridge University Press, 2018. On specific historical figures: *The Mystical Experience in Abraham Abulafia*, by Moshe Idel. Albany, NY: SUNY Press, 1988; *Physician of the Soul, Healer of the Cosmos: Isaac Luria and His Kabbalistic Fellowship*, by Lawrence Fine. Stanford: Stanford University Press, 2003; *The Light and Fire of the Baal Shem Tov*, by Yitzhak Buxbaum. New York: Bloomsbury Academic, 2013; *A Palace of*

Pearls: The Stories of Rabbi Nachman of Bratslav, retold by Howard Schwartz. New York: Oxford University Press, 2018.

24. Hermits in Medieval and Later Islam

The MacDonald quote is from *Development of Muslim Theology, Jurisprudence and Constitutional Theory*, by Duncan B. MacDonald. New York: Scribner, 1903, p. 125 and https://archive.org/details/developmentofmux00macduoft/. MacDonald further argues that from the example of the hermits "sprang the asceticism of Islam and that asceticism grew and developed into quietism and then into mysticism," which eventually culminates in Sufism. On earlier Islam generally: *Encyclopedia of Islam, 3rd ed.*, edited by Kate Fleet et al. Leiden: Brill, 2016; *Encyclopedia of Islam*, by Juan Eduardo Campo. New York: Facts on File, 2016. On specific figures: *The Philosophy of Ibn Arabi*, by Rom Landau. London: Routledge, 2008; *Creative Imagination in the Sufism of Ibn Arabi*, by Henry Corbin. (Bollingen series, 91) Princeton: Princeton University Press, 1969; *Morals and Mysticism in Persian Sufism: a History of Sufi-futuwwat in Iran*, by Lloyd V. J. Ridgeon. New York: Routledge, 2014; *The Essential Rumi* (new expanded edition), translated by Coleman Barks and John Moyne. New York: Harper, 2004; *Rumi's Mystical Design: Reading the Mathnawi, Book One*, by Seyed Ghahreman Safavi and Simon Weightman. Albany, NY: SUNY Press, 2009; *Ibn Tufayl's Hayy ibn Yaqzan: a Philosophical Tale*, translated by Lenn Evan Goodman. Chicago: University of Chicago Press, 2009.

25. Hermits in Hindu India

On ancient India: *An Introduction to Hinduism*, by Gavin D. Flood. Cambridge: Cambridge University Press, 2017; *The Roots of Hinduism: The Early Aryans and the Indus Civilization*, by Asko Parpola. Oxford: Oxford University Press, 2015; *India's Ancient Past*, by R. S. Sharma. Delhi and Oxford: Oxford University Press, 2007; *The Rigveda*, translated by Stephanie W. Jamison and Joel P. Brereton. London and New York: Oxford University Press, 2014. 3 volumes; *Manu's Code of Law*, critical edition and translation of the *Mānava-Dharmásāstra*, by Patrick Olivelle and Suman Olivelle. New Delhi and New York: Oxford University Press, 2006; *The Asrama System: the History and Hermeneutics of a Religious Institution*, by Patrick Olivelle. Oxford and New York: Oxford University Press, 1993; *The Rāmāyaṇa of Vālmīki: An Epic of Ancient India*, translated by Robert P. Goldman. Princeton, NJ: Princeton

University Press, 1985-2017, 7 volumes; *Rāmāyana*, translated by William Buck. Berkeley, CA: University of California Press, 1976 and reprints; *The Ramayana of Valmiki*, translated by Hari Prasad Shastri. London: Shanti Sadan, 1952 and https://archive.org/details/The.Ramayana.of.Valmiki. by.Hari.Prasad.Shastri/; *Mahabharata*, translated by William Buck. Berkeley, CA: University of California Press, 1973 and reprints; *Mahabharata, the Epic of Ancient India*, translated by Romesh Chunder Dutt. London: Dent, 1907 and https://archive.org/details/RamayanaTheEpicOfRamaPrinceOfIndiaCondensedIntoEnglishVerseBy/; *Upanisads*, translated by Patrick Olivelle. Oxford: Oxford University Press, 2008; *Principal Upanishads*, edited and translated by Sarvepalli Radhakrishnan. NewYork: Harper, 1953 and https://archive.org/details/PrincipalUpanishads/; *The Bhagavad Gita*, translated by W. J. Johnson. Oxford: OxfordUniversity Press, 2009; *The Vairagya-Satakam, or The Hundred Verses on Renunciation* [by] Bhartrhari, edited by Swami Madhavananda. Calcutta: Advaita Ashrama, 1963 and https://archive.org/details/Vairagya.Satakam.of.Bhartrihari; *Rules and Regulations of Brahmanical Asceticism: Yatidharmasamuccaya of Yādava Prakāśa*, translated by Patrick Olivelle. Albany, NY: SUNY Press, 1995; on Patanjali: *The Yoga Sutra of Patanjali: a Biography*, by David Gordon White. Princeton: Princeton University Press, 2014; *Yoga, Discipline of Freedom: the Yoga Sutra Attributed to Patanjali*, translated with commentary by Barbara Stoler Miller. Berkeley, CA: University of California, Press, 1996; on Shankara: *Shankara and Indian Philosophy*, by Natalia Isayeva. Albany, NY: SUNY Press, 1993; *The Ethics of Sankara and Santideva: a Selfless Response to an Illusory World*, by Warren Lee Todd. London and New York: Routledge/Taylor & Francis Group, 2016.

26. Hermits in Jain India

General works include *Outlines of Jainism*, by Jagomandar Lal Jaini, edited by Frederick William Thomas. Cambridge and New York: Cambridge University Press, 2013 (reprint of 1940 ed.); *The Assembly of Listeners: Jains in Society*, by Michael Carrithers and Caroline Humphrey. Cambridge: Cambridge University Press, 1991. A primary source is *The Lives of the Jain Elders*, translated by R. C. C. Fynes. Oxford and New York: Oxford University Press, 1998. On Gymnosophists: *Plutarch's Lives*, translated by John Dryden, revised by Arthur Hugh Clough. New York: Modern Library, p. 847; *The Anabasis of Alexander*, by Arrian, translated by E. J. Chinnock. London: Hodder and Stoughton, 1884, p. 371; Chinnock translates Gymnosophists as "the naked sect of

Indian philosophers;" and https://archive.org/stream/cu31924026460752/
cu31924026460752_djvu.txt.

27. Buddhist Hermits of Tibet

General works on Tibetan Buddhism include *Sources of Tibetan Tradition*,
edited by Kurtis R. Schaeffer, Matthew Kapstein, and Gray Tuttle. New
York: Columbia University Press, 2013; *The Spirit of Tibetan Buddhism* by
Sam Van Schaik. New Haven: Yale University Press, 2016; *Introducing Tibetan
Buddhism*, by Geoffrey Samuel. New York: Routledge, 2012; *Introduction to
Tibetan Buddhism*, by John Powers. Ithaca, NY: Snow Lion Publications,
2007; *Essential Tibetan Buddhism*, by Robert A. F. Thurman. San Francisco:
HarperSanFrancisco, 1997. On Milarepa: *The Life of Milarepa*, by Tsangn-
yon Heruka, translated by Andrew Quintman. New York: Penguin, 2010;
Tibet's Great Yogi, Milarepa: a Biography from the Tibetan; being the *Jetsun-Kahbum
or Biographical History of Jetsun-Milarepa*, according to the Late Lama Kazi
Dawa-Samdup's English Rendering, edited by W.Y. Evans-Wentz, foreword
by Donald S. Lopez, Jr. New York: Oxford University Press, 2000, reprint of
1928 ed.; *The Hundred Thousand Songs of Milarepa: The Life-Story and Teaching
of the Greatest Poet-Saint Ever to Appear in the History of Buddhism*, translated
and annotated by Garma C. C. Chang. Boston: Shambhala, 1999; *The Yogin
& the Madman: Reading the Biographical Corpus of Tibet's Great Saint Milarepa*,
by Andrew Quintman. New York: Columbia University Press, 2014; *Songs
of Milarepa*, edited by Donald Herder. Mineola, NY: Dover, 2003, reprint of
1958 ed.; quotes: "monastery of the uninhabited mountain," p. 5; on Patrul
Rinpoche: *The Words of My Perfect Teacher, by Patrul Rinpoche*, translated by the
Padmakara Translation Group. Boston: Shambhala, 1998 (rev. ed.); *Enlightened
Vagabond: the Life and Teachings of Patrul Rinpoche*, by Matthieu Ricard, edited
by Constance Wilkinson. Boulder: Shambhala, 2017. The anecdote about
Zhong Chi is described in the *Wudong Huiyuan* (or, *Compendium of the Five
Lamps*), translated in *Zen's Chinese Heritage: the Masters and Their Teachings*, by
Andrew Ferguson. Boston: Wisdom Publications, 2000, p. 17; on Orgyan
Chopyi: *Himalayan Hermitess: The Life of a Tibetan Buddhist Nun*, by Kurtis R.
Schaeffer. Oxford and New York: Oxford University Press, 2005.

28. Shabkar, Tibetan Buddhism's "Perfect Hermit"

The Life of Shabkar: Autobiography of a Tibetan Yogin, translated by Matthieu
Ricard, edited by Constance Wilkinson, Michal Abrams, and the Padmakara
Translation Group. Albany, NY: SUNY Press, 1994: quotes, 'if you aspire…,'

p. 29; "Wander from one…," p. 108; "I bow down…," p. 191; "Meditate like the rishis…," p. 417; "In the pleasant groves…," p. 528.

29. Buddhist Hermits of Sri Lanka

General works on Buddhism in Sri Lanka include: *The Buddhist Revival in Sri Lanka: Religious Tradition, Reinterpretation and Response*, by George Doherty Bond. Columbia, SC: University of South Carolina Press, 1988; *The Buddha in Sri Lanka: Histories and Stories*, by Gananath Obeyesekere. London and New York: Routledge/Taylor & Francis, 2018; *Theravada Traditions: Buddhist Ritual Cultures in Contemporary Southeast Asia and Sri Lanka*, by John Clifford Holt. Honolulu: University of Hawaii Press, 2017; *The Heritage of the Bhikkhu*, by Rahula Walpola, translated by Edmund F. Perry. New York: Grove Press, 1974; *The Forest Monks of Sri Lanka: an Anthropological and Historical Study*, by Michael Carrithers. Oxford: Oxford University Press, 1983; for Buddhaghosa: *Visuddhimagga: The Path of Purity*, by Buddhaghosa, translated by Pe Maung Tin. Oxford: Pali Text Society, 2003 and *The Path of Purification: Visuddhimagga*, translated by Bhikkhu Nanamoli. Onalaska, WA: Pariyatti Publishing, 2003; on the historical chronicle *Mahavamsa: The Mahavaṃsa or the Great Chronicle of Ceylon*, translated by Wilhelm Geiger. London: Pali Text Society, 2001 and *Reading the Mahavaṃsa: the Literary Aims of a Theravada Buddhist History*, by Kristin Scheible. New York: Columbia University Press, 2016.

30. Buddhist Hermits of Thailand

Many sources on Buddhism in Thailand focus on social and political contexts, such as *Sangha, State, and Society: Thai Buddhism in History*, by Yoneo Ishii. Honolulu: University of Hawaii Press, 1986 and *World Conqueror and World Renouncer: a Study of Buddhism and Polity in Thailand Against a Historical Background*, by Stanley Jeyaraja Tambiah. Cambridge: Cambridge University Press, 1976; on thudong are two books by Kamala Tiyavanich: *Forest Recollections: Wandering Monks in Twentieth-Century Thailand*. Honolulu: University of Hawaii Press, 1997, and *The Buddha in the Jungle*. Seattle, WA: University of Washington Press, 2003, reissued as *In the Cool Shade of Compassion: The Enchanted World of the Buddha in the Jungle*. Boulder: Shambhala, 2018; *With Robes and Bowl: Glimpses of the Thudong Bhikkhu Life*, by Bhikkhu Khantipalo. 1965 and http://www.buddhanet.net/pdf_file/robes-bowl6.pdf; books by Ajahn Chah: *A Still Forest Pool: The Insight Meditation of Achaan Chah*, compiled by Paul Breiter and Jack Kornfield. Wheaton, IL: Quest Publications, 2004 (reprint of 1985 ed.), *Food for the Heart: the Collected Teachings of Ajahn Chah*.

Somerville, MA: Wisdom Publications, 2002, and *Being Dharma: the Essence of the Buddha's Teachings*. Boston: Shambhala 2001; most collections available at the BuddhaNet website https://www.buddhanet.org; quote "Unfettered, like a deer…," from *Sutta Nipāta*,1.3: "Rhinoceros."

31. Eremitism in China: Confucius & Taoism

The best informal introductions to the hermits of China are *Road to Heaven: Encounters with Chinese Hermits*, by Bill Porter. San Francisco: Mercury House, 1993, reprinted Berkeley: Counterpoint, 2009, and the documentary film *Amongst White Clouds: Buddhist Masters of China's Zhonghan Mountains*, directed and produced by Edward A. Burger, 2007. *The I Ching or Book of Changes*, edited by Richard Wilhelm, translated by Cary F. Baynes. Princeton: Princeton University Press (Bollingen Series), 1967); *I Ching*, translated by James Legge. New York: Dover, 1963 and reprints, and https://archive.org/details/I-Ching/; *The Book of Songs*, translated by Arthur Waley. New York: Grove Press, 1956; quote: "When words are…." p. 171; and https://archive.org/details/bookofsongs00wale/; "The Book of Documents" in vol. 3, pt. 1 of *The Chinese Classics*, translated by James Legge. London: Treubner, 1865; quote: "withdraw to the wilds," p. 276; "withdraw from public life," p. 209; *The Analects*, by Confucius, translated by Raymond Dawson. Oxford: Oxford University Press, 2008; *The Analects of Confucius*, translated by Burton Watson. New York: Columbia University Press, 2007;

The Ssu-ma Chien quote is from *Ssu-ma Chien, Grand Historian of China*, by Burton Watson. New York: Columbia University Press, 1958, p. 157. Scholarly sources are *Men of the Cliffs and Caves: the Development of the Chinese Eremitic Tradition to the End of the Han Dynasty*, by Aat Vervoorn. Hong Kong: Chinese University Press, 1990, and *Patterns of Disengagement: The Practice and Portrayal of Reclusion in Early Medieval China*, by Alan J. Berkowitz. Stanford: Stanford University Press, 2000; on individuals: *Mencius*, translated by Irene Bloom, edited by Philip J. Ivanhoe. New York: Columbia University Press, 2003; *Mo Tzu: Basic Writings*, translated by Burton Watson. New York: Columbia University Press, 1963; *Han Fei Tzu: Basic Writings, translated by Burton Watson. New York: Columbia Uni*versity Press, 1964; *Tao Te Ching*, by Lao Tzu, translated by D. C. Lau. New York: Columbia UniversityPress, 2001; *Tao Te Ching*, by Lao Tzu, translated by Gia-FuFeng and Jane English. New York: Vintage, 1972; *Lao-tzu's Tao Te Ching*, translated by Red Pine. San Francisco: Mercury House, 1996 and Port Townsend, WA: Copper Canyon Press, 2010; *Tao Te Ching*, by Lao Tzu, translated by David Hinton.

Washington, DC: Counterpoint Press, 2000; *The Complete Works of Zhuang-zi*, translated by Burton Watson. New York: Columbia University Press, 2013; *Zhuang-zi: Basic Writings*, translated by Burton Watson. New York: Columbia University Press, 1996 (2d ed.); *Chuang-tzu: The Inner Chapters*, translated by David Hinton. Washington, DC: Counterpoint Press, 1998. On the Tillers: "The Nung-chia School of the Tillers and the Origins of Peasant Utopianism in China," by A. C. Graham in *Bulletin of the School of Oriental and African Studies, University of London*, v. 42, 1979, p. 68-100. For the *Huainanzi* of An Liu: *The Huainanzi: a Guide to the Theory and Practice of Government in Early Han China*, edited and translated by John S. Major, and others. New York: Columbia University Press, 2010. The chief historical primary source for the period is the *Shih chi of Sima Qian: Ssu-ma Chien, Grand Historian of China*, translated by Burton Watson. New York: Columbia University Press, 1958, reprinted 1993-1995, and *The Grand Scribe's Records*, edited by William H. Nienhauser, Jr., multiple translators. Bloomington, IN: Indiana University Press, 2018- (multivolume); general secondary source history: *Ancient China: a History*, by John S. Major and Constance A. Cook. London; New York: Routledge, 2017; *Early China: a Social and Cultural History*, by Feng Li. Cambridge: Cambridge University Press, 2014; on Ch'in dynasty history, *Records of the Grand Historian*, by Qian Sima, translated by Burton Watson, volume 1. New York: Columbia University Press, 1993; *Courtier and Commoner in Ancient China: Selections from the History of the Former Han, by Gu Ban*, translated and edited by Burton Watson. New York: Columbia University Press, 1974, additional historical sources in next section; on the Hundred Schools: *An Introduction to Chinese Philosophy*, by Karyn Lai. Cambridge: Cambridge University Press, 2017; *History of Chinese Political Thought From the Beginnings to the Sixth Century, A.D.*, by Kung-chuan Hsiao [Gongquan Xiao], translated by Frederick W. Mote. Princeton: Princeton University Press, 2015 (reprint of 1979 ed.); *History of Chinese Philosophy*, by Bo Mou. London and New York: Routledge, 2014; *The Dynamics of Masters Literature: Early Chinese Thought from Confucius to Han Feizi*, by Wiebke Denecke. Cambridge, MA: Harvard University Press, 2011; *Studies in Chinese Philosophy and Philosophical Literature*, by C. Graham. Albany, NY: SUNY Press, 1990; quotes: "Excellent men of old…," p. 175 of *Confucius: The Analects*, translated by D. C. Lau. New York: Penguin, 1979; "hermit-scholars hiding in their caves…," p. 105 of *Ssu-ma Chien's "The Biography of Po Yi and Shu Ch'i,"* translated by Burton Watson in *Anthology of Chinese Literature: From Early Times to the Fourteenth Century*, edited by Cyril Birch. New York: Grove Press, 1965. As Griet Vankeerberghen notes in *The Huainanzi and Liu An's Claim to Moral Authority*. Albany, NY: SUNY Press, 2001, p. 205, "The absence of hermits was often seen as a sign of good government" and quotes the *Huainanzi* (20/211/23): "When a sage rule occupies the highest position … there are no hermits;" quote: "Xu You, Fang Hu…," from *The Huainanzi: A Guide to the Theory and Practice of Government in Early Han China*, by An Liu, edited by John S. Major. New York: Columbia University Press, 2010, p. 105.

32. Eremitism in China: Han Dynasty

Additional historical sources: *The Early Chinese Empires: Qin and Han*, by Mark Edward Lewis. Cambridge, MA: Belknap Press, 2007; *The Cambridge History of China, Vol. 1: The Chin and Han Empires, 221 BC-AD 220*, edited by Denis Twitchett and Michael Loewe. Cambridge: Cambridge University Press, 1986; *Crisis and Conflict in Han China, 104 BC to AD 9*, by Michael Loewe. London and New York: Routledge/Taylor & Francis, 2005 (reprint of 1974 ed.); *Fire Over Luoyang: a History of the Later Han Dynasty, 23-220 AD*, by Rafe De Crespigny. Boston: Brill, 2017; *Worlds of Bronze and Bamboo: Sima Qian's Conquest of History*, by Grant Hardy. New York: Columbia University Press, 1999; on Zhuang Zun, "Zhuang Zun: A Daoist Philosopher of the Late First Century B.C.," by Aat Vervoorn in *Monumenta Serica: Journal of Oriental Studies*, vol. 38, issue 1, 1988, p. 69-94. In *Patterns of Disengagement: The Practice and Portrayal of Reclusion in Early Medieval China*, by Alan J. Berkowitz. Stanford: Stanford University Press, 2000, the author notes (p. 160) that after Huang Mi's *Gaoshi zhuan* ("Biographies of Lofty Men") successive works in the genre included only hermits and recluses, though most of these imitative works are no longer extant. Berkowitz also enumerates the many post-Han Taoist eccentric recluses. "The Moral Hero: A Pattern of Reclusion in Traditional China," by Alan J.Berkowitz, in *Journal of Oriental Studies*, v. 40, 1992, issue 1, p. 1-32; "The Wives of the Han Recluses," by Tan Soon Cheng in *International Journal of the Asian Philosophical Association*, v. 2, Jan. 2009, p. 35-51 and http://www.asianpa.net/assets/upload/articles/hPI1T8LoKTJvvqnK.pdf.

33. Eremitism in Medieval China: The Poets

Individual poets: Hsieh Ling-yün: *The Mountain Poems of Hsieh Ling-Yun*, translated by David Hinton. New York: New Directions, 2001; J. D. Frodsham: *The Murmuring Stream: Life and Works of Hsieh Ling-yun*. Kuala Lampur: University of Malaya Press, 1967; Tao Chien: *The Selected Poems of T'ao Ch'ien*, translated by David Hinton. Port Townsend, WA: Copper Canyon Press, 1993; *The Transport of Reading: Text and Understanding in the World of Tao Qian (365-427),*by Robert Ashmore. Cambridge, MA: Harvard University Asia Center, 2010; *The Classic of Mountains and Seas* ("Shan Hai Jing"),translated by Anne Birrell. London and New York: Penguin, 1999; Tu Fu: *The Selected Poems of Du Fu,* translated by Burton Watson. New York: Columbia University Press, 2002; *The Selected Poems of Tu Fu,* translated by David Hinton. New York: New Directions, 1989 and expanded and newly translated ed. 2020; *Awakened Cosmos: the Mind of Classical Chinese Poetry* [about Tu Fu], by David Hinton. Boulder, CO: Shambhala, 2019; Hanshan: *Cold Mountain Poems: Zen Poems of Han Shan, Shih Te [Shide], and Wang Fan-chih [Fanzhi Wang],* translated by J. P. Seaton. Boulder: Shambhala, 2009; *The Complete Cold Mountain: Poems of the Legendary Hermit Hanshan,* translated by Kazuaki Tanahashi and Peter Levitt. Boulder: Shambhala, 2018; *Cold Mountain Poems: Twenty-Four Poems by Han-Shan,* translated by Gary Snyder. Berkeley: Counterpoint Press, 2013; *The Collected Songs of Cold Mountain,* translated by Red Pine. Port Townsend, WA: Copper Canyon Press, 2000; *Cold Mountain: 100 Poems by the Táng Poet Han-Shan,* translated by Burton Watson. New York: Columbia University Press, 1970; *The Poetry of Hanshan (Cold Mountain), Shide, and Fenggan,* translated by Paul Rouzer, edited by Christopher M. B. Nugent. Boston: Walter de Gruyter, 2017 and https://library.oapen.org/bitstream/handle/20.500.12657/27418/9781501501913.pdf; Po Chu-i (Bai Juyi): *Po Chü-i: Selected Poems,* translated by Burton Watson. New York: Columbia University Press, 2000; *The Life and Times of Po Chü-I, 772-846 A.D,* by Arthur Waley. New York: Macmillan, 1949; *The Selected Poems of Po Chu-i,* translated by David Hinton. New York: New Directions, 1999; Li Po: *The Selected Poems of Li Po,* translated by David Hinton. New York: New Directions, 1996; *The Banished Immortal: A Life of Li Bai (Li Po),* by Ha Jin. New York: Vintage Books, 2019; Wang Wei: *The Selected Poems of Wang Wei,* translated by David Hinton. New York: New Directions, 2006; *Wang Wei: Poems,* translated by G. W. Robinson. London: Penguin, 1973, reissued 2015; Shihwu, or Stonehouse: *The Mountain Poems of Stonehouse: Poems and Talks of a Fourteenth–Century Chinese Hermit,* translations and commentary by Red Pine. Port Townsend, WA: Copper Canyon Press, 2014; quote: "out of touch…," "Mountain Poems," 37.2, ibid., p. 21; on *tzu–jan* and the rivers–and–mountains poets: *Mountain Home: the Wilderness Poetry of Ancient China,* translated by David Hinton. Washington, DC: Counterpoint, 2002. Other Chinese poets: *Poems of the Masters: China's Classic Anthology of T'ang* *and Sung Dynasty Verse*, translated by Red Pine. Port Townsend, WA: Copper Canyon Press, 2003; *Classical Chinese Poetry: an Anthology*, translated and edited by David Hinton. New York: Farrar, Straus and Giroux, 2008.

34. Eremitism in Medieval China: The Painters

Art in China, by Craig Clunas. Oxford and New York: Oxford University Press, 1997; *Poetry and Painting in Song China: The Subtle Art of Dissent*, by Alfreda Murck. Cambridge, MA: Harvard University Asia Center, 2002; *The Art of Southern Sung China*, by James Cahill. New York: Asian House, 2002; *Parting at the Shore: Chinese Painting of the Early and Middle Ming Dynasty, 1368–1580*, by James Cahill. New York: Weatherhill, 1978; *The Distant Mountains: Chinese Painting of the Late Ming Dynasty, 1570–1644*, by James Cahill. New York: Weatherhill, 1982; *Writing an Image: Chinese Literati Art*, by Shuishan Yu. Rochester, MI: Oakland University Art Gallery, 2009 and https://pdfs.semanticscholar.org/0e39/ae0c3f19926f41bd98d8ff2db16ac66f43f3.pdf; *Shitao: Painting and Modernity in Early Qing China*, by Jonathan Hay. Cambridge: Cambridge University Press, 2001; "The Ten Oxherding Pictures," translated by D. T. Suzuki, in his *Manual of Zen Buddhism* Kyoto: Eastern Buddhist Society, 1934, London: Rider, 1950, and New York: Grove Press, 1960, p. 150–171.

35. Eremitism in Shinto Japan

Shugendo: Essays on the Structure of Japanese Folk Religion, by Hitoshi Miyake; edited by H. Earhart. Ann Arbor, MI: University of Michigan Press, 2001; *Mountain Mandalas: Shugendo in Kyushu*, by Allan G. Grapard. London and New York: Bloomsbury Academic, 2016; *Shugendo: The Way of the Mountain Monks*, by Shokai Koshikidake with Martin Faulks. London: Faulks Books, 2015; *En no Gyōja: The Legend of a Holy Man in the Twelve Centuries of Japanese Literature*, by Linda Klepinger Keenan. (dissertation, University of Wisconsin-Madison, 1989).

36. Eremitism in Buddhist Japan: The Poets

Overview: *The Aesthetics of Discontent: Politics and Reclusion in Medieval Japanese Literature*, by Michael F. Marra. Honolulu: University of Hawaii Press, 1991; *The Karma of Words: Buddhism and the Literary Arts in Medieval Japan*, by William R. LaFleur. Berkeley, CA: University of California Press, 1986; *Seeds in the Heart: Japanese Literature from Earliest Times to the Late Sixteenth Century*, by Donal Keene. New York: Holt, 1993; two influential literary works, fifth century and eighth century: *Wen xuan or Selections of Refined Literature*, by Xiao

Tong, translated by David R. Knechtges. Princeton, NJ: Princeton University Press, 1982-96 (3 vols.) and *1000 Poems from the Manyoshu: The Complete Nippon Gakujutsu Shinkokai Translation.* New York: Columbia University Press, 1965; Mineola, NY: Dover, 2005 and https://archive.org/details/Manyoshu; on Kamo no Chōmei: *Kenko and Chomei: Essays in Idleness and Hojoki,* translated by Meredith McKinney. London: Penguin, 2013; *Hojoki,* in *Anthology of Japanese Literature From the Earliest Era to the Mid-Nineteenth Century,* edited by Donald Keene. New York: Grove Press, 1960; *Hojoki* in *Four Huts: Asian Writings on the Simple Life,* translated by Burton Watson. Boulder, CO: Shambhala, 1994; "Recluses and Eccentric Monks: Tales from the *Hosshinshu* by Kamo no Chomei," translated by Marian Ury, in *Monumenta Nipponica, v*ol. 27, no. 2 (Summer, 1972), pp. 149-173; on Ippen: *No Abode: the Record of Ippen,* translated by Dennis Hirota. Honolulu: University of Hawaii Press, 1997 (rev. ed.); on Kenko Yoshida: *Kenko and Chomei: Essays in Idleness and Hojoki,* translated by Meredith McKinney, op. cit.; *Essays in Idleness: the Tsurezuregusa,* translated by Donald Keene. New York: Columbia University Press, 1967; on Saigyō: *Saigyō: Poems of a Mountain Home,* translated by Burton Watson. New York: Columbia University Press, 1991; *Awesome Nightfall: the Life, Times, and Poetry of Saigyō,* by William R. LaFleur. Boston: Wisdom Publications, 2003; on Bashō: *Bashō: the Complete Haiku,* translated and annotated by Jane Reichhold. New York: Kodansha, 2013; *On Love and Barley: Haiku of Bashō,* translated by Lucien Stryk. London and New York: Penguin, 2003; *The Narrow Road to the Deep North And Other Travel Sketches,* by Bashō Matsuo, translated by Nobuyuki Yuasa. London: Penguin, 2005 (reprint of 1967); *Narrow Road to the Interior And Other Writings, by Matsuo Bashō,* translated by Sam Hamill. Boston: Shambhala, 2019; *The Narrow Road to Oku,* by Matsuo Bashō, translated by Donal Keene. New York: Kodansha, 2017; *Bashō's Haiku: Selected Poems of Matsuo Bashō,* translated by David Landis Barnhill. Albany, NY: SUNY Press, 2004; on Ryokan: *Great Fool: Zen Master Ryokan: Poems, Letters, and Other Writings,* translated with essays by Ryuichi Abe and Peter Haskell. Honolulu: University of Hawaii Press, 1996; *Ryokan, Zen Monk-Poet of Japan,* translated by Burton Watson. New York: Columbia University Press, 1977; *One Robe, One Bowl: the Zen Poetry of Ryokan,* translated by John Stevens. Boston: Weatherhill, 2006; *Dewdrops on a Lotus Leaf: Zen Poems of Ryokan,* translated by John Stevens. Boston: Shambhala, 2004; *Sky Above, Great Wind: the Life and Poetry of Zen Master Ryokan,* by Kazuaki Tanahashi. Boston: Shambhala, 2012; *The Zen Poems of Ryokan,* translated by Nobuyuki Yuasa. Princeton: Princeton University Press, 1981.

37. Aesthetics of Eremitism: *wabi, sabi, aware, yugen*

Overview: *Stanford Encyclopedia of Aesthetics: Japanese Aesthetics* (revised 2018) and https://plato.stanford.edu/entries/japanese-aesthetics; *Evanescence and Form: an Introduction to Japanese Culture*, by Charles Shiro Inouye. New York: Palgrave Macmillan, 2008; *Japanese Hermeneutics: Current Debates on Aesthetics and Interpretation*, edited by Michael F. Marra. Honolulu: University of Hawaii Press, 2002; *Ikigai & Other Japanese Words to Live By*, by Mari Fujimoto. London: Modern Books, 2019; article "Wabi-Sabi, Mono no Aware, and Ma: Tracing Traditional Japanese Aesthetics Through Japanese History," by Lauren Prusinski on https://castle.eiu.edu/studiesonasia/documents/seriesIV/2-Prusinkski_001.pdf; on yugen: "Zeami and the Transition of the Concept of Yugen: A Note on Japanese Aesthetics," by Andrew A. Tsubaki, in *The Journal of Aesthetics and Art Criticism*, v. 3, no. 1, Fall 1971, p. 55-67, and https://kuscholarworks.ku.edu/bitstream/handle/1808/1139/CEAS.1971.n10.pdf; Zeami's essay "On Attaining the Stage of Yugen" is reproduced in *On the Art of the No Drama: The Major Treatises of Zeami*, translated by J. Thomas Rimer and Yamazaki Masakazu. Princeton: Princeton University Press, 1984; on Shinkei: *Murmured Conversations: A Treatise on Poetry and Buddhism by the Poet-Monk Shinkei*, translation [of his *Sasamegoto*], by Esperanza Ramirez-Christensen. Stanford: Stanford University Press, 2008; *Emptiness and Temporality: Buddhism and Medieval Japanese Poetics*, by Esperanza Ramirez-Christensen. Stanford: Stanford University Press, 2008; *Heart's Flower: The Life and Poetry of Shinkei*, by Esperanza Ramirez-Christensen. Stanford: Stanford University Press, 1994. The quote from Shinkei "You find mystery…," is from *Modern Japanese Aesthetics: A Reader*, edited by Michael F. Marra. Honolulu: University of Hawaii Press, 1999 (rev. ed.), p. 151; the quote from T. D. Suzuki "the experience of the…," is from his *Zen and Japanese Culture*. New York: Pantheon, 1959 (rev. ed., Bollingen Series 64), p. 220-221; R. H. Blyth's comment in his *A History of Haiku*. Tokyo: Hokuseido Press, 1964, v. 1, p. ix; Basho quotes: "you must leave your subjective…," from *Basho: The Narrow Road to the Deep North and Other Travel Sketches*, translated by Nobuyuki Yuasa. New York: Penguin, 1966, p. 33, and "Saigyō in traditional poetry…," ibid., p. 71-72; on wabi and sabi: *Wabi-Sabi for Artists, Designers, Poets & Philosophers*, by Leonard Koren. Point Reyes, CA: Imperfect Publishing, 2008; *Wabi Sabi: the Japanese Art of Impermanence*, by Andrew Juniper. North Clarendon, VT: Tuttle, 2010.

38. Aesthetics of Eremitism: Japanese Painting

On religion: "The Hermit at Court: Reclusion in Early Fifteenth-Century Japanese Zen Buddhism," by Joseph D. Parker, in *The Journal of Japanese Studies*, v. 21, no. 1 (Winter 1995), p. 103–120; *In Search of the Way: Thought and Religion in Early-Modern Japan, 1582–1860*, by Richard Bowring. Oxford: Oxford University Press, 2017; on painting: *Politics of Reclusion: Painting and Power in Momoyama Japan*, by Kendall H. Brown. Honolulu: University of Hawaii Press, 1997; *Scholar Painters of Japan: the Nanga School*, by James Cahill. New York: Asia Society, 1972; *The Eyes of Power: Art and Early Tokugawa Authority*, by Karen M. Gerhart. Honolulu: University of Hawaii Press, 1999; *77 Dances: Japanese Calligraphy by Poets, Monks, and Scholars, 1568-1868*, by Stephen Addiss. Boston: Weatherhill, 2006; on literature: *Aesthetics of Discontent: Politics and Reclusion in Medieval Japanese Literature*, by Michael F. Marra. Honolulu: University of Hawaii Press, 1991; *World Within Walls: Japanese Literature of the Pre-modern Era, 1600-1867*, by Donald Keene. New York: Columbia University Press, 1976; on Kinoshita Choshoshi: *Some Japanese Portraits*, by Donald Keene. Tokyo: Kodansha, 1978, p. 79-86; on Shokado: *The Painting of Shokado Shojo: Crosscurrents in Early Seventeenth-Century Japanese Painting*, by Kendall H. Brown. University of California-Berkeley, 1985 dissertation; *Kanshi: The Poetry of Ishikawa Jozan and Other Edo-Period Poets*, translated by Burton Watson. San Francisco: North Point Press, 1990; on Jozan: *Shisendo, Hall of the Poetry Immortals*, by J. Thomas Rimer. New York: Weatherhill, 1991.

39. From Hermits to Solitude in Early Modern Europe

English-language version of Tirso de Molina's *El Condenado por desconfiado* is available in *Three Plays by Tirso de Molina*, translated by Raymond Conlon as *A Sinner Saved, a Sinner Damned*. Jefferson, NC: McFarland, 2017; *The Life of Lazarillo de Tormes*, translated by W. S. Merwin. New York: NYRB, 2004; *The Complete Works of Francois Villon*, translated by Anthony Bonner. New York: David McKay, 1960; Ariosto quote: canto 2.14, p. 43, in *The Orlando Furioso* by Ludovico Ariosto, translated by William Stewart Rose. London: Bohn, 1858 and https://archive.org/details/orlandofuriosotr01ario/; *The Complete Fables of Jean de La Fontaine*, translated by Norman R. Shapiro. Champaign, IL: University of Illinois, 1960; La Fontaine's "The Rat Who Retired from the World," and "The Arbitrator, Almoner, and Hermit," in *The Fables of LaFontaine*, translated by Walter Thornbury. London and New York: Cassell,

Petter, and Galpin, 1886, p. 381-382 and p. 833-837; *Ivanhoe*, by Walter Scott. London and New York: Penguin, 2012, quote "lusty hypocrite" from chapter 20; Cowper's poem is no. 160 in *The Golden Treasury*, edited by Francis T. Palgrave. London: Macmillan, 1875, reprinted in bartleby.com: https://www.bartleby.com/106/160.html; *Robinson Crusoe*, by Daniel Defoe. Oxford and New York: Oxford University Press, 2007; Gibbon, op. cit.; the Scipio quote is recorded by Cicero in his "De Officiis," III. Lyric 1, in *Ethical Writings of Cicero*, translated by Andrew P. Peabody. New York: Little, Brown, 1887, p. 170; Seneca quote from "Epistle 6," in *Seneca's Morals by Way of Abstract*, by Roger L'Estrange. Edinburgh: Gavin Alston, 1774, p. 321.

40. Roger Crab: Early Modern Hermit

The two essays of Roger Crab have been reprinted separately, and published together as *The English Hermite and Dragon's Downfall,* all editions edited byAndrew Hopton. London: Aporia, 1990.

41. In Defense of Solitude: Petrarch to Rousseau

Deschamps quoted by J. Huizinga in his *The Waning of the Middle Ages.* Harmondsworth: Penguin, 1955, p. 36 and https://archive.org/details/in.ernet.dli.2015.100122/. *The Life of Solitude*, by Petrarch, translated by Jacob Zeitlin. Urbana: University of Illinois Press, 1924 and Westport, CT: Hyperion Press, 1978 reprint; *On Religious Leisure: De otio religioso*, edited and translated by Susan S. Schearer. New York: Italica Press, 2002; "Petrarch's Constructions of the Sacred Solitary Place in *De vita solitaria* and Other Writings," by Karl A. E. Enenkel, in *Solitudo: Spaces and Places of Solitude in Late Medieval and Early Modern Cultures*, edited by Karl A. E. Enenkel and Christine Gottler. Leiden: Boston: Brill, 2018, p. 29-80; "*De vita solitaria* and *De otio religioso*: the Perspective of the Guest," by Unn Falkeid, in *The Cambridge Companion to Petrarch*. Cambridge: Cambridge University Press, 2015, chapter 9, p. 111-119;on Antonio de Guevara: "Menosprecio de corte" Read as a Picaresque Text," by Sean McDaniel in *Hispanic Journal*, v. 26, no. 1/2 (Spring-Fall, 2005), p. 23-34. The *Menosprecio…* has not been translated into English. *Essays*, by Michel de Montaigne. New York: Viking, 1993 and *Michel de Montaigne: The Complete Essays*, edited and translated by M. A. Screech. London: Penguin, 1993 and 2013 reprint; Montaigne's essay on solitude is in Book 1, no. 39, p. 266-278; *The Complete Essays of Montaigne*, translated by Donald M. Frame. Stanford: Stanford University Press, 1958, and https://archive.org/details/essaysofmontaign03mo/; Montaigne's favorite reading is clearly Seneca, among whose Stoic themes of the philosopher's mean, the wisdom of withdrawal from the world, and the primacy of virtue, are all reflected in his *Essays*; Seneca quote: "… chained to fortune…," in "On Tranquility of Mind," p. 93 in *The Stoic Philosophy of Seneca: Essays and Letters of Seneca*, edited and translated by Moses Hadas. Garden City, NJ: Doubleday, 1958, p. 75–106; Descartes quote: "live without being…," p. 33, in *Discourse on the Method of Rightly Conducting One's Reason …*, by Rene Descartes, translated by John Veitch. Chicago: Open Court, 1913; "A Great City is a Great Solitude": Descartes's Urban Pastoral," by Kevin Dunn, in *Yale French Studies*, 1991, no. 80, p. 93–107; La Bruyere's *Dialogues sur le Quiétism* (often titled *Dialogues posthumes sur le quietisme*) has not been translated into English; Fénelon quote: "Christ Himself…," p. 31 of *The Maxims of the Saints*, by François Fénelon. London: Allenton, 1903 and https://archive.org/details/in.ernet.dli.2015.23470/; *Pascal's Pensées*, translated by W. F. Trotter. New York: Dutton, 1958, and https://archive.org/details/penseestheprovin013046mbp/; Pascal on happiness: section 139, p. 48; on Rousseau: *The Cambridge Companion to Rousseau*, edited by Patrick Riley. Cambridge: Cambridge University Press, 2000; *Rousseau's Political Philosophy: Stoic and Augustinian Origins*, by Christopher Brooke. Cambridge: Cambridge University Press, 2012; *Rousseau: Stoic & Romantic*, by Kennedy F. Roche. London and New York: Routledge, 2019, reprint of 1974 ed.; works by Rousseau: *Rousseau: The Discourses and Other Early Political Writings*, edited and translated by Victor Gourevitch. Cambridge: Cambridge University Press, 1997; *Rousseau, The Basic Political Writings: Discourse on the Sciences and the Arts, Discourse on the Origin of Inequality, Discourse on Political Economy*, [et al.], translated and edited by Donald A. Cress. Indianapolis, IN: Hackett, 2011 (2nd ed.); *Rousseau, The Reveries of the Solitary Walker*, translated by Charles E. Butterworth; Indianapolis, IN: Hackett Publishing, 1992; *Rousseau: Reveries of the Solitary Walker*, translated by Peter France. London and New York: Penguin, 1995; *Jean-Jacques Rousseau: Reveries of the Solitary Walker*, translated by Russell Goulbourne. Oxford and New York: Oxford University Press, 2011; quote: "From the disdain…" and "The conclusion I am able to draw…," in *The Confessions of J.J. Rousseau With The Reveries of the Solitary Walker*. London: J. Bew, 1783, [pt.2], p. 147 and p. 237–238; *On the Happiness of the Philosophic Life: Reflections on Rousseau's Reveries in Two Books*, by Heinrich Meier, translated by Robert Berman. Chicago: University of Chicago Press, 2016; "*Le Promeneur Solitaire*: Rousseau and the Emergence of the Post-Social Self," by David Gauthier in *Social Philosophy and Policy*, v. 8, no. 1, 1990, p. 35–58;

Jean-Jacques Rousseau and the Sources of Self, edited by Timothy O'Hagan. Aldershot: Avebury, 1997; Barbara Taylor juxtaposes Hume and Rousseau in "Philosophical Solitude: David Hume versus Jean-Jacques Rousseau," by Barbara Taylor, in *History Workshop Journal*, v. 89, Spring 2020, p. 1–21, and https://academic.oup.com/hwj/article/doi/10.1093/hwj/dbz048/5714185, with these epigraphic quotes: "A perfect solitude is, perhaps, the greatest punishment we can suffer. Every pleasure languishes when enjoyed apart from company, and every pain becomes more cruel and intolerable." –David Hume (1711–76), *A Treatise of Human Nature*, 1739–401. "I bless heaven for making me ... a hermit ... rather than a philosopher!–Jean-Jacques Rousseau (1712–78), 'Letter to Mme d'E pinay', 1757.

42. Hermits in Renaissance Art

For works of art, see the Hermitary Gallery website: www.hermitary.com/gallery/art/.

43. Eremitism in Eighteenth Century Britain

Overview: *Literary Loneliness in Mid-Eighteenth-Century England*, by John E. Sitter. Ithaca, NY: Cornell University Press, 1982; "Solitude and the Neoclassicists," by Raymond D. Havens, in *ELH: English Literary History*, v. 21, no. 4, Dec. 1954, p. 251-273. The Eighteenth-Century Poetry Archive lists seventy poems of the era on the subject of solitude, under the theme of "retirement": https://www.eighteenthcenturypoetry.org/works/#themes/. Cowley's poem "On Solitude," and https://cowley.lib.virginia.edu/small/solitudo.htm; his essay "On Solitude" in *The Essays and Other Prose Writings, by Abraham Cowley*, edited by Alfred B. Gough. Oxford: Clarendon Press, 1915 and http://www.archive.org/stream/essaysandotherpr00cowluoft#page/128/mode/2up; Parnell's poem "The Hermit" in *Collected Poems of Thomas Parnell*, edited by Claude Rawson and F. P. Lock. London: Associated Universities Press and Newark, DE: University of Delaware Press, 1989, and in the Eighteen-Century Poetry Archive: https://www.eighteenthcenturypoetry.org/works/o4106-w0190.shtml; Goldsmith's "Edwin and Angelina: a Ballad" in the Eighteenth Century Collections Online at https://quod.lib.umich.edu/e/ecco/004781641.0001.000/1:1?rgn=div1;view=fulltext; Beattie's "The Hermit" in https://www.eighteenthcenturypoetry.org/works/o4986-w0140.shtml; *The Hermit of Warkworth: a Northumberland Ballad*, by Thomas Percy, London: Davies and Leacroft, 1771 and https://archive.org/details/hermitofwarkwort00percuoft/; Robinson's "Anselmo, The Hermit of the Alps" in *Poetical Works of the Late Mrs. Mary Robinson*. London: Phillips, 1824, p. 94-96 and https://archive.org/details/ThePoeticalWorksOfTheLateMrsMary/page/n101/mode/2up?q=anselmo; Johnson's *The Hermit of the Forest, and the Wandering Infants*. Newcastle: Hodgson, 1807and https://archive.org/details/hermitofforestor00johniala/; *Bewick's Woodcuts* … by Thomas Hugo. London: Reeve, 1870 and https://archive.org/download/bewickswoodcutsi00hugo/bewickswoodcutsi00hugo.pdf); "Dorrington's Quarll" in Evans Early American Imprint Collection: https://quod.lib.umich.edu/e/evans/N21527.0001.001/1:3?rgn=div1;view=fulltext; *Fairburn's Cabinet of Instruction*. London: Fairburn, 1819; "The Hermit," p. 28-34, the quote on p. 28 at https://archive.proxyof.pro/details/fairburnscabinet00londiala; *The Every–Day Book and Table Book, or Everlasting Calendar of Popular Amusements* …, by William Hone. London: Tegg, 1826, in three volumes, and later reprints, and volume 1: https://archive.org/details/everydaybooktabl01honeuoft/, volume 2: https://archive.org/details/everydaybookorgu02hone, and volume 3: https://archive.org/details/everydaybooktabl03honeuoft.

Different printings over the years reflect different titles, subtitles, and numbers of volumes. The hermit-saints are described in volume 1, Billy Butterworth in volume 2; Francis Kimberley in volume 3. *The English Eccentrics*, by Edith Sitwell. London: Faber & Faber and Boston: Houghton Mifflin, 1933; Harmondsworth: Penguin, 1972, and https://archive.org/details/in.ernet.dli.2015.13144/; *The Hermit in the Garden: from Imperial Rome to Ornamental Gnome*, by Gordon Campbell. Oxford: Oxford University Press, 2014; *The Figure in the Landscape: Poetry, Painting, and Gardening during the Eighteenth Century*, by John Dixon Hunt. Baltimore, MD: Johns Hopkins University Press, 1976, reprinted 1989 and https://archive.org/details/figureinlandsca00hunt/; see especially chapter 1: "Hermit in their Landscapes"; in his *Hermits: The Insights of Solitude*, p. 87, where Peter France mentions the popularity of William Wright's *Grotesque Architecture, or, Rural Amusement*. London: Webley, 1767 and https://archive.org/details/grotesquearchite00wrig/, which presents construction plans for a variety of huts and hermitages.

Chapter 8. Eremitism in the Romantic era

Illuminating for an understanding of solitude as alienation, specifically among the literati of eighteenth and nineteenth century Europe, are the sociological premises of *Solitude in Society,* by Robert Sayre. Cambridge: Harvard University Press, 1978, reprinted 2014) and https://archive.org/details/solitudeinsociet0000sayr.

44. Eremitism & Romanticism: England

The *Complete Poetical Works by William Wordsworth*, introduction by John Morley. London: Macmillan, 1888 and https://www.bartleby.com/br/145.htm); *The Complete Poetical Works of Samuel Taylor Coleridge,* edited by Ernest Hartley Coleridge. Oxford: Clarendon Press, 1912 and https://www.gutenberg.org/ebooks/29090; *Samuel Taylor Coleridge: The Complete Poems,* edited by William Keach. London and New York: Penguin, 1997; *Lord Byron: The Complete Poetical Works,* edited by Jerome J. McGann and Barry Weller. Oxford: Clarendon Press; New York: Oxford University Press, 1980-1993; *The Complete Poetical Works of Percy Bysshe Shelley,* edited by George Edward Woodberry. Cambridge: Riverside Press; Boston: Houghton Mifflin, 1901 and in https://www.bartleby.com/139/; Shelley's "Alastor": https://archive.org/details/alastororspirito00shel/; *The Poetical Works of John Keats,* notes by Francis T. Palgrave. London: Macmillan, 1884 and Keats' "O Solitude" in https://www.bartleby.com/126/20.html; *Frankenstein,* by Mary Shelley (1818 text), edited by Marilyn Butler. Oxford: Oxford University Press, 2009 and *Frankenstein,* by Mary Shelley (1831 text), edited by M. K. Joseph. Oxford: Oxford University Press, 2008 and https://archive.org/details/frankensteinorm02shelgoog/ and https://archive.org/stream/Frankenstein1818Edition/frank-a5_djvu.txt; "A Forced Solitude: Mary Shelley and the Creation of Frankenstein's Monster," by Marcia Tillotson, in *The Female Gothic,* edited by Julian E. Fleenor. Montreal: Eden, 1983, p. 167-75 and http://knarf.english.upenn.edu/Articles/tillot.html; Shelley quotes from the 1818 edition: "elementary principles…," p.vi; "I shunned the face…," p. 92; "an imperfect and solitary being," p. 118; "solitary and detested," p. 142; *The Poems of Emily Brontë,* edited by Derek Roper and Edward Chitham. Oxford: Clarendon Press; New York: Oxford University Press, 1995; *The Complete Poems of Emily Brontë,* edited by Clement King Shorter and W. Robertson Nicoll. New York: Hodder and Stoughton, 1908 and https://archive.org/details/completepoemsofe01bronuoft;

Gondal's Queen; a Novel in Verse, by Emily Brontë. Austin, TX: University of TexasPress, 1983; Emily Brontë quote is from "Why Ask To Know the Day, the Clime?" in *Gondal Poems by Emily Jane Bronte*, edited by Helen Brown and Joan Mott. Oxford: Shakespeare Head Press, 1938, reprint Norwood, PA: Norwood Editions, 1978, p. 35-47 and https://en.wikisource.org/wiki/ Why_Ask_To_Know_The_Date%E2%80%94The_Clime%3F.

45. Eremitism & Romanticism: France

Translations: *French Romantic Prose*, edited by W.W. Comfort [includes Chateaubriand's *Rene*, Senancourt's *Obermann*, Vigny's *Stello*]. New York: Scribner, 1928 and https://archive.org/details/frenchromanticpr0000comf; *Stello: A Session with Doctor Noir*, by Alfred de Vigny, translated by Irving Massey. Whateley, MA: Noumena Press, 2015; the quote translated from *Stello*, by le Comte Alfred de Vigny. Paris: Charpentier, 1841, p. 309 and https:// archive.org/details/stello00goog/page/n8; *Lamartine: The Meditations Poetiques* (English and French), translated by David Hillery. Durham, UK: University of Durham, 1993. The quote from Victor Hugo's *Notre Dame* is in Book 2. Chapter 6: https://www.gutenberg.org/ebooks/2610 and https://www. bartleby.com/ebook/adobe/312.pdf. "Solitude" in *Baudelaire, His Prose and Poetry*, by Charles Baudelaire, translated by T. R. Smith. New York: Boni and Liveright, 1919, p. 74-75, and https://archive.org/details/baudelaire-hispro00baudiala/

46. Eremitism & Romanticism: Germany

Overview: *The Hermit in German Literature from Lessing to Eichendorff*, by John Fitzell. Chapel Hill, NC: University of North Carolina Press, 1961, reprint New York: AMS Press, 1969 and https://archive.org/details/hermitingermanli00fitz; *An Anthology of German Literature of the Romantic Era and Age of Goethe*, edited by Klaus-Peter Hinze and Leonard M. Trawick. Lewiston, NY: Edwin Mellen Press, 1993; selected translations: *Parzival*, by Wolfram von Eschenbach, translated by AS. T. Hatto. New York: Penguin,1980; *Parzival and Titurel* by Wolfram von Eschenbach, translated by Cyril Edwards. London and New York: Oxford University Press, 2006; *The Adventures of Simplicius Simplicissimus*, by Hans Jakob Christoffel von Grimmelshausen, translated by J. A. Underwood. London and New York: Penguin, 2018; *Simplicissimus*, by Hans Jakob Christoffel von Grimmelshausen, translated by Mike Mitchell. London: Dedalus, 1989; *The Adventurous Simplicissimus*, first English translation, by A. T. S. G. London: Heinemann, 1912 and http://www.gutenberg.

org/ebooks/33858; other works: *Confessions and Fantasie* by Wilhelm Heinrich Wackenroder, translated by Mary Hurst Schubert. University Park, PA: Pennsylvania State University Press, 1971; *Franz Sternbald's Wanderings* by Ludwig Tieck is unavailable in English translation; *Henry of Oftendingen, a Romance, from the German of Novalis*. Cambridge: Owen, 1842 and http://www.gutenberg.org/ebooks/31873; "Christianity or Europe" in *Novalis: Philosophical Writings*, translated by Margaret Mahony Stoljar. Albany, NY: SUNY Press, 1997, p. 137-153; "Romantic Cosmopolitanism: Novalis's *Christianity or Europe*," by Pauline Kleinfeld in *Journal of the History of Philosophy*, v. 46, no. 2, April 2008, p. 269-284; *Goethe's Satyros and Prometheus*, translated by John Gray. Glasgow: Glasgow Goethe Society, 1898; *Faust, Part One*, translated by David Luke. Oxford and New York: Oxford University Press, 2012; and https://archive.org/details/faustpartsiii00goetuoft/; *Oberon: A Poem*, by Christoph Martin Wieland, translated by William Sotheby. London: Cadell and Davies, 1798 and https://archive.org/details/oberonapoem01sothgoog/; *Henry of Ofterdingen, A Romance*, by Novalis. Mineola, NY: Dover, 2015 and https://archive.org/details/henryofterdinge00schlgoog/; *Konig Eginhard* by Ludwig Uhland is unavailable in English translation; *Heimatlosen* by Justinus Kerner is unavailable in English translation; *Peter Schlemihl*, by Adelbert von Chamisso, edited by Henry Morley. London: Cassell, 1889 and http://www.gutenberg.org/ebooks/5339; *Eine Meerfahrt*, by Joseph Eichendorff is unavailable in English translation; The poem "Der Eremit" by Gotthold Lessing is unavailable in English translation; *Nathan the Wise: A Dramatic Poem in Five Acts*, by Gotthold Lessing, translated by William Taylor. London: Cassell, 1893 and https://archive.org/details/nathanwisedramat00lessuoft/; *Die Kleiner* and *Walderbruder* by Jakob Lenz are unavailable in English translation; "Storm and Stress," by Friedrich Maximilian Klinger, translated by Betty Senk Waterhouse in *Sturm und Drang*, edited by Alan C. Leider. New York: Continuum, 1992, p. 123-180; *Zwillinge*, by Friedrich Maximilian Klinger unavailable in English translation; *Faustus: His Life, Death, and Descent into Hell*, by Friedrich Maximilian Klinger, translated by George Borrow. London: Constable, 1924 and https://archive.org/details/faustushislifed01klingoog/; *Erwin und Elmire*, by Goethe, *Godwi*, by Clemens Brentano, *Walter*, by Annette von Droste–Hulshoff are unavailable in English translation; *Hyperion, or The Hermit in Greece*, by Friedrich Hölderlin, translated by Howard Gaskill. Cambridge: Open Publishers, 2019 and https://www.openbookpublishers.com/product/941; Wakenroder's "A Wondrous Oriental Fairy Tale of a Naked Saint" in *German Literary Fairy Tales*, edited by Frank G. Ryder and Robert

M. Browning, translated by Robert M. Browning. New York: Continuum, 1983, p. 47-51; "The Story of Serapion" in *The Serapion Brethren* by E. T. A. Hoffmann, translated by Alexander Ewing. London: Bell, 1886, p. 10-24 and https://archive.org/details/serapionbrethre00ewingoog/; Lenau's "Die Marionetten" is not available in English translation; Grimm: "The Hut in the Forest" in *Household Tales*, by Jacob and Wilhelm Grimm, translated by Margaret Hunt. London: Bell, 1884, no. 169, p. 261-265 and https://archive. org/details/grimmshouseholdt2grim/; "Lowenberg: The Wild Hunt," p. 122-123 of *Legends of the Rhine*, by H. A. Guerber. New York: Barnes, 1895, and https://archive.org/details/legendsofrhine00guer/; *The Wild Huntsman's Chase*, from the German of [Gottfried August] Burger. London: British Library, 1911, reprint of London: Sampson Low, 1797.

47. Eremitism & Romanticism: United States

Overview: "The American Hermit and the British Castaway: Voluntary Retreat and Deliberative Democracy in Early American Culture," by Coby Dowdell, in *Early American Literature*, v. 46, no. 1, 2011, p. 121-156; *American Eccentrics: One Hundred Forty of the Greatest Human Interest Stories Ever Told*, by Carl Sifakis. New York: Facts on File, 1984 (reprint New York: Galahad, 1994); *Hairy Men in Caves: True Stories of America's Most Colorful Hermits*, by Marlin Bressi. Mechanicsburg, PA: Sunbury Press, 2015; Kelpius: "The Hermits of the Wissahickon," by Oswald Seidensticker, in *The Pennsylvania Magazine of History and Biography*, v. 11, no. 4 (Jan. 1888), p. 427-441 and https://www.jstor.org/stable/pdf/20083229.pdf; "More About the Hermit of the Ridge, John Kelpius," by Oswald Seidensticker in *The American Historical Record*. Philadelphia: Samuel P. Town, 1873, v. 2, no. 13, p. 1-6 and no. 15, p. 127; *An Account of the Wonderful Old Hermit's Death and Burial, Aged Two Hundred Twenty Eight Years*. Worcester, MA: Printed [by Isaiah Thomas, 1788] in *Evans Early American Imprint Collection*: https://quod.lib.umich. edu/e/evans/N16301.0001.001/1:1?rgn=div1;view=fulltext; *The Pennsylvania Hermit: A Narrative of the Extraordinary Life Of Amos Wilson*. Philadelphia: Smith and Carpenter, 1839, including "The Sweets of Solitude," by Amos Wilson, p. 14-24 and https://archive.org/details/pennsylvaniaherm00phil/; *Life and Adventures of Robert, The Hermit of Massachusetts...* Providence, RI: H. Trumbull,1829 and https://archive.org/details/lifeadventuresof00voor/; *An Account of the Discovery of a Hermit, Who Lived about 200 Years in a Cave, at the Foot of a Hill, 73 Days Journey Westward of the Great [Allegheny] Mountains, by James Buckland and John Fielding*, 1786, by various publishers, variant titles:

https://graphicarts.princeton.edu/2017/04/18/probably-the-best-seller-of-1786/; *The Hermit: or, An Account of Francis Adam Joseph Phyle* ..., by John Atkinson. New Jersey: Atkinson, 1811 and https://archive.org/details/hermit__01atki/; various sources re Sarah Bishop, including https://www.sarahbishop.org/about-sarah-bishop/.

48. Johnny Appleseed: Americana Hermit

Johnny Appleseed: the Man, the Myth, the American Story, by Howard B. Means. New York: Simon & Schuster, 2011; *Johnny Appleseed: Man & Myth*, by Robert Price. Urbana, OH: Urbana University Press, 2001; *The Frontier in American History: Essays*, by Frederick Jackson Turner. New York: Holt, 1920 and https://archive.org/details/cu31924016878013; *Alone in America: The Stories That Matter*, by Robert A. Ferguson. Cambridge, MA: Harvard University Press, 2013.

49. Romanticism & Solitude: United States

Overview: Ferguson, ibid.; *Cultures of Solitude: Loneliness, Limitation, Liberation*, edited by Ina Bergmann and Stefan Hippler. New York: Peter Lang, 2017; re Emerson: *The Collected Works of Ralph Waldo Emerson*, edited by Robert Ernest Spiller and others. Cambridge, MA: Belknap Press, 1971-2013; *The Essential Writings of Ralph Waldo Emerson*, edited by Brooks Atkinson. New York: Modern Library, 2000; *The Portable Emerson*, edited by Jeffrey S. Cramer. New York: Penguin, 2014; *An Uneasy Solitude: Individual and Society in the Work of Ralph Waldo Emerson*, by Maurice Gonnaud, translated by Lawrence Rosenwald. Princeton, NJ: Princeton University Press, 2016; Emerson quotes, from *Solitude and Society*. London: Sampson, Low, Son, & Marston, 1870 and https://archive.org/stream/societyandsolitu00emeriala: "shuffle off my...," p. 3; "necessity of isolation...," p. 4; "either habits of...," p. 5; "clothed with society...," p. 7; "dressed in arts...," p. 8; "solitude is impracticable ...," p. 12; "small doses...," p. 10; quotes from *The Essay on Self-reliance*. West Aurora, NY: Roycrofters, 1908 and https://archive.org/details/selfrelianceessay00emerrich/: "Trust thyself...," p. 8; "Whoso would be...," p. 15; "What I must do...," p. 18; "It is easy...," p. 19; "For non-conformity...," p. 21; "let us affront...," p. 26; "The world has been...," p. 28; "... divine fact," p. 38; "Your isolation must...," p. 39; "... disease of the intellect," p. 47; "fool's paradise...," p. 50; "Insist on yourself...," p. 51; "Nothing can bring you peace...," p. 59; quotes from *Nature, and Selected Essays*. New York: Penguin, 2003: "Nature is a discipline...," p. 55; "Nature is made…," p. 65; quote from "Literary Ethics," in *The Works of Ralph Waldo Emerson*… London: G. Bell, 1904, "The poets who have lived…," p. 422 and https://www.bartleby.com/90/0104.html; quote from "Friendship," in *Selected Writings of Emerson*. London: Scott, 1888, "I chide society…," p. 136 and https://www.bartleby.com/90/0206.html; on Thoreau: *Walden, Walking*, and *A Week*… are available in standard imprints and *Walden*: https://archive.org/details/waldenorlifeinwo1854thor/, *Walking* (part of *Excursions*): https://archive.org/details/excursionhenry00thorrich/, and *A Week*… https://archive.org/details/aweekonconcorda00thorgoog/; for the *Journal: The Journal of Henry David Thoreau, 1837-1861*, edited by Damion Searls. New York: NYRB, 2009 and https://www.walden.org/collection/journals/; *Henry David Thoreau: A Life*, by Laura Dassow Walls. Chicago: University of Chicago Press, 2017; Walls specifically states that while "Thoreau was no hermit" the multi-faceted Thoreau "could of course be icy, prickly, occasionally hermitous, and even a nag…," p. xx-xxi; elsewhere Walls describes Thoreau as "the iconic hermit of American lore," p. 231; quote: "Spartan-Buddhist…," p. 233; re *Solitude*, by Johann Georg Zimmermann: https://www.gutenberg.org/ebooks/55898; quotes from *Walden: An Annotated Edition*. Boston: Houghton Mifflin Harcourt, 1995, "I never found…," p. 132; "Not till we are lost…," p. 167; quotes from *Journal: The Writings of Henry David Thoreau: Journal*, edited by B. Torrey. Boston: Houghton, Mifflin, 1906, "By my intimacy with nature…," (July 26, 1852, p. 258); from *I to Myself: An Annotated Selection from the Journal of Henry D. Thoreau*. New Haven, CT: Yale University Press, 2007, "I thrive best…,"(December 28, 1856, p. 298); "I feel the necessity of deepening…," (August 2, 1854, p. 228-229); "I do not know if I am singular…," (November 25, 1857, p. 347); "I am tired of frivolous society…," Torrey op. cit., (July 11, 1855, p. 417); on Dickinson: *The Complete Poems of Emily Dickinson*. Boston: Little, Brown, 1924 and 1960, edited by Thomas H. Johnson: https://archive.org/details/in.ernet.dli.2015.185786/; *Emily Dickinson's Poems as She Preserved Them*, edited by Cristanne Miller. Cambridge, MA: Belknap Press, 2016; poems cited, with chronological enumeration, from 1960 Johnson ed.: "There is a solitude of space…," 1695, p. 691; "The soul selects her own society…," 303, p. 143; "To put this World down…," 527, p. 692; "Those dying then…," 1551, p. 646; "Growth of Man…," 750, p. 367; "How many Flowers…," 404, p. 192; "Take all away from me…" 1640, p. 672; "The Only News I know…" 827, p. 401; "Sweet hours have perished here…," 1767, p. 714; Sewall quote: "abstinence, endurance, and renunciation," p. 692; Dickinson quote: "yielded up" p. 679, in *The Life of Emily Dickinson*, by Richard Benson Sewall. Cambridge, MA: Harvard University Press, 1994, in two volumes: New York: Farrar, Straus & Giroux, 1974 and https://archive.org/details/lifeofemilydicki0001sewa; on Poe: *Complete Stories and Poems of Edgar Allan Poe*. New York: Doubleday, 1966 and https://archive.org/details/in.ernet.dli.2015.499306/; "Alone," composed 1829, published in *Scribner's Monthly*, Sept. 1875: https://en.wikisource.org/wiki/Alone_Poe; "Silence" [poem], published in *Saturday Courier* [Philadelphia], Jan. 1840: https://en.wikisource.org/wiki/The_Works_of_the_Late_Edgar_Allan_Poe/Volume_2/Silence; "Silence: A Fable," published in *Baltimore Book*, 1838 as "Siope": https://en.wikisource.org/wiki/Silence_(Poe,_short_story); "Fall of the House of Usher," published in *Burton's Gentleman's Magazine*, Sept. 1839: http://www.gutenberg.org/ebooks/932; on Hawthorne: *Hawthorne: A Study in Solitude*, by Herbert Sherman Gorman. New York: Biblo and Tannen, 1966, reprint of New York: Doran, 1927; "Fragments": https://www.gutenberg.org/ebooks/9247, "Adamant": https://www.gutenberg.org/ebooks/9240; on Melville: *Solitude and Society in the Works of Herman Melville and Edith Wharton*, by Linda Costanzo Cahir. Westport, CT: Greenwood Press, 1999; *Herman Melville: Complete Shorter Fiction*. New York: Everyman's Library, 1997; *Moby Dick*: https://www.gutenberg.org/ebooks/2701 and https://archive.org/details/mobydickorwhale01melvuoft/; quote: from *Moby-Dick, or, The Whale*. London: Constable, 1922, "They were nearly all Islands…," v. 1., p. 149; *Mardi and A Voyage Thither*. New York: Harper Brothers, 1849, "…with whom to mingle sympathies," p. 15; article: "Writing a Durable Mark: A Community of Isolatoes in *John Marr and Other Sailors*," by Yoshiaki Furui in *Leviathan*, v. 19, no. 2, June 2017, p. 52-70; quote: "I'd strike the sun…," *Moby-Dick*, ibid., v. 1, p. 204; "When I think of this life…," v. 2, p. 328; *Bartleby the Scrivner*: http://www.gutenberg.org/ebooks/11231.

50. Romantic Art and Solitude: Early Nineteenth Century

For works of art, see the Hermitary Gallery website: www.hermitary.com/gallery/art/. Friedrich painting and Samuel Beckett: https://www.bl.uk/collection-items/two-men-contemplating-the-moon-by-caspar-david-friedrich

51. Eremitism and Literature: Britain and Europe

Overview: *Solitude in Society: A Sociological Study in French Literature*, by Robert Sayre. Cambridge, MA: Harvard University Press, 2014 reprint of 1978 ed.; on Andersen: "The Silent Book," in *The Complete Andersen*, translated by Jean

Hersholt. New York: Heritage Press, 1948, section 2, p. 69-71 and http://
www.andersen.sdu.dk/vaerk/hersholt/TheSilentBook_e.html; on Reade:
The Cloister and the Hearth. London: Trubner, 1861 and http://www.guten-
berg.org/ebooks/1366; on Wilde: *The Complete Works of Oscar Wilde*: vol. 1,
Poems and Poems in Prose, edited by Bobby Fong and Karl Beckson. Oxford
and New York: Oxford University Press, 2000 and http://www.gutenberg.
org/ebooks/1338; on Maupassant: "The Hermit" in *The Works of Guy de
Maupassant*. New York: National Library Co., 1909, v. 4, p. 322-331 and
http://www.gutenberg.org/ebooks/17377, "Solitude" in *The Complete Short
Stories of Guy de Maupassant*. New York: Collier, 1903 and https://archive.
org/details/completeshortsto1903maup, p. 652-655; on Tolstoy: "Three
Questions" in *What Men Live By and Other Tales, by Leo Tolstoy*, translated by
Louise and Aylmer Maude. Bodton: Stratford, 1918, p. 34-38, and https://
archive.org/details/cu31924026397202/; "Three Hermits" in *The Com-
plete Works of Count Tolstoy: Fables for Children...*, translated by Leo Wiener.
Boston: Estes, 1903, p. 363-374 and https://archive.org/details/Three-
Hermits_LevTolstoy); on Chekhov: "The Bet" in *The Bet and Other Stories by
Anton Tchekhov*, translated by S. Koteliansky and J. N. Murry. Boston: Luce,
1915, p. 1-12 and https://archive.org/details/betotherstories00chekiala/; on
Kipling: "The Miracle of Purum Bhagat" in *The Works of Rudyard Kipling: The
Second Jungle Book*. New York: Doubleday Page, 1914, p. 35-60 and https://
archive.org/details/secondjungleboo03kiplgoog/; on Ewing: *The Trinity
Flower, and Other Stories* by Juliana Horatia Ewing. Boston: Knight, 1897, p.
1-21 and https://archive.org/details/trinityfloweroth00ewin/; on Smith:
"Hermit's Cave," p. 183-188 and "Chrysanthemum Hermit," p. 287-290, in
Ancient Tales and Folklore of Japan. London: Black, 1908 and https://archive.
org/details/ancienttalesandf00gordrich; on Twain: *A Connecticut Yankee in
King Arthur's Court*. New York: Webster Co.,1889 and https://archive.org/
details/connecticutyanke1889twai. The quote is from p. 280.

52. "The Temptation of St. Anthony" in Art

The Temptation of Saint Anthony, by Gustav Flaubert, translated by Lafcadio
Hearn. NewYork: Modern Library, 2001 and https://archive.org/details/
temptationofstan00flauuoft/; *Thaïs*, by Anatole France, translated by Ernest
Tristan. NewYork: Modern Library, 1902: https://archive.org/details/
in.ernet.dli.2015.350988/; translated by Robert B. Douglas. London: Lane,
1924; *On Ugliness*, by Umberto Eco, translated by Alastair McEwen. New
York: Rizzoli, 2007, specifically Chapter 2: "Passion, Death, Martyrdom,"

p. 43-72. For art works, visit the Hermitary Gallery: www.hermitary.com/
gallery/art.

53. Philosophers of Solitude: Kierkegaard to Nietzsche

Overview: *The Seventh Solitude: Man's Isolation in Kierkegaard, Dostoevsky, and
Nietzsche*, by Ralph Harper. Baltimore: Johns Hopkins University Press, 1965
(also subtitled "Metaphysical Homelessness in Kierkegaard, Dostoevsky,
and Nietzsche"): https://archive.org/details/seventhsolitudem00harp; on
Kierkegaard: *The Essential Kierkegaard*, edited by Howard V. Hong and Edna
H. Hong. Princeton: Princeton University Press, 2000; *Kierkegaard's Writings*
(26 vols.), Howard V. Hong & Edna H. Hong, series editors. Princeton:
Princeton University Press, 1990-2000; quote, "If you have never been
solitary…," from *Works of Love*, translated by David F. Swenson and Lillian
Marvin Swenson. Princeton: Princeton University Press, 1946, p. 309; on
Schopenhauer: *The World as Will and Presentation*, v. 1, translated by Richard
E. Aquila. London; New York: Routledge, 2008, quote: "overcomers of
the world…," p. 129; the quote from *Counsels and Maxims* is from chapter 2,
section 12 of "Our Relations to Ourselves," p. 27: https://www.gutenberg.
org/ebooks/10715 and https://archive.org/stream/counselsandmax-
im033505mbp/counselsandmaxim033505mbp_djvu.txt; the quote from
The Wisdom of Life is from section 1, "Division of the Subject," p. 7:
http://www.gutenberg.org/cache/epub/10741/pg10741.txt and https://
archive.org/details/wisdomoflife01scho/; on Dostoyevsky: "The Grand
Inquisitor" is book 5, chapter 5, p. 246-264 of *The Brothers Karamazov*, translated by Richard Pevear and Larissa Volokhonsky. San Francisco: North
Point Press, 1990; Constance Garnett translation: *The Brothers Karamazov*, by
Fyodor Dostoevsky. New York: Modern Library, 1996 and https://archive.
org/details/brotherskaramaz00dost/; *Notes from Underground*, translated by
Richard Pevear and Larissa Volokhonsky. New York: Everyman Library,
1993, reprinted New York: Vintage, 1994; quote: "the tragedy lies…,"
quoted in *Dostoevsky and the Novel*, by Michael Holquist. Princeton: Princeton
University Press, 2015, p. 30; quote: "The best thing is to do nothing…,"
Notes from Underground, translated by Mirra Ginsberg. New York: Bantam,
1983, p. 42 and https://archive.org/details/notesfromundergr00dost_0;
on Chernyshevsky: *A Vital Question; or, What Is To Be Done?* by Nikolay
Chernyshevsky, translated by Nathan Haskell Dole and S. S. Skidelsky. New
York: Crowell, 1886 and https://archive.org/details/cu31924096961036;
on Nietzsche: In letters to a friend Peter Gast, Nietzsche refers to "the

lonely sylvan hermitage of which I am the hermit" (July 18, 1880, p. 127), notes that he applies "the themes of my hermit theories to practical life" (Sept. 3, 1883, p. 169); reassures Gast re visiting not to be "fearing that you would not be *enough* of a hermit here" (Dec. 10, 1885, p. 175), recounts to a friend a visit to Jakob Burkhardt, renowned historian: "A great advantage I enjoyed there was the genial relations existing between Jakob Burkhardt and myself; something quite unusual on the part of that hermit-like thinker, who lived a very retired life." (April 10, 1888, p. 341) from *Selected Letters of Friedrich Nietzsche*, translated by Anthony M. Ludovici, edited by Oscar Levy. Garden City, NY: Doubleday, Page, 1921 and https://archive.org/details/selectedletterso00nietuoft/; calls himself the "hermit of Sils Maria" in a letter to Peter Gast (1884, p. 230) and twice in the same letter to Malwida von Meysenbug (Sept. 4,1886, p. 256), to Malwida he also writes: "Solitude with most solitary nature has been till now my solace, my medicine." (May 12, 1887, p. 265-266) in *Selected Letters of Friedrich Nietzsche*, edited and translated by Christopher Middleton. Indianapolis: Hackett, 1969; quote: "I go to solitude…," from *The Dawn of Day*, [or *Daybreak*] by Friedrich Nietzsche, translated by John McFarland Kennedy. London: Allen & Unwin; New York: MacMillan, 1911, Book V, Aphorism 491, p. 300 and http://www.gutenberg.org/files/39955/39955-pdf.pdf; quote: "One must avoid chance…" from "Why I Am So Clever" in *Ecce Homo*, in *Genealogy of Morals [and] Ecce Homo*, translated by Walter Kaufmann. New York: Random House, 1967 and New York: Vintage, 1989, p. 242; quote: "born, sworn, jealous friends…" from *Beyond Good and Evil*, edited by Rolf-Peter Horstmann, translated by Judith Norman. Cambridge: Cambridge University Press, 2002, p. 42; quote: "No stranger to me…," from *Thus Spoke Zarathustra* in *The Portable Nietzsche*, translated by Walter Kaufmann. New York: Penguin, 1954, reprinted 1976; p. 122; quote: "Flee, my friend,…" p. 163; quote: "the courage of hermits and eagles…" from part 4, chapter 13, "The Higher Man" section 4, p. 400; quote: "All honor to…" from essay 3, "What is the Meaning of Ascetic Ideals?" section 26, p. 158, in *Genealogy of Morals*, from *Genealogy of Morals [and] Ecce Homo*, op cit., "Nothing is true, everything is permitted…" p. 150.

54. Eremitism in British Literature

"An Hour with the Hermits," by Marybella Macaulay, in *The Irish Monthly*, v. 21 (August, 1893), p. 443-446; "The Hermits of the Sierra Morena," by Herbert Vivian, in *World Wide Magazine*, 1900, p. 184-189 and http://www.digitalhistoryproject.com/2011/08/sons-of-wildnerness-hermit-monks-of.

html; *The Spirit of Place, and Other Essays*, by Alice Meynell. London and New York: John Lane, 1899 and https://archive.org/details/spiritofplaceot00meyn/; *The Poetics of Space*, by Gaston Bachelard, translated by Maria Jolas. Boston: Beacon Press, 1969 and New York: Penguin, 2014; "On a Hermit Whom I Knew" in *On Nothing & Kindred Subjects*, by H[ilaire] Belloc. London: Methuen, 1908, p. 197-206, and https://archive.org/details/onnothingkindre00bellgoog/; "The Case for Hermits" in *The Well and the Shallows*, by G. K. Chesterton. London: Sheed & Ward, 1935, p. 41–414 and http://gutenberg.net.au/ebooks13/1301661h.html#ch6; "The Fairy Tale of Father Brown" from *The Wisdom of Father Brown*, in *The Complete Father Brown Stories*, by G. K. Chesterton. New York: Penguin, 2012, p. 304-315 and https://ebooks.adelaide.edu.au/c/chesterton/gk/c52fb/chapter24.html; Arthur Conan Doyle: "The Coming of the Huns" in *The Last of the Legions, and Other Tales of Long Ago*. New York: Doran, 1922, p. 47–68, and https://www.gutenberg.org/files/26153/26153-h/26153-h.htm; "Hermits, Ancient and Modern," by Charles Dickens, Jr., in *All The Year Round: a Weekly Journal*, March 24, 1894, vol. 11, third series, p. 282-285 and https://archive.org/details/allyearround07dickgoog/page/n298; Powys quote: "True lovers are twin–hermits...," p. 184; "What is advisable...," p. 76, in A *Philosophy of Solitude*, by John Cowper Powys. London: J. Cape and New York: Simon & Schuster, 1933 and https://archive.org/details/in.ernet.dli.2015.260410; on J. C. Powys: *"I Am Myself Alone": Solitude and Transcendence in John Cowper Powys*, by Janina Nordius. Goteborg, Sweden: Acta Universitatis Gothoburgensis, 1997; T. F. Powys quote: "I, too, for a long time...," p. 45; "peacefully planting cabbages," p. 79, in *Soliloquies of a Hermit*, by Theodore Francis Powys. London: Melrose, 1918, and https://archive.org/details/soliloquiesofher00powy; on Conrad: *Solitude Versus Solidarity in the Novels of Joseph Conrad: Political and Epistemological Implications of Narrative Innovation*, by Ursula Lord. Toronto: McGill-Queen's University Press, 1998; "Joseph Conrad and the lure of solitude," by John Gray, in *New Statesman*, Oct. 2015, https://www.newstatesman.com/culture/books/2015/10/joseph-conrad-and-lure-solitude; quote from *The Arrow of Gold*, London: Unwin, 1919, p. 62 and https://archive.org/details/arrowofgoldstory00conr/; quote from *Chance*, Leipzig: Tauchnitz, 1913, p. 149 and https://archive.org/details/Chance_by_Joseph_Conrad; quote from *Lord Jim*, London: Blackwood, 1900, p. 347 and https://archive.org/details/lordjimtale00conrrich/; quote from *Under Western Eyes*, New York: Harper, 1911, p. 358 and https://archive.org/details/underwesterneye00conrgoog; quote from *The Nigger*

of the Narcissus. New York: Doubleday, 1914, p. 189 and https://archive.
org/details/niggernarcissus00conrgoog; quote: "invincible solidarity" in
Preface to *The Nigger of the Narcissus*, p. 12; quote from *Victory: An Island
Tale*. Paris: Conard, 1916, p. 97; quote from *Heart of Darkness*. Garden City,
NY: Doubleday, Page, 1916, p. 24 and https://archive.org/details/ost-en-
glish-conrad_joseph_1857_1924_heart_of_darkness.

55. Eremitism in European Literature

The existentialism succeeding the collapse of Romanticism and Romantic
solitude begins formally with Kierkegaard, Dostoyevsky, and Nietzsche in
the nineteenth century. In the twentieth century, literature, philosophy, and
religion overlap with existential themes affecting solitude, the individual,
and the nature of society. Overviews of this period include works of Walter Kaufmann: *Existentialism from Dostoevsky to Sartre*. New York: Penguin,
2004, revised and expanded 1975 ed.; *Religion from Tolstoy to Camus*. New
Brunswick, NJ: Transaction, 1994; *From Shakespeare to Existentialism: Studies
in Religion, Poetry, and Philosophy*. Boston: Beacon Press, 1960, reprinted Princeton: Princeton University Press, 1980; the Kafka quote "I need solitude..."
from June 6, 1913 entry in *Letters to Felice*, by Franz Kafka, translated by
James Stern and Elisabeth Duckworth. New York: Penguin, 1974, p. 156;
Kafka's stories are collected in *Franz Kafka: The Complete Stories*, edited by
Nahum N. Glatzer. New York: Shocken Books, 1973 and https://archive.
org/details/completestories00kafk; on Rilke: Freud's essay "On Transience"
at https://www.sas.upenn.edu/~cavitch/pdf-library/Freud_Transience.
pdf. About "vast steppes of Russia," etc., Robert Hass, "Introduction"
(p. xi-xliv) in *Selected Poetry of Rainer Maria Rilke*, edited and translated by
Stephen Mitchell, introduction by Robert Hass. New York: Vintage, 1986,
reprint of New York: Random House, 1982; Rilke quotes: "Love your solitude...," p. 39; "Your solitude will be...," p. 40; "The necessary thing...," p.
45; in *Letters to a Young Poet*, translated by M. D. Hester Norton. New York:
Norton, 1954 and https://archive.org/details/letterstoyoungpo00rilk/;
"Everything is far and long gone by...," p. 37 in *Poems*, translated by Jessie
Lemont. New York: Wright, 1918; *The Fairy Tales of Hermann Hesse*, trans-
lated by Jack Zipes. New York: Bantam, 1995 and http://hesse.projects.
gss.ucsb.edu/works/maerchen-blurb.pdf; *Wandering: Notes and Sketches*, by
Hermann Hesse, translated by James Wright. New York: Farrar, Straus &
Giroux, 1972; *Siddhartha*, by Hermann Hesse, translated by Hilda Rosner.
New York: Bantam, 1981; translated by Stanley Appelbaum. Mineola, NY:

Dover, 1998; The quote "surrounded by..." and "neat, pedantic and wise Sinicism," p. 248 in *The Glass Bead Game (Magister Ludi)*, by Hermann Hesse; translated by Richard and Clara Winston. New York: Holt, Rinehart, and Winston, 2002, reprint of New York: Bantam, 1969 and https://archive. org/details/isbn_0553139568; Pessoa quotes: "To be born free...," section 283; "All I ask...," section 399, in *The Book of Disquiet*, by Fernando Pessoa, edited and translated by Richard Zenith. New York: Penguin, 2002. Using a different assembly of Pessoa's fragments is *The Book of Disquiet*, by Fernando Pessoa, translated by Margaret Jull Costa, edited by Jeronomo Pizarro. New York: New Directions, 2017; on Huysmans, Sayre comments on p. 80, op. cit.; *Against Nature (A Rebours)*, by Joris-Karl Huysman, edited by Patrick Mcguiness, translated by Robert Baldick. New York: Penguin, 2004; *Against the Grain*, by J. K. Huysmans, translated by John Howard. Mineola, NY: Dover, 1969, reprint of New York: Lieber & Lewis, 1922 and https://archive. org/details/cu31924088939974; *Monsieur Teste*, by Paul Valery, edited and translated by Jackson Mathews Princeton: Princeton University Press, 1973 and https://archive.org/stream/MonsieurTestePaulValery/Monsieur%20 Teste_Paul%20Valery_djvu.txt; *Hell*, by Henri Barbusse, translated by Robert Baldick. London: Chapman & Hall, 1966 and New York: Turtle Point Press, 1995; *In Search of Lost Time*, by Marcel Proust, edited by William C. Carter, translated by C. K. Scott-Moncrieff. New Haven: Yale University Press, 1913-2018, 3 of 7 vols.; *In Search of Lost Time*, by Marcel Proust, translated by C. K. Scott-Moncrieff and Terence Kilmartin, edited by D. J. Enright. New York: Random House, 1992 and Modern Library, 2003; Proust quote: "an inviolable solitude,..." p. 14, in *Swann's Way, Volume 1*, translated by C. K. Scott Moncrieff. New York: Holt, 1922; *Collected Poems of W. B. Yeats*. New York: Macmillan, 1950: from "Innesfree," p. 39, from "The Three Hermits," p. 111, from "Symbols," p. 235, from "Meru," p. 287, and https://archive.org/details/WBYeats-CollectedPoems1889-1939; Gibran quotes: "dwell in the solitude of your heart..." "On Talking," p. 68, in *The Prophet: His Parables and His Poems*. New York: Knopf, 1923 and https://archive.org/details/in.ernet.dli.2015.536146/; quotes: "The I in me, my friend...," "My Friend," p. 11, "Where the seeds are few,..."("The Pomegranate," p. 36, "left that sea to seek..." "The Greater Sea," p. 56 in *The Madman: His Parables and Poems*. New York: Knopf, 1918 and https:// archive.org/details/madmanparables00gibrrich/; "The King-Hermit" in *The Forerunner: His Parables and Poems*. New York: Knopf, 1920, p. 17-21, "The Hermit and the Beasts" p. 16-17, "The Hermit-Prophet," p. 32,

"Finding God," p. 48, in *The Wanderer: His Parables and Poems*. New York: Knopf, 1932; "The Tempest," p. 3-26, in *The Secrets of the Heart*, translated by Anthony Rizcallah Ferris, edited by Martin L. Wolfe. New York: Philosophical Library, 1947, reprinted New York: Jaico Publishing, [1947] and https://archive.org/details/SecretsOfTheHeartKhalilGibran; *The Hermit*, by Eugene Ionesco, translated by Richard Seaver. London: Deutsch and New York: Holt, 1987; Ionesco quote: "Solitude seems to oppress me..." p. 19 in *Rhinoceros*, by Eugene Ionesco, translated by Derek Prouse. New York: Grove Press, 1960; reprinted Harmondsworth: Penguin, 1962; quotes from: *The Hermit*, a novel, by Eugene Ionesco, translated by Richard Seaver. London: Calder, 1983, New York: Viking, 1974: "What are my desires?..." p. 28; "Time went by..." p. 151, "I was billions..." p. 153.

56. Philosophers of Solitude: Wittgenstein to Berdyaev

On Wittgenstein: *Language and Solitude: Wittgenstein, Malinowski and the Habsburg Dilemma*, by Ernest Gellner. Cambridge: Cambridge University Press, 1998. Quote: "poem to solitude" is the partial title of section 11; *Tractatus Logico-Philosophicus*, by Ludwig Wittgenstein, translated by C. K. Ogden. London: Kegan Paul and New York: Harcourt Brace, 1922; *Philosophical Investigations*, by Ludwig Wittgenstein, translated by G. E. M. Anscombe. Oxford: Blackwell, 2001; Camus quote: "There are no more deserts..." from the essay "The Minotaur, or The Stop in Oran," p. 155, in *The Myth of Sisyphus and Other Essays*, by Albert Camus, translated by Justin O'Brien. New York: Vintage, 1955; other works Camus: *The Stranger*, translated by Gilbert Stuart. New York: Knopf, 1946; *The Plague*, translated by Gilbert Stuart. New York: Vintage, 1948; *The Rebel*, translated by Anthony Bower. New York: Vintage, 1948; Sartre's work: *Nausea*, translated by Lloyd Alexander. New York: New Directions, 1964, and *Nausea*, translated by Robert Baldick. Harmondsworth: Penguin, 1965; *Being and Nothingness*, translated by Hazel E. Barnes. New York: Washington Square Press, 1953; *Existentialism and Humanism*, translated by Philip Mairet. London: Methuen,1948 (other translations titled *Existentialism Is a Humanism* and *Existentialism and Human Emotion*); *No Exit*, translated by Gilbert Stuart. New York: Knopf, 1946 and https://archive.org/details/NoExit); on Heidegger: "On Solitude and Loneliness in Hermeneutical Philosophy," by Adrian Costache, in *Research in Hermeneutics, Phenomenology, and Practical Philosophy*, v. 5, no. 1, June 2013, p. 130-149; *Being and Time*, by Martin Heidegger, translated by John McQuarrie and Edward Robinson. New York: Harper & Row, 1962; *The Fundamental Concepts of Metaphysics:*

World, Finitude, Solitude, translated by William McNeill and Nicholas Walker. Bloomington, IN: Indiana University Press, 1995; Heidegger quote: "that solitariness…," p. 6; *Solitude and Society*, by Nikolai Berdyaev, translated by George Reavey. London: G. Bles, 1938 and https://archive.org/details/in.ernet.dli.2015.1274/.

57. Simone Weil, Philosopher of Solitude

Overview: *Stanford Encyclopedia of Philosophy: Simone Weil* (revised 2018): https://plato.stanford.edu/entries/simone-weil/; works of Weil: *Oppression and Liberation*. London: Routledge, 2001, p. 102-114; quotes: "Rome is the…," p. 167, "Society is the…," p. 165, "A society like the Church…" p. 166, "relationship breaks its way out…," p.165 from "The Great Beast" in *Gravity and Grace*, translated by Emma Crawford and Mario von der Ruhr. New York: Routledge, 2002; "Gregorian chant…," and "What is sacred…, from "Human Personality" p. 55, and "Love is more or less …," from "The Great Beast," p. 121 in *Simone Weil, an Anthology*, edited by Sian Miles. New York: GrovePress, 2000; "Meditation on the social mechanism…" from *The Notebooks of Simone Weil*, translated by Arthur Wills. New York: Routledge, 2004, p. 311; "essentially anonymous," "Gregorian chant…," "What is sacred in science…" on p. 55, "impersonality is only reached…," p. 56, of "Human Personality," "Love is more or less…" p. 121, "pseudo-immortality," p. 273, "Do not allow yourself…" in "Love," p. 275 in *Simone Weil, An Anthology*, edited by Sean Miles. New York: Grove Press, 2000; "Keep your solitude…" p. 67 of "To Desire Without an Object" in *Gravity and Grace*, op. cit.; "Solitude. Where does it…," p. 121 of "Attention and Will" in *Gravity and Grace*, op. cit.; "rooted in the absence…," p. 300 of *Notebooks of Simone Weil*. op. cit.; "It is necessary to…," p. 86 of "Decreation" in *Gravity and Grace*, op. cit.

58. Romantic Eremitism in American Literature

Burroughs quotes from *The Writings of John Burroughs, v. 8: Indoor Studies*. Boston: Houghton Mifflin, 1905, p. 233-242: "Hermits generally…," p. 234 and https://archive.org/details/writingsofjohnbu08burriala/; Jewett quotes: "a nun or hermit person…," p. 103; "something mediaeval…," p. 110; "crossed in love…," p. 103, from *The Country of the Pointed Firs*, by Sarah Orne Jewett. Boston: Houghton Mifflin, 1896 and https://archive.org/details/countryofpointed00jewerich; "To Him Who Waits," in *Options*, by O. Henry. New York: Harper, 1909, p. 147-155 and in *The Complete Works of O. Henry*. Garden City, NY: Doubleday, 1953, p. 739-747 and https://archive.org/details/completeworksofo00henr; "A Hermit of Carmel" in *A Hermit of Carmel and Other Poems*, by George Santayana. New York: Scribner, 1901, p. 3-42, and https://archive.org/details/hermitofcarmel00santrich/; "The Hermit and the Wild Woman," in *The Hermit and the Wild Woman, and Other Stories*, by Edith Wharton. New York: Scribner, 1908, p. 3-42, and https://archive.org/details/hermitandwildwo00whargoog/; Wharton's poem "Ogrin" was published in the December 1909 issue of *Atlantic Magazine*: https://www.theatlantic.com/magazine/archive/1909/12/ogrin-the-hermit/376201/ and in *Edith Wharton: Selected Poems*, edited by Louis Auchincloss. New York: Library of America, 2005.

59. Realist Eremitism in American Literature

The Frost quote "a lump in the throat..." from a letter to editor Louis Untermeyer, in *The Letters of Robert Frost to Louis Untermeyer*. New York: Holt, Rinehart & Winston, 1963, p. 22 and https://archive.org/details/lettersofrobertf00fros; quotes from poems are from *The Poetry of Robert Frost*, edited by Edward Connery Lathem. New York: Holt, Rinehart and Winston, 1969, also issued as *The Poetry of Robert Frost: The Collected Poems, Complete and Unabridged*: quoted poems, from *A Boy's Will*: "Into My Own," p. 5, "Ghost House," p. 5, Storm Fear," p. 9, "To the Thawing Wind," p. 11, "Dream Pang," p. 16, "My Butterfly," p. 28, "Reluctance," p. 29; from *North of Boston*: "TheWood-Pile, p. 101; from *Mountain Intervals*: "Birches," p. 121, "Out Out—," p. 136; from *New Hampshire*: "Two Witches," p. 202, "The Pauper Witch of Grafton," p. 207, "The Lockless Door," p. 240; "The Need of Being Versed in Country Things," p. 241; *A Way Out: a One-Act Play*, by Robert Frost in *Seven Arts* (Feb. 1917), p. 347-362, not published individually until 1929 by New York: Harbor Press; quote: "overcasts my poetry...," p. 210 in *Family Letters of Robert and Elinor Frost*, edited by Arnold Grade, foreword by Lesley Frost. Albany, NY: SUNY Press, 1972; quote: "My disease I guess...," cited on p. 55-56 in *Robert Frost: The Later Years, 1938-1963*, by Lawrance Roger Thompson and R. H. Winnick. New York: Holt, Rinehart and Winston, 1966; Jeffers poems cited, not quoted: "Divinely Superfluous Beauty," p. 23," "Excesses of God," p. 23, "Point Joe," p. 31, "Boats in a Fog," p. 163, "De Rerum Virtute," p. 176-178, in *The Wild God of the World: An Anthology of Robinson Jeffers*, selected by Albert Gelpi. Stanford, CA: Stanford University Press, 2003; "Meditation on Saviors," p. 222-226, "Dear Judas," p. 225-265 in *The Selected Poetry of Robinson Jeffers*.

New York: Random House, 1938 and https://archive.org/details/select-edpoertyof029969mbp; *The Selected Poetry of Robinson Jeffers*, edited by Tim Hunt. Stanford, CA: Stanford University Press, 2001; quotes from Random House edition: "one must forgive nature…," p. 79; quotes from "Fog, p. 162; "why a lone bird..." p. 166; "No matter what happens to men…" p. 167; "paid my birth–dues, p. 262; "Men moulding themselves to the anthill..." p. 269; "I need, therefore, nothing..." p. 193; "I hope..." p. 194; "hardly a friend of humanity," p. 459; "how to be human again..." p. 574; "will not wind himself,..." p. 577; "the enormous invulnerable…," p. 598; "Integrity is wholeness…," p. 594; "tormented persons want truth…," p. 614; "annul the suffering,..." p. 615; "loved landscapes and solitude," p. 695; quotes from *The Double-axe & Other Poems, Including Eleven Suppressed Poems*, by Robinson Jeffers. New York: Liveright, 1977: "the rejection of human solipsism,..." p. xxii; "the devaluation of human–centered illusions," p. 171; "Turn away from each other." p. 173; quote from 2001 edition: "loved landscapes and solitude," from "On An Anthology of Chinese Poems," p. 695. Secondary sources: *Robinson Jeffers: Poet and Prophet*, by James Karman. Stanford, CA: Stanford University Press, 2015; *Robinson Jeffers and the American Sublime*, by Robert Zaller. Stanford, CA: Stanford University Press, 2012; *The Cliffs of Solitude: A Reading of Robinson Jeffers*, by Robert Zaller. Cambridge: Cambridge University Press, 2009; *Invisible Man*, by Ralph Ellison. New York: Random House, 1952 and Vintage, 1972. In the Nov. 1981 "Introduction" to a Vintage printing, Ellison indicates that "I associated him [the protagonist], ever so distantly, with the narrator of Dostoevsky's *Notes from Underground*…," p. xv; quote: "I am an invisible man…," p. 3-4, "hibernation, a covert preparation...," p. 13, "not all sickness is unto death…," p. 14, "I could only move ahead…," p. 571.

60. West Meets East: Eremitic Journeys

The Bhagvat-Geeta, or Dialogues of Kreeshn and Arjoon, by Charles Wilkins. London: Nourse, 1875 and https://rarebooksocietyofindia.org//book_archive/bhgvtgtordialog00compgoog.pdf; *Oupnek'hat (id est, Secretum tegendum)*, [translated and edited by M. Anquetil-Duperron]. Argenrorati: Levrault, 1801; Zend-Avesta, ouvrage de Zoroastre... partie 2: Vie de Zoroastre, [translated and edited by] M. Anquetil-Duperron. Paris: Tilliard, 1771 and https://archive.org/details/zendavestaouvrag02anqu/page/n8; *Sacred Books of the East*, edited by F. Max Muller. Oxford: Clarendon Press, 1879-1910; *Friedrich Max Müller and the Sacred Books of the East*, by Arie L. Molendijk. Oxford:

Oxford University Press, 2016; works by H. P. Blavatsky: *Isis Unveiled: a Master-key to the Mysteries of Ancient and Modern Science and Theology.* New York: J. W. Bouton, 1877; *The Secret Doctrine: the Synthesis of Science, Religion and Philosophy.* London: Theosophical Society, 1888, and *The Key to Theosophy.* London: Theosophical Society, 1889; *The Fourth Way: a Record of Talks and Answers to Questions Based on the Teaching of G.I. Gurdjieff,* by P. D. Ospenskii. London: Routledge & K. Paul, 1967; *Meetings With Remarkable Men,* by George Gurdjieff. London: Routledge & K. Paul; New York: Dutton, 1963; Works by Alexandra David-Neel: *With Mystics And Magicians In Tibet,* by Alexandra David-Neel, translated by A. D'Arsonval. London: Lane, 1931 and https://archive.org/details/in.ernet.dli.2015.40665/, published as *Magic and Mystery in Tibet.* New York: Claude Kendall, 1933: https://www.theosophy.world/resource/ebooks/magic-and-mystery-tibet-alexandra-david-neel; quotes from the 1933 edition: p. 75: "often chosen as dwelling-places....," "mountaineers called...," "visiting the gomchen...," "about whom so many..."; quotes from p. 76: "this lama...," and "I had no definite plan...," p 72: "I feel that the hermit's life...."; *My Journey to Lhasa.* London: Heinemann, 1927 and https://archive.org/details/in.ernet.dli.2015.40184/; Brunton quotes: "useless to society...," p. 126, "Starched uncomfortable...," p. 158, "fitting to a hermit...," p. 157 "modern habits for...," p. 94, "use solitude but...," p. 199, in *A Hermit in the Himalayas: the Journal of a Lonely Exile,* by Paul Brunton. New York: Rider, 1937 and https://archive.org/details/in.ernet.dli.2015.81502/; *The Razor's Edge,* by W. Somerset Maugham. London: Heinemann and New York: Doubleday, Doran, 1944. The quote "commodification of...," is from "Somerset Maugham's Swami," by David Shaftel in the July 22, 2010 issue of the *New York Times Book Review.* https://www.nytimes.com/2010/07/25/books/review/Shaftel-t.html; *Clearing the Path: Writings of Ñaṇavira Thera (1960-1965),* edited by Samonerea Bodhesako and Forrest Williams. Colombo: Path Press, 1987 and https://www.nanavira.org/libraries/ctp_book_v1.pdf; revised and enlarged edition: *Clearing the Path (1960-1965),* by Nanavira Thera, edited by Bhikku H. Nanasuci. Ijssel, Netherlands: Path Press, 2010; *The Hermit of Bundala: Biography of Ñaṇavira Thera, With Reflections on His Life and Work,* by Bhikkhu Hiriko. Ijssel, Netherlands: Path Press, 2014; quotes: "something of a solitary by nature...," January 24, 1964 letter: https://nanavira.org/index.php/letters/post-sotapatti/1964/116-l-03-11-january-1964; "solitaire, not...," August 25, 1963 letter: https://www.nanavira.org/index.php/letters/post-sotapatti/1963/90-l-62-25-august-1963; on Le Saux: *Ascent to the*

Depth of the Heart: The Spiritual Diary (1948-1973) of Swami Abhishiktananda, edited by Raimon Panikkar, translated by David Fleming and James Stuart. Delhi: ISPCK, 1998; *Ascent to the Depth of the Heart: The Spiritual Diary (1948-1973) of Swami Abhishiktananda*. Delhi: ISPCK, 1998; *Guru and Disciple: an Encounter with Sri Gnanananda, a Contemporary Spiritual Master.* London: SPCK, 1974; later revised 1990 and enlarged 2012; *Swami Abhishiktananada: Essential Writings*, selected by Shirley Du Boulay. Maryknoll, NY; Orbis Books, 2007; *Swami Abhishiktananda: His Life Told Through His Letters*, by James Stuart. Delhi: ISPCK, 1989; *The Cave of the Heart: The Life of Swami Abhishiktananda*, by Shirley Du Boulay. Maryknoll, NY: Orbis Books, 2005. Quote: "In serene solitude…," from "Diary," November 25, 1956, p. 131, in *In the Bosom of the Father: The Collected Poems of a Benedictine Mystic Swami Abhishiktananda*, translated by Jacob Riyeff. Eugene, OR: Wipf and Stock, 2018; "living alone with oneself…," from "Diary," November 29, 1956, p.184, and "The solitary is all alone…," from "Diary," November 13, 1962, p. 246-247, from *Ascent to the Depth of the Heart,* ibid.; on Christian–Hindu religious dialogue generally, with references to Buddhism, and later figures such as Foucauld and Merton, written from a Christian/Catholic point of view: *The Way of the Hermit: Interfaith Encounters in Silence and Prayer*, by Mario Aguilar. London and Philadelphia: Jessica Kingsley Publishers, 2017; on Bede Griffiths: *Bede Griffiths: Essential Writings*, selected by Thomas Matus. Maryknoll, NY: Orbis Books, 2004; *Beyond the Darkness: A Biography of Bede Griffiths*, by Shirley Du Boulay. New York: Doubleday, 1998; *A Sense of the Sacred: A Biography of Bede Griffiths*, by Kathryn Spink. Maryknoll, NY: Orbis Books, 1989; *Yogins of Ladakh: A Pilgrimage Among the Hermits of the Buddhist Himalayas*, by John Crook and James Low. Delhi: Motilal Banarsidass, 2007; *The Hermits of Rishikesh: a Sociological Study*, by Augusthy Keemattam. New Delhi: Intercultural Publications, 1997; *Cave in the Snow: Tenzin Palmo's Quest for Enlightenment*, by Vicki Mackenzie. London and New York: Bloomsbury, 1998 (paperback edition subtitled *A Western Woman's Quest for Enlightenment).* Works by Bill Porter: *Road to Heaven: Encounters with Chinese Hermits*. San Francisco: Mercury House, 1993 and Berkeley, CA: Counterpoint Press, 2009 reprint; *Finding Them Gone: Visiting China's Poets of the Past.* Port Townsend, WA: Copper Canyon Press, 2016 (the poets of the latter work are hermits, from Tao Chien to Tu Fu, Cold Mountain to Stonehouse); *Amongst White Clouds: Chinese Buddhist Hermit Monks*, directed and produced by Edward A. Burger, (documentary film, 2005), Oakland, CA: Festival Media/Buddhist Film Foundation (DVD), 2007; *Hermits*, directed by He Shiping and Fu Peng (documentary film, 2015), Sichuan, China: Emei Film Channel, https://www.youtube.com/watch?v=3R0h3dvL73w; *Summoning the Recluse*, produced by Max Duncan and Ellen Xu, (documentary film, 2017). Aeon Media Group: https://aeon.co/videos/why-some-chinese-millennials-are-taking-up-the-hermit-s-life-in-the-mountains

61. Charles de Foucauld: Hermit of Contradiction

Meditations of a Hermit: the Spiritual Writings of Charles de Foucauld, a Hermit of the Sahara and Apostle of the Tuaregs, translated by Charlotte Balfour. London: Oates & Washbourne, 1930, reprinted New York: Orbis Books, 1981; *Memories of Charles de Foucauld, Explorer and Hermit, Seen in His Letters*, translated by Donald Attwater, edited by George Gorree. London: Burns, Oates & Washbourne, 1938; *Charles de Foucauld: Writings*, selected by Robert Ellsberg. Maryknoll, NY: Orbis, 2005; *Hidden in God: Discovering the Desert Vision of Charles de Foucauld*, by Bonnie Thurston. Notre Dame, IN: Ave Maria Press, 2016; quote: "solitary little house…," cited in *The Quest of Solitude*, by Charles F. Anson. London: Dent, New York: Dutton, 1932, p. 254, and https://archive.org/details/in.ernet.dli.2015.75798; to the Nazareth prioress: "France, in spite of appearances, is still the France of Charlemagne, St. Louis, and Jeanne d'Arc; the old soul of the nation lives on in our generation..." cited on p. 337 in *Charles De Foucauld: Hermit and Explorer*, by René Bazin, translated by Peter Keelan. New York: Benziger, 1923, and https://archive.org/details/charlesdefoucaul00bazi/; intent to canonize: https://www.catholicnewsagency.com/news/pope-francis-to-canonize-french-missionary-bl-charles-de-foucauld-79665.

62. The Renaissance of Eremitism in Hindu India

On Ramakrishna and Vivekananda: *The Life of Ramakrishna*, by Romain Rolland, translated by E. F. Malcom-Smith. Calcutta: Advaita Ashrama, 1929; *The Life of Vivekananda and the Universal Gospel*, by Romain Rolland, translated by E. F. Malcolm-Smith. Almora, Uttarakhand, India: Advaita Ashrama, 1931. Ramakrishna quote "one should pray…," p. 1159 and "think of God…," p. 1164 of *The Gospel of Ramakrishna*, [compiled] by Mahendranath Gupta, translated by Swami Nikhilananda, introduction by Aldous Huxley, edited by Joseph Campbell. New York: Ramakrishna-Vivekananda Center, 1942; Vivekananda quote: "The ideal man…," in "Karma-Yoga," Chapter 1: "Karma In Its Effect on Character," *Complete Works of Swami Vivekananda*, v. 1, p. 34 Calcutta: Advaita Ashrama, 1907 and https://archive.

org/details/in.ernet.dli.2015.94806/; Tagore's poem "Deeno Daan" is not included in the standard *Collected Poems And Plays of Rabindranath Tagore*. London: Macmillan, 1920, but found at https://scroll.in/article/969579/there-is-no-god-in-that-temple-said-the-hermit-rabindranath-tagore-wrote-this-poem-in-1900; Aurobindo quotes: "We must not make...," from *Essays Divine and Human: Writings from Manuscripts 1910-1950*. Pondicherry: Sri Aurobindo Ashram, 1997, p. 58; "A meditative mind turned...," from *The Message of the Gita*. London: Allen & Unwin, 1946, p. 193; "The endless difficulties...," from *Synthesis of Yoga*. Pondicherry: Sri Aurobindo Ashram, 1957, p. 30; Ramana Maharshi quotes: "the state of being free ...," p. 64, "Restraint of speech...," p. 234, "The perfection of Solitude...," p. 162, "the sage who...," p. 44, "the Self is that where...," p. 42; "Silence is the highest and most perfect form...," p. 86 in *The Collected Works of Ramana Maharshi*, edited by Arthur Osborne. London: Rider, 1959, reprinted 1968 and https://archive.org/details/CollectedWorksOfRamanaMaharishi/; J. Krishnamurti quotes: "Can the man who belongs...," from Bombay public talk, 1955: http://www.jkrishnamurti.org/content/bombay-1st-public-talk-16th-february-1955/Bombay%201955%20Bombay%201st%20Public%20Talk%2016th%20February%201955; "The hermit and the monk are never alone...," January 31, 1962 entry in *Krishnamurti's Notebook*. Ojai, CA: Krishnamurti Publications, 2003; "For the total development of the human being...," *Life Ahead: On Learning and the Search for Meaning*, by J. Krishnamurti. Novato, CA: New World Library, 2005, reprint of 1963, p. 8.

63. The Hermit in the Tarot

The Hermits and Anchorites of England, by Mary Rotha Clay. London: Methuen, 1914 and https://archive.org/details/hermitsanchorite00clay/; *The Pictorial Key to the Tarot*, by Arthur Edward Waite, illustrations by Pamela Colman Smith. London: Rider, 1911; Boston: Weiser, 2000; New York: Dover, 2005 and https://archive.org/details/A.EWaiteThePictorialKeyToTheTarot/ and http://www.sacred-texts.com/tarot/pkt/; quote: "artificial and arbitrary," from Weiser ed., p. 287; *The Symbolism of the Tarot*, by P. D. Ouspensky, translated by A. L. Pogossky. St. Petersburg, Russia: Trood, 1913; New York: Dover, 1976, and http://www.sacred-texts.com/tarot/sot/; quoted text of "Card IX: The Hermit," p. 53-54 of Dover ed. For art works, see the Hermitary Gallery: www.hermitary.com/gallery/art/.

64. Rehabilitation of Hermits in the West

The Man Who Planted Trees, by Jean Giono, illustrated by Michael McCurdy. Post Mills: VT: Chelsea Green, 1995, (translation of 1953 French ed.) and https://archive.org/details/manwhoplantedtre00gion Planted_Trees); video: Frederic Back, producer. Canadian Broadcasting Corporation (CBC), National Film Board, and Société Radio-Canada, 1987; Microcinema International (DVD), 2005: https://archive.org/details/TheManWhoPlantedTrees; *The Solitude of Compassion*, by Jean Giono, translated by Edward Ford. New York: Seven Stories Press, 2002. Availability of web-based resources about Basili Girbau varies. Articles on the Maronite Order and its hermits: "The Maronite Eremitical Tradition: a Contemporary Revival," by Guita G. Hourani & Antoine B. Habachi in *Heythrop Journal* v. 45, 2004, p. 451-465; "A Spiritual Odyssey: The Maronite Self-Image in the Twenty-First Century," by Emma Loosley, in *Bulletin of the Royal Institute for Inter-Faith Studies*, v. 7, no. 2 (Sept. 2005), p.183-191; quote from p. 188: "Within the last twenty years, there has ... been a renewal in the Maronite eremitical tradition that was so successful ... in the Middle Ages." *The Hermit of Lebanon: Father Sharbel: a First Essay on the Servant of God*, by Joseph Eid. New York: Paulist Press, 1952; *A Cedar of Lebanon*, by Paul Daher. Dublin, Ireland: Browne and Nolan, 1956 and reprinted New York: Philosophical Library, 1957; on Thomas Merton, key works on solitude and eremitism include his *Thoughts in Solitude*. New York: Farrar, Straus and Cudahy, 1958; "Preface" to *Alone with God*, by Dom Jean Leclercq, translated by Elizabeth McCabe, preface by Thomas Merton. New York: Farrar, Straus and Cudahy, 1961, reprinted in *Camaldolese Extraordinary: The Life, Doctrine, and Rule of Blessed Paul Giustiniani*, by Jean Leclercq. Bloomingdale, OH: Ercam, 2002, second ed., 2008); quote: "demand that there be hermits," in *Disputed Questions*. New York: Houghton, Mifflin, 1985, p. 162; *Dans le desert de Dieu*. Saint-Léger-Vauban: La Pierre-qui-vire, 1955; quote: "divertissement," *Disputed Questions*, ibid., p. 178; quote: "out of pity for the universe...," p. 194; "material and physical poverty..." and "eremitical solitude...," p. 201; quote: "You will never find interior solitude..., p. 84 of chapter 12 "The Pure Heart" in New Seeds of Contemplation. New York: New Directions, 1972, reprint of 1961 ed.; *The Solitary Life: a Letter of Guigo*, introduced and translated from the Latin by Thomas Merton. Worcester, UK: Stanbrook Abbey Press, 1963; quote: "Follow my ways...," from the poem "Song: If You Seek" in *Emblems of a Secret Fury*. New York: New Directions, 1963, cited in The *Collected Poems of Thomas Merton.* New York: New Directions, 1980, p. 340; quotes: "The life of the hermit is…" and "myth not of eremitical solitude…," *Disputed Questions,* op. cit., p. 201; "You will never find interior solitude…," *Seeds of Contemplation.* London: Burns & Oates, 1962, p. 65; quotes in *The Wisdom of the Desert.* New York: New Directions, 1970: "Whatever you see your soul…," p. 7; "much more in common with…," p. 9; and "primitive anarchic…," p. 19; quote: "Chuang Tzu is not concerned with…," *The Way of Chuang Tzu.* New York: New Directions, 1965, p. 11; quote: "regard sparsity and moderation…," *Mystics and Zen Masters.* New York, Farrar, Straus and Giroux, 1967. p. 11; *Zen and the Birds of Appetite.* New York: New Directions, 1968. Daisetsu Teitaro (D. T.) Suzuki (1870-1966), prolific author of works on Zen Buddhism; Kitarō Nishida (1870-1945), philosopher interested in Zen Buddhism and modern Western thought. Secondary source: *Solitude in the Thought of Thomas Merton,* by Richard Anthony Cashen. Kalamazoo, MI: Cistercian Publications, 1981; *A Search for Wisdom and Spirit: Thomas Merton's Theology of the Self,* by Anne Carr. Notre Dame, IN: University of Notre Dame Press, 1988; on Robert Lax: *A Catch of Anti-Letters, Letters by Thomas Merton and Robert Lax.* Kansas City: Sheed, Andrews, 1977; Merton quotes re Robert Lax, "prophet without rage," from *Seven Storey Mountain.* New York: Harcourt, Brace, 1998, p. 198 and quote: "meditated on some incomprehensible woe," cited in *Thomas Merton, Spiritual Master: The Essential Writings,* selected by Lawrence S. Cunningham. New York: Paulist Press, 1992, p. 66; on Robert Lax: *Pure Act: The Uncommon Life of Robert Lax,* by Michael N. McGregor. New York: Fordham University Press, 2015; *Hermits: The Insights of Solitude,* by Peter France. New York: St. Martin's Press, 1997, chapter 8: "A Hermit for Our Time: Robert Lax on Patmos," p. 192-212.

65. Rehabilitation of Hermits in the United States

Kerouac quotes: "no characters, alone, isolated…, in *Desolation Angels,* by Jack Kerouac. New York: Riverhead Books, 1995, p. 14; "Desolation Adventure finds me…, p. 68; "vision of the freedom of eternity…, in *Dharma Bums,* by Jack Kerouac. London: Flamingo, 1994, p. 203; *Wake Up: A Life of the Buddha,* prepared by Jack Kerouac, introduction by Robert A. F. Thurman. New York: Viking, 2008; quote: "the word and the way…," p. 430 in *Jack Kerouac: Selected Letters: vol. 1, 1940-1956,* edited by Ann Charters. New York: Viking, 1995; essay: "The Vanishing American Hobo" in *Holiday Magazine,* March 1960, reprinted in *Lonesome Traveler,* by Jack Kerouac. New York:

McGraw-Hill, 1960, and in *Jack Kerouac: Road Novels 1957-1960*, edited by Douglas Brinkley. New York: Library of America, 2007, "Lonesome Traveler," p. 621-774; a French translation of *Lonesome Traveler* is resonantly titled *Le vagabond solitaire*; on Abbey: *Epitaph for a Desert Anarchist: The Life and Legacy of Edward Abbey*, by James Bishop, Jr. New York: Simon & Schuster, 1994 and https://archive.org/details/epitaphfordesert00jame; "Mythic Landscapes: The Desert Imagination of Edward Abbey," chapter 4, in *Landscapes of the Sacred: Geography and Narrative in American Spirituality*, by Belden C. Lane. Baltimore: Johns Hopkins University Press, 2002, p. 124-130; *Desert Solitaire: A Season in the Wilderness*, by Edward Abbey. New York: McGraw-Hill, 1968 and https://archive.org/details/desertsolitaires00abbe/; on California hermits, the November 21, 1938 issue of *LIFE Magazine* is archived at https://books.google.com/books?id=Zk0EAAAAMBAJ&dq=nov+21+1938; the "Cuckooland" article begins p. 50; on Noah John Rondeau: *Noah John Rondeau, Adirondack Hermit*, by Maitland C. De Sormo. Utica, NY: North Country Books, 1969; *The Hermit And Us: Our Adirondack Adventures with Noah John Rondeau*, by William J. O'Hern. Camden, NY: In the Adirondacks, 2014; *New York Times* obituary: https://www.nytimes.com/1967/08/26/archives/the-hermit-of-the-adirondacks-noah-john-rondeau-dead-at-84.html; on Ray Phillips: "Eden & Ruin: Monhegan's Island Shepherd," by Taylor Cunningham, in *The Maine Journal of Conservation and Sustainability*, May 2017: https://umaine.edu/spire/2017/05/04/cunningham/; *New York Times* obituary: https://www.nytimes.com/1975/05/11/archives/ray-phillips-celebrated-hermit-of-maine-coast-island-is-dead-built.html; on Robert E. Harrill: *The Reluctant Hermit of Fort Fisher*, by Daniel Ray Norris and Fred Pickler. Carolina Beach, NC: Slapdash Publisher, 2014; about the Everglades hermits: *Hermits from The Mangrove Country of The Everglades (Prop Roots, v. 2)*, by Larry and Jeri Green and Everglades High School students. Everglades City, FL: Collier County Historical Society, 1980: https://archive.org/details/HERMITS; *ThePhony Hermit*, by Al Seely, edited by Elizabeth M. Perdecizzi. Marco Island, FL: Caxambas, 2010; on Willard: *The Hermit of Gully Lake: The Life and Times of Willard Kitchener MacDonald*, by Joan Baxter. Lawrence town Beach, NS, Canada: Pottersfield Press, 2005; on Bernard Wheatley: The December, 1959 issue of *Ebony Magazine* is archived at https://books.google.com/books?id=-afILxQ2isIC&q=wheatley#v=snippet&q=wheatley&f=false); the article on Bernard Wheatley is titled "The Doctor Who Lives as a Hermit," p. 29-42; on Richard Proenneke: *One Man's Wilderness:*

An Alaskan Odyssey, by Sam Keith and Richard Proenneke. Anchorage, AK: Alaska Northwest Publication Co., 1973, reprinted Portland, OR: Graphic Arts Center, 2013.

66. Contemporary Men Hermits Around The World

Dunstan Morrissey: article "Your Cell Will Teach You Everything," by Dunstan Morrissey, in *Parabola*, v. 25, no. 3, p. 33-38; biographical: http://www.skyfarm.org/about-us; on Richard Withers: "A City Dweller Chooses the Life of Religious Hermit," by Gustav Niebuhr. *New York Times*, Oct. 30, 2001: https://www.nytimes.com/2001/10/30/us/a-city-dweller-chooses-the-life-of-religious-hermit.html; on Charles Brandt: https://www.hakaimagazine.com/features/the-oracle-of-oyster-river/; https://vancouversun.com/opinion/columnists/stephen-hume-the-life-of-oyster-river-hermit-frater-charles-brandt-celebrated-in-campbell-river and http://islandcatholicnews.ca/news/2014/12/hermit-charles-brandt-life-conservation-and-contemplation; *Meditations From the Wilderness*, by Charles Brandt. Toronto: HarperCollins, 1997; on Daniel Bourguet: http://danielbourguet.org; on Maxime Qavtaradze: https://www.huffpost.com/entry/katskhi-pillar-monk-georgia-maxime-qavtaradze_n_3950192 and video: https://thestylite.com/; on Norman Davies: "Dedicated Jewish Contemplatives," by Norman R. Davies, in *European Judaism: A Journal for the New Europe*, v. 41, no. 1, Spring 2008, p. 131–147; quote from Dec. 2009 blog entry in https://jewishcontemplatives.blogspot.com/; on Jake Williams: https://www.independent.co.uk/life-style/health-and-families/features/life-as-a-hermit-my-life-is-a-great-adventure-7771209.html and https://www.thesun.co.uk/archives/news/751301/we-meet-movie-hermit-who-kips-in-a-caravan/; film: *Two Years at Sea*, directed by Ben Rivers. Cinema Guild, 2013 (DVD); on Masafumi Nagasaki: http://nagasaki.docastaway.com; on Pietro Lentini: documentary film *Coming Home*, directed by Emmanuele Pecorar and produced by Peter Cook, 2011 and https://www.cultureunplugged.com/documentary/watch-online/play/9947/Coming-Home and https://www.ilgiornalepopolare.it/meglio-soli-con-i-tempi-che-corrono/; on Faustino Barrientos: https://www.vice.com/en_us/topic/faustino-barrientos; on Robert Kull: *Solitude: Seeking Wisdom in Extremes—A Year Alone in the Patagonia Wilderness*, by Robert Kull. Novato, CA: New World Library, 2009 and http://www.bobkull.org; on Neil Ansell: *Deep Country: Five Years in the Welsh Hills*, by

Neil Ansell. London: Hamish Hamilton, 2011 and London: Penguin, 2012; *The Last Wilderness: A Journey into Silence*, by Neil Ansell. London: Tinder Press, 2018; https://www.theguardian.com/environment/2011/mar/27/neil-ansell-my-life-as-hermit; on *David Glasheen: The Millionaire Castaway: The Incredible Story of How I Lost My Fortune but Found New Riches Living on a Deserted Island*, by Dave Glasheen with Neil Bramwell. South Melbourne, Australia: Affirm Press, 2019; https://www.theaustralian.com.au/weekend-australian-magazine/david-glasheen-exmillionaire-and-his-tropical-island-refuge/news-story/c25cc64f24d08e7ecf99dde883e5bf02, https://www.dailymail.co.uk/travel/travel_news/article-8244725/Millionaire-Castaway-David-Glasheen-reveals-tips-living-isolation.html, and https://www.youtube.com/watch?v=sL34Fw7dPWI; on Mauro Morandi: https://www.cnn.com/travel/article/italy-hermit-coronavirus/; https://www.mnn.com/lifestyle/eco-tourism/blogs/79-year-old-enjoys-life-solitude-deserted-italian-island"; video: https://www.greatbigstory.com/amp/mauro-island; autobiography: *La poltrona di ginepro. Abbandonare il mondo per la libertà: la mia vita sulla Spiaggia Rosa*, Mauro Morandi con Gianpaolo Melani. Milan: Rizzolli, 2019; ebook of photography: *8: Un'isola* di Mauro Morandi. Amazon Media EU, Kindle format; https://www.theguardian.com/world/2021/apr/26/mauro-morandi-budelli-island-italy-robinson-crusoe. Other modern men hermits: Brendon Grenshaw: https://www.dailymail.co.uk/news/article-2135299/Brit-bought-cut-price-island-Seychelles-50-years-ago—lives-blissful-solitude.html; Pedro Luca: https://www.ctvnews.ca/lifestyle/extreme-man-cave-argentine-hermit-lives-in-cavern-for-40-years-1.3009654; Tom Neale: *An Island to Oneself: the Story of Six Years on a Desert Island*, by Tom Neale. London: Collins, 1966, and reprints; "Pete": https://www.rnz.co.nz/news/the-wireless/373999/what-it-s-like-to-be-a-hermit-in-new-zealand; "Viktor": https://www.reuters.com/article/us-russia-hermit/russian-hermit-seeks-peace-in-remote-siberia-idUSKCN1TM1LC; Nikolai Gromov: https://www.newsweek.com/hermit-siberia-murder-1461810; Carlos Sanchez Ortiz: https://www.telegraph.co.uk/news/worldnews/europe/italy/11983786/Long-lost-doctor-discovered-living-like-a-hermit-in-the-woods-of-Tuscany.html; Mang Emigdio: https://www.gmanetwork.com/news/lifestyle/healthandwellness/727020/why-did-this-man-choose-to-live-inside-a-cave-for-30-years/story/; Chris McCandless: *Into the Wild*, by Jon Krakauer. New York: Anchor Books, 1997; *The Wild Truth*, by Carine McCandless.

New York: HarperOne, 2014; *Back To The Wild: Photographs and Writings of Christopher McCandless.* [no place of publication]: Twin Star Press, 2011; feature film: *Into the Wild*, directed by Sean Penn. Paramount, 2007 (DVD); Christopher Knight: *The Stranger in the Woods: The Extraordinary Story of the Last True Hermit*, by Michael Finkel. New York: Knopf, 2017.

67. Contemporary Women Solitaries Around The World

Pinions: *Wind on the Sand: The Hidden Life of an Anchoress*, by Pinions. London: SPCK, 1980 and New York: Paulist Press, 1981; Rachel Denton: http://www.stcuthbertshouse.co.uk; https://www.independent.co.uk/news/people/sister-rachel-denton-why-i-founded-a-one-nun-hermitage-a6706916.html; Mother Thekla: https://www.theguardian.com/world/2002/apr/16/gender.uk; https://www.telegraph.co.uk/news/obituaries/religion-obituaries/8698853/Mother-Thekla.html; Julia Bolton Holloway: http://www.umilta.net; http://www.florin.ms; https://colorado.academia.edu/JuliaBoltonHolloway; https://www.amazon.com/Julia-Bolton-Holloway/e/B001IYXNEW; Wendy Beckett: https://www.pbs.org/wgbh/sisterwendy/meet/; https://www.bfi.org.uk/films-tv-people/4ce2bb187a3cd; https://www.nytimes.com/2018/12/26/obituaries/sister-wendy-beckett-dead.html; Sister Laurel O'Neal: https://notesfromstillsong.blogspot.com; by Sara Maitland: *How to Be Alone (The School of Life Series)*. New York: Picador, 2014; *A Book of Silence*. Berkeley, CA: Counterpoint, 2008, and http://www.saramaitland.com; *The Wisdom of Solitude: A Zen Retreat in the Woods*, by Jane Dobisz. San Francisco: HarperSanFrancisco, 2003, reprinted as *One Hundred Days of Solitude: Losing Myself and Finding Grace on a Zen Retreat.* Boston: Wisdom Publications, 2007; *Forty Days: The Diary of a Traditional Solitary Sufi Retreat*, by Michaela Ozelsel. Brattleboro, VT: Threshold Books, 1996, reprinted Boston: Shambhala, 2002. *Journal of a Solitude*, by May Sarton. New York: Norton, 1973; *Fifty Days of Solitude*, by Doris Grumbach. Boston: Beacon Press, 1995; *Pilgrim at Tinker Creek*, by Annie Dillard. New York: Harper's Magazine Press, 1974 and New York: Harper Collins, 2013; *Epicurean Simplicity*, by Stephanie Mills. Washington, DC: Island Press, 2002; *Woodswoman: Living Alone in the Adirondack Wilderness*, by Anne LaBastille. New York: Dutton, 1976 and New York: Penguin, 1991; on Jane Carter: "Girl Friday Lives Hermit Existence On Storm-Lashed Island," British Pathé newsreel: https://www.britishpathe.com/video/VLVA4DYRGH-5J1HRCAOQQEK6HU1MIG-AUSTRALIA-GIRL-FRIDAY-LIVES-HERMIT-EXISTENCE-ON-STORM-LASHED/;

Emma Orbach: https://www.dailymail.co.uk/news/article-2254397/Oxford-graduate-quit-mainstream-society-live-hobbit-style-existence-mud-hut-Welsh-hills.html; Tamsin Calidas: *I Am An Island*, by Tamsin Calidas. London and New York: Doubleday, 2020.

Appendix
Hermit Dwelling–places: Hut, Cell, and Cabin

On Adam's House in Paradise: The Idea of the Primitive Hut in Architectural History, by Joseph Rykwert. New York: Museum of Modern Art, 1972; The *Hermit's Hut: Asceticism and Architecture in India (Spatial Habitus)*, by Kazi K. Ashraf. Honolulu: University of Hawaii Press, 2013; *Metamorphoses*, by Ovid, translated by Frank Justus Miller. Cambridge, MA: Harvard University Press (Loeb Classical Library) ,v. 1, and https://archive.org/details/metamorphoses01ovid/; quote: "that old house of theirs ... was changed into a temple," p. 455; Heraclitus Fragment 121 (119 in some sources) is *"ethos anthropoi daimon"*; *The Fragments of the Work of Heraclitus of Ephesus on Nature*, translated by Ingram Bywater. Baltimore: Murray, 1889, p. 112 and https://archive.org/details/thefragmentsofth00herauoft/. Heidegger translates the fragment as "A man's character is his *daimon*." Other translations: "character determines fate" or *"ethos* equals *daimon*." The proper state of a person's virtue approximates the universal order, the life force. Further, Heidegger sees the root meaning of the Greek *ethos* as "abode," such that self and its inclusion or home is in Being, its relationship to *daimon*. "Here, too, the gods are present" means the gods attest to the virtue of the hut occupant who in turn identifying with wisdom in Being, the hut represents the dwelling-place or abode of self within existence. Heidegger notes the *"Kai entautha*, "even here," at the stove, in that ordinary place where every thing and every condition, each deed and thought is intimate and commonplace, that is, familiar [*geheuer*], "even there" in the sphere of the familiar, *einai theous*, it is the case that "the gods come to presence." Heidegger's references to Heraclitus are in the essay "Letter on Humanism" in *Basic Writings*, by Martin Heidegger, edited by David F. Krell. New York: Harper & Row and London: Routledge & K. Paul,1977; quote from 2008 ed., p. 258; Aristotle on Heraclitus: "De Partibus Ani*malium i 5.645a17-23;* in *Parts of Animals, Movement of Animal, Progression of Animals*, translated by A. L. Peck and E. S. Forster. Cambridge,

MA: Harvard University Press (Loeb Classical Library), 1937; *The Fruit of the Homeless Life: the Samaññaphala Sutta,* translated by Silachara. London: Buddhist Society of Great Britain and Ireland,1917, and https://archive. org/details/fruitofhomelessl00silarich/; Lu-Yun poem in *A Hundred and Seventy Chinese Poems,* translated by Arthur Waley. London: Constable, 1918, p. 69, and https://www.gutenberg.org/files/42290/42290-h/42290-h.htm;

    The Poetics of Space, by Gaston Bachelard, translated by Maria Jolas. Boston: Beacon Press, 1969 (reprint of 1964 ed.), quote: "The hermit is before God...," p. 32; *Life of Anthony by Athanasius* in *Early Christian Lives,* translated by Carolinne White. London and New York: Penguin, 1998, p. 1-69; Evagrios the Solitary in *Philokalia,* op. cit. (section 19); Po Chu-i (Bai Juyi) in *Four Huts: Asian Writings on the Simple Life,* translated by Burton Watson. Boston: Shambhala,1994, p. 1-22; Stonehouse, op.cit. (section 33); Yasutane, *Four Huts,* ibid., p. 23–49; Saigyō, op. cit. (section 35); Bashō, *Four Huts,* ibid., p. 115-132, and section 35; Kamo no Chōmei, *Four Huts,* ibid., p. 51-119 and section 35; *Shobogenzo: The Treasure House of the Eye of the True Teaching,* translated by Hubert Nearman. Mount Shasta, CA: Shasta Abbey Press, 2007 and https://archive.org/details/ShobogenzoComplete; quotes: "Living alone ...," p. 386; "Thatched hermitages and cottages...," p. 390; "built a thatched hermit's hut...," p. 396; "An Account of My Journey to the East," in *Classical Japanese Prose: An Anthology,* edited by Helen Craig McCullough. Stanford, CA: Stanford University Press, 1991, p. 421-445; Ryokan, op. cit. (section 35); Ippen (section 35); on Pure Land Buddhism: religion scholar Mark MacWilliams notes that Pure Land pilgrimage tales depict the holy man moving beyond impermanence, and the hermit's hut as standing outside of impermanence. Pure Land holy men and hermits are not wanderers but seek a suitable setting for a temple promoting Kannon. The sacred space is denoted by signs: miraculous clouds, wonderful fragrance, celestial music, beautiful nature sounds, and mystical light. The eremitic experience is thus secondary to the Kannon devotion in Pure Land Buddhism: "The Holy Man's Hut as a Symbol of Stability in Japanese Buddhist Pilgrimage," by Mark W. MacWilliams, in *Numen* v. 47, 2000, p. 387–416; quote of Toyohara Sumiaki cited by Ashraf, op. cit., in note 13, p. 202: *Tea in Japan: Essays on the History of Chanoyu,* edited by Paul Varley and Kumakura Isao: "The Development of Chanoyu before Rikyü," by Murai Yasuhiko. Honolulu: University of Hawaii, 1989; Thoreau: *Walden,* op. cit. and section 48; quotes from *Walden:* "I went to the woods...," p. 98; "in undisturbed solitude...what the Orientals..., p. 122; "my furniture...," p.

71; "I had three chairs…," p. 152, "I experienced sometimes…," p. 142, "I left the woods…," p. 345; quote from *Journal:* "Why I left the woods? …," *Journal,* v. 3, chapter 4, Jan. 22, 1852, p. 214 in *The Writings of Henry David Thoreau: Journal,* edited by Bradford Torrey: v. 3: September 16, 1851–April 30, 1852. Boston: Houghton Mifflin, 1906 and https://www.google.com/books/edition/Journal_ed_by_B_Torrey_1837_1846_1850_NoFP0rAQAA-IAAJkptab=editions&gbpv=1; Nietzsche at Sil Maria: https://nietzschehaus.ch/en/; quote: "I should like to have…" from letter to Freiherr Karl Von Gersdorff, June 28, 1883, in *Selected Letters of Friedrich Nietzsche,* edited by Oscar Levy, translated by Anthony M. Ludovici. Garden City, NY: Doubleday, Page, 1921, p. 153-154; Robert Hass in "Introduction" p. xi-liv, in *Selected Poetry of Rainer Maria Rilke,* op. cit.; Wittgenstein: quote: "Throughout his life…" from *Times* obituary, May 2, 1951: https://www.thetimes.co.uk/archive/find/wittgenstein/w:1951-05-02~1951-05-02; "On the Trail to Wittgenstein's Hut: the Historical Background of the *Tractatus Logico-Philosophicus,*" by Ivar Oxaal. Piscataway, NJ: Transaction Publishers, 2010; 'Showing the way out of the fly bottle: searching for Wittgenstein in Norway," by Jan Estep, in *Cultural Geographies in Practice,* v. 15 (2008), p. 255-260; "Ludwig Wittgenstein's exile in Skjolden," multiple articles, in *Einarlunga* (2010): https://einarlunga.wordpress.com/2010/02/20/wittgenstein-in-skjolden/; "The Philosopher's Home from Home," by Lesley Chamberlain, in *Standpoint Magazine* (2011): https://standpointmag.co.uk/features-october-11-the-philosophers-home-from-home-lesley-chamberlain-ludwig-wittgenstein-hut-norway-skjolden; *Philosophical Investigations / Philosophische Untersuchungen,* by Ludwig Wittgenstein, translated by G. E. M. Anscombe. London and New York: Macmillan,1953; references to hut and text: 85. "A rule stands there like a sign-post. Does the sign-post leave no doubt open about the way I have to go? Does it shew which direction I am to take when I have passed it …" (118). "Where does our investigation get its importance from, since it seems only to destroy everything interesting, … as it were all the buildings, leaving behind only bits of stone and rubble. What we are destroying is nothing but the houses of cards and we are clearing up the ground of language on which they stand." (309) "What is your aim in philosophy?–to shew the fly the way out of the fly-bottle."; on Heidegger: *Heidegger's Hut,* by Adam Sharr. London and Cambridge, MA: MIT Press, 2006; "Letter on Humanism" in *Pathmarks,* by Martin Heidegger, edited by Edward McNeill. Cambridge: Cambridge University Press, 1998 reprint of 1976 ed., p. 239-275; reference "path" theme: *Martin Heidegger,* by George Steiner. Chicago:

University of Chicago Press, 1991, p. 18; connection to Eastern "path" theme: *Heidegger and Asian Thought*, edited by Graham Parkes. Honolulu: University of Hawaii Press, 1998; "Why Do I Stay in the Provinces," in *Heidegger: The Man and the Thinker*, edited by Thomas Sheehan. Chicago: University of Chicago Press, 1981, London and NewYork: Routledge, 2009, reprint of 1981 ed., p. 27-29, and https://archive.org/details/heideggermanthin0000unse/. A critical view of Heidegger's hut: in *Building and Dwelling: Ethics for the City*, by Richard Sennett. New York: Farrar, Straus and Giroux, 2018, p. 127-128.

INDEX

domincula, 25
Donatists, 18, 173
Dong Zhongshu, 73
Dorothea von Montau, 26
Dorrington, Edward, 115
Dostoyevsky, Fyodor, 163-165, 170, 188, 193, 207-208, 214
Doyle, Arthur Conan, 173
Droste–Hulshoff, Annette von, 129
Duperron, Anquetil, 211

E

Eckhart *see* Meister Eckhart
Eco, Umberto, 161
Eichendorff, Joseph, 121
Elazar ben Moshe Azikri, 50
Eliade, Mircea, xx
Elijah (Prophet), 6, 9, 50
Ellison, Ralph, 199, 207-209, 326
Emerson, Ralph Waldo, 135, 139-142, 149, 197, 211, 274-275
Emigdio, Mang, 253
Enno Gyoja, 85-86
Epictetus, 5, 282
Epicurus, 5, 258
eremos, xiv, xvii, 4, 7, 102
Ernst, Max, 162
Esau (son of Jacob), xviii, 6
Escobar, Dario (Fr.), 237
Essenes, 6, 250
Estanislau (Fr.), 235
Etteilla, 229
Eucharius of Lyon, 19
eudaimonia, 5
Euphrosyne, 22
Euthymios, 43
Evagrius Pontius, the Solitary, xv, 11, 44, 264
Eve of St. Martin, 26
Everglades hermits *see* Florida Everglades hermits
Ewing, Juliana Horatia, 157
existentialism, 163, 174, 188, 191, 214, 238

F

Fachia *see* Legalists
Fairburn, John, 115
Fantin–Latour, Henri, 161
Felix, *Life of St. Guthlac*, 20
Fenggan ("Big Stick"), 78, 96
Ferguson, Robert A., 135
Fielding, John, 134
fields–and–gardens poetry, 79
Finkel, Michael, xvii, 254
Five Scholars–at–Home, 74
Flaubert, Gustave, 10, 13, 161, 181, 182
Florida Everglades hermits, 247-248
fool, 11, 13, 34, 96, 114, 183-184, 230
Fort Fisher hermit *see* Harris, Robert E.
Foucauld, Charles, 223-224
Four Graybeards, 74, 96
France, Anatole, 13, 161
Freud, Sigmund, 177, 203, 248, 281
Friedrich, Caspar David, 150
Frost, Robert, 199-203
Frumentius of Tyre, 49
Fujiwara Seika, 97

G

Gellner, Ernest, 189-190
Geoffrey Chaucer, 34
Geoffrey of Monmouth, 31-32
Gibau, Basili *see* Basili (Fr.)
Gibbon, Edward, 104, 265
Gibran, Kahlil, xiv, 185-187
Gil Vicente, 102
Giono, Jean, 233-234
Glasheen, David, 252-253
Gnädinger, Manfred, 250-251
Gnanananda, 216
Godric (or Goderic), 20
Goethe, Wolfgang, 125, 128
Goldsmith, Oliver, 113, 128
gomchen, 212-213
Goscelin of St. Bertin, 24, 26
Grand Inquisitor, 164
Graybeards see Four Graybeards
Gregory Nazianzus, 14
Greybeards *see* Four Graybeards
Griffiths, Bede, 217

Robert Rodriguez spent forty years as a librarian in university, college and public libraries. He is the founder of the Hermitary website (hermitary.com) and editor since its 2002 inception.

CPSIA information can be obtained
at www.ICGtesting.com
Printed in the USA
BVHW031300060323
659771BV00001B/124